ADVANCES IN LIBRARY ADMINISTRATION AND ORGANIZATION

ADVANCES IN LIBRARY ADMINISTRATION AND ORGANIZATION

Series Editors: Delmus E. Williams, James M. Nyce and Janine Golden

ADVANCES IN LIBRARY ADMINISTRATION AND
ORGANIZATION   VOLUME 28

ADVANCES IN LIBRARY ADMINISTRATION AND ORGANIZATION

EDITED BY

DELMUS E. WILLIAMS
University of Akron, Akron, OH, USA

JAMES M. NYCE
Ball State University, Muncie, IN, USA

JANINE GOLDEN
Texas Woman's University, Denton, TX, USA

United Kingdom – North America – Japan
India – Malaysia – China

Emerald Group Publishing Limited
Howard House, Wagon Lane, Bingley BD16 1WA, UK

First edition 2009

British Library Cataloguing in Publication Data
A catalogue record for this book is available from the British Library

ISBN: 978-1-84950-579-6
ISSN: 0732-0671 (Series)

Awarded in recognition of
Emerald's production
department's adherence to
quality systems and processes
when preparing scholarly
journals for print

INVESTOR IN PEOPLE

CONTENTS

v

LIST OF CONTRIBUTORS

Stephen H. Aby	The University of Akron Libraries, Akron, OH, USA
Bella Karr Gerlich	Dominican University Library, River Forest, IL, USA
Donald L. Gilstrap	University of Oklahoma Libraries, Norman, OK, USA
Lisa K. Hussey	Graduate School of Library and Information Science, Simmons College, Boston, MA, USA
Catherine Maskell	Leddy Library, University of Windsor, Windsor, Ontario, Canada
Jean K. Mulhern	S. Arthur Watson Library, Wilmington College, Wilmington, OH, USA
Barbara J. Stites	Florida Gulf Coast University, Ft. Myers, FL, USA

INTRODUCTION

From the beginning, *Advances in Library Administration and Organization* has sought to develop a body of research literature that could, at once, contribute to the base of organizational theory upon which library administrators rely. The intention is to bring to light good scholarship that strengthens and reinforces the base of knowledge library administrators have on hand. Librarians are very good at working pragmatically to solve difficult problems, but they have been less good at explaining to themselves and to others how and why they do what they do and what they contribute to the common good. That was why I jumped at the chance to provide an article for Volume 2 of the series, agreed to help edit ALAO beginning with Volume 13, and now, along with my co-editors, present to you Volume 28. Through these many years, I have enjoyed the opportunity to help make this series what it has become, in addressing the challenge it has presented to find people who think about how libraries and library administrators work and to bring their ideas to the public. This volume follows a pattern to which you have become accustomed. It includes seven studies from the United States and Canada on topics relating to problems library managers face and strategies that might be of value in addressing those challenges. As always, we the editors hope that you find them interesting and as thought-provoking as we have.

The lead article by Donald L. Gilstrap is a case study designed to provide insight into how research librarians address change. He interviewed 17 librarians working for a member of the Association of Research Libraries using a clustering technique and semi-structured interviewing and then incorporated the resulting data using a collective case method. The result is an interesting read about competing tensions between the physical and the virtual environments, the speed of change, the search for professional meaning, and coping with the experiences of professional change. The study explores the nuances of coping with a hypercritical organization operating within a complex system.

An article drawn from a very different study done by Jean K. Mulhern follows. Jean leads a small college library and has been a key player in the organization of OPAL, a consortium founded specifically to allow small colleges in Ohio to participate in and benefit from a statewide network called OhioLINK. She explores whether this and other consortia are agile organizations with the leadership capacity to respond quickly to changes in the environment. Her case study talks about the organization of the network and then expands to consider how the consortia and its development opened its members to new ideas and served as a bridge to expanded opportunities for those libraries and those they serve. Jean does a good job of explaining the "coming together" process and gives insight into both the vision and the practicality of molding these libraries into a group. In addition, as a participant, she offers a bird's eye view of the impact this kind of association can have on the development of small, isolated institutions and those who work in them.

Catherine Maskell's work then continues with a different kind of discussion relating to consortial activity among academic libraries. Specifically, she asks whether library consortia are a public good or whether their activities as purchasing agents for groups of libraries are leading toward anti-competitive activities. She contends that most university librarians view the work of consortia as something that helps them provide more information to more people more efficiently. However, she offers an alternative view that, in their efforts to interact with publishers both as consumers and as aggregators of information themselves, they may be changing the relationship between academic libraries and publishers. This change tests the balance between libraries' roles as consumers of information and competitors in the dissemination of information in a way that could attract the attention of those who make policy regarding competition. This discussion takes place in a Canadian context, but it addresses an interesting and intriguing question for any of us who live in countries where the market economy is valued and where cartels are regulated.

Lisa K. Hussey's article represents an abrupt change in direction as she tackles questions related to diversity within Library and Information Science. She notes that, while our profession has long recognized the need for diversity, more needs to be done to determine how we might recruit more minorities to the field. She interviewed students from protected classes in several library schools, asking them why they decided to become librarians and what might motivate others to join them. Her findings about the relationship between recruitment, identity, and acculturation are useful and offer insights into this important topic.

Barbara J. Stites is concerned with the need to keep librarians abreast of the many changes that are occurring in our community. It has often been stressed that librarians must continuously upgrade their skills by participating in library organizations and professional development activities, and this emphasis has increased in recent years. Stites sees an urgency in efforts to enhance our understanding of what we are doing and a need to examine what we are doing to train those with whom we work to insure its effectiveness. Her study documents evaluation practices currently used in library training and continuing education programs for library employees to determine how they evaluate training, what kind of training evaluation practices are in place, and how they determine the return-on-investment of programs that are mounted and supported by the organization.

Stephen H. Aby in his article then looks at faculty unionization as it pertains to librarians. Unionization in academic libraries is growing, and, while there is some literature available that talks about its impact on salaries and benefits, there is little available about how well collective bargaining contracts address the sometimes unique nature of library faculty work. This article explores how well existing contracts in a number of Ohio universities and from selective institutions around the country accommodate the professional and work-related needs of librarians, dealing with issues like governance, academic freedom, workload, salary, and the retention, tenure, and the promotion of faculty.

In the final article, Bella Karr Gerlich addresses the fact that reference services are changing and that we need to develop a better understanding of their current state, particularly in a networked environment. Her study is designed to investigate those circumstances and conditions that bear – directly and indirectly – on changes in the nature, form, substance, and effects of those services as seen through the eyes of reference librarian. She has assessed the causes and impact of changes in reference services in the context of a medium-sized private university with a national reputation for successfully integrating information technologies into the educational process with a view toward developing metrics that might be used in evaluating those services and the personnel who provide them.

This volume, like most of the others produced in this series, is unapologetically eclectic. While it may lack a theme, it is not lacking in content, and we hope that you will find here thought-provoking ideas that will inform and challenge.

Delmus E. Williams
Co-Editor

LIBRARIANS AND THE COMPLEXITY OF INDIVIDUAL AND ORGANIZATIONAL CHANGE: CASE STUDY FINDINGS OF AN EMERGENT RESEARCH LIBRARY

Donald L. Gilstrap

ABSTRACT

The purpose of this case study was to increase the knowledge base of how research librarians experience and cope with the turbulence of change within their library system. A library belonging to the Association of Research Libraries was selected for case study investigation. Seventeen librarians participated in on-site interviews, utilizing a protocol composed of a clustering technique and semi-structured interviewing. Instrumental case studies of each individual were then developed through a collective case method. The findings presented in this chapter include: the competing tensions between the physical and virtual environments, the speed of change, the search for professional meaning, and coping with the experiences of professional change. Analysis of the findings suggest: the emergence of a hypercritical state, the limiting nature of negative feedback, a complex systems framework for professional thinking, and coping in the hypercritical organization.

Advances in Library Administration and Organization, Volume 28, 1–58
Copyright © 2009 by Emerald Group Publishing Limited
All rights of reproduction in any form reserved
ISSN: 0732-0671/doi:10.1108/S0732-0671(2009)0000028004

INTRODUCTION

Now, think back to the first day on your current job. How did it change from your first job to your present job? How has your current job changed from day one to today? How has it changed from last week? Is the last statement tongue in cheek? Sarcastic? We don't think so. Our jobs are changing so rapidly it may seem as if we are, like Kirk and Scott, hurtling through space at warp speed and we sometimes think, as Scotty was always fond of saying, we 'canna take any more.' (Osif & Harwood, 1999, p. 224)

It is little secret that academic librarians have seen several major changes within their libraries over the past 20 years. These changes have been driven primarily by different external and internal shifts in access to information and expectations by academic and stakeholder communities. Librarians are faced with challenges to their traditional services with the rise in consumer use of virtual resources, the proliferation of search engines that link to gray literature, and new publishing and pricing models for academic research. Librarians are additionally confronted with decreased funding from federal and state agencies, leading to difficult decisions on which services, programs, and collections to maintain (De Rosa et al., 2005). Moreover, librarians now use technology to a high degree in the dissemination and diffusion of knowledge among scholarly publishers and users of university research. But the rapid technological integration of new tools for research while maintaining traditional print collections places demands on librarians for continual learning that sometimes appear both complementary and contradictory. Major differences in viewing these challenges over the past few years from previous decades, however, are the increasing speed and complexity that are now associated with changes in academic libraries. Librarians might describe their evolving professional life at present as an environment of turbulence: a paradox of "commotion, agitation, or disturbance" that concurrently "is of natural conditions" (Simpson & Weiner, 2001); one that breaks from the traditional history of equilibrium, control, and stability. These rapid and increasing changes have created environments of uncertainty for academic librarians and suggest shifts in professional and organizational thinking.

Changing Roles of Librarians

Roles of academic librarians now include more substantially the need for educating students, faculty, and themselves to keep up with the evolving aspects of research and information resources in a technological environment. The Internet has created increased student reliance on a tremendous amount of gray literature that professionals argue has led to a crisis of quality information (Williams, 2001). At the same time students and sometimes even faculty, who are unfamiliar with the critical analysis methods for web-based resources often begin or perform research entirely with search engines such as Yahoo or Google (De Rosa et al., 2005). And the use of online search engines has led students to rate their self-efficacy of academic research at much higher levels than their actual ability to perform this research has shown (Dunn, 2002; Maughan, 2001). Many academic libraries now incorporate library instruction and information literacy programs that help students critically analyze and use different mediums of research information. In spite of these efforts, "librarians are put in the unfortunate position of telling people to eat their spinach, that fast food searching isn't enough" (Wilson, 2004, p. 11).

Librarians are also dealing with the graying of the profession. Fewer students are matriculating from library science graduate programs in relation to population demands. Oftentimes, their absence in these programs reflects general student misperceptions of what the academic library world is like. Potential students sometimes view librarians through stereotypical frameworks of bibliophiles who are concerned with rules and order over access and management of information through the use of technology. This phenomenon has made recruitment efforts to fill positions that have come open due to retirements difficult (Fennewald & Stachacz, 2005; Unabashed librarian, 2003). Moreover, the increased need for academic librarians to have both broad and specific technology skill sets has led at least one library pundit, James Neal, to argue that "there will be fewer librarians working in academic libraries because of a significant increase in the number of technical staff" (Riggs, 1997, p. 6). In addition to the stress of this uncertain future, while librarians deal with many new changes in their environments, they are frequently working understaffed while trying to fill open positions or are dealing with setbacks from attrition or retrenchment (Rogers, 2004; White, 1985).

There has also been an exponential growth of scholarly information produced by the research community. Higher expectations for publication among university faculty combined with the power technology brings to conduct and present research contribute to this trend. Managing these growing collections and providing access to the overwhelming amount of new electronic resources that become available on a daily basis has become a daunting challenge for librarians, and traditional models of collection development are, therefore, beginning to crumble. Moreover, escalating subscription prices for scholarly publications, primarily in the hard sciences, have forced librarians to make tough decisions about the maintenance of expensive print collections (Glogoff, 2001). Frequently, this is conflicted with the expectations of those faculty who tend to focus on the maintenance of traditional printed mediums while, at the same time, expect expanded access to electronic resources (Jankowska, 2004; Wisneski, 2005). Research librarians additionally struggle with their professional obligation to preserve the human record of scholarly research while trying to lead their libraries into a digital future. Consequently, these issues bring about a "disconnect between the library's organizational self-understanding and the institution's understanding about the library" (Stephens & Russell, 2004, p. 246).

Responding to Change

Librarians now deal with heightened emotional responses to shifts in the profession. However, some argue these professional shifts might be necessary for the survival of libraries (Glogoff, 2001; Weiner, 2003). Researchers in library science have noted that the changes that are coming in the future will be transformative professional and organizational changes that will challenge the core philosophies and structures of research libraries (Goble, 1997; Riggs, 1997, 1998, 2001; Weiner, 2003). In their view, librarians can no longer react to the changes that are taking place through incremental approaches. Much like the case with most technology-oriented organizations, "libraries that select comfortable, traditional, but increasingly marginal, roles risk becoming more marginalized and increasingly irrelevant to the central focus of information access and scholarly discourse" (Weiner, 2003, p. 70).

Some library organizational development theorists would go so far as to argue that this debate has ensued for much of the twentieth century. Ranganathan (1963) first proposed an organic view of libraries as living systems during the mid-century. He suggested that libraries function much like an ecosystem, responding to controlling and amplifying feedback. In the Association of Research Libraries (ARL), Webster (1973) developed a guide for library administrators that challenged traditional organizational ways of thinking. Relying on contemporary organizational development theorists such as Argyris (1971) and McGregor (1960), he suggested a transformative approach to organize libraries and management decision-making that called into question many of the common practices of the time. Yet, research libraries were slow to adopt these new systems-oriented concepts until the end of the twentieth century.

Technological advancements in libraries have equally increased the speed of change exponentially. Some research librarians have managed to face this turbulent environment and lead their libraries into a brighter technological future. Historically, many librarians have been leaders on campuses in adopting and implementing new technologies, converting their card catalog systems to online catalogs during the 1980s. Academic librarians were also some of the first people on campuses to capitalize on web-based resources, transferring collections to electronic formats, implementing online databases, and moving technology centers to their own buildings. Evidence of these technological and organizational changes has led some researchers to argue that libraries are actually changing faster than their universities (Riggs, 1997). As Goble (1997) notes, "change is not new to librarians. What is different is that change is no longer intermittent. It is constant, and its pace is accelerating" (p. 151). However, the multitude of disparate changes and competing tensions librarians face is somewhat overwhelming (Osif & Harwood, 1999). Moreover, little is actually known about how librarians experience and cope with these changes.

These factors have led academic librarians to respond to this changing environment in different ways. Some librarians have been more reactive, focusing on traditional organizational structures and collection policies as an attempt to harness this changing environment in incremental steps (Stephens & Russell, 2004; Weiner, 2003). Librarians at other institutions have taken more progressive approaches in implementing radical changes in organizational structures, communication patterns, and methods of delivery for library services. These types of changes have often been identified through "fundamental paradigm shifts" that focus on the process of innovation which "has value in providing a means to an end beyond itself" (Weiner, 2003, p. 74). Some of these librarians have incorporated organizational structures that are more organic in nature and are able to adapt more easily to rapid decision-making (Giesecke, Michalak, & Franklin, 1997; Kascus, 2004; Phipps, 2004).

Statement of the Problem and Purpose of Study

Many academic librarians are, therefore, undergoing turbulent and transformative changes in their libraries. These changes are brought on largely by shifts in scholarly mediums of publication, dissemination, and access to information, but they are also influenced by changing educational practices, competing external resources, decreased funding, and conflicting expectations of information needs by students and faculty. As Stacey (2003) has argued, "human emotions ... are thus all social processes individually experienced through variations" (p. 326). However, much of the research has focused on libraries as "things" while ignoring librarians as human beings.

At the same time, practices among many academic librarians continue not only to focus on but also to promote the organizational management concepts of Frederick Taylor (1911) (Stueart & Moran, 2002). As a result, these traditional management concepts of control, efficiency, and stability are not designed to encourage librarians to lead transformative changes, and they oftentimes limit the ability of librarians to expedite change at the rate needed for long-term, organizational survival (Goble, 1997; Kaarnst-Brown, Nicholson, von Dran, & Stanton, 2004; Phipps, 2004; Stephens & Russell, 2004). Consequently, there have been many emerging paradoxes in the research librarian community, similar to Morgan's (1997) concept of competing tensions that lead to organizational environments of uncertainty and unpredictability.

According to Stephens and Russell (2004), librarians now require models that focus on adaptation to the environment while studying cases that manifest the connection between individual and organizational transitions. Although there is an increasing amount of new literature recommending a shift in organizational structures and leadership philosophy, research shows our knowledge is to be extremely limited with respect to the effects of these shifts librarians. It was the purpose of this research to increase the knowledge base of how research librarians experience and cope with the turbulence of change within their library. This research also examined the issues that surround the organizational structures and leadership of transformative change in a research library.

Research Questions

- What experiences do librarians associate with an environment of rapid change, uncertainty, and turbulence?
- What specific changes do they regard as having the most profound effects on their work lives?
- How do research librarians respond to their organizational structure?
- In what ways do librarians as individuals contribute to the leadership of the library?

The findings in this chapter *specifically* address the first two research questions, but it should be noted that a more comprehensive examination of all these issues is also available (Gilstrap, 2007b).

LITERATURE REVIEW

The literature review that accompanies this study contains a broad theoretical base, including complexity theory, organizational theory, leadership theory, library organizational development theory, and individual change theory. The intent of this researcher was to incorporate a wide range of theories that can help in understanding and interpreting the complex phenomena that emerge while studying a research library going through change. The evolution of these theoretical frameworks is included to develop the contextual and philosophical foundations for later data analysis and interpretation of findings. For the confines of this chapter, a general taxonomy is described, and further exploration of these theoretical frameworks and numerous studies that support these theories is encouraged.

Theories X, Y, and Z move from an authoritarian and confrontational relationship between worker and administrator toward a democracy-centered and inclusive framework of organizational dynamics (Argyris, 1957, 1960; McGregor, 1960; Ouchi, 1981). Normative and transactional theories rely on the identification of behavioral traits and the implementation or reciprocal relationships in the workplace (Avolio & Bass, 2002; Blake & Mouton, 1978, 1981, 1985; Blake, Mouton, & Williams, 1981; Burns, 1979, 2003). Situational leadership includes assessing worker willingness and readiness while subsequently adjusting leader responsiveness (Hersey & Blanchard, 1969/1993). Shared leadership focuses on the team environment, where individuals become accountable for the leadership and organizational development of the group through structures and processes (Carew, Parisi-Carew, & Blanchard, 1986; Yukl, 2002). Transformational leadership moves organizational development away from individual wants and needs, reflecting group purposes more developed than self-actualization (Avolio & Bass, 2002; Bass, 1998; Burns, 1979, 2003).

Systems theories of individual and organizational development and change are engineered from natural, ecological processes that reflect the relationships of humans within the larger environment of the organization (Ackoff, 1981, 1994; Argyris, 1990, 1992; Argyris & Schön, 1974, 1978; Ashby, 1956; Holloway, 2004; Lewin, 1951; Ranganathan, 1963; Schön, 1971, 1991; Senge, 1994, 2004; Stephens & Russell, 2004; von Bertalanffy, 1968/1973; Webster, 1973). Transitional and transformational theories of development highlight the psycho-social processes inherent among individuals within an organization going through significant change (Abraham & Gilgen, 1995; Bergson, 1911; Bridges, 2004, 2003; Buch, 1997; Burlingame, Fuhriman, & Barnum, 1995; Carver & Scheier, 1998; Dewey & Bentley, 1975; Goerner, 1995;

Mezirow, 1991). And complexity science theories extend the systems theoretical framework, identifying the concepts of emergence, interconnectedness, turbulence, and self-organization in groups operating as dissipative, chaotic, or complex systems (Bak, 1996; Bateson, 1972; Gallagher & Appenzeller, 1999; Davis, 2005; Doll, 1993; Fleener, 2002; Gilstrap, 2007a; Lorenz, 1963; Mandelbrot, 1975; Morgan, 1997; Osberg & Biesta, 2007; Pascale, Millemann, & Gioja, 2000; Prigogine & Stengers, 1984; Stacey, 1992, 2003; Waldrop, 1992).

METHODOLOGY

An ARL institution library was identified for participation in this case study as exemplifying the transformative change process among research libraries. This library ranked near the ARL median and had participated in two organizational restructuring activities within the past 15 years. A preliminary survey dealing with professional changes was sent to all librarians, and approximately half of these librarians responded. As Denzin and Lincoln (1994) have consistently suggested in qualitative research, purposive sampling was conducted based on the responses to the preliminary survey. Seventeen librarians (Table 1) were chosen for on-site interviewing based on the richness of description of their responses, and on-site interviews consisted of an open-ended clustering technique where participants were asked to draw

Table 1. Demographic Information of Case Study Participants.

Demographic	n
Female	8
Male	9
Mean age	51
Median age	56
Youngest participant age	36
Oldest participant sge	63
Mean years of experience as an academic librarian	21
Number holding second subject masters or Ph.D. in addition to M.L.S.	10
Administrators or managers	7
Supervisors	5
Nonsupervisors	5
Number of branch librarians	3
Number in collections or technical areas	7
Number in public services areas	8

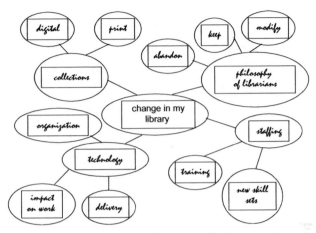

Fig. 1. Example of Clustering Technique Used during Interviews.

a concept map around the phrase, "change in my library" (Fig. 1). After the clustering portion of the interview was completed, semi-structured questions from the interview protocol were asked of each participant. Owing to institutional review board policies at both the participating institution and the institution of the researcher, anonymity of this research library and the librarians is further preserved through the use of pseudonyms. Case study instrumental and intrinsic data (Stake, 1995) were iteratively analyzed through a broad theoretical framework included in the literature, and four major themes that emerged through this analysis are reported in the following findings section.

RESEARCH FINDINGS

Introduction: Intrinsic Case Study Findings of the Organization

Six main themes emerged during intrinsic case study analysis of the East Coast University (ECU) Libraries as an organization from data collected from on-site instrumental case study interviews (Fig. 2). These themes spanned the breadth of experiences each librarian attributed to change, given his or her individual perspectives on the organization. The first two main research questions for this study are: (1) "What experiences do librarians associate with an environment of rapid change, uncertainty, and turbulence?" and (2) "What specific changes do librarians regard as having

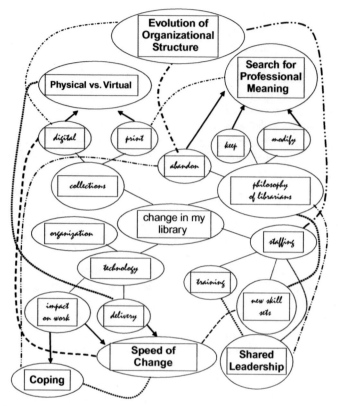

Fig. 2. Concept Map of Intrinsic Themes Emerging from Instrumental Case Clustering.

the most profound effects on their work life?" The four themes responding to the first two research questions on which this chapter is focused include: Competing tensions between the physical and the virtual environments, the speed of change, the search for professional meaning, and coping with the experiences of professional change.

Theme One: Competing Tensions between the Physical and Virtual Environments

Research librarians have begun the new century with many challenges facing the future directions of the profession. One of the most apparent issues for librarians, the users of library resources, and university administrators has been a significant shift in focus from the print to the virtual library. In the past, research librarians defined themselves by print collections and boasted about the size of these physical collections. As more and more digital resources became available at the ECU Libraries, the maintenance of a print environment became an increasing challenge for the librarians. As a result, the ECU Libraries have significantly slowed collection development of print resources, moving toward a model of electronic-only where possible. Granted, this shift excludes the library's special collections, and, rather, integrates digital objects along side the preservation of rare items. But changes in the focus of overall collection development have led almost all librarians to respond with some emotion in favor of or against this trend. And the decrease in maintenance of print items challenges librarians to think in new ways about how to use the physical library building in the future.

Since the ECU Libraries have taken an active role in the shift from the physical to the virtual environment, this new focus has been a major catalyst for change within the organization. The library has decided to forego the purchase of a remote storage facility, since librarians at ECU have watched their peers at other institutions fill these storage units quickly while still running out of space. As a result, librarians at ECU have made a conscious decision to select electronic items over print and discard duplicate print copies. Library staff members have traditionally processed the print item, but work is now focused on providing access to electronic resources. The ECU Libraries outsource much of their processing of the remaining print items to receive "shelf-ready" materials from their book vendors. Though many academic libraries focus fully on cataloging data in the international standard MAchine Readable Cataloging (MARC) format, the ECU Libraries now have time to integrate an increasing amount of non-MARC metadata, using the extensible markup language (XML) and the Dublin Core standards. However, this shift in focus requires continual re-training to enrich data associated with the new digital resources.

Space issues have in recent years been of major concern in research libraries. In some ways, this trend could be viewed as a microcosm of the space issues faced by the university at large, as the number of students and faculty has increased on most comprehensive university campuses. At ECU, every campus in the state system has been asked to implement new programs, but, physically, where to place the students in these new programs has been perceived by some to have reached a critical level. So administrators identify the library at their campus as one solution to their space dilemmas. As an example, Paul, who manages a branch library, recognizes this growing tension between librarians and campus administrators and points out that, "they walk around and ask, 'isn't it true people don't use books anymore, and isn't it true a whole lot of your space is taken up with book stacks?' Well ... yeah [laughing]." At the same time, Paul presents a challenging argument to campus administrators that if they walk around several of the classrooms on campus, they will find many empty at any given hour and day of the week. For the same reasons that research libraries have to confront space issues through new services and technologies, this trend in libraries might signal a broader need to analyze the use of space, and subsequent scheduling, on university campuses in general.

The administration of current physical and virtual environments has also challenged librarians to differentiate between the library as place versus doing something in the building. If students primarily go to the library to get a cup of coffee and find a corner in which to study, then the purpose of the library as a physical space shifts dramatically. Moreover, if journal subscriptions and books move increasingly to electronic access, then storage of items in the physical building becomes somewhat obsolete with the exception of maintaining physical items to support statistical rankings. On this issue, Bill, who has administered work with both print and digital items processing, suggests that most physical items can be stored in off-site storage facilities while being shared by several research libraries in a consortium. But given that the shift to a virtual library is taking place at the ECU Libraries, he questions how the space that is left will be utilized most effectively.

This emphasis on digital over print resources has become a critical aspect of the ECU librarians' vision of the future. The library previously had a consultant come in who asked how much of their collection budget was devoted to electronic-only purchases. After the library's administration proudly remarked, 70 per cent, the consultant asked "why isn't that one hundred percent?" This was a fairly reasonable question to ask of research libraries in the age of digital resources, but events like this reflect marker events in individual librarians' professional lives. As an example, librarians had spent many years developing the print collections and watching them grow. James, a mid-career librarian who has worked with collection development and library instruction, indicates that ECU librarians were now given the difficult task to begin weeding out the collection at a much more dramatic pace than in the past:

> It's one of those traditional librarian roles that just never was much fun in the past. And now it's definitely not something that anyone is excited about doing. But it's just as critical as it has always been ... we have a real space crunch.

The reference unit in the ECU Libraries is another area that has been affected by the shift from print to electronic resources, impacting the psychological perceptions of librarians working in this unit. In the past years, the reference department proudly proclaimed how many thousands of volumes were in the reference collection, and these librarians had spent a considerable number of years building up that collection. Almost overnight the collection was cut in half in favor of online reference sources. Elizabeth, a young librarian new to her work in instructional services but with experience in other university academic units, argues that the decision to do this was critical for the survival of the ECU Libraries. However, some librarians at ECU now feel lost and are having a hard time transitioning away from the collection of physical items.

A parallel view of space issues also emerged during the discussion of the shift from the print to the virtual environment. Although freeing up space in the library by weeding out books has been successful at ECU, the demands for digital resources have placed a new set of requirements on the virtual spaces found on the library's networked servers. In effect, the space issue has not disappeared; rather it has shifted from the physical building to networked infrastructure. And this requires a new focus on how administrative decisions are made to support this digital environment. The new challenge has evolved toward trying to find enough server storage space and resources to house the digital items that have been created at the ECU Libraries. Robert, who works primarily with digital resources, notes for example that this will become an even more critical issue as the ECU Libraries expand access to information in online video and audio used for course reserves and special collections. Consequently, as the ECU librarians respond to physical space issues in the future, this demand for virtual space will continue to grow.

Theme Two: The Speed of Change

Many of the specific issues surrounding both changes at the individual level and how librarians cope with these transitions involve the speed of change itself. Though some librarians find the speed to be too fast, others find the speed slow and rigid. However, technology serves as a catalyst for the speed of the changing environment at the ECU Libraries in both proscribed and unintentional ways that lead to further complexity of the services and resources librarians provide to the university community. Limitations in the university structure, capital and human resources, and the external business community also prohibit librarians from affecting change at a faster pace. And at the same time, the rapidity and constancy of the changing organizational environment increases levels of professional tension among the librarians.

Technology as a Catalyst for Change

Technology understandably contributes to many of the service shifts in academic librarianship today. As new library technologies emerge on a daily basis, librarians respond to the changing external environment to provide services and resources in a contemporary fashion. Equally, the integration of new technologies is applied to help transform the organizational structure of the ECU Libraries through continual adaptation to the changing student body. The librarians in this study indicate that technology has been a major impetus for change at the ECU Libraries, but they also note that it encompasses several different aspects of a changing profession. On the one hand, technology has been a very empowering tool for freeing up space in the library and making daily tasks more efficient. On the other, technology makes librarians somewhat nervous about the future, because it confronts the core values of librarianship. As an example, Elizabeth, who is new to the career of librarianship and who works in an educational role, shows how the use of electronic databases has entirely changed the way library instruction is taught at the ECU Libraries in the course of only a few years:

> I find myself with instruction shifting the way I talk about things. From, 'you better know how to find it in print', to 'let's go looking for it in full text, but don't forget there might be print if you *have* to use it.' It's a totally different way of talking about things, of thinking about things.

These shifts in professional thinking as a result of technology cause librarians to speculate whether the changes at ECU are more successful because of technology or if sometimes technology drives the change.

Although technology has solved problems brought on by growing collections and services, it has brought, at the same time, new problems that are equally, if not more, complex in nature. Technology has greatly assisted the librarians at ECU to transition into the future, and most of the librarians self-identify their preference for the use of new technologies. However, all of these changes have required new equipment, new training, new network architectures, and an increasingly complex communication network with appropriate university officials: from carpenters to network technicians to legal counsel. And, because this network of both hardware and the people required to implement it is now so complicated, librarians have to be very selective in what they choose to integrate. Furthering this argument, Laura, who supervises a unit that oversees technology used for public services, states that it becomes critical to plan for the obsolescence of old practices to integrate the new technologies. But, due to the limitations in librarians' abilities to predict far into the future, a significant challenge comes in knowing what to give up, when to do it, and how to plan for that abandonment.

Adding value to services that are provided primarily through the World Wide Web also becomes problematic. As librarians do not always know how to transfer skill sets in new, technologically oriented ways, grounding user expectations in the academic setting becomes increasingly difficult. As an example, Ted, who has worked in a branch library for many years, questions whether student use of certain technological products drives the changes taking place at the ECU Libraries. He states that he wonders whether RSS feeds and facebook.com pages in research libraries add any value to services. At the same time traditional collection development practices do not exist on the Web, and incorporating strategies that adapt to student and faculty use of technology becomes more critical in convincing the university community that librarians do something that adds value; or, as Ted comments, "that you're not an appendage of the Internet." Phillip, the library's director, extends this perspective by arguing that disseminating information in ways that are commonly used in society is crucial for the future of academic librarianship. If librarians do not embrace these changes, they will continue to lose ground at academic institutions, because library users will find ways to get the information they need if the library does not provide it in a contemporary fashion.

Technology can also be seen as a panacea for dealing with the inefficiencies of the print environment. With the rise in newer student expectations for a Web framework in which everything is in full text, some librarians believe that the library should abandon print collections wherever possible. Christina, for example, who is new to the profession and fully embraces technological change, states that she has become increasingly frustrated with any continued focus on collecting print resources. Although the ECU Libraries have been particularly active in this collection development strategy, she states that academic librarianship as a profession cannot break free from the frame of reference of the print environment:

> [The ECU Libraries] are OK with not buying a print copy of a book if it's online. And if the online goes down for a couple of hours, nobody in this library is going to die ... I don't know how any librarian could *not* feel that way; this whole idea that you need to retain print.

Katherine, a librarian new to the ECU Libraries who primarily works with technology, equally sympathizes with this shift in collection development. She comments that, "honestly, when I'm at the reference desk, I don't want to send people to the paper stacks if I can possibly avoid it."

Limitations in Affecting Change
One of the particularly frustrating issues that accompanies change at the ECU Libraries has to do with the actual purchase of new products or technology. A large amount of time may be spent on evaluating and making recommendations for new software that will help improve the ECU Libraries' further transition into a digital environment. But once the selection has been made, librarians note that months can transpire in the university's purchasing or legal units before the product is actually implemented. Whereas some might argue that the library is not changing fast enough, librarians argue just as often that the university's bureaucracy cannot keep up with changes the ECU Libraries need to make. As a result, ECU librarians comment that they are given an unfair reputation of being resistant to change when in actuality the university structure prevents them from becoming more effective change agents.

Technology also becomes a system agent that adds further complexity when trying to move the library into the future. Again, many librarians note that they bear the brunt of criticisms by students and faculty about the library's technology when it cannot compete with enterprise technologies like Yahoo or Google. As an example, James, who has contributed to the ECU Libraries' migrations to two different integrated library management systems, states that online catalog systems supplied by corporate vendors continue to use technology that is "straight out of the 70s." Librarians at ECU know the improvements that need to be made to this technology and, as beta partners, provide the knowledge and feedback to the vendors to make these changes on a weekly basis. Moreover, there is a tremendous investment made in these products, and, since the library has little ability within the overall structure of the university to pursue litigation, many librarians believe there is no way to confront the failure of these vendors.

There is a paradox that emerges in observing research libraries that try to compete with large corporations for similar product development. One of the most frustrating elements of being a research librarian is that much of the knowledge needed to create new products already exists among librarians. However, there is a lack of time and resources to implement these services. As an example, the librarians at ECU have many of the technological skills and the desire to be able to implement online audio and video for course reserves, adding more value to services that would expand access to these resources for students and faculty regardless of time or geographic location. Equally, this model could effectively replace physical nonprint items that are currently held on reserve. Moreover, as information resources in research libraries evolve beyond traditional text-based items, the library's ability to support these new mediums of information will become critical. But the required equipment and product development are cost prohibitive for research libraries let alone smaller academic libraries.

Many ARL libraries become beta-sites for vendors to develop products as a way to address the lack of in-house resources. Some of these vendors give the ECU Libraries discounts in pricing in return for their agreeing to become a beta-site. But in reality, the ECU Libraries do significant product development of vendor software, including a large investment of human resources and intellectual capital from which the vendors benefit later on with other libraries. Christina, who brings experience from having worked in the corporate technology sector, laughs as she describes this model, arguing that any other company in the same situation would actually be *paid* to be a beta-site, rather than merely receiving discounts. Moreover, there oftentimes are no other vendors that provide better services, so being a beta-site is one of the only methods librarians believe they have to bring the vendors up to speed with the technology needs of twenty-first century research libraries. The frustrations that arise from this situation are highlighted by Elizabeth, who deeply questions the slowness of change when teaching library research, in her response to vendor limitations:

> If change is so good and so essential, why isn't it just happening? Why aren't we in the twenty-second century with technology, and why aren't librarians inventing the technology? ... Change is certainly possible, but you can't just will it, however passionate you are about change.

Although the open source movement has received great attention recently in research libraries (Breeding, 2007a, 2007b; Pace, 2006), many ARL libraries do not have the capital to invest in equipment, people, and resources to create products that compete with vendors in the business community. Or, conversely, strategic priorities might move in this direction in the near future.

Another feature that emerged through the course of interviews concerned how quickly librarians are able to respond to change with the rise of so many communication technologies. Granted, email, wikis, listservs, and intranets have massively integrated and provided access to information in ways that enable librarians to absorb and share a great deal of knowledge in much faster ways. Several librarians comment that the real challenge comes when the involvement of so many people actually slows down the process of implementing change, as Lisa, a library administrator in a public services area, recounts:

> Sometimes change is very slow. You can't always have an impact, and it doesn't always go smoothly when you're working with a group of people. It also feels like the process can be slow, because you're consulting everyone.

At the broader professional level, research libraries have not been able to create and implement standards fast enough to keep up with technology due to the involvement of so many people in different online working groups. Robert, as an example, commented that he first chose to pursue an MLS because of the predicted mass digitization that was soon to take place. However, 10 years later, many of the metadata standards that apply to both the academic and private sectors are still in nascent stages, so many research libraries are left on their own to create or enhance locally the standards associated with metadata.

Limitations in decision-making are also connected to the basic limitations of the strategic planning process in the ECU Libraries, as well as in higher education in general. The ECU Libraries, like most research libraries, follow a yearly strategic planning process where library-wide goals and objectives are developed with input from all personnel in the library. However, technological developments in the ECU libraries now happen so quickly that by the time the library's goals and objectives have been finalized, emerging technologies have already shifted the focus of the librarians. Katherine describes her own frustrations with how this process slows down the ability of librarians to make periodic changes throughout the year:

> Librarians aren't necessarily thinking in that cycle. They're thinking, we need to do this, and we need to do it now. They're not thinking in terms of 'well in two months I'll be able to propose goals and objectives for the next strategic planning cycle.'

And as universities continue to use these traditional strategic planning models, rapid changes in research libraries will be further limited by this annual cycle.

The Speed of Change is Rapid and Constant

Many librarians see continual change taking place at their libraries, ranging from the introduction of new technologies to the incorporation of new information sources. The literature in library science shows that many research libraries approach change as an incremental process. However, those librarians working at ECU frequently describe change as rapid and constant, and they note that change no longer happens at a pace consistent with generations. Rather, technology in libraries has created an environment where something new comes out literally every day. And because of the rapid and turbulent speed of change, librarians at ECU are affected by this speed in their abilities to respond to change. Lisa, who works daily to help her colleagues move further toward a digital environment, highlights this feeling of being constantly pulled in different directions as a result of so much change:

> This change is beyond a proliferation, it's an explosion. I can't finish doing one thing before I've got five more that need to be done yesterday. Looking at my calendar this week and last week, if I have two hours together without a meeting, somebody's waiting to fill that time ... It's like being on a treadmill.

The ECU Libraries are making significant progress in their transformation to an organization that relies predominantly on providing information and services in a virtual environment. However, several librarians comment that the speed of change happens so quickly that there seems to be little time to enjoy the successes that the ECU Libraries experience due to an immediate shift in focus toward the next project. As an example, Laura describes the turbulence of change in her own professional life:

> Change is happening so fast, and flying at us at such a pace, that you constantly feel like you don't have time to get your foot down before you're moving on to the next thing ... And while we don't have the kind of financial support that the commercial sector would have, we still have to provide things in ways that are comfortable and convenient for the population in other areas of their lives.

Laura, who also suggested that librarians plan for the obsolescence of past practices, is an avid supporter of all the changes the ECU Libraries have made in the past few years. But she asks somewhat rhetorically if there is a way to control the speed of change that hits everyone's desk on a daily basis. Although she knows this probably cannot be accomplished, she recommends to the profession that, "there does have to be the voice that says, I embrace change, but there has got to be a way to do this that is not going to kill everybody."

Another phenomenon that emerged related to this theme pertains to the abandonment of old practices. The ability to increase the speed of change at the ECU Libraries is often slowed down, again, by trying to maintain both a physical and a virtual library. New digital resources and services compute to new work that has been added on top of the librarians' existing work, while new staff to handle these services are not added to the library. At the same time, however, Patricia, who administers a unit that processes many of the print and digital resources of the ECU Libraries, notes that librarians are not willing to give up this work even if it is no longer needed. Consequently, this dilemma is exacerbated, since some librarians are very much in favor of continuing to add more and more digital resources while *maintaining* their work in the print environment. Several other librarians comment, however, this is just not an option for the ECU Libraries. So while librarians have been given permission to abandon their old work, passive aggressiveness toward change sometimes emerges regarding the protection of obsolete work. And, moreover, the necessity of this change becomes critical, because the library will not be viewed on campus as being an innovator or a partner in educational and research processes.

Theme Three: The Search for Professional Meaning

The search for professional meaning emerged as a philosophical under-current associated with change at the ECU Libraries. This theme ranged in diversity and depth of responses by librarians which showed that, although the ECU Libraries operate with a shared vision and team environment, the concept of change was not necessarily a conformist ideal accepted by all of the librarians. Rather, levels of its acceptance were connected to each person's individual experiences and desire to make sense of the phenom-enon. This search for professional meaning leads librarians into a period of simultaneous uncertainty and discovery. Bridges (2004) describes this search as the "forest dweller" stage where an individual leaves the comfort of his or her previously stable settings and introspectively explores alternative perspectives of career meaning.

For some librarians at ECU, this journey does not include a change in professional philosophy. Rather, it implies the need for librarians to choose aspects of the philosophy that respond more readily to new environments while communicating their own professional relevance to the university community. For other librarians, this response to the external environment requires radical shifts in philosophical thinking to ensure the long-term survival of the profession. This search for professional meaning also brings the question of dehumanization in the profession to the surface, as some librarians fear that the implementation of new technologies without the presence of human interaction with students and faculty will create increased stress and uncertainty not only for librarians but for the academic community in general. Still other librarians suggest that the search for professional meaning includes active competition with the business community in future product development. ECU librarians also suggest that internal professional crises precipitate the need to shift away from traditional librarian specializations altogether, requiring radical shifts in library science curriculum to provide the skill sets necessary to manage emerging virtual libraries. Moreover, the absence of these external opportunities for development requires research libraries in the future to promote professional transformation through the precipitation of organizational transformation.

Communicating Professional Relevance

In an online environment, the concept of communicating the relevance of the library becomes more and more difficult. Users access online resources to which the library subscribes, oftentimes without realizing the work that has gone on behind the scenes to provide a seamless gateway to these resources. As an example, Lisa, who previously questioned the continuation of outdated practices, notes the greater importance librarians attribute to the perception of the library by the academic institution. She describes this scenario as continually exacerbating the concept of communicating the library's importance:

> You have to continue to prove your relevance, but you have to do it in ways you didn't do in the past. Volume counts aren't important anymore. When researchers get grants and rely on the electronic resources of the library, and they don't identify those resources with the library or the people that work there, how do you keep them aware of that?

Furthermore, the physical library used to be viewed as a central intellectual center on campus, but university administrators now see this central role disappearing due to the increasing demand for electronic information. And, while the library continues to pay for these digital subscriptions, researchers do not always identify the library with the information resources available to the university community.

Changes in the ECU Libraries might also be attributed to dysfunctional communication patterns among the librarians. Some librarians find themselves disconnected from the university community and from other academic librarians. As an example, Elizabeth, who previously questioned how slow change sometimes takes place, challenges librarians to communicate their relevance by tearing down both the physical and metaphorical walls that separate librarians from the university community. Moreover, this framework for understanding can help expose the dilemmas of libraries as similar symptoms of universities at large. Elizabeth argues that libraries epitomize the ivory towers on campus:

> Libraries have always been a tower within a tower. And often literally, *literally*, a library is that building that looks like a tower in the middle of the campus.

In her view, the metaphorical significance of this image subsequently leads to a convent-like mentality among librarians. Because of their physical spaces, librarians allow themselves to be cloistered from the university community outside the walls of the library and from their own colleagues within the building.

The Question of Dehumanization in the Profession
Many of the problems the ECU Libraries face are equally representative of the same dilemmas encountered by other academic units on campus. As an example, many university employees take Information Technology (IT) departments for granted and do not realize the significant amount of work that goes into maintenance of the campus IT infrastructure. And this problem is exacerbated in IT units, since many of the people who work within them are never seen by the campus community. Elizabeth comments that librarians have in the same vein been unable to find ways to legitimize and advocate for themselves professionally. In her view, the human side of libraries continues to have importance even in a digital age:

> You could erase the people, and we could hide ourselves underground, right? There would still have to be people hidden someplace like moles or gophers actually doing things to make that possible. We'll still be around. But it would be nice not to have to be buried in a hole. It would be nice to market ourselves.

The search for professional meaning in the age of commercial search engines becomes problematic when trying to project an image of human interaction into the future of librarianship. Some of the attributes of the profession happen philosophically behind the scenes but are not realized by many who use the ECU Libraries. As an example, Ann states that she feels the human focus of the profession has been taken for granted. Research librarians have a societal obligation to preserve history for the future while concurrently incorporating new technologies to make this happen. "It is sort of a dichotomy we've been faced with for 20 years or more at least, and it's not an easy one." However, Ann, like Elizabeth, fears that a research future that does not involve human interaction seems dark and desolate.

The Need to Respond to the External Environment
The search for professional meaning is a challenge that also shifts thinking in more rapid ways to respond to the real world experiences of library users. Librarians at ECU argue that librarians should learn to provide services and resources that are more in line with what people experience in their lives. Although Laura describes herself as an older, long-term career librarian,

many of the challenges in exposing the deeper issues of professional meaning are related to generational divides among older and younger librarians. The ECU Libraries are moving into the digital environment at a fast pace, but her experiences with librarians in other libraries have shown her that the profession is reaching a critical juncture. Laura, who has worked in different libraries for many years, argues that change in most libraries is happening at a slow rate that is unsustainable if librarians continue to force rigid structures of control and guardianship on the university community:

> Mostly in other libraries, the change doesn't come as fast as it does here, and it's not well received. There's a lot of older librarians in more hierarchical places who don't get it. They don't get it that, if they don't change, their whole institution may well disappear.

This argument does not imply that research libraries can do without older professionals. On the contrary, these librarians could lend a great deal of knowledge to the further development of the profession by beginning new individual searches for professional meaning. This dilemma becomes frustrating for many librarians when apathy toward a shift in professional thinking threatens job security. However, as Laura comments:

> My sons, who are in their 20s and 30s, tell me, 'Mom, you have got to get a new profession. Libraries are going away. Nobody in their right mind goes to a library anymore.' That's an epidemic way of thinking in the population as a whole and not necessarily inappropriate I think … It's a huge issue, and it really needs to be put out there especially for the benefit of the people who don't think their jobs are in danger or that libraries will go away.

Librarians at ECU also note that responding to the external environment must begin by reflecting on practice, and the practice of librarianship relies on understanding the educational and personal experiences of the library user. As Richard notes this includes recognizing what it is like to be a university student today and that many students are just as busy between work, school, and family lives as are librarians. What an incredible advantage it is for these students to be able to access the library's resources late at night after the family has gone to bed.

The divide between library user expectations and traditional frames of reference for the library profession can be particularly frustrating in an age of enterprise level search engines. Many of the students entering ECU now have lived through much of their educational careers with online search engines. As a result, they are accustomed to this type of searching and do not feel that library databases meet their expectations as far as user interfaces go. As one example, Christina notes that some of her colleagues take an adversarial position against the use of online search engines, and she states that any librarian's quest for professional meaning should specifically address the failure of library resources to meet the Google expectation. Students now have choices and do not need to rely on librarians to find information. If librarians want to be able to compete with these types of search engines in the future, they must compete now, and that can only come with a new professional philosophy that tries to surpass the performance of Yahoo or Google. Students and faculty continue to view librarians as "kindly" and "intellectual," but these qualities will not suffice when librarians are no longer the people students and faculty turn to when they need information.

David, who has been a librarian for many years and administers technology in the ECU Libraries, argues that librarians have lost touch with the foundations of librarianship and need a recursive view of the founding philosophies:

> It certainly doesn't have to do with books, and it has nothing to do with libraries – it has more to do with access to information. It's really what it was all about in the first place, but I think we've always gotten hung up by the book on the shelf itself.

This is the unfortunate circumstance within which librarians have placed themselves. Some would argue that librarians have focused on the book and have therefore shifted their thinking toward things rather than people. In effect, librarians have created for themselves the very crisis from which they are trying to escape. If librarians can begin marketing their own value, they have a chance to find a place for themselves in a future where physical items are less important and human beings are more valued in a profession that continues to compete with the private sector.

Identified Needs for Change in the Philosophy of Librarianship

Changes in professional and organizational structures are happening so fast that there have been significant shifts in how research libraries of the future are even discussed. Teresa notes, for example, that there has been a subtle conversation among ARL directors that in the future, there might only be a handful of research libraries, and the remaining libraries will end up merging in virtual environments with, or subsequently absorbing, other academic libraries. If the former occurs – all of the prestige that formally came with the title of being a research librarian will start to disappear – leaving many wondering what this future will hold. Research universities in general might subsequently follow this trend. As Teresa states, "I think the profession will probably continue to have an identity crisis [laughing]." Moreover, Teresa questions, like many of her colleagues, if there will even be research librarians as we know them now in the future. If there are, the stereotype of librarians liking books will completely disappear, and the concept of managing electronic resources will be less understandable to those outside the profession.

The uncertainty that the profession will evolve quickly enough to meet the challenges facing it increases occupational angst. At ECU, the librarians have done a very good job in reaching out to the new generation of students coming into the university, but this shift in focus has not been easy. As librarians note, they need to have people in the library who understand this generation. And the ECU Libraries have accomplished this to a large degree by actually going physically and virtually to where the students are. Librarians go to the students to provide services, whether that means the dorms, the individual colleges and departments, or the student union building. Equally, in a virtual environment, the librarians use wikis, blogs, podcasting, and Facebook to reach out to students. Lisa, as an example, challenges research librarians to understand how important this is, arguing that librarians need to look deeply at the relevance of their organization to the current and future university. "You definitely need to get a strong idea of what your institution is thinking about you and what it's expecting from you." And that means librarians have to make difficult choices. They can no longer continue to perform tasks that the institution perceives as irrelevant or wait to react to changing needs.

Increasing retirements taking place in research libraries can also be viewed as a catalyst for a new process of discovery of professional meaning. The ECU Libraries, like many other research libraries, have had difficulties recruiting librarians with newly needed skill sets. As an example, Christina states that, librarians disagree with the librarian stereotype, but the stereotype still fits to a large extent. "I think the people who are attracted to becoming 'a librarian' in quotes are not necessarily the type of people we need." The ECU Libraries seek out librarians who are willing to create and promote an environment where students can get access to library resources from commercial search engines without ever coming to a physical library. The problem in her view is that research librarians often want to work primarily with graduate students when the vast majority of most campuses at ARL institutions are composed of undergraduate students who use the library far more frequently than their graduate level colleagues. As Christina argues, "I don't think we like a lot of our users. I think we don't connect with them, and it's a problem."

Organizational Transformation Accompanied by Professional Transformation
For many research librarians, organizational changes serve as a catalyst for accompanying professional changes. These shifts in thinking require

librarians to generate their own professional evolution by relying on the continual acquisition of new skill sets. Librarians at ECU highlight changes in their own professional philosophies by focusing on the organizational redesigns that have occurred at the ECU Libraries over the past 15 years. It becomes critical for research libraries to evolve continuously, otherwise members of the university community will find different ways to get the information they need through methods that reflect practice in contemporary society. As an example, Philip sees how the organizational structure of the ECU Libraries has gone through significant changes in philosophy by encouraging openness to new ideas. And this means individuals must take on leadership roles that promote this continual evolution. However, librarians can sometimes be reluctant to initiate change without direction and may express resistance to giving up obsolete to take on new challenges. Although the ECU Libraries have been particularly successful in recruiting librarians with these skill sets, many librarians were hired to perform work in a traditional print environment. And, equally, many of these people were hired to do very specific tasks. Consequently, Philip states:

> I see the disconnects between the skills that we have at hand, and the skills that we need ... And I think that's our single biggest challenge ... There will always be a call for the digital object itself, but I truly believe we're looking at a really different future at some point.

Another concept that emerged during the course of this study suggests that a change in professional philosophy should really be centered on the concept of coping with change. These librarians note that everyone responds to change differently, and, perhaps, there is a tendency for people in general to react negatively to change during the beginning of the process. The ECU Libraries have been active in facilitating an educational process that helps train people to develop new skill sets and to question current practices. This change process at the ECU Libraries typically has to be explored at the individual level which generates its own set of problems. When individuals ask themselves whether their own work needs to continue to be performed, they feel threatened. Ann, who works in an educational capacity where she helps librarians repurpose their skill sets, jokes that "it's like the first rule of holes: the first thing you have to do is quit digging." When librarians refocus their views toward the opportunities that the changes bring, however, they recognize that holding on to the past actually creates more stress for themselves than letting go and embracing new ideas.

Having worked at different ARL institutions, Ann recognizes that other research libraries share some of the same professional challenges that the

ECU Libraries faces. And these challenges often come in the form of a paradox between professional thinking about the printed and virtual environments. Research libraries have an obligation to preserve the past to make this information available for future examination. At the same time, research libraries are obligated to incorporate digital resources that streamline the research process for faculty and students. But regardless of the medium of exchange, the need for human experience and interaction will continue to be critical for the success of the research library in the future.

Theme Four: Coping with the Experiences of Professional Change

Significant turbulence in a person's life can greatly influence how she/he responds to change. And certainly there are significant changes taking place at many research libraries across the country. However, there is little in the literature that addresses how librarians cope with and experience change in academic libraries. During the course of interviews at the ECU Libraries, librarians described several different experiences and coping mechanisms they use when responding to change. The concept of increased stress and tension as a result of rapid change and increased workloads emerged frequently, and the phenomenon of stress as a shared experience also was identified by the librarians in this study. Subsequently, coping strategies were identified by the participants which included communicating change, learning new skills, and adapting workflows. Equally, the necessity of coping at the individual level and through dialogue with other individuals becomes important to establish what Schön (1991) would describe as new theories in use. It became clear during the course of these interviews that dealing with change focuses more on the individual's own experiences, and his or her coping mechanisms manifest themselves in ways relevant to these experiences.

Coping by Communicating Change
It has been suggested by several researchers in the social and behavioral sciences that leaders should communicate the issues that surround needed changes in organizations as a strategy that helps individuals deal with organizational shifts (Birnbaum, 2000; Burns, 2003; Shaw, 1999; Yukl, 2002). At the ECU libraries, several librarians extend this perspective of communicating changes at all levels as an effective coping strategy. By letting colleagues know that changes are coming before they happen gives the librarians an opportunity to confront and make sense out of those changes. As an example, Teresa, who has participated in both library organizational

restructuring activities, sees communication as the most important aspect of coping with change. Change for many people in her area is uncomfortable and frustrating since they require that outdated practices be phased out. The perception among staff can sometimes be that change is being pushed on them. But in her view, the ECU Libraries have been particularly successful at communicating changes throughout the organization and getting people involved in discussion. As a result, in addition to the library-wide opportunities for communicating change, in her own area Teresa tries to begin dialogue among colleagues as early as possible.

This process of allowing participants to verbalize their frustrations and share in this discomfort is a strategy for coping that helps employees move toward the change, similar to Bridges' (2003, 2004) description of the individual transition process. Occasionally, the changes are so dramatic that library personnel find themselves in a situation Mezirow (1991) would describe as a disorienting dilemma. For some, the change is insurmountable, and, in spite of opportunities to train for new skill sets, these employees see retirement as the only option for coping with change. Conversely, employees also go through a similar transformation of perspective that enables them to move into a more highly developed frame of reference for coping with change. Moreover, Teresa states that their involvement in communicating the change process is sometimes more important than the change itself, a phenomenon Ouchi (1981) has observed in corporate organizations.

Coping with change is also viewed from a different framework when discussing individuals outside of the ECU Libraries. Several librarians accept the changes that have taken place in at the ECU Libraries very positively. Adding further to this idea, James, who works in an educational capacity, states that communicating change is essential to help *faculty and students* cope with the shifts taking place at the ECU Libraries. Students, in particular, find it difficult to engage in instructional sessions on library research, because the amount of information is somewhat overwhelming for them and because their experiences are so different from those of students working 10 years ago. Consequently, it becomes more difficult to learn critical reflection skills in a dynamic rather than a static environment, as the traditional structures of research and learning are starting to disappear. Therefore, librarians constantly change lesson plans and supporting materials as a way to communicate shifts in higher education that subsequently help students and faculty cope with these changes.

Communicating change can also be used in subtle ways that help individuals accomplish their goals. Librarians who are relatively new to the ECU Libraries might use a naive approach to communicate change. As an example, Robert, who has been at the ECU Libraries for a few years now, notes that much of the perception of the resistance or inability to cope with change at the ECU Libraries can be attributed to the idea that these conversations are "probably gossip enhanced to make the library more interesting." Consequently, since it is more difficult for someone perceived as an outsider by long-time employees to be accepted and thereby affect change, newness and the naivetée that comes with it can break down these otherwise judgmental attitudes through the recognition that someone is new and does not know any better. This in turn allows librarians to be less reactive and reflect critically on the new ideas proposed by someone who has not been influenced by the traditions in the organization.

Coping with Change through Learning
Several ECU librarians identify the concept of learning as an integral strategy for coping with all of the changes taking place at their library. As an example, Lisa notes her own way of confronting change has incorporated new learning strategies to prepare for the future:

> I have had to "come to Jesus" as it were. You know I have had to fight the same personal issues that a lot of people do. I just have to be prepared for change and that it's a part of my life all the time. What we did well six months or a year ago may be different. So looking forward helps me not to get blind-sided.

Consequently, the brown bag lunches the ECU Libraries hold periodically have been a very effective method for her to incorporate continual learning into her coping strategies. These brown bag lunches usually cover a specific aspect of new technologies and give participants opportunities to discuss and understand the changes these technologies bring. Lisa also points out that no matter how much she might discuss the constancy of change at the ECU Libraries, "that doesn't give anyone any comfort." Rather the ability of individuals to experience and understand change through learning makes the change less uncomfortable, as well as provides new skills that will help during the change process.

Conversely, learning as a strategy to cope with change can also make increasing stress more problematic. Gaining new knowledge is integral to several of the ECU librarians' evolving perspectives on the changing library profession. However, this quest for knowledge can be very time consuming, because the team environment contributes to a considerable number of meetings. Moreover, if training or learning activities are not geared toward immediate use, people will forget their new skill sets or will not be able to see the bigger picture of their application toward contributing to change.

Elizabeth, who works in an educational capacity with many web technologies, also expands on this idea, arguing that using learning to cope with change involves an incredible investment of time and a conscious decision to *choose* what to learn:

> Someone could spend 40 hours a week going to informational meetings just trying to keep up with what's going on. I mean really, it's just so overwhelming. How do you balance learning new things with actually trying to get some work done [laughing]. It's difficult some times.

So, although learning can be an effective method for coping with change, it can also contribute to the increasing stress levels associated with change.

Coping by Adapting Workflows
Mechanisms for coping with stress can also be attributed to more direct methods in the workplace. For several librarians at ECU, adaptations in their professional lives include such concepts as organization, choice, and disengagement. For each librarian, adaptation in the workplace brings either positive or negative outcomes and sometimes a combination of the two. Many librarians note that they are better able to cope with change by drawing from one of the key philosophical components of librarianship: staying organized. The high volume of e-mails, meeting requests, and daily priorities are almost overwhelming for several of the librarians interviewed in this study. Recently, the ECU Libraries hosted a day of learning where time management and organizational skills were taught. As an example, Laura, who must use several different technologies in the area she supervises, found this very beneficial, as she now coordinates her e-mail with documents in her PC and Intranet folders to keep a connected map of her workflows. By taking this organizational approach, she believes she is able to replicate her thought processes about task development regardless of the medium of information or its location. Taking the extra time up front to enhance this information on project schedules turns out to be a long-term investment which prevents stressful cycles of trying to reach deadlines while trying to connect all of the data on individual computers.

Interruptions during the normal workday are also some of the more frustrating outcomes of continual change in libraries. Since many of the work responsibilities associated with professional librarianship are largely intellectual, there is an increased need for finding both the time and space for concentrated thinking about change. Organizational development theorists suggest one coping strategy that can be used is to review and answer e-mail only at a certain time of the day. However, e-mail traffic is typically nonstop during most of the day at the ECU Libraries, and librarians note that waiting too long to respond leads to their being overwhelmed by the volume of e-mail. And interruptions to concentrated thought will become more and more significant as impairments for librarians to be able to adapt to change. As an example, Bill, who processes a great deal of communication in the area he oversees, finds himself closing the door to his office more frequently as a coping strategy. However, since the ECU librarians' work lives are so busy, people still constantly knock on his closed door to ask questions or report findings. Librarians, consequently, have growing levels of stress, since it becomes difficult to find time to think about complex decisions that need to be made quickly. Furthermore, in the case of Bill, he has shifted this time and space of concentrated thought to his home life, early in the morning or late in the evening, but he notices that having to do these cuts further into his personal life. Christina, who is involved with large team projects, also notes that she finds herself taking more and more work home, since she has little opportunity for concentrated effort during the work day. However, she feels that she is sometimes neglecting her family by working at home rather than spending time with them. In effect, both have carried over into their personal lives the cycle of stress from which they have difficulty escaping in their professional lives.

Overwhelming feelings of information overload can also contribute to the change of workflows at a philosophical level as a way to cope with change. As has been previously stated, several librarians describe the stress and tension that occur as a result of so much change at ECU. Realizing that he simply cannot keep up with everything, Richard, who works in a cross-functional manner with several different library units, now chooses to focus specifically on those changes that affect his area while ignoring some of the changes in tertiary areas. With the proliferation of information, it is virtually impossible for any single person to keep abreast of everything that is going on. Consequently, Richard has learned to filter information that does not pertain specifically to the tasks at hand:

> The pace of innovation and change is everywhere, and you can't be part of it all. Or I can't be, because I just have too much to do ... I think there's a good deal of rhetorical cynicism about some of the changes, but I think it's a fairly easy cynicism. The gap between ideal and reality is all around us in our lives, and it's here in the library.

A strategy of disengagement extends the philosophical strategies used to cope with the stress of the changing library environment. As an example, Tony, who has participated in both library reorganizations, laughs when he states the only way to cope realistically with these changes is through "therapy!" He notices his own coping strategy has been to disengage from commitments to the organization and to the profession, focusing primarily on the tasks that surround his local area. As another example, Ted, who has actively worked to help the ECU Libraries continually evolve, jests that, "there's probably something that will cause change that I'm either blocking or ignoring!" However, both Tony and Ted try consciously to see the changes taking place at the ECU Libraries as positive which they feel helps them to cope.

Environmental settings are an equally effective method for coping with change. Issues such as access to external light and separation from others in office spaces can contribute to positive coping strategies. Librarians note that office spaces can be constructed in a way where there are constant interruptions which makes it very hard to stay focused. Philip, the library's director, notes for example that his office is located at the end of a suite of offices. Because of the physical layout, no one comes to his office unless it is his or her destination. Equally, this office is surrounded by windows to the outside. As a result, Philip finds that this environment lends greatly to productivity on concentrated work where creativity is involved and, therefore, helps to decrease the stress and tension of everyday work life.

Coping as an Individual
Coping with change ultimately can be tied to the experiences of the individual. Librarians at ECU identify that coping most usually requires each person to respond in a manner most conducive to his or her own situation. Having worked in several research libraries, Ann says that, during her career, she was forced to go through a transformative experience when she was moved out of an administrative position. Much like Mezirow's (1991) description of the "disorienting dilemma," Ann went through several stages of reactions to this event and eventually realized that she was not coping productively with change when this event started to affect her personal life. When Ann sees this phenomenon taking place at the individual level at the ECU Libraries, she is able to draw from past experiences to encourage librarians to move toward positive reference points which will help them cope with change:

> Despite 1000s of years of development, deep in our reptilian brains, we are still "fight or flight." So much of what we do during that very first reaction to change is still based on that. And we can't control that, but we can realize what it is.

As a result, helping colleagues develop frames of reference that relate to an individualized view of change subsequently enables people to build a broader perspective of others in the library going through similar transitions.

Another method used to cope with change is to project a positive image at the individual level. Some librarians at ECU note that this is sometimes difficult but believe this positive image helps others respond in ways that are beneficial to the group environment. As an example, Patricia sometimes finds it frustrating to deal with the people that she supervises when "they complain just to complain." This is one of the most difficult aspects of her job because of her deep affection for her colleagues. By focusing less on failures and more on success, librarians see the positive effects of her individual attempts. In turn, Patricia feels personal gratification which enables her to continue to adapt to the changes in her own work.

Exercise is another strategy that can be used to cope positively with change. Interestingly, the concept of exercise as a coping mechanism was not identified by a majority of the librarians interviewed at ECU, although it is stressed by many in the social and behavioral sciences (Austin, Shah, & Muncer, 2005; Morse & Walker, 1994; Puetz, O'Connor, & Dishman, 2006; Taylor-Piliae, Haskell, Waters, & Froelicher, 2006). This researcher found that those librarians who identified exercise as one technique they used for coping tended to have positive attitudes about change while dealing with stress in constructive ways. As an example, Bill states that he originally began exercising everyday for health reasons, but now that he has done it for so long, he recognizes that it has become an aspect of how he copes with change, noting, "I do feel better, I feel more energetic." As another example, Patricia comments that, in addition to contributing to her general well-being and positive attitude, she notices that exercise gives her an opportunity to clear her head from competing ideas, enabling her to focus more deeply on the critical issues that need immediate attention. Equally, Philip argues that he has to exercise everyday to deal with the stress of his job and that his exercise regimen allows him to think more positively about his work. Additionally, he recommends to all librarians that, when tension is starting to build up during the day, they should get up and walk around the library to cope with stress in the workplace.

Coping through Dialogue with Other Individuals

Although communicating change is one method used to cope with stress in the workplace, dialogue with others suggests a broader focus on giving meaning to organizational change. As many organizational theorists have argued, communicating with others on the crises or dilemmas affecting an individual in his or her professional life provides the group with a context to generate deeper meaning about their own on circumstances (Abraham & Gilgen, 1995; Bridges, 2004; Mezirow, 1991; Stacey, 2003). Librarians at ECU also concur that conversations with others about the stress of their work life has been an effective personal strategy to cope with all of the changes taking place at their library. As an example, Tony, who is nearing retirement, notes that being able to share the same frustrations with his colleagues enables him to decrease his own angst about professional changes. Equally, Lisa, who is somewhat new to the ECU Libraries, shares this belief, stating that "being honest about the fear of change when that is what is happening enables everyone to learn ways to deal with it better." And Patricia, who has worked at the ECU Libraries for several years, comments that personal stories can be used to help others both learn and teach from the experiences of others, helping everyone to reflect further on their own individual coping strategies.

The open meetings at the ECU Libraries also help to encourage group communication that contributes to coping with change at the individual level. Since not all of the ECU librarians deal with change in the same way, the open forums for discussion have been very effective for helping other librarians see the different perspectives of their colleagues. Ted suggests, for example, that all research libraries should integrate this style of communication:

> Go ahead and talk about it. If you don't like it, bring it up. For someone upon whom change is being imposed, talk about it. If it's negative, if it's positive, at least it's expressed.

Therefore, reflections become less focused on the change itself than on the need for the voices of individuals to be heard, reflecting Ouchi's (1981) work on *Theory Z*. As another example, Laura argues that territorial boundaries tend to lend to negative misperceptions about "what the other guy does." Now her entire department meets informally with other ECU librarians outside of her area which has allowed all librarians involved to develop "broad spectrum" coping strategies across individuals working in various areas within the ECU Libraries.

The ECU Libraries' administration has moved toward being as transparent as possible when addressing upcoming changes at the library. This helps staff tremendously, as they like to know what is going to happen, when it will take place, and how changes will affect their own work. Equally, the ECU

Libraries have implemented a program that helps train staff for new responsibilities, and this has been viewed positively by library staff. In this program, staff are presented with scenarios for the future, and work that will be de-emphasized is discussed, as well as why the work will be phased out. Philip, as an example, has found this program to be valuable, as many staff want to be successful in their new work, and the more time they are given to explore options and talk about them, the better they are able to succeed.

The comfort that comes from communicating the stress associated with the workplace can also be found in relationships with spouses and partners. A few of the librarians identified this as the most effective way for them to cope with change. As an example, Lisa comments that she speaks with her husband every night about problems, frustrations, or achievements made by and within the ECU Libraries. She also notes that she has the added benefit of having a partner working in higher education, enabling her to have an actual dialogue with someone outside her own work environment. As another example, David, who has been married for many years, believes it is essential for this researcher to understand that he feels he is really only able to cope with the stress caused by working in the library by expressing his concerns and joys with his wife:

> I have somebody that I can talk about changes in the library with, and decompress them, and put them into some kind of real situation. That's on a very personal note, but I think it's important. I don't know how I could do it without her. It would be so relentless; I wouldn't be able to step away from it.

As a result, both Lisa and David find that having a trusted confidant outside the library serves as a successful way to cope with the increasing stress and turbulence that comes from working in an organization undergoing transformative change.

INTERPRETATION OF FINDINGS

Introduction

Academic librarians are faced with dramatic changes in their libraries. The turbulence and rapidity of these changes are manifested in the study of the ECU Libraries. Librarians at ECU's main and branch libraries have experienced many significant changes, ranging from the shift from the physical to the virtual library to organizational restructuring activities that focus on continual change in the thinking and practices of the participants.

This study reveals significant findings pertaining to the experiences of these librarians, and each participant provides an individual interpretation of organizational phenomena that are integrated into a systemic picture of the ECU Libraries.

An interpretive framework of complex systems was used as the main method for analysis of the phenomena that emerged through case study research. This researcher also included a broad literature base on change theory, organizational theory, leadership theory, and library organizational development theory in the analysis of findings. Complexity theory "emphasizes a nonlinear, even emergent approach to dealing with organizational challenge" and "provides an integration point for many disciplines," sometimes even those that seem to be at odds with each other (Bütz, 1997, pp. 184, 223–224). Using this wide range of theories, therefore, enabled the researcher to analyze and interpret recursively the findings of this study through the lens of complexity theory while grounding the study in the main theoretical literature pertaining to individual and organizational change. This chapter, therefore, presents the experiences of the ECU librarians under study by generating interpretive results that include: the emergence of a hypercritical state; the limiting nature of negative feedback mechanisms in relation to change; a complex systems framework for professional thinking; and coping in a hypercritical organization.

The Emergence of a Hypercritical State

The concept of paradox in group dynamics has been presented by several different researchers during the twentieth and twenty-first centuries (Abraham & Gilgen, 1995; Mitleton-Kelly, 2003; Morgan, 1997; Stacey, 2003). Morgan (1997) has described the paradoxes in organizational life through various ideas, ranging from power and influence to adoption and resistance. In organizations, paradox often is manifested through competing tensions between organizational cultures, norms, and experiences. It is in this discovery of paradox that one is able to see an organizational place that might exist "between the status quo and alternative future states" (p. 271). At the same time, the results of these changes contribute to further complexity in the organizational lives of the individual participants in this study, increasing the competing tensions surrounding organizational paradox. Consequently, a hypercritical state has become evident at the ECU Libraries, contributing to the transformative changes in both individual and organizational dynamics.

For many ECU librarians, their experiences with change, uncertainty, and turbulence contribute to competing tension between the emergences of their future state while trying to maintain the traditional roles of research librarianship. The shift from the print to the digital research library has not taken place as quickly as many librarians had previously expected at the ECU Libraries. Equally, many external constituents – from faculty and students to university administrators and alumni – have identified the shift to the virtual library at ECU as a panacea for decreasing the costs of running libraries in the future. Although this is possible, it is not the planned outcome, and ECU librarians have continuously encountered this misinterpretation, not as a result of resistance to change, but rather as the slow progress made so far that is a consequence of the growing complexity with which librarians now deal when financing and providing digital services and resources.

It is apparent that the shift away from print resources allows the ECU librarians to focus less on the expenses and resources associated with maintaining print collections. Human involvement with printed materials is greatly reduced if there is not as much need to have library personnel process, check-out, and re-shelve physical items. Equally, fewer facilities expenses arise if there is less physical square footage that must be maintained. Conversely, in a digital environment, many of the costs and resources associated with the maintenance of print collections shift to the maintenance of items in digital form. Research information and the technology needed to provide it still cost money in a virtual environment. Moreover, humans are still needed to help faculty and students address and match their research needs with the electronic resources that are purchased by the university or are otherwise available. However, the library as a physical place and the physical items within it change in importance on campus which bring emotional and psychological challenges to the librarians at ECU. This shift from the physical to the digital library at the ECU Libraries might provide a glimpse of the future that can be extended to other libraries. For several librarians at ECU, particularly those who have been in the profession for many years, the shift from print to digital environments manifests individual changes that are accompanied by discomfort, heightened emotional responses, and feelings of confusion about the future. Moreover, these changes represent a time of closure in the provision of print-based services that librarians had embraced throughout their careers.

There is, as in the earlier section, unique similarity to Bridges' (2003, 2004) stages of transition in that several librarians are now confronted with a professional "ending" to a large aspect of their careers. During the previous reorganization at the ECU Libraries, the maintenance of both the print and virtual environments allowed librarians to avoid confronting this stage. But in very recent years, the impetus to move away from print altogether has thrust several librarians into the "neutral zone," a period described by Bridges (2003) as one filled with confusion and doubt. At the same time, a significant finding in this study suggests that the heightened levels of stress associated with the rapid and turbulent environment of change are related to the current reality that the ECU librarians still maintain both print and virtual environments. The next stage in this transition process is the time for "new beginnings" that one could speculate might possibly represent the evolution of philosophical and professional thinking among librarians.

When interpreting these phenomena through the lens of complexity theory, it can be noted that Prigogine and Stengers (1984) have identified this period as one existing between a chaotic state and a bifurcation point. Accordingly, when agents operating as a system move through a chaotic state, there is a period right before bifurcation when chaotic activity appears to dissipate in a period doubling cycle where the internal resonance or balance of agents within the system seem to be at their most harmonic state (Ravindra & Mallik, 1994). Metaphorically speaking, one can find similarities to the absence of turbulence found in the eye of a hurricane. In a dissipative structure, the outcome of this bifurcation has the potential to be either negative or positive, and the system will evolve with higher development and structure, bringing the system back toward an equilibrium state.

There are similarities between the observations that take place in physical and life systems and the observations of change within the ECU Libraries. Individuals in this study have moved into a level of professional turbulence and uncertainty that creates a chaotic organizational state. Bak (1996) has described this hypercritical state in physical systems through the concept of self-organized criticality, and this state has also been shown to emerge among individuals in group and organizational settings (Breu & Benwell, 1999; Gilstrap, 2008; Lichtenstein, 2000; Smith & Comer, 1994). Some researchers in the social and behavioral sciences have argued that it is necessary for individuals to remain in this state without moving toward a bifurcation point (Carver & Scheier, 1998; Pascale et al., 2000). Other researchers have argued that it is critical for people to move beyond this phase for organizational transformation to take place (MacIntosh & MacLean, 1999, 2001). In the case of the ECU Libraries, both situations seem to have occurred. During the library's first reorganization, transformative structural change led the librarians through individual and organizational bifurcation points where the organizational operations, culture, and thinking have been transformed at a level with which Osberg and Biesta (2007) have described as *strong emergence*. During the library's second reorganization, structures were put into place that both influence and limit librarians' abilities to operate in far-from-equilibrium conditions while simultaneously preventing movement into periods of unbounded chaotic activity.

The speed of change was a major contributor to the feelings of uncertainty and turbulence among the study's participants. Several librarians identified technology as a critical component that greatly affects this speed and, subsequently, is associated with heightened emotional responses among the participants. Continual learning and the implementation of expanding forms of communication with the ECU Libraries' constituents also contributed to the speed of change through more rapid rates of information processing at the individual level. Consequently, the information taken in by librarians is then used to generate rapid and consistent change at the organizational level, reflected in the statement of one librarian that, "change happens faster here than at other libraries."

In the case of ECU, these librarians deal with increasing amounts of information on which they must make decisions. These rapid and fluid information flows lead each librarian to process and reprocess information in interconnected ways that are shared among the members of the group. Likewise, a qualitative characteristic of a dissipative system is its ability to take in and exchange information at faster and more comprehensive rates than systems moving toward equilibrium states. Ashby (1956) first described this phenomenon through requisite variety in cybernetics, where a system's ability to reflect internal variety at levels comparative to the external environment becomes critical for its survival. Stacey (1992, 2003) has also argued that a dissipative system's absorption of increasing amounts of information leads to further diversity among individual system agents.

The Limiting Nature of Negative Feedback Mechanisms

In contrast to the stress associated with the rapidity and turbulence of change, certain limitations identified by the ECU librarians act to inhibit their abilities to affect change at a faster pace. These limitations include slowness in university purchasing and strategic planning, vendor production failures, and the lack of capital, physical, and human resources to develop library technology within the ECU Libraries. As several researchers in the social and behavioral sciences have observed, such limitations can be viewed as negative feedback mechanisms (Checkland, 1999; Flood, 1999; Stacey, 1992; von Bertalanffy, 1973). It was assumed by this researcher that during the course of this study much of the negative feedback would result internally, either at the individual level through resistance to change or at the administrative level. However, as detailed in the following section, librarians identified negative feedback controls primarily as originating outside of the library system. In complex systems, these negative control mechanisms move individuals toward equilibrium and stability (Stacey, 1992, 2003). More importantly, over time, the damaging effects of negative control mechanisms can move systems toward obsolescence (Pascale et al., 2000). It must be noted that the university structure at ECU supports creativity and growth in intellectual thought and educational change which is evidenced in its support of the ECU Libraries' organizational restructuring activities. However, it is equally important to note that, while this support exists, institutional limitations to the ECU Libraries' continual evolution still occur within the framework of negative feedback in organizational systems.

One of the strongest negative feedback mechanisms identified by the ECU librarians pertains to the strategic planning process. Strategic planning in most institutions of higher education is typically performed on an annual, two-, or five-year cycle that is repeated after goals and objectives have been achieved. On the one hand, this mechanism prevents academic departments and units from shifting goals and objectives too quickly, preventing an environment of unbounded chaos (Morgan, 1997; Stacey, 1992). On the other hand, when changes do need to be made at a faster rate that responds to the external environment, longer cycles limit an organization's ability to respond and adapt to the changing environment (Cutright, 2001; Weick, 1985). Strategic planning largely evolved from the Management By Objectives (MBO) movement of the 1950s and 1960s and was fully integrated into the academy by the 1980s. It has since been criticized as an ineffective and unproven strategy by major management theorists in both the higher education and business communities (Birnbaum, 2000; Mintzberg, 1994). However, this periodic cycle of strategic planning continues to be used to a high degree by institutions of higher education for, as some might argue, lack of a better model.

The strategic planning process at the ECU Libraries is problematic to the complex systems framework. The annual cycle is linear in nature, with the creation of goals and objectives taking place at the beginning of the cycle followed by a report on goal and objective progress or completion at the end of the cycle. Little room is given for deviation from this linear process when new or changed goals arise as a result of the changing environment. Equally, similar to the single-order learning organization (Argyris, 1992; Argyris & Schön, 1978; Schön, 1991), reflection on practice during a strategic planning cycle while in process often involves the same information or practices that originally created system errors. Although this model can still be viewed as an open system in complex adaptive systems due to the absorption of external influences on a periodic cycle of planning and replanning, the limiting aspects of strategic planning can prevent an organization from reaching its full potential. Some researchers even suggest that traditional forms of strategic planning in higher education should be abandoned and replaced by newer models that continually adapt to the changing environment (Cutright, 2001). This phenomenon challenges all academic librarians to reflect more critically on how timely and effectively the strategic planning process contributes to the organization's adaptation to the environment, whereas considering or proposing alternative forms of planning, such as scenario probability development, that reflect the nonlinear dynamics inherent in the library as a system.

The university purchasing process also contributes negative feedback from the environment external of the ECU Libraries. Technology evolves at an exponential rate, however, a typical purchase for any high dollar item involves a lengthy process including: bid, response review, contract negotiation, legal review, and implementation, which takes about six months before the technology is in full production. Equally, if the product is needed at the time but deviates from the strategic planning process, the purchase must be delayed until it can be added into the next cycle.

Failures of library technology vendors have also contributed to the limiting aspects of the ECU Libraries' organizational development. As ECU librarians pointed out, technology used in most integrated library management systems is outdated and does not compete with enterprise technologies in the private sector. This trend of poor performance by library technology vendors has also been documented in the library science literature most recently (Antelman, Lynema, & Pace, 2006; Breeding, 2007a, 2007b; Pace, 2006). Although the open source software movement has gained attention, it has not fully been embraced by information technology units in higher education. This reluctance can be explained in complexity theory through Arthur's (1994) concept of increasing returns: adoption of software models becomes difficult with which to compete the longer products have been on the market and have been mainstreamed by individuals; even when better and less expensive software exists. Consequently, the librarians at ECU are left with few options to provide technology that competes with the private sector without further investment in human and capital resources for product development. And, since many comprehensive universities have in the past few years faced significant funding restraints at the federal and state levels, this issue must be discussed at a broader level in the research library community. If librarians at individual institutions are unable to fund product development, it might be beneficial for research libraries to expand on their consortial partnerships to promote collaborative technology product development that can be shared at the regional or national levels.

The limiting nature of both university purchasing cycles and technological development points to the recreation of Prigogine's (1967, 1980) concept of dissipative structures. In these cases, the organization is limited in the amount of resources it is able to take in from the external environment and subsequently dissipate entropy, or rather random and unused energy, as a way to adapt to the environment. Equally, if the dynamics taking place among the ECU librarians exhibit the characteristics of dissipative structures, then the external negative controls could be said to operate as the boundary parameters that prevent the organization of the library from moving toward bifurcation points. However, as a result of the negative feedback mechanisms at the macrolevels that have a tendency to move systems toward equilibrium conditions, stress and turbulence at the microlevel of the individual librarian is heightened to a state where potential bifurcations emerge from within the organization.

This observation of dissipative structures activity among the ECU librarians leads to Prigogine's (1980) theory of order through fluctuations. Observations of this activity in physical systems show the spontaneous generation of self-organization among individual agents within a system. Bak (1996) furthers this idea through the study of self-organized criticality. When negative feedback mechanisms prevent a system at the macrolevel from interacting with its external environment, internal perturbations at the microlevel can contribute to self-organization among individual agents within the system where critical system states emerge (Gilstrap, 2008). In organizations, Stacey (2003) has also observed this type of dissipative structures activity in similar terms through the amplification of system diversity. This appears to be a major finding of this study, because the librarians at ECU have been able to institute transformative changes in spite of these external limitations, showing that the phenomenon of self-organization, and subsequent self-organized criticality, might be taking place and contributing to the change process.

Trends in scholarly publishing also contribute to negative feedback mechanisms for librarians at ECU. The control mechanisms of publishing models emerged frequently during participant interviews. However, scholarly publishing inflation has been copiously cited in the library science literature. On the surface, this issue does not present new knowledge for the findings of this study. But as one librarian commented, "change is sneaky ... you must peel back the layers to understand." Therefore, a major finding for this study suggests, in general, that librarians, faculty, and administrators inadvertently contribute positive feedback to this trend of scholarly publishing inflation, particularly in regard to academic journals in print and electronic format. As has been stated previously, scholarly publishing inflation rates – particularly in science, medicine, and technology – far outpace the Consumer Price Index (Bureau of Labor Statistics, 2007; EBSCO Information Services, 2007; Van Orsdel & Born, 2007). Although librarians and university administrators have been active in addressing this for many years now (Crow, 2002; Edwards & Shulenberger, 2003), the trend continues to take place as an aspect of this positive feedback.

At the microlevel, faculty members at comprehensive institutions in many disciplines are required to research and publish in the highest tiered and subsequently most expensive journals for consideration for promotion and tenure. Resources for faculty to conduct this research and writing are primarily provided through tuition and fees, state tax revenues, and tax sponsored federal grants and programs. After faculty publish the results of their findings in journals produced by for profit publishing companies, the information is then sold back to university libraries at an extremely high cost. In effect, the revenues universities receive from the public subsidize many highly successful sectors of the scholarly publishing industry in the form of new knowledge provided by faculty. And universities again subsidize the publishing industry when purchasing the information written by university faculty to be held in the form of journals in institutional libraries (Edwards & Shulenberger, 2003).

Librarians and administrators have been advocates for bringing attention to this paradox between academic expectations for faculty and increasing inflation rates in scholarly publishing. Albeit, this has been conducted somewhat idiosyncratically among teaching faculty, institutions have participated in economies of scale consortium arrangements for many years now to try to drive down inflation rates on scholarly journals. And some suggest that attempts to maintain both print and electronic formats of journals have contributed to this problem from both the public and private sectors (Johnson & Luther, 2007). At the national level, most recently, the U.S. Congress initiated legislation to promote open access to government-funded research which primarily appears in science, medical, and technology journals (National Institutes of Health, 2005, 2008). In the case of several academic libraries, librarians have instituted negative feedback mechanisms in the form of canceling subscriptions where possible; yet many of these publications can be considered essential to the academic programs of the university.

From a complex systems framework, this phenomenon represents a constant flux of negative and positive feedbacks between the higher education community and the private publishing sector. Converse to what would seem to be the natural order of market-driven economies, university libraries generate positive feedback to the external publishing community by paying high inflation rates for information that has been produced by faculty and is integral to university teaching and research. The publishing community, understandably, faces rising production costs and subsequently increases subscription prices each year, which, in turn, serves as an external negative feedback mechanism imposed at the institutional level, creating continued financial dilemmas.

A Complex Systems Framework for Professional Thinking

The call for a philosophical evolution of academic librarianship serves as another challenge for participants at the individual level. Some librarians are able to transfer the philosophy of librarianship to the newly emerging research library. They argue that the philosophy has not changed; rather, many librarians have lost touch with their professional philosophy by focusing entirely on the physical item. Other librarians see a need for a critical shift in thinking about how research libraries operate in the future, including a shift toward services and technologies that reflect contemporary society.

These observations by the librarians at ECU reflect the work of Argyris (1990, 1992), Argyris and Schön (1974, 1978), Schön (1971, 1991), and Senge, (1994, 2004) on organizational learning. In single-order learning environments, librarians would correct errors within the environment by applying rules that already exist within the organization. In the long run, this type of learning environment becomes problematic, because the same system structures that contributed to the errors are integrated into problem-solving situations. In second-order learning environments, librarians identify the key philosophical issues that contribute to the causes of error by critically reflecting on existing theories in use and by subsequently developing new theories in use that respond to changes in the environment. The ECU librarians' recognition that the need for change in professional philosophy, or a recursive reflection on the original philosophy, highlights their incorporation of a second-order learning organization. Although single-order learning still exists in the organization, it reflects the paradox that emerges in the move away from constrained, linear learning toward an environment of self-organizing learning described by Aram and Noble (1999). Equally, the observation that second-order learning is often taking place among librarians is significant, because it signals that the ECU Libraries are in a continually recursive process of movement toward the organizational learning and complex systems learning environments described by Senge (1994), Doll (1993), and Fleener (2002). This learning environment at ECU reflects the openness of librarians to external influences that continually challenge librarians to think in a complex systems framework. This observation is also significant, because it challenges the academic library community to identify whether single-order learning is a dominant learning function of several contemporary research libraries. If that is the case, it implies that some libraries have moved increasingly toward a closed system framework which could be contributing to the professional perception that academic librarianship might be coming to an end.

Several tacit outcomes of the changing environment at the ECU Libraries have also had profound effects on librarians' professional thinking. Communicating the relevance of the library becomes more difficult when resources are provided in digital formats and are not necessarily branded in ways that associate the library with the resources. The ECU Libraries' recruitment of recent graduates of library science programs who not only possess the technological skill sets to operate in a digital environment but who also understand the complexities these technologies bring when providing virtual services continues to be difficult. Along these same lines, from interviews with the ECU librarians, it can be inferred that recruitment by library science programs which continue to admit students who are "bookish" might prove problematic for the profession. This is particularly challenging when research libraries are reaching a time when many librarians from the baby boomer generation will be retiring. As a result, librarians at ECU identified that the profession will need to become more flexible, more adaptable, promote strategies of continual change, and reflect more critically on the future rather than the past. This finding is important, because the ECU librarians have suggested that faculty and students *will* find other places from which to receive their information. And this is particularly the case if librarians miss opportunities to transfer important aspects of professional thinking toward the digital environment by focusing their energies on the physical items in their library.

Finding analogy with the work of Lewin (1951) in field theory, it can be said that the ECU librarians paint the picture of research librarianship as a current state of being "frozen." Extending this perspective to complexity theory, the maintenance of the status quo reflects professional thinking that is designed to promote stability and equilibrium in academic libraries. Although stability might be a desired aspect of individuals operating within organizations, the unfortunate long-term consequence of this approach in organizations is that equilibrium jeopardizes the survival of the system (Pascale et al., 2000; MacIntosh & MacLean, 1999, 2001). If this is the case for research libraries, the future of these organizations might appear much bleaker to those both outside and inside these institutions.

Coping in the Hypercritical Organization

The movement toward far-from-equilibrium conditions also brings increased levels of individual as well as group stress, and the experiences of the ECU librarians equally reflect this phenomenon. On the surface, observations of heightened individual stress suggest a negative analysis. But even though stress levels are high among the ECU librarians, the activities associated with this stress actually reflect a healthy organization that responds to its environment. As Stacey (1992, 2003) has found, individuals interacting with high levels of energy lead to the amplification of system feedback. The reverberations of this feedback throughout the organization contribute to the creation of a critical state where organizational learning continues to fold in on itself, presenting the possibility for transformative development to take place with each iteration. Breu and Benwell (1999) have observed this same phenomenon in organizational studies, where individuals actually reach states of "hyperactivity" that challenge each person to seek out learning opportunities to help understand the experiences of stress associated with change. It is at this stage that hyperactivity appears sometimes to be without formal structures or outcomes. If individuals enter this state and seek out opportunities for new learning, however, the organization has the ability for "strong emergence" (Osberg & Biesta, 2007) to take place where radically novel shifts in professional thinking can lead to further organizational transformation.

To reiterate previous discussion, Bak (1996) describes this phenomenon in the natural world as self-organized criticality. Supercritical interaction among individual agents leads to a system's ability to create emergent internal structures. When individual agents within a system reach this state, there is a point where the system can fluctuate between predictable outcomes and chaotic activity. In Bak's (1996) view, this observation highlights the characteristics of a complex system. It can be said that the individual stress associated with rapid change at the ECU Libraries reflects this hypercritical state where the emergence of more highly developed professional thinking is taking place. However, the potential for unbounded chaos implies that this emergence could take either positive or negative forms. Although recognizing that this phenomenon is a natural occurrence within complex systems (Prigogine, 2000; Prigogine & Stengers, 1984), it is at the juncture between this stress and organizational turbulence that it becomes critical for librarians to learn coping mechanisms that limit the ability of unbounded chaos to take hold within the system as a response to negative individual psycho-social bifurcations.

Coping mechanisms for dealing with change are varied at the ECU Libraries. One observation that took place during the course of this study is that those librarians who identified more developed methods for coping with change exhibited lower levels of stress even when significant change was taking place in their areas. As Wheatley (1994) has noted in organizational dynamics, we often confuse "control with order" (p. 22). Consequently, lower levels of stress came from those librarians who released the psychological desire to control situations that bring turbulence and uncertainty. Additionally, the concept of communicating change at the organizational level was viewed by a majority of librarians who *receive* this information as an effective method of coping, but it was not reflected in general as contributing to lower levels of stress when viewed in the context of the wide range of responses by each librarian at the individual level. Of interest, however, were those librarians who commented that communicating change was an effective method they used to help *others* – both internal and external to the organization – cope with the stress of the changing library environment, similar to Karpiak's (2000) finding of a "call to community" in mid-career professionals. Moreover, these librarians tended to project a level of stress that was well managed in spite of the turbulence surrounding them. Additionally, these librarians did not identify themselves as "change agents" but were instrumental in helping their colleagues who did project high levels of stress cope with change. This was observed in both their own and their colleagues' responses. Returning to the theory of dissipative structures, complex systems dissipate increasing levels of entropy, or unused random energy, as the system moves away from equilibrium and toward a chaotic state (Prigogine, 1980, 1964). Taking this observation further, it can be said that these librarians dissipated the stress associated with change by helping colleagues and external constituents cope with their own individual responses.

Conversely, dialogue on individual frustrations associated with change was also identified as an effective coping mechanism. Librarians in this group tended equally to exhibit lower levels of stress in their descriptions of the ECU Libraries. Although other factors might be involved in the phenomenon such as disengagement that emerged for this group, in individual transition theory (Bridges, 2004), perspective transformation theory (Mezirow, 1991), and complexity theory (Stacey, 2003), humans enter a state of confusion where discussion of a cathartic event helps that person to cope with and deal with the changes taking place in his or her life. Extending this approach to group therapy in psychology, Burlingame et al. (1995) expand on the reciprocal process of dialogue among individuals within organizations:

> It is readily apparent that the psychotherapeutic process is not only characterized but influenced by multiple levels. These levels exist within the intrapersonal sphere, the interpersonal sphere, and the global sphere. Although no one level may be individually preeminent, each could potentially be connected to or influence another, thus contributing to process change and evolution. (Burlingame et al., 1995, p. 90)

The appearance of this phenomenon at the ECU Libraries, therefore, suggests that, at the microlevel, individuals can cycle through periods of stress and stability whereas, at the macrolevel, the library as a system can be exhibiting concurrent or conflicting periods of stress and stability. Equally, extending these same types of dialogue that take place between two or three people to larger groups provides a generative framework to further the process of individual and organizational change while contributing to positive coping methods in academic libraries.

In a similar vein, coping with change through the projection of a positive attitude was another strategy identified to help others deal with the stress of a turbulent environment. In complexity theory, this might be interpreted as a positive feedback mechanism which is integral to self-organizing, open systems. As Bütz (1997) has found "positive emotional communication ... appears similar to positive feedback loops" (p. 157). Amplifications of the positive aspects of the transitions through which the ECU Libraries are moving are integrated back into the organization by the librarians who, in turn, amplify the system's positive feedback. Using the metaphor of the strange attractor in chaotic systems (Fig. 3) increased levels of positive feedback cause individuals within the ECU Libraries system to move toward

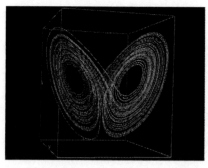 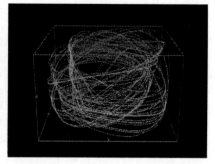

Fig. 3. Lorenz and Duffing Chaotic Attractors. *Source:* Fair use of the *Chaos Hypertextbook* is encouraged. http://hypertextbook.com/contact.shtml

basins of attraction that stimulate growth (Gilstrap, 2005). As these cycles loop into themselves, the energy created by the positive feedback causes subtle transitional states to grow stronger with each iteration, leading to high levels of energy production and entropy dissipation.

Several other coping strategies for dealing with the turbulence of change in the organizational environment were proposed by the study's participants, including exercise, disengagement, and isolation. Although not identified by a majority of librarians in this study, exercise was perceived as critical to a few individuals at ECU. Much literature exists on the positive benefits of exercise in relation to work attitude and performance (Austin et al., 2005; Puetz et al., 2006; Taylor-Piliae et al., 2006). More research would be needed to investigate this concept further, but these findings suggest that academic libraries consider encouraging employee wellness programs as an additional strategy for coping with change. A strategy of disengagement was also identified by a few of the ECU librarians as successful, since they were receiving so much information and had more new work responsibilities to accomplish. This is an understandable reaction to change at the ECU Libraries, and Carver and Scheier (1998), in their research on the self-regulation of behavior, suggest that disengagement is sometimes a necessary process to help individuals struggle through self-verification; or, rather, "confirming their view of themselves" (p. 211). Conversely, they note that it can contribute to self-destructive patterns of behavior. In the case of research librarians, disengagement as a coping method can lead to possible anomie among colleagues and implies that this strategy for coping might follow the same phases at research libraries that incorporate either traditional hierarchies or flattened organizational structures. At the same time, other ECU librarians identified that they had less and less time in the workplace for uninterrupted, concentrated thought. These librarians also noted that they had begun seeking out opportunities for this type of isolated thinking in their home lives, adding further stress to both their professional and personal lives. This paradox between practiced disengagement and needed isolation will most likely continue, and the phenomenon taking place at the ECU Libraries might signal an emerging challenge for librarians at research libraries in general.

Opportunities for learning were also identified by many librarians as effective methods for coping with change, but, at the same time, this learning created more stress among participants. Activities ranged from self-directed learning and brown bag lunches to formal workshops on new technological and workflow skill sets. Intrinsically, these learning opportunities are important for most librarians to keep up with the changes happening at the ECU Libraries. However, learning was not observed to decrease levels of stress among the ECU librarians in general terms; rather, learning opportunities appeared to increase stress levels among many librarians. In the study of nonlinearity in psychology, proportionality in relationships between psychosocial responses are not always congruent (Goerner, 1995). As is the case for learning opportunities among the ECU librarians, this suggests that it is not necessarily a correlative relationship where increases in produced knowledge lead to linear decreases in stress levels. Conversely, the environment of learning contributed to further amplification of chaotic periods among study participants by their hypercritical consumption of information. As Prigogine (2000) has argued, in a networked society, "the imperatives of the connected collective overwhelm the individual's ability to make choices" (p. 36). Primarily, there were so many different learning opportunities in which individuals could or felt they needed to engage at the ECU Libraries that increasing amounts of knowledge began to contribute to these individual librarians' confusion over selecting which learning was most relevant to their work. Furthermore, the abilities of these librarians to retain new knowledge became problematic if the new skill sets were not immediately applicable, increasing the amount of individual stress as a result of investing in learning that did not contribute to the tasks at hand. These findings suggest that, although boundary conditions can exist to keep an organization from moving toward unbounded chaos, at the individual level these boundaries appear to be less defined. Consequently, although coping with change is necessary at the individual level, systemic mentoring opportunities to learn how to cope with change might be idiosyncratic in many academic libraries.

IMPLICATIONS AND CONCLUSION

The findings of this research present significant new knowledge concerning the librarians and the organization that make up the ECU Libraries. Responding to the two research questions in this chapter, these librarians are making significant shifts from a print to a digital environment, but a paradox emerges that challenges traditional ways of thinking about libraries. Possible implications for academic librarians therefore include: the challenge of emerging resources needs, associating digital resources and services with the library, a radical shift in professional thinking, and learning how to cope with change at the organizational level.

The implications for a shift from the physical library as place to a virtual environment that integrates many new mediums of information to support research, teaching, and learning suggest the emergence of a more complex set of resource challenges. Librarians must be able to provide the hardware, network infrastructure, and human knowledge to make future transformations successful. Current librarians need continual learning of new and relevant skill sets, and hiring librarians with the high-level skill sets needed for even entry level positions will be difficult. Equally, the implications of shifting to a digital environment might create further issues of professional relevance for academic librarians. Associating resources and services in a digital environment – particularly those that are highly expensive – with the work of librarians is problematic when library users find it much more difficult to distinguish between the free and subscription-only aspects of the World Wide Web. Moreover, librarians will be challenged to market the resources and services they provide to the academic community in nontraditional ways that focus much more on becoming part of the external environment, using methods that may have yet to be explored.

The incorporation of new technologies and the organizational changes taking place at the ECU Libraries cause heightened emotional responses and apparent increases in stress levels that may not exist in other academic and administrative units in the university system. Most importantly, the findings of this study suggest that much of the individual stress at the ECU Libraries is not due to resistance to change but, rather, can be associated with attempts to maintain concurrently a print *and* a digital library. This dual environment creates additional work and added stress for librarians who already deal with an exponential amount of growth in scholarly research and services.

A significant implication for this study, therefore, suggests that a radical shift in professional thinking might be required for academic librarians. For this study's participants, this change represents what Bridges (2004) describes as an "ending" in the history of the ECU Libraries. Choosing which aspects of our professional stance can be transferred to a digital environment – while recognizing that certain aspects of the philosophy should be modified or abandoned altogether – can contribute to library organizational development that focuses on continual change and adaptation to the external environment. However, promoting the relevance of librarians in the academic community will continue to be problematic if campus constituents do not congruently reflect on practice in ways that question whether similar professional shifts in thinking are needed in other units of higher education.

The efforts on the part of the ECU librarians to cope with the turbulence and rapid change in their library environment are another significant finding of this study. Stress levels among librarians varied, but, in general, a heightened intensity of stress was observed through this research. Inference can be made that the transformative changes that take place at the ECU Libraries contribute heavily to this stress. Subsequent coping mechanisms were intended to help librarians respond to the experiences attributed to change in active and positive ways. These coping strategies utilized among the ECU librarians ranged from adapting workflows and dialogue with others to learning new skill sets and the projection of positive feedback into the organizational environment.

The implications for the study's participants suggest that coping mechanisms are still somewhat misunderstood among academic librarians. Continued high levels of stress at the individual level can have negative effects on organizations over the long term, and ways to deal with this stress at the individual level can contribute to resources and energy being devoted to nonessential functions in the library. In particular, coping strategies might be promoted in idiosyncratic ways or are primarily driven at the individual level. Although this is both expected and necessary, academic librarians will continue to be challenged to find methods that promote coping with change in positive, mentoring, and supporting ways at the macro-organizational level.

In summary, interpreting the experiences of individuals interacting and responding to change within the ECU Libraries highlights the complex systems nature of the organization. The 17 librarians who participated in the main part of this research study bring experiences that might be shared by academic librarians in general and that are also unique to their own individual environmental responses to the ECU Libraries over the past few years. The findings of this study suggest that librarians at ECU have critically reflected upon the experiences of turbulent change and have developed new perceptions of research libraries and professional librarianship in the future.

It should be reinforced that this journey has not been easy for even the most willing of participants in the change process. Conversely, the changes that have occurred in this library have empowered librarians and provided opportunities for them to facilitate professional shifts that they note otherwise would have been very difficult for them to accomplish. Moreover, the deep reflection on errors or misperceptions on previous theories in use has moved the ECU librarians' thinking away from *being* in a library that focuses on the eminency of the physical object. Librarians are now in the process of *becoming* professionally, as they learn to accept or embrace the necessity of responding and adapting to the external environment through a continual and natural flux of order and disorder.

REFERENCES

Abraham, F. D., & Gilgen, A. R. (Eds). (1995). *Chaos theory in psychology.* Westport, CT: Greenwood Press.

Ackoff, R. L. (1981). *Creating the corporate future: Plan or be planned for.* New York: Wiley.

Ackoff, R. L. (1994). *The democratic corporation: A radical prescription for recreating corporate America and rediscovering success.* New York: Oxford University Press.

Antelman, K., Lynema, E., & Pace, A. (2006). Toward a twenty-first century library catalog. *Information Technology and Libraries, 25*(3), 128–139.

Aram, E., & Noble, D. (1999). Educating prospective managers in the complexity of organisational life: Teaching and learning from a complexity perspective. *Management Learning, 30*(3), 321–342.

Argyris, C. (1957). *Personality and organization: The conflict between system and the individual.* New York: Harper & Row.

Argyris, C. (1960). *Understanding organizational behavior.* Homewood, IL: Dorsey Press.

Argyris, C. (1971). *Management and organizational development.* New York: McGraw-Hill.

Argyris, C. (1990). *Overcoming organizational defenses: Facilitating organizational learning.* Englewood Cliffs, NJ: Prentice Hall.

Argyris, C. (1992). *On organizational learning.* Cambridge, MA: Blackwell Publishers.

Argyris, C., & Schön, D. A. (1974). *Theory in practice: Increasing professional effectiveness.* San Francisco: Jossey-Bass.

Argyris, C., & Schön, D. A. (1978). *Organizational learning: A theory of action perspective.* Reading, MA: Addison-Wesley.

Arthur, B. (1994). *Increasing returns and path-dependence in the economy.* An Arbor, MI: University of Michigan Press.

Ashby, R. W. (1956). *An introduction to cybernetics.* New York: Wiley.

Austin, V., Shah, S., & Muncer, S. (2005). Teacher stress and coping strategies used to reduce stress. *Occupational Therapy International, 12*(2), 63–80.

Avolio, B. J., & Bass, B. M. (Eds). (2002). *Developing potential across a full range of leadership: Cases on transactional and transformational leadership.* Mahwah, NJ: Lawrence Erlbaum Associates, Publishers.

Bak, P. (1996). *How nature works: The science of self-organized criticality.* New York: Copernicus.

Bass, B. M. (1998). *Transformational leadership: Industrial, military, and educational impact.* Mahwah, NJ: Lawrence Erlbaum Associates, Inc.

Bateson, G. (1972). *Steps to an ecology of mind.* New York: Ballantine Books.

Bergson, H. L. (1911/1975). *Creative evolution.* Westport, CT: Greenwood Press.

Birnbaum, R. (2000). *Management fads in higher education: Where they come from, what they do, why they fail.* San Francisco: Jossey-Bass.

Blake, R. R., & Mouton, J. S. (1978). *The new managerial grid* (2nd ed). Houston, TX: Gulf Publishing Company.

Blake, R. R., & Mouton, J. S. (1981). *Productivity, the human side: A social dynamics approach.* New York: AMACOM.

Blake, R. R., & Mouton, J. S. (1985). *The managerial grid III.* Houston, TX: Gulf Publishing Company.

Blake, R. R., Mouton, J. S., & Williams, M. S. (1981). *The academic administrator grid: A guide to developing effective management teams.* San Francisco, CA: Jossey-Bass.

Breeding, M. (2007a). An update on open source ILS. *Computers in Libraries, 27*(3), 27–29.

Breeding, M. (2007b). An industry redefined: Private equity moves into the ILS, and open source emerges. *Library Journal, 132*(6). Available at http://libraryjournal.com/article/CA6429251.html. Retrieved on 1 October.

Breu, K., & Benwell, M. (1999). Modelling individual transition in the context of organisational transformation. *Journal of Management Development, 18*(6), 496–520.

Bridges, W. (2003). *Managing transitions: Making the most of change* (2nd ed). Cambridge, MA: Perseus Books.

Bridges, W. (1980/2004). *Transitions: Making sense of life's changes* (2nd ed). Cambridge, MA: Perseus Books.

Buch, K. (1997). Managing the human side of change. *Library Administration & Management, 11*(3), 147–151.

Bureau of Labor Statistics. (2007). Consumer price index history table. Table Containing History of CPI-U U. S. All Items Indexes and Annual Percentage Changes from 1913 to Present. Available at http://www.bls.gov/cpi/. Retrieved on 24 September.

Burlingame, G. M., Fuhriman, A., & Barnum, K. R. (1995). Group therapy as a nonlinear dynamical system: Analysis of therapeutic communication for chaotic patterns. In: F. D. Abraham & A. R. Gilgen (Eds), *Chaos theory in psychology.* Westport, CT: Greenwood Press.

Burns, J. M. (1979). *Leadership* (1st ed). New York: Harper & Row.

Burns, J. M. (2003). *Transforming leadership: The new pursuit of happiness.* New York: Atlantic Monthly Press.

Bütz, M. R. (1997). *Chaos and complexity: Implications for theory and practice.* Washington, DC: Taylor & Francis.

Carew, D. K., Parisi-Carew, E., & Blanchard, K. H. (1986). Group development and situational leadership: A model for managing groups. *Training and Development Journal, 40*(6), 46–50.

Carver, C. S., & Scheier, M. F. (1998). *On the self-regulation of behavior.* Cambridge, UK: Cambridge University Press.

Checkland, P. (1999). *Soft systems methodology: A 30-year retrospective.* New York: Wiley.

Crow, R. (2002). The case for institutional repositories: A SPARC position paper. The Scholarly Publishing & Academic Resources Coalition. Available at http://www.arl.org/sparc/bm~doc/ir_final_release_102.pdf. Retrieved on October 10, 2007.

Cutright, M. (2001). *Chaos theory & higher education: Leadership, planning, & policy.* New York: Peter Lang.

Davis, B. (2005). Interrupting frameworks: Interpreting geometries of epistemology and curriculum. In: W. E. Doll, J. M. Fleener, D. Trueit & J. St. Julien (Eds), *Chaos, complexity, curriculum, and culture: A conversation.* New York: Peter Lang.

Denzin, N. K., & Lincoln, Y. S. (1994). *Handbook of qualitative research.* Thousand Oaks, CA: Sage Publications.

De Rosa, C., Cantrell, J., Cellentani, D., Hawk, J., Jenkins, L., & Wilson, A. (Eds). (2005). *Perceptions of libraries and information resources: A report to the OCLC membership.* Dublin, OH: OCLC Online Computer Library Center, Inc.

Dewey, J., & Bentley, A. F. (1949/1975). *Knowing and the known.* Westport, CT: Greenwood Press.

Doll, W. E., Jr. (1993). *A post-modern perspective on curriculum.* New York: Teachers College, Columbia University.

Dunn, K. (2002). Assessing information literacy skills in the California State University: A progress report. *Journal of Academic Librarianship, 28*(1), 26–35.

EBSCO Information Services. (2007). Five year journal price increase history (2003–2007). Available at http://www2.ebsco.com/en-us/InfoProfs/serialspriceproj/Pages/index.aspx. Retrieved on 24 September.

Edwards, R., & Shulenberger, D. (2003). The high cost of scholarly journals (and what to do about it). *Change, 35*(6), 10–19.

Fennewald, J., & Stachacz, J. (2005). Recruiting students to careers in academic libraries. *College & Research Libraries News, 66*(2), 120–122.

Fleener, M. J. (2002). Curriculum dynamics: Recreating heart. In: J. L. Kincheloe & S. R. Steinberg (Eds), *Counterpoints: Studies in the postmodern theory of education* (Vol. 200). New York: Peter Lang Publishing.

Flood, R. L. (1999). *Rethinking the fifth discipline: Learning within the unknowable.* London: Routledge.

Gallagher, R., & Appenzeller, T. (1999). Complex systems. *Science, 284*(5411), 79–109.

Giesecke, J., Michalak, S., & Franklin, B. (1997). Changing management roles for associate directors in libraries. *Library Administration & Management, 11*(3), 172–179.

Gilstrap, D. L. (2005). Strange attractors and human interaction: Leading complex organizations through the use of metaphors. *Complicity: An International Journal of Complexity and Education, 2*(1), 55–69.

Gilstrap, D. L. (2007a). Dissipative structures in educational change: Prigogine and the academy. *International Journal of Leadership in Education, 10*(1), 49–69.

Gilstrap, D. L. (2007b). *Librarians and the emerging research library: A case study of complex individual and organizational development.* Doctoral dissertation, University of Oklahoma, Norman, OK. Dissertation Abstracts International (Publication no. ATT 3284303).

Gilstrap, D. L. (2008). Dialogic and the emergence of criticality in complex group processes. *Journal of the Canadian Association of Curriculum Studies, 6*(1), 91–112.

Glogoff, S. (2001). Information technology in the virtual library: Leadership in times of change. *Journal of Library Administration, 32*(3/4), 61–84.

Goble, D. S. (1997). Managing in a change environment. *Library Administration & Management, 11*(3), p. 152.

Goerner, S. J. (1995). Chaos and deep ecology. In: F. D. Abraham & A. R. Gilgen (Eds), *Chaos theory in psychology.* Westport, CT: Greenwood Press.

Hersey, P., & Blanchard, K. H. (1969/1993). *Management of organizational behavior: Utilizing human resources* (6th ed). Englewood Cliffs, NJ: Simon & Schuster.

Holloway, K. (2004). The significance of organizational development in academic research libraries. *Library Trends, 53*(1), 5–16.

Jankowska, M. A. (2004). Identifying university professors' information needs in the challenging environment of information and communication technologies. *Journal of Academic Librarianship, 30*(1), 51–66.

Johnson, R. K., & Luther, J. (2007). *The e-only tipping point for journals: What's ahead in the print-to-electronic transition zone.* Washington, DC: Association of Research Libraries.

Kaarnst-Brown, M. L., Nicholson, S., von Dran, G. M., & Stanton, J. M. (2004). Organizational cultures of libraries as a strategic resource. *Library Trends, 53*(1), 33–53.

Karpiak, I. E. (2000). The 'second call': Faculty renewal and recommitment at midlife. *Quality in Higher Education, 6*(2), 125–134.

Kascus, M. A. (2004). *Effect of the introduction of team management on the leadership role and skills needed to lead teams: A case study.* Doctoral dissertation, Simmons College, December. Dissertation Abstracts International (Publication no. ATT 3159376).

Lewin, K. (1951). *Field theory in social science.* New York: Harper & Row.

Lichtenstein, B. B. (2000). Self-organized transitions: A pattern amid the chaos of transformative change. *Academy of Management Executive, 14*(4), 128–131.

Lorenz, E. (1963). Deterministic non-periodic flow. *Journal of Atmospheric Science, 20*, 130–141.

MacIntosh, R., & MacLean, D. (1999). Conditioned emergence: A dissipative structures approach to transformation. *Strategic Management Journal, 20*(4), 297–316.

MacIntosh, R., & MacLean, D. (2001). Conditioned emergence: Researching change and changing research. *International Journal of Operations and Production Management, 21*(10), 1343–1357.

Mandelbrot, B. B. (1975). *Les object fractals: Forme, hasard, et dimension.* Paris: Flammarion.

Maughan, P. D. (2001). Assessing information literacy among undergraduates: A discussion of the literature and the University of California-Berkeley assessment experience. *College & Research Libraries, 26*(1), 71–85.

McGregor, D. (1960). *The human side of enterprise.* New York: McGraw-Hill.

Mezirow, J. (1991). *Transformative dimensions of adult learning.* San Francisco: Jossey-Bass.

Mintzberg, H. (1994). *The rise and fall of strategic planning.* New York: Free Press.

Mitleton-Kelly, E. (Ed.) (2003). *Complex systems and evolutionary perspectives on organisations: The application of complexity theory to organizations.* Kidlington, Oxford: Elsevier Science.

Morgan, G. (1997). *Images of organization* (2nd ed). Thousand Oaks, CA: Sage Publications.

Morse, A., & Walker, R. (1994). The effects of exercise on psychological measure of the stress response. *Wellness Perspectives, 11*(1), 39–46.

National Institutes of Health. (2005). Policy on enhancing public access to archived publications resulting from NIH-funded research. Available at http://grants.nih.gov/grants/guide/notice-files/NOT-OD-05-022.html. Retrieved on October 1, 2007.

National Institutes of Health. (2008). NIH public access policy. Available at http://publicaccess.nih.gov/. Retrieved on 11 August.

Osberg, D., & Biesta, G. J. J. (2007). Beyond presence: Epistemological and pedagogical implications of 'strong' emergence. *Interchange, 38*(1), 31–35.

Osif, B. A., & Harwood, R. L. (1999). Change challenges and coping. *Library Administration & Management, 13*(4), 224–228.

Ouchi, W. (1981). *Theory Z: How American business can meet the Japanese challenge.* Reading, MA: Addison-Wesley Publishing Company, Inc.

Pace, A. (2006). Technically speaking: Giving homegrown software its due. *American Libraries, 37*(10), 50–51.

Pascale, R. T., Millemann, M., & Gioja, L. (2000). *Surfing the edge of chaos: The laws of nature and the new laws of business.* New York: Crown Business.

Phipps, S. E. (2004). The system design approach to organizational development: The University of Arizona model. *Library Trends, 53*(1), 68–111.

Prigogine, I. (1967). *Thermodynamics of irreversible processes.* New York: Wiley.

Prigogine, I. (1980). *From being to becoming: Time and complexity in the physical sciences.* San Francisco: W. H. Freeman and Company.

Prigogine, I. (2000). The future is not given, in society or nature. *NPQ: New Perspectives Quarterly, 17*(2), 35–37.

Prigogine, I., & Stengers, I. (1984). *Order out of chaos: Man's new dialogue with nature.* New York: Bantam Books, Incorporated.

Puetz, T. W., O'Connor, P., & Dishman, R. K. (2006). Effects of chronic exercise on feelings of energy and fatigue: A quantitative synthesis. *Psychological Bulletin, 132*(6), 866–876.

Ranganathan, S. R. (1963). *The five laws of library science.* Bombay: Asia Publishing House.

Ravindra, B., & Mallik, A. K. (1994). Role of nonlinear dissipation in soft Duffing oscillators. *Physical Review E, 49*(6), 4950–4954.

Riggs, D. E. (1997). What's in store for academic libraries? Leadership and management issues. *Journal of Academic Librarianship, 23*, 3–8.

Riggs, D. E. (1998). Visionary leadership. In: T. F. Mech & G. B. McCabe (Eds.), *Leadership and academic libraries.* The Greenwood Library Management Collection. Westport, CT: Greenwood Press.

Riggs, D. E. (2001). The crisis and opportunities in library leadership. *Journal of Library Administration, 32*(3/4), 5–17.

Rogers, M. (2004). Where are all the library jobs? *Library Journal, 129*(15), 14–15.

Schön, D. A. (1971). *Beyond the stable state.* New York: Random House, Inc.

Schön, D. A. (1991). *The reflective practitioner: How professionals think in action.* Averbury, UK: Ashgate Publishing Limited.

Senge, P. (1994). *The fifth discipline: The art and practice of the learning organization.* New York: Doubleday.

Senge, P. (2004). *Presence: human purpose and the field of the future.* Cambridge, MA: Society for Organizational Learning (SoL).

Shaw, K. A. (1999). *The successful president: "Buzzwords" on leadership.* Phoenix: AZ: Oryx Press.

Simpson, J. A., & Weiner, E. S. C. (Eds). (2001). *Oxford English dictionary.* Oxford, UK: Clarendon Press. OED online Oxford University Press. Available at http://dictionary. oed.com. Retrieved on 1 November.

Smith, C., & Comer, D. (1994). Self-organization in small groups: A study of group effectiveness within non-equilibrium conditions. *Human Relations, 47*(5), 553–581.

Stacey, R. (1992). *Managing the unknowable: Strategic boundaries between order and chaos in organizations.* San Francisco: Jossey-Bass.

Stacey, R. (2003). *Complexity and group processes: A radical social understanding of individuals.* New York: Brunner-Routledge.

Stake, R. E. (1995). *The art of case study research.* Thousand Oaks, CA: Sage Publications.

Stephens, D., & Russell, K. (2004). Organizational development, leadership, change, and the future of libraries. *Library Trends, 53*(1), 238–257.

Stueart, R., & Moran, B. B. (2002). *Library and information center management* (6th ed). Greenwood Village, CO: Libraries Unlimited.

Taylor, F. W. (1911). *The principles of scientific management.* New York: W. W. Norton.

Taylor-Piliae, R. E., Haskell, W. L., Waters, C. M., & Froelicher, E. S. (2006). Change in perceived psychosocial status following a 12-week Tai Chi exercise programme. *Journal of Advanced Nursing, 54*(3), 313–329.

Unabashed librarian. (2003). *Library Journal, 128*(5), p. 48.

Van Orsdel, L. C., & Born, K. (2007). Serial wars: As open access gains ground, STM publishers change tactics, and librarians ask hard questions. *Library Journal, 132*(7). Available at http://www.libraryjournal.com/article/CA6431958.html. Retrieved on 1 October.

von Bertalanffy, L. (1973/1968). *General system theory: Foundations, development, applications* (Revised edition). New York: George Braziller, Inc.

Waldrop, M. M. (1992). *Complexity: The emerging science at the edge of order and chaos.* New York: Simon & Schuster.

Webster, D. E. (1973). *Library management review and analysis program: A handbook for guiding change and improvement in research library management* (Vol. 2). Washington, DC: Office of University Library Management Studies. Association of Research Libraries.

Weick, K. E. (1985). Sources of order in unorganized systems: Themes in recent organizational theory. In: Y. S. Lincoln (Ed.), *Organizational theory and inquiry: The paradigm revolution.* Beverley Hills, CA: Sage Publications.

Weiner, S. G. (2003). Resistance to change in libraries: Application of communication theories. *Portal: Libraries and the Academy, 3*(1), 69–78.

Wheatley, M. J. (1994). *Leadership and the new science: Learning about organization from an orderly universe.* San Francisco: Berrett-Koehler Publishers, Inc.

White, H. (1985). Library turf. *Library Journal, 110*(7), 54–55.

Williams, J. F. I. (2001). Leadership evaluation and assessment. *Journal of Library Administration, 32*(3/4), 145–167.

Wilson, A. (Ed.) (2004). *The 2003 OCLC environmental scan: Pattern recognition. A report to the OCLC membership.* Dublin, OH: OCLC Online Computer Library Center.

Wisneski, R. (2005). Investigating the research practices and library needs of contingent, tenure-track, and tenured English faculty. *Journal of Academic Librarianship, 31*(2), 119–133.

Yukl, G. A. (2002). *Leadership in organizations* (5th ed). Upper Saddle River, NJ: Prentice-Hall.

AN EXPLORATORY CASE STUDY OF LEADERSHIP FOR ORGANIZATIONAL AGILITY IN A CONSORTIUM OF SMALL PRIVATE COLLEGE LIBRARIES

Jean K. Mulhern

ABSTRACT

Are library consortia agile organizations? That is, do they have the leadership capacity to respond quickly to or drive change in complex environments? To explore the related issues of library consortium agility and leadership, the author developed a case study of the Ohio Private Academic Libraries (referred to hereafter as OPAL) consortium, 1998–2007. This chapter describes the OPAL experience and summarizes her findings, conclusions, and recommendations.

BACKGROUND

Both Gray (1989) and Huxham and Vangen (2005) found that, in general, consortia rarely move outside or beyond their original objectives because reaching consensus among members on additional common objectives is

Advances in Library Administration and Organization, Volume 28, 59–79
Copyright © 2009 by Emerald Group Publishing Limited
All rights of reproduction in any form reserved
ISSN: 0732-0671/doi:10.1108/S0732-0671(2009)0000028005

difficult. The shared and negotiated nature of consortial governance may hinder agility and mire this type of organization in a state of inertia, making it vulnerable to disintegration.

However, critics have decried the apparent lack of responsiveness and agility among today's library consortia and local libraries given the rapid changes in the economy, technology, publishing, and the Internet (Beyerlein, Freedman, McGee, & Moran, 2003; De Rosa, Dempsey, & Wilson, 2004; Peters, 2001). They question whether library consortial leadership can sustain member support as local needs shift and opportunities emerge elsewhere. They have predicted the demise of some consortia and mergers among others because of the failure of consortial leadership to move with agility (De Rosa et al., 2004; Hirshon, 1999).

The leadership of library consortia is a topic that challenges common understandings about the nature of organizational leadership. In voluntary library consortia, independent organizations commit significant local resources toward working together, motivated by the goal of achieving local advantages not possible through individual library effort. The test of a successful consortium is whether, based on perceptions of local benefit, its member libraries decide to continue to provide strong levels of support.

In such consortia, leadership is not associated with any one individual or even one organization (Huxham & Vangen, 2005). Leadership power and influence are diffused among members and their representatives. Even when consortia employ administrators to manage group activities, the locus of power within the group remains with the member organizations that supply and control the financial resources and the expertise that the consortium needs to function (Huxham & Vangen, 2005). Member representatives make group decisions about how the consortium will function, choose how resources will be invested, and evaluate those who are asked to administer the group (Huxham & Vangen, 2005). Consensus, tempered by useful exchanges of ideas, is critical to the health of the consortium.

RESEARCH OBJECTIVE

In 1995, OHIONET, a nonprofit library membership service organization, explored how they might help many of its small independent college library members join the OhioLINK academic library consortium despite their lack of sufficient resources. OHIONET had long been the broker in Ohio for OCLC services, and, as such had developed a long-standing relationship with many of these libraries, provided technical expertise and training for their employees. OhioLINK had been formed and was funded directly by the Ohio Board of Regents to facilitate resource sharing, first, among libraries in state universities and two large private research universities. OhioLINK resource sharing was later extended to support community colleges and the branch campuses of state universities across the state. It then decided to expand further by offering membership to the many private colleges in Ohio on condition that they purchase the integrated library system (henceforth referred to as ILS) that all of the state supported colleges had in place. Initially, despite the obvious advantages of joining OhioLINK, many of the small colleges declined because they did not have sufficient resources or expertise to purchase the system specified and operate it on their home campuses.

OHIONET proposed a shared ILS for the libraries volunteering to form the Ohio Private Academic Libraries (OPAL, 2008) consortium. The tremendous burst of collaborative energy among 17 libraries and OHIONET staff during the formation of OPAL in late 1997 quickly produced a high-functioning ILS that could be shared by a large group of libraries. It also resulted in a high-functioning collaborative environment among the participating library staffs. Nevertheless, despite evidence of continued interest in additional shared projects, OPAL did not expand its agenda (its program of policies, procedures, and activities) beyond the shared ILS between 1998 and 2007. Could one conclude, therefore, that this failure to expand its agenda was evidence that OPAL was not agile, that it had entered into a state of inertia?

To address questions about agility and inertia, this research focuses on the capacity of the OPAL consortium's leadership to demonstrate agility. The author explores how the OPAL leadership processes that were used to structure the collaborative and to set its agenda between 1998 and 2007 fit with the tenants of organizational agility. Huxham and Vangen (2005) had identified these two processes as the most significant factors in the shared leadership of consortia of social service, health, and government organizations.

CASE STUDY RESEARCH DESIGN

The author selected OPAL for her case study in 2004 because it had been well established since 1998 and was attracting new members. OPAL, as the least complex type of consortium identified by Gray (1989) and Huxham and Vangen (2005), presented few confounding factors in data analysis of its internal leadership processes. Its member libraries were of a single-type, participated voluntarily, and provided all consortium financing. Existing unique factors included operating under the legal umbrella of OHIONET and its member libraries, being enabled to join OhioLINK as an OPAL benefit, and participating in the OhioLINK shared catalog via the shared OPAL catalog in addition to optional OhioLINK activities. Because the author was a director of one of the founding OPAL libraries, she had a long-term participant perspective, the necessary access to data, and the trust of the various participants.

The author, as a *complete insider/researcher*, combined the qualitative research strategies of personal journaling, participant observation, document analysis, and participant interviews in a process of heuristic inquiry. She gathered extensive documentation, dating from 1994, including correspondence, meeting reports and minutes, background papers, and electronic mail archives. The author supplemented the historical documentation with meeting observations between 2004 and 2007 and interviews with selected OPAL directors and OHIONET personnel in 2007, both of which provided the sources for the quotations used in this report. She subjected the compiled research data to concept *chunk* description and analysis on a series of spreadsheets. Data were presented both in historical narratives and on timelines that could be sorted by keywords to trace changes in structure and agenda in the context of other relevant events in the consortium environment. Descriptive analysis of change trajectories aligned with the historical narratives of OPAL structuring and agenda setting led to the research findings.

BACKGROUND OF THE OPAL CONSORTIUM

The Ohio Board of Regents formed OhioLINK in the late 1980s as a consortium to facilitate academic library resource sharing (OhioLINK, 2008). The early success of OhioLINK in increasing resource sharing among large university libraries and publicly funded community colleges attracted the interest of private colleges eager to be included in the project that so effectively and efficiently boosted patron access to resources. Participation in OhioLINK was seen as essential for offering high-quality library services and competing successfully for students and faculty. OhioLINK's shared catalog, paperless, unmediated lending and borrowing system, and statewide daily delivery service using a private contractor assured speedy intrastate resource exchange. OhioLINK's "big deal" consortium pricing for electronic content purchases and subscriptions was an attractive bonus benefit that by 2008 was offering more than 140 databases and several electronic content archives at prices that were substantially less than could be found in the open market.

Ohio's smaller independent college libraries were invited to join the OhioLINK shared catalog and delivery service beginning in 1996, provided that they met certain costly technology requirements – namely that they equip themselves with a specific ILS package provided by Innovative Interfaces, Inc. Four private institutions, Denison University, Kenyon College, Ohio Wesleyan University, and College of Wooster, joined together in a consortium called CONSORT to share a single system and qualify for membership in OhioLINK. CONSORT provided the technology model of a shared ILS as a cost effective way for smaller institutions to join the larger consortium. A few other institutions also used the OhioLINK invitation as an incentive to convert to the preferred system and joined as individual institutions. But the majority of small colleges in the state held back because of the expense.

OHIONET, originally a broker for OCLC products and training, expanded its services to include library technical training workshops, consulting, and group pricing for library-specific equipment and supplies. It built a reputation among potential OPAL members as a solid organization able to meet the needs of its member libraries, especially in the area of technology. The staff of OHIONET explored the replication of the CONSORT model of centrally housed computer equipment and system support staff and then asked the small colleges of the state whether they would be interested in joining together for this purpose. The Ohio Association of Independent Colleges and Universities assisted in this effort by providing the institution presidents information about the potential benefits of participation. Commitment from at least five libraries was needed to make the proposed project cost effective.

There was substantial interest. In December 1997, OHIONET finalized the formation of OPAL under the CONSORT model with 17 small private institution libraries signing the original contracts for service. Two-thirds of the founding OPAL member libraries abandoned stand-alone library systems to join OPAL. For the remaining members, OPAL provided their first automation system with several needing to complete retrospective record conversion projects through OCLC.

OPAL Consortium Profile

For six months before the signing of formal contracts, staff from the original group of libraries worked together with OHIONET staff to develop the technical platform for the new OPAL consortium. Member libraries agreed to common ILS module profiles so that they could share the ILS bibliographic, patron, and library management databases. They agreed to share equally in the costs of hardware and software purchase, maintenance, and upgrades, technical and administrative support, and financial management and to require memberships in OCLC and OHIONET.

At first, OPAL library users needed to consult the OPAL catalog to request items from other OPAL libraries and the OhioLINK catalog to request items from non-OPAL OhioLINK member libraries. In 2006, OhioLINK activated III Agency software that enabled these users to request items from all libraries through the OhioLINK system, giving them full functionality in the OhioLINK central catalog. They continue to use the OPAL local catalog to manage their personal library accounts, view local reserve collections, and search local holdings only. In addition to their strong collections in the areas of religion and philosophy, the OPAL libraries in aggregate offer the largest undergraduate collection in OhioLINK and have always been a net lender system to the OhioLINK community.

By 2008, after 10 years of efficient and effective operation as a shared ILS system, OPAL grew from 17 to its maximum system capacity of 24 member libraries with an aggregated collection of more than 3.7 million items available to almost 40,000 active local borrowers. The OPAL system handled 353,000 borrower loans from OPAL and OhioLINK libraries in the 2007–2008 academic year. The individual OPAL member libraries are profiled in Table 1.

Beyond the OhioLINK resource exchange and access to a few databases provided by state funds, OPAL libraries obtained a membership bonus option that enabled them to spend their own local funds to participate in the purchase of additional OhioLINK member-funded databases for access to 12,000 journal titles. By 2008, OPAL libraries were participating in OhioLINK resource sharing activities, which included patron access to 46 million items in 87 library collections, daily delivery service, and shared electronic repositories for electronic books, journals, dissertations, media, and digitized documents and instructional objects. An OPAL director offered his perception of the local benefit of the OPAL/OhioLINK relationship, "Oh, that's how I viewed it, shared catalog and everything else is frosting on the cake!"

OPAL Contract Requirements

From the start, each OPAL member institution contracted individually with OHIONET for access to and technical and financial administration of the

Table 1. Profile of Ohio Private Academic Libraries (OPAL), Member Institutions, 2006–2007.

Institution (Date Joined OPAL)	Carnegie Classification[a]	Library Staff[b]	Students[c]
Antioch College including McGregor [University in 2008] (1998)	Baccalaureate/arts and science	8	910
Athenaeum of Ohio (1998)	Special/faith	4	242
Baldwin-Wallace College[d] (1998)	Masters/large	19	4,349
Bluffton University[d,e] (1998)	Baccalaureate/diverse	8	1,154
Columbus College of Art and Design (1999)	Special/arts	10	1,581
Defiance College[d] (1998)	Baccalaureate/diverse	7	996
University of Findlay[d,e] (1998)	Masters/large	8	5,263
DeVry Institute/Columbus[d] (withdrew in 2002)	Proprietary		
Franciscan University of Steubenville (1998)[d]	Masters/medium	9	2,387
Heidelberg College[d,e] (1998)	Masters/small	9	1,570
Lourdes College[d] (2001)	Baccalaureate/diverse	4	1,879
Malone College[e] (1998)	Masters/small	10	2,296
Mercy College of Northwest Ohio (Nursing)[d] (2004)	Special/health	3	780
Methodist Theological School – Ohio[d] (2006)	Special/faith – Graduate	3	244
Mt. Carmel College of Nursing[d] (1998)	Special/health	6	628
Mt. Union College[d,e] (1998)	Baccaluareate/arts and science	12	2,193
Muskingum College[e] (1998)	Masters/medium	7	2,165
Otterbein College[d,e] (1998)	Masters/medium	13	3,184
Pontifical College Josephinum[d] (2006)	Special/faith	3	173
Tiffin University[d] (1998)	Masters/medium	4	1,977
Trinity Lutheran Seminary[d] (2006)	Special/faith – Graduate	5	177
Urbana University (1999)	Baccalaureate/diverse	4	1,568
Walsh University[d] (2003)	Masters/small	9	2,405
Wilberforce University (1998)	Baccalaureate/diverse	4	863
Wilmington College[d,e] (1998)	Baccalaureate/diverse	7	1,678
Total 24		176	40,662

Note: All OPAL members are private, not-for-profit, four-year or above postsecondary institutions.
[a]From Carnegie Foundation. (2008). Carnegie classification, 2005 edition updated. Available at http://www.carnegiefoundation.org/classifications. Retrieved on 6 January.
[b]Head count. From OPAL. (2007a). OPAL staff directory. Available at http://staff.opal-libraries.org/resources/index.php/staff-directory. Retrieved on 17 November.
[c]Head count includes undergraduate and graduate students. From National Center for Education Statistics. (2007). The Integrated Postsecondary Education Data system (IPEDS), 2006–2007. Available at http://nces.ed.gov/collegenavigator/. Retrieved on 15 November.
[d]Had an ILS before joining OPAL.
[e]Federal Depository Library Program.

consortium. In the three contract cycles between December 1997 and June 2008, individual library costs actually decreased as the total number of members increased. Member contracts were identical in terms of costs and responsibilities, assuring member equity in power and responsibility for the consortium. Though OPAL did not employ a consortium administrator, the OHIONET Director of Consortium and Technology Services fulfilled that role ex officio, to ensure that OHIONET met its contract obligations to OPAL members.

As per contract, OPAL members were expected to organize as a self-directing consortium under the OHIONET umbrella. OPAL bore responsibility for determining the consortium vision, direction, and agenda, and for adjusting the governance structure as needed. OPAL needed to shape its governance structure to speak with *one voice* in its relationship with OHIONET concerning ILS issues, enhancements, and other interests. As an aside, OPAL does *not* speak with one voice with OhioLINK except through its OHIONET systems administrator on technical compatibility issues. OPAL member libraries pay individual membership fees to OhioLINK and all OPAL library directors serve on the OhioLINK Private Colleges Directors Council (DC). OPAL library staff members who are elected by the private college sector to various OhioLINK committees represent all 47 private colleges, not just the 24 OPAL member colleges. OPAL encourages its library staff members to stand for election on the various committees and the Library Administrative Council (LAC) (a group that includes the Deans and Directors of the original OhioLINK members, with representatives from two year and private colleges) but does not as a group endorse a particular candidate.

Beyond the responsibility for group governance outlined in the OPAL contracts, a long-range plan for structuring the organization was not developed initially; changes were made based on consensus of the need for change. In late 1998, OPAL began what became an eight-year incremental structuring journey toward self-governance. In 2007, one director recalled, "I think initially we said we weren't going to set up a lot of stuff unless we saw a need for it. Well, one thing that changed from the first year was that we actually do have structure!"

Changes in the OPAL Agenda

Having successfully implemented the ILS in just one year, OPAL members began to consider adding to the consortium agenda to build on the success of their new collaborative relationship. When the author evaluated the 29 concepts for additions to the OPAL agenda proposed between 1998 and 2007, she observed an interesting pattern of approval and implementation. Each of the 29 items responded to the local needs of members or opportunities to share in group purchases as presented by OhioLINK. Every proposal enjoyed positive and often enthusiastic initial interest among the directors. However, just 16 of the 29 potential projects were approved and implemented by OPAL. Fourteen of the 16 approved projects directly enhanced the ILS. The other two approved projects used OPAL funds to participate in OhioLINK group purchases of databases, a short-lived funding model.

New projects approved to enhance the effectiveness of the ILS included enhancements to records in the ILS and adding the government documents shared cataloging program, catalog authority control, functional listservs, a website with group calendar, archive, and training resources, purchase of shared inventory scanners, a book cover and summary service for the ILS, and an Internet conferencing service. OPAL libraries cooperated in a library-shared statistics program facilitated by one member director, though this was not a project approved by the OPAL DC.

Despite initial interest, the projects that were not approved by OPAL had two things in common. First, although the failed proposals addressed important member needs, they did not enhance the effectiveness or operational efficiency of the OPAL shared catalog. Second, although attractive, all rejected proposals would have required the expenditure of additional local energy and financial resources at the same time that issues related to sharing the OPAL ILS continued to make demands on local staff time. Projects not approved included shared offsite storage, OPAL electronic book collections, a shared disaster recovery plan, OPAL bibliographic instruction modules, an audio book service, digitization, serials management software, shared interlibrary loan software, and an OPAL marketing program.

FINDINGS

This section describes the author's findings relating to the governance of OPAL and its ability to adapt to changing circumstances (i.e., its agility) based on her analysis of the case study data on changes within OPAL during this period. OPAL experienced the following changes related to its leadership's capacity for agility.

Transformation from Informal to Formal Governance

OPAL governance transformed from a loosely connected group of informal roundtables to a formalized and centralized hierarchy of representative committees that operated with increasing equity, cohesiveness, independence, and productivity. Hindsight allows the OPAL structuring journey between 1998 and 2007 to be described in several phases: OHIONET administered coordination, 1996–1998; informal cooperation, 1998–1999; semi-formal collaboration, 1999–2001; and formal collaboration, achieved in two phases between 2002 and 2006. In reality, the phases are historical constructs since changes in OPAL structure did not result from a long-range or linear plan.

At first, OPAL operated as a flat, informal organization with six functional committees of volunteers loosely linked to a member directors' roundtable called the Administrative Committee. That group elected officers in 1998 and changed its name to DC. The OPAL DC approved an essentially open and flexible mission statement in September 1999 after nine months of consultation and nearly two years after the formation of OPAL, stating that:

> OPAL (Ohio Private Academic Libraries) is a consortium of libraries in independent institutions of higher education in the State of Ohio. ... Its mission is to enable cooperation among, enrich the collections in, and enhance the support of its member libraries. ... This mission is achieved through maintenance of a union catalog of its member libraries, sharing of resources from those libraries, links to additional resources within and beyond those libraries, and other related activities.

The author found that the ongoing changes in OPAL's structure corresponded to the increasing need for more formal and inclusive communication processes as issues with the shared ILS emerged and as additional members joined OPAL. It became evident that the processes of sharing an ILS among 17+ independent college libraries were much more complex than anticipated by the founding librarians. More than 175 local staff members had ILS system privileges, not including the several hundred part-time student library employees. Such a large number of ILS operators and the normal ongoing employee turnover within member libraries created the need to continually clarify and strengthen policies, procedures, standards, and training to confront the threat of chaos in the shared environment and to increase the quality of shared records in the ILS.

To meet this challenge, OPAL added activities to facilitate communication among employees of the member libraries, among OPAL committees, and between OPAL and related organizations including OHIONET,

OhioLINK, and its ILS vendor. Team-building activities included multiple electronic lists, an annual conference for staff members, annual service awards, three-year strategic planning cycles, and participation in system user groups. One director summed up the OPAL structural transformation:

> And I think it has benefited everyone whether it's the participants on the committees ... knowing how their voice or how their input is determined, what their role is within the committee and within the larger organization; the directors ... I think [the formal structure] has reaffirmed their role as the leaders and the guiders, the guiding body of this organization; and for OHIONET, in terms of giving OPAL the control and allowing [OPAL] to say this is the way we want things to operate. I think that is obviously one of the most critical changes in the past.

At first changes in OPAL governance structure were reactive, made in response to problems. After the OPAL DC approved its own bylaws in 2001, it made more changes proactively, beginning with an intensive and purposeful reorganization of the committee structure, and conducted two rounds of strategic planning in 2002 and 2005 that identified priorities.

In 2005, after a four-year process of restructuring, OPAL implemented a new streamlined, formal committee structure with just three standing committees charged with oversight of specific ILS-based library functions. The standing committees were Cataloging, Circulation, and User Services Advisory. Task forces and interest groups were authorized to address cross-committee initiatives and niche interests. In practice, OPAL made extensive use of limited-scope task forces. All subgroups reported to the OPAL DC that used its Executive Committee (EC) in a servant role to expedite consortium affairs between quarterly meetings and work closely with the OHIONET Director of Consortium and Technology Services.

By design, most EC officers and standing committee officers held just one-year terms and none exceeded two years in the same office. The resulting *weak* governance model diluted the potential power and influence of any one library representative and empowered shared decision-making as the OPAL leader substitute. One member director interviewed about the changes in governance structure said that, "It's really made OPAL much more effective as an organization – all of the organization and policies and strategic planning. At first we flew by the seat of our pants and that's the only word for it. We would have the Directors council meeting and oh, here's another crisis!" Another director described the results of the OPAL changes in structure as follows:

> I think OPAL would not be as successful as [we] are today if [we] were not formal. Because the problem with collaborative models, if you are not organized, the person that

talks the most and loudest generally gets their way and that is not always the best way so you need some formal structure where everyone can be heard. Everyone has the right to say something and then you evaluate the process, and in my mind, without that structure, you have chaos. And believe me, in this profession, you have people who speak passionately about things that they believe in, and if they believe strongly, they will drown out those ideas that differ. So you need structure so there is common ground for everyone to be heard.

Shared Leadership through Structuring

OPAL member directors exerted shared leadership power and influence through decision-making on structure. They made decisions by consensus during the first four years and by formal vote after the approval of bylaws. Their shared decisions on the OPAL agenda complemented changes in structure by providing supportive policies, procedures, and projects and by building on structuring changes in two successive triennial strategic plans in 2002 and 2005. Because the increasingly formal OPAL structure effectively privileged the shared ILS, these incremental changes directed consortial and member resources toward the shared ILS as the highest common priority of the collaboration.

Close Interpretation of the Mission Statement

The OPAL directors and members of the standing committees considered many proposals for additional shared projects related to the OPAL mission of *sharing resources* or *other related activities* (OPAL mission statement, September 1999). Despite active consideration of expanding the OPAL agenda beyond the narrow scope of the ILS, decision-making on structure by the OPAL DC had the apparent effect of a close interpretation of the OPAL mission statement with a keen focus on the ILS. The OPAL consortium participants transformed from a group eager to add many shared services to a group organized to focus intensely on the ILS as the one clear and strongly supported group purpose. Concerning this narrowed focus, one OPAL director observed "The focus on the ILS – I didn't realize that, but when you look back and think about it, that's what we did!"

The incremental changes in OPAL's structure increased the effectiveness of its growing collegial support system for library management problem solving, training, and professional development. The support system improved both the shared ILS and the quality of related local operations. As examples, the elected member at large of the OPAL EC was charged with assuming the role of Training and Mentoring Coordinator. The vice chairperson was charged with being the Communications Coordinator, to expedite communications among OPAL committees and with OHIONET staff. The EC was charged with reviewing all proposals and preparing the DC meeting agendas. The annual OPAL conference became an opportunity for functional peer networking among libraries' staff members as well as a showcase of local staff expertise. Each year OPAL honors one local staff member who has contributed significant service to OPAL through standing committee, task force, and project accomplishments. OPAL sponsors the honoree at the next national ILS users' group conference, which draws locally sponsored representatives as well. Finally, the standing committees developed formal policy and procedure manuals for circulation, cataloging, and collection weeding and a resource exchange program to maintain bibliographic records in the ILS and strengthen local collections.

As OPAL became more formal, proposals for expanding the agenda with new shared projects unrelated to the operation of the ILS were not approved, despite their attractiveness and the flexible mission statement. Data showed that of the 16 new projects eventually implemented by OPAL between 1998 and 2007, 12 of the ideas were first discussed by OPAL directors before 2002, before they agreed to the first set of OPAL bylaws, its first strategic plan, and the restructuring of the committees. The OPAL formal structure that evolved did not emphasize innovation or pilot projects. One participant told the author that OPAL had "no mechanism for ideas to move up the organization ... If you don't have a mechanism to bring them [new ideas] to the larger body, they get lost."

Another OPAL participant shared a different perspective on the role of innovation in OPAL. That person said that:

> I don't see us as an incubator of new ideas. I see us as maybe seeing how we could tweak things and maybe be a little more efficient or as [the OhioLINK executive officer] likes to say, rearrange the deck chairs. But new, no, I really do not see us [OPAL] as cutting edge new.

Development in a Rich, Complex Environment

The OPAL governance transformation to a formal structure occurred within and contributed to an increasingly complex environment of other organizations also engaged with OPAL and its individual member libraries (Fig. 1).

The case study data demonstrated how OPAL participants increasingly began to develop the consortium agenda within the broader context of

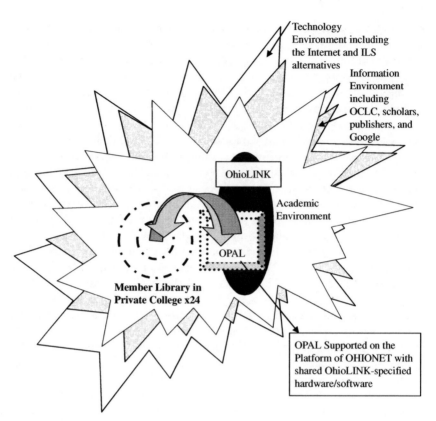

Technology
Environment including
the Internet and ILS
alternatives
Information
Environment
including
OCLC, scholars,
publishers, and
Google

OhioLINK

Academic
Environment

OPAL

Member Library in
Private College x24

OPAL Supported on the
Platform of OHIONET with
shared OhioLINK-specified
hardware/software

Fig. 1. The Complex OPAL Collaboration Environment Required OPAL Partici-
pants to Bridge Multiple Organizational Relationships. The OPAL Consortium was
Co-Created by Member Libraries on a Platform Supported by OHIONET. Both
OPAL and OHIONET Developed Relationships with the OhioLINK Consortium.

support provided by OhioLINK and OHIONET's relationship with
OhioLINK, OPAL, and individual OPAL libraries. The complex relationship between OPAL and OhioLINK greatly improved local library services
in OPAL libraries. Numerous formal and informal proposals to add new
shared projects emerged from discussions among OPAL members between
1998 and 2007 but were overshadowed by similar OhioLINK projects that
had the advantages of being on a larger scale. As an example, OPAL's early
program of "pick up anywhere in OPAL" was replaced several years later
by a similar broader program in OhioLINK. In the same vein, shared online

reference was proposed among members, but proved to be easier to implement among the many more libraries participating in OhioLINK.

As OPAL participants gained more experience with their linked participation in OPAL and OhioLINK, they transferred most of their expectations (and local energy and resources) for new shared activities and products to their OhioLINK membership. Today, as a direct benefit of OPAL membership, OPAL member libraries enjoy a high-quality, dependable, and very affordable shared local ILS. They also enjoy OhioLINK's daily direct delivery from the circulating collections of all 87 OhioLINK libraries, opportunities to subscribe to more than 140 databases and the Electronic Journal Center through group discounts, access to the Digital Media Center, the Digital Repository, the Digital Dissertation Center, a resource exchange, and shared marketing resources. OPAL members had also discussed shared storage, electronic book collections, shared databases, and marketing programs but found it easier to join with the larger OhioLINK membership in bringing these programs to fruition. In addition, in 2006 and 2007, OPAL experimented with a hybrid model of funding new OhioLINK database subscriptions with OPAL funds. This model was abandoned because of lack of common interest in the databases and because OhioLINK agreed to calculate individual library costs to participate.

Despite the fact that the mission of OPAL did not expand, the addition of the 24 OPAL member libraries to OhioLINK drove change in that consortium that further benefited OPAL libraries. The OhioLINK selection processes for committee representation were formalized, assuring that staff members from OPAL libraries had opportunities to serve and thereby to develop professionally. The OhioLINK algorithm calculations controlling loan requests became more complex to assure equity of participation after it became clear that some OPAL libraries were experiencing excessive demands on their collections. In turn, other OhioLINK member libraries benefited from access to the OPAL undergraduate collections for more copies of popular titles and the OPAL specialty collections in such areas as equine studies, nursing, religion and philosophy, literature, and Asian studies. In short, OPAL libraries were exposed to the full expertise represented within OhioLINK and earned the respect of the entire membership of OhioLINK as full partners in the larger consortium.

OPAL also drove change in OHIONET, which reorganized in 2002 to create a new administrative department, Consortium and Technology Services. That change helped OHIONET take advantage of its increasing staff expertise in technology. By 2008, OHIONET was negotiating and managing some group purchases for OhioLINK and had formed an additional consortium of up to 10 OhioLINK members, mostly community colleges, which shared a hardware platform and technical support for their independent local systems.

Strong, Sustained Support

OPAL member libraries provided strong, sustained support for their consortium through contributions of financial and human resources between 1998 and 2007. The case study findings demonstrated that through 10 years of incremental change, mainly in the OPAL structure, OPAL member libraries sustained their local support for the consortium with conscientious attendance at committee meetings and mutual assistance through active listservs. OPAL members committed the time and energy of their library directors and staff members to the development of consortium governance and ILS enhancement projects. As examples, between 1998 and 2007, elected committee officers came from 16 member libraries including 9 DC chairpersons from 8 member libraries. Quarterly meetings drew 85% or more of directors, even on days with hazardous weather. OPAL institutions approved without objection three generations of membership contracts with OHIONET (a similar fourth contract was approved in 2008).

Beyond the shared collections, directors have cited as benefits to their local libraries these direct economic advantages obtained from OPAL consortium participation: robust system hardware, timely software upgrades expertly implemented with minimal downtown, data archiving, long-term financial planning, management of the ILS vendor relationship, local library staff training, and responsive technical support from the OHIONET staff and from OPAL colleagues. OPAL member representatives also increasingly participated in a variety of OhioLINK and OHIONET elective positions with the effect of strengthening ties among the three-member-driven organizations.

CONCLUSIONS

The intent of the case study was to explore the OPAL processes of structuring and agenda setting with attention to the issue of organizational leadership for agility. To assess agility in OPAL's first decade, the author compared the OPAL research data with characteristics for proactive leadership for agility identified by Mische (2001) who contended that an organization with responsible leadership demonstrates both agility and excellence.

OPAL exhibited the following leadership characteristics suggested by Mische (2001) as it made incremental decisions to change its structure: (a) throughout this period OPAL read its market well through continuous learning, a broad base of knowledge and experience, a global perspective, customer focus, and strong knowledge of competition; (b) it mobilized its resources well by sharing power and empowering its committees; and (c) finally, it positioned itself openly in its environment by being accessible and flexible in relationships with other organizations, building its own network, and creating coalitions with other organizations. Through its open positioning, OPAL incorporated the opportunities presented to its members by OhioLINK and OHIONET as an agile response to its environment, enabling the local libraries to expand resources and services to local constituents while more narrowly focusing the structure of the consortium on the OPAL ILS. Research data confirmed that OPAL mobilized its resources through sponsorship of initiatives or innovation directly related to its ILS but not for initiatives unrelated to the ILS. Instead, individual members of OPAL, freed from the considerable costs and responsibilities of operating independent systems and stimulated by consortium networking, had increased financial and motivational capacity to seize opportunities to participate in OhioLINK's innovative projects, especially in the areas of electronic content and online reference.

Since OPAL demonstrated all the characteristics associated with organizations that have agile leadership, the author concluded that OPAL demonstrated organizational agility appropriate to its specific environment. It achieved agility primarily through responsive incremental changes in governance structure that sharpened participant focus on the necessary processes of sharing the ILS and the pursuit of excellence in the ILS. Given the limited personnel and financial resources of its small college members, OPAL achieved a sustainable agenda.

OPAL members had the luxury of enhancing their founding consortium objective of the shared ILS because, by virtue of their membership in OPAL, they also could become engaged in Ohio's lively environment of overlapping consortia. The complementary nature of OPAL, OhioLINK, and OHIONET enabled OPAL to become a *niche* consortium for ongoing development of a shared ILS for small college libraries and for staff support, training, and mentoring. Given access to OhioLINK by virtue of their OPAL membership, member libraries found in OhioLINK the means to meet their other important local library needs through its economies of scale with deeper discounts on information products and more broadly shared risks of innovation.

IMPLICATIONS

The author's research findings and conclusions have three implications. First, although well-organized, strongly supported, and appropriately agile, OPAL remained *temporary by definition* of the consortium type of organization (Gray, 1989; Huxham & Vangen, 2005). Consortia more often lose effectiveness through waning member interest than abrupt failure.

OPAL was and is completely dependent on voluntary member support in its environment of unpredictable change. The lifespan of OPAL as a consortium depends on sustaining each individual member's agreement that the OPAL collaboration continues to provide the local library with unique and high-priority advantages that justify ongoing investment of local funds and human resources. OPAL succeeds as long as its member libraries can equate the consortium with helping them achieve agility at the local level.

In the case of OPAL, by increasing the focus on the ILS, resisting temptations to expand its own agenda, and enabling members to participate in the 87-member OhioLINK consortium, OPAL sustained high member satisfaction over the 10 years studied. Very high and high satisfaction with OPAL among 100% of OPAL member directors was verified by a 2007 director survey using the Wilder Collaboration Inventory (Mattessich, Murray-Close, & Monsey, 2001). The broader and very advantageous environment of OhioLINK and OHIONET was the essential factor in member comfort with the narrow focus of OPAL although members remained open to further consideration of an expanded agenda for OPAL. Said one director concerning adding to the agenda, "So anytime from now on there could be something done … By the way, when I say group purchasing, I mean OPAL as OPAL, not OPAL through OhioLINK … But the new ideas, I think we are ready for them if they are generated and come up."

OPAL's shared ILS itself also remained a *temporary* solution in this library age where nothing can be taken for granted because everything is subject to change. Since the formation of OPAL, members have included features of Drucker's (1992) *planned abandonment* in their contracts and financial policies. OPAL planned for additions or losses in membership and for transition to the next, still-unidentified generation technology in library systems that may or may not include a consortium approach.

The second implication of the research was that the OPAL process of structuring aligned closely with the characteristics of organizational leadership for agility identified by Mische (2001). These characteristics provided a rubric useful for assessing the capacity of OPAL's leadership for agility and potentially useful in research of leadership in other consortia.

Finally, this research implies that the role of structuring in OPAL shared leadership, in effect, as a leader substitute, differed from findings of researchers of social services consortia, in which structure was established as a condition of formation to provide a platform for other shared leadership strategies (Huxham & Vangen, 2005). For OPAL, decisions on governance structure became the principal venue for shared leading of the consortium. The incremental changes in the structure of OPAL shaped the consortium vision and objectives and established its essential, unduplicated place in Ohio's library multiconsortium landscape.

DISCUSSION

In this research project, the author was concerned with leadership and agility in the OPAL consortium. She concluded that the leadership capacity for agility in the OPAL consortium was realized through its process of incremental shared decision-making on consortium structure. As a result of changes in structure, the consortium became more formal to accommodate membership expansion, increase channels of communication, and facilitate inclusiveness. Changes in structure enhanced ILS-related training, mentoring, and professional development. Changes in agenda complemented structuring with new services and activities focused on enhancing the effectiveness and efficiency of the shared ILS as the highest consortium priority.

The research conclusions suggest that the agility of the OPAL consortium and concerns with whether it might disintegrate or be subject to merger were secondary to the fundamental agility of the local member library. The primary question about OPAL was whether each member library was agile locally by virtue of membership in one or more consortia. Each OPAL member voted continuously and positively on that question by directing staff energy, expertise, and resources toward the operation of OPAL governance and increasingly toward enhancement of the shared ILS. Further, each member library provided change leadership in its own institution based on its association with OPAL, OhioLINK, OHIONET, and sometimes additional consortia. Given that small libraries in general are impeded in their efforts to implement change because of resource limitations, OPAL offered a dramatic opportunity for its member libraries to gain access to an expanding and innovative array of resources at a price they could afford and to take risks in the development of collections, services, and technologies within the context of OPAL and OhioLINK that would have been difficult if they were acting alone. The end result of the efforts of this consortium working in concert with OHIONET within the context of OhioLINK has been access to a library program and resources well beyond what one might expect to find in a typical small college library.

The implications of this research can be interpreted as four *lessons learned*. First, a consortium providing low-priority benefits, however worthy, would fail as support withered. In contrast, OPAL member institutions were highly motivated to provide ongoing and extensive resource support to OPAL and other related consortia based on perceptions of strong relevancy and important benefits for the local campuses. Second, regardless of group planning, consortium success results from group action. How individual OPAL member libraries allocated campus-based staff energy and time determined OPAL's strengths and priorities. OPAL members dedicated extraordinary staff time and expertise to their shared ILS while ignoring other suggested or planned initiatives. Third, offering access to more resources requires more skillful local staff members. OPAL participation empowered member librarians to become local campus change leaders by providing both formal and informal professional development along with affordable access to formerly unobtainable resources and services. Finally, consortium form (structure) follows function. OPAL members sustained the consortium during its first 10 years with high levels of trust and low levels of formal organization. Members increased organizational formality only when growth led to the need for more coordination and communication.

The author suggests that this research project on the OPAL consortium provides the foundation of two themes for additional research. First, she recommends that her case study design that focused on the history and context of consortium structuring and agenda setting could be useful as a template for additional case studies of other consortia to deepen general understanding of the issues of consortium leadership and agility. Second, she notes that Mische's (2001) characteristics of organizational leadership for agility are similar to those identified with Senge's (1990) learning communities. To focus on the nexus between learning community and leadership in library consortia, she suggests exploration of the role of consortium culture, including the concept of learning community, to build on her research of OPAL consortium leadership.

Finally, this research project on OPAL provides the basis for research on the impact of participation in OPAL and OhioLINK on individual member libraries and their constituents. The author recommends exploration of the impact of OPAL or other library consortium membership, along with the peer influence resulting from participation in group decision-making, on the capacity of individual consortium member libraries to change in ways that respond agilely to the changing environment.

REFERENCES

Beyerlein, M. M., Freedman, S., McGee, C., & Moran, L. (2003). *Beyond teams: Building the collaborative organization.* San Francisco: Jossey-Bass.

De Rosa, C., Dempsey, L., & Wilson, A. (2004). *The 2003 OCLC environmental scan: Pattern recognition, a report to the OCLC membership.* Dublin, OH: OCLC Online Computer Library Center, Inc.

Drucker, P. T. (1992). The new society of organizations. *Harvard Business Review, 70*(5), 95–104. Retrieved October 7, 2007, from EBSCO Business Source Complete database.

Gray, B. (1989). *Collaborating: Finding common ground for multiparty problems.* San Francisco: Jossey-Bass.

Hirshon, A. (1999). Libraries, consortia, and change management. *Journal of Academic Librarianship, 25,* 124–126.

Huxham, C., & Vangen, S. (2005). *Managing for collaborative advantage: The theory and practice of collaborative advantage.* London: Routledge.

Mattessich, P. W., Murray-Close, M., & Monsey, B. R. (2001). *Collaboration, what makes it work: A review of research literature.* St. Paul, MN: Amherst H. Wilder Foundation.

Mische, M. A. (2001). *Strategic renewal: Becoming a high-performance organization.* Upper Saddle River, NJ: Prentice Hall.

Ohio Private Academic Libraries. (2008). Website. Available at http://www.opal-libraries.org/. Retrieved on 14 July.

OhioLINK (2008). Website. Available at http://www.ohiolink.edu. Retrieved on 14 July.

OHIONET (2008). Website. Available at http://www.ohionet.org/. Retrieved on 14 July.

Peters, T. A. (2001). Agile innovation clubs [inaugural column on academic library consortia]. *Journal of Academic Librarianship, 27,* 149–151.

Senge, P. (1990). *Fifth discipline.* New York: Doubleday.

CONSORTIA ACTIVITY IN ACADEMIC LIBRARIES: ANTI-COMPETITIVE OR IN THE PUBLIC GOOD?

Catherine Maskell

ABSTRACT

Academic library consortia activity has become an integral part of academic libraries' operations. Consortia have come to assert considerable bargaining power over publishers and have provided libraries with considerable economic advantage. They interact with publishers both as consumers of publishers' products, with much stronger bargaining power than individual libraries hold, and, increasingly, as rival publishers themselves. Are consortia changing the relationship between academic libraries and publishers? Is the role of academic library consortia placing academic libraries in a position that should and will attract the attention of competition policy regulators? Competition policy prohibits buying and selling cartels that can negatively impact the free market on which the Canadian economic system, like other Western economies, depends. Competition policy as part of economic policy is, however, only relevant where we are concerned with aspects of the market economy. Traditionally, public goods for the greater social and cultural benefit of society are not considered part of the market economic system. If the activities of academic library consortia are part of that public good perspective,

Advances in Library Administration and Organization, Volume 28, 81–151
ISSN: 0732-0671/doi:10.1108/S0732-0671(2009)0000028006

competition policy may not be a relevant concern. Using evidence gained from in-depth interviews from a national sample of university librarians and from interviews with the relevant federal government policy makers, this research establishes whether library consortia are viewed as participating in the market economy of Canada or not. Are consortia viewed by librarians and government as serving a public good role of providing information for a greater social and cultural benefit or are they seen from a market-economic perspective of changing power relations with publishers? Findings show government has little in-depth understanding of academic library consortia activity, but would most likely consider such activity predominantly from a market economic perspective. University librarians view consortia from a public good perspective but also as having an important future role in library operations and in changing the existing scholarly publishing paradigm. One-third of librarian respondents felt that future consortia could compete with publishers by becoming publishers and through initiatives such as open source institutional repositories. Librarians also felt that consortia have had a positive effect on librarians' professional roles through the facilitation of knowledge building and collaboration opportunities outside of the home institution.

INTRODUCTION

Academic library consortia activity has become an integral part of how academic libraries are acquiring resources and providing services for their respective communities. Consortia are involved across a broad span of academic libraries' operations, including purchasing content for collections, building, and maintaining technical infrastructures; delivering services such as interlibrary loan and document delivery; developing resource sharing agreements; and establishing institutional repositories. From the internal perspective of academic libraries, and the librarians who manage them, with each passing year, consortial obligations are demanding a larger share of each member library's budget, human resources, time, and attention.

Considering the roles consortia play in academic libraries, a crucial question to consider is if and how consortia may be changing the role of the academic library? How might consortia be affecting the relationship between academic libraries and publishers? How could the consortia activity in which we are all so intimately involved be affecting what we do, or should be doing, as libraries in support of our institutions and as librarians meeting our obligations to our profession?

What makes this picture of academic library management, and the evolution of academic library consortia, in particular, more complex is that it is part of the overall picture of the scholarly publishing cycle, a cycle intimately involved with information, and thus intersecting with established intellectual property regimes, specifically copyright. The scholarly publishing cycle, particularly as the information economy matures in the twentieth and twenty-first centuries, is also a cycle that is part of the overall market economy of Western nations such as Canada. Competition is a dominant element within the market system. In Canada, like other countries with developed market economies, competition policy has been developed and lays out a legal regime to protect the competitive structure of markets. Recent views on the intersection between Canadian competition policy and intellectual property rights suggest that the two are complementary. Both seek to promote innovation in the economy. Though intellectual property law may restrict access to or use of information in the short term, its purpose of stimulating innovation and research contributes over the long term to growth and development.

If viewed as cartels of purchasers, might library consortia be characterized as a direct competitive response by academic libraries (buyers) to counter the increasing monopolistic control of commercial publishers (sellers)? Might this then be interpreted under Canadian competition policy as anti-competitive activity by academic libraries? Is consortia activity necessarily placing Canadian academic libraries in a market economic framework that includes competition policy and possibly subjecting them to anti-competitive practices scrutiny?

Using evidence gained from in-depth interviews from a national sample of Canadian University Librarians (i.e., Directors of Canadian university libraries) and from interviews with relevant Canadian federal government policy makers, this chapter examines academic library consortia activity in the broad context of the scholarly publishing cycle from the competing perspectives of the market economy and the public good. The research presented considers whether consortia are viewed by librarians and government as serving a public good role of providing information for a greater social and cultural benefit or are they seen from a market-economic perspective of changing power relations with publishers? The principles of competition and copyright are used to define the theoretical premise of the research.

Competition policy becomes a concern only where there is a concern about the competitive marketplace. Where, on the contrary, the issue at hand concerns the traditional public good and resources that are non-commodifiable, competition concerns do not arise. In the economic literature, the concept of a market economy and private property are taken as a given and "public goods," within those givens, are resources or materials that cannot be commodified. The concept of "public good" also arises in the context of the cultural public good, a notion that is also frequently referred to as the "commons." This notion describes areas of society or culture, as well as resources that should not be defined and managed by a market definition of resource development, commodification, and sale.

If academic library consortia activity is properly characterized as part of the notion of the cultural public good, that is, as an attempt by academic libraries to wield their influence over the scholarly publishing cycle through a more effective realization of the ideal of information as a public good, competition policy considerations would not arise. Such a characterization should occur if the goal of consortia activity is to ensure that the control of commercial scholarly publishers does not expand to the point that information becomes entirely a commodity and access to that information is based totally on ability to pay.

However, if academic consortia are best characterized as a type of buying club applying competitive pressure against publishers to achieve greater market strength for academic libraries, then such activity should be considered in the context of a direct attempt by participating libraries to affect the control of commercial publishers over the scholarly publishing record. Such activity within the context of the market economy of academic publishing should attract competition scrutiny if academic libraries are acting as buyer cartels and, in an anti-competitive manner, overwhelming the bargaining position of publishers, either by giving academic libraries an undue control over price or product (or both) as consumers or by unfairly competing as publishers directly with the existing commercial publishers.

Distinguishing between the market economic view of library consortia and the public good perspective, I focus on the following central theme:

> How do the University Librarians who have created and maintain the academic library consortia in Canada view these consortia? How do the federal government actors responsible for providing funding to the national consortium and regulating competition view them?

In examining the university librarians' views, I also explore which of four organizational models best represents the mental model of consortia activity held by these librarians because each of these models, by definition, assists in discriminating between consortia viewed from a public good perspective and viewed from a market economic perspective. Finally, in analyzing the views of these librarians about academic library consortia, I make observations concerning these librarians' views of the effect of consortia activity on the professional roles of librarians.

The views of academic librarians were gleaned from in-person interviews with 30 university librarians from across Canada, a national sample of the 64 academic libraries originally involved in Canadian National Site Licensing Project (CNSLP),[1] and drawn from the four academic library regions of Canada (the West, Ontario, Quebec, and the Atlantic provinces) as well as representing all sizes of library systems. The government perspective was obtained from interviews with representatives of key federal government policy agencies involved with information policy, the federal funding of universities in projects like the CNSLP, and in the administration of Canada's competition policy are.

ACADEMIC LIBRARY CONSORTIA: A BRIEF BACKGROUND

Academic library consortia, and the cooperation between libraries they engender, are not recent inventions. Library consortia have existed for more than a century, as groups of libraries have agreed on policies for services such as interlibrary loan and reciprocal borrowing (Kopp, 1998; Weber, 1976). In a study of 125 academic consortia formed in the United States between 1931 and 1972, Ruth Patrick (1972) found that the five most common activities undertaken by consortia were reciprocal borrowing privileges (78%), expanded interlibrary loan service (64%), union catalogs or lists (62%), photocopying services (58%), and reference services (40%). Weber (1976) notes that at least one or two academic library consortia were formed in the United States every year from 1930 until 1960. After 1960, Weber goes on to note, there was a sharp increase in consortia formations with over 105 consortia formed between 1964 and 1970 inclusive.

James Kopp (1998) fills in the more recent historical details of academic library consortia activity in the United States with the observation that although the number of consortia continued to increase throughout the 1970s and 1980s, the activity by academic libraries within those consortia was diminishing because individual libraries began to concentrate on emerging technological imperatives such as establishing and implementing in-house online integrated systems, establishing links with huge multi-national bibliographic utilities such as the Ohio College Library Center (OCLC), and dealing with the beginnings of an era of reduced budgets and decreasing buying power.

The late 1980s and early 1990s saw a resurgence of consortia activity as the trends of more pervasive technological innovation and even more severe resource constraints, which had emerged in the early 1980s, increased. These trends were coincident with political and social pressures for increased access and accountability. The most significant reason for the resurgence of consortia was most likely the impact of new technologies and the emergence of the Internet on the ability of libraries to access and deliver resources.

Hirshon (1999) lists several environmental factors that contributed to the need for, and growth of, academic library consortia. These factors include increased demand for customized patron services; the need to balance content acquisitions between traditional print resources and the rapidly growing demand for digital resources; organizational changes that require new partnerships and collaborations as a regular way of doing things; and constantly changing technology demands that place the library on the forefront of information technology and information provision.

Allen and Hirshon (1998) state that the new goals of academic library consortia reflect the opportunity libraries have with respect to technology as well the impact of other environmental constraints such as fiscal restraint, political pressures, and resource availability and costs. They list the three reasons for these new goals as being able to leverage resources through shared collections, being able to reduce costs through the consortium acting as buying agent, and being able to affect the future of scholarly information by collective efforts to affect national policies such as copyright policy, and to pressure information providers such as commercial publishers to control costs and pass those cost savings on to libraries.

Ball and Pye (1998) identify four major benefits of library consortia membership: financial savings; opportunities to affect the marketplace and make known the commitment to affect real change in pricing schemes and product design; an increasing awareness and knowledge of the procurement process, market dynamics, and the power of group purchasing; and finally, an increase in the level of cooperation and partnership between libraries and other partners to open up new opportunities and achieve new benefits. They point to the effects on the marketplace as the most significant of the four stating that library consortia have "radically affected the marketplace ... Suppliers now realize that libraries will band together and, more importantly, will demonstrate their commitment to such associations by moving their business to recommended suppliers" (p. 7).

By all accounts, academic library consortia activity seems to be well integrated into library operations, playing an important role in libraries' abilities to acquire the resources they need and in turn serve their respective communities. Consortia activity appears to be affecting collections decisions, budget decisions, the activities of professional librarians, inter-library cooperation and collaboration, and, on an even broader scale, the relationship between libraries and other key players in the scholarly publishing cycle.

THE SCHOLARLY PUBLISHING CYCLE

The scholarly publishing cycle, also referred to as the information chain (Owen & van Halm, 1989), is one in which academic research is developed, published, collected, disseminated, and reinvested in the research process (Garvey, 1978; Lancaster & Smith, 1978). The role of the academic library in this process is a dual one. Through knowledge of how information is published and arranged, and through knowledge of a faculty member's specific research interests, the library assists faculty members in finding the information necessary to support their research. The academic library is also responsible for collecting, organizing, and disseminating published research both to support future research and to preserve the scholarly research record (Garvey, 1978). This scholarly publication process, based historically on print products and traditional relationships between scholar, university, publisher, and library, has been very stable for many decades but recently has come under scrutiny for various reasons. Owen (2002) states that the motivations and perceived role of commercial publishers with respect to scholarly publishing are changing, with publishers' focus shifting to profit and the outcome of commercialization resulting in unacceptably high costs, restrictive copyright practices, and a lack of technical innovation. He goes on to state that the collaboration between academics and scholarly publishers is breaking down with publishers being perceived more as adversary than partner.

Oppenheim, Greenlaugh, and Rowland (2000) note that the scholarly publishing industry has been described as displaying the characteristics of monopolistic competition. Once a publisher controls a specific journal title, there is no competition for that title from other publishers. A buyer, such as a library, must purchase that journal from that publisher. The library cannot shop around and hope to find the same content in another journal owned by another publisher and selling for a better price. The publisher of a journal can also increase that journal's subscription cost without worrying about a significant decrease in demand because they know that libraries cannot get that title anywhere else. Libraries, as purchasers of journals, have no recourse against rapidly increasing journal prices. They become trapped in a cycle of increasing journal prices, increasing demand from its users (the

Fig. 1.   The Traditional Scholarly Publishing Continuum.

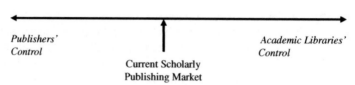

Fig. 2.   A Scholarly Publishing Continuum with More Power for Academic Libraries.

researcher and student) and budgets that are decreasing, stagnant, or, at best, increasing, but at a rate less than the serials price increases it is facing.

If viewed as a continuum of market control, with publishers as suppliers of scholarly content at one end, and academic libraries as purchasers of scholarly content on the other, with the continuum representing market strength (the ability to control price, new market entries, product design, and delivery), then the traditional state of scholarly publishing should probably be placed as a point on the continuum much closer to publishers' end of the continuum than to the academic libraries' end (Fig. 1).

Within this broad perspective of the traditional scholarly publishing cycle weighted in favor of publishers, academic library consortia currently may be having an effect on the location of academic libraries on the continuum. Consortia are groups of libraries coming together to acquire resources or services at lower costs and can be considered as a type of buying club applying competitive pressure against publishers to achieve greater market strength for academic libraries, and in effect shifting the "current scholarly publishing market" (arrow in Fig. 2) in academic libraries' favor.

The information that libraries provide is traditionally considered as not falling within the market economy, not subject to normal market conditions of buying and selling, and therefore, not subject to market principles of competition. However, as library consortia gain bargaining power, it is possible that consortia will come to be viewed as buying cartels, and the product purchased, information, will be seen as a commodifiable resource, subject to market regulatory frameworks such as competition policy.

CONSORTIA, THE MARKET ECONOMY
AND COMPETITION POLICY

One of the primary purposes of academic library consortia cited in the literature is the leveraging of library budgets to purchase more resources (mainly digital resources) than could be purchased by any one member institution (Rowse, 2003; Baker & Sanville, 2000; Alexander, 1999; Allen & Hirshon, 1998). The economic value of consortia for individual member libraries lies in the ability of those libraries to take their budgets farther, spending less and getting more. Consortia have been described as providing cartel buying power for members (Helmer, 2002), allowing libraries to reduce costs of operations through the negotiation of lower prices for acquisitions (Allen & Hirshon, 1998). In an article describing the history of consortia development, Bostick (2001) describes the over-arching goal of consortia as economies of scale with some consortia developed for the sole purpose of acting as "buying clubs" for their members. Consortia may be a means to make the market more competitive and ultimately to make it easier for libraries to purchase what they need to support their constituents. Academic library consortia place academic libraries as significant participants in the market economy, with scholarly publications as the market resource being bought and sold.

Competition is considered a dominant element within the market system (Doern, 1996). The ideology behind the fostering of competition is that there is an equilibrium between buyer and seller such that if a seller raises prices or decreases quality or service, buyers can choose to take their business elsewhere. Practices such as collusion between sellers to fix prices or divide up markets are viewed as anti-competitive. Similarly, if buyers group together to obtain a lower price (perhaps lower than the supplier can bear), this would also be seen as anti-competitive. On either the buyer or the seller side, society may have enshrined in law that it is a violation of competition policy to come together as a group to achieve and maintain market control (Trebilcock, Winter, Collins, & Iacobucci, 2002).

Competition law in Canada generally seeks to prevent business practices that "unduly or substantially lessen or prevent competition and so diminish the efficiency and competitiveness of the Canadian Economy" (Director of Investigation and Research, 1995). The focus of Canadian competition policy lies in the enforcement of the federal Competition Act (1985). Article 1.1 of the Act describes its purpose as fourfold: (1) maintaining and encouraging competition in Canada to promote the efficiency and adaptability of the Canadian economy; (2) expanding opportunities for Canadian participation in world markets while also recognizing the role of foreign competition in Canada; (3) ensuring that small- and medium-sized enterprises have an equitable opportunity to participate in the Canadian economy; and (4) providing consumers with competitive prices and product choices. Of those four reasons, the first, economic efficiency, is recognized as the most important (Trebilcock et al., 2002).

With respect to academic library consortia, what makes a competition perspective more complex is that the product in question is the scholarly output or intellectual property of scholars around the world. The primary intellectual property device affecting academic library consortia is copyright. Copyright artificially creates a property right in the expression of a person's intellectual labor in a fixed form (Wilkinson, 1996). It establishes a time-limited monopoly on the sale, distribution, and use of these fixed works. When a scholar has finished his or her research, and written an article describing that research, he or she passes the article to a publisher for peer review and consideration for publication. If the article is accepted for publication, it is normally the case that the author signs the control of the copyright for that article over to the publisher. In such a manner, publishers become the rights holders of the majority of scholarly material being produced.

It had traditionally been thought that intellectual property rights stood apart from competition policy. By definition, copyright allows rights holders an exclusive or monopoly right with respect to their intellectual property. The goal of competition policy, on the contrary, as described above, is to protect competition in markets, against among other things, monopoly control. The two seem to be in direct conflict (Ullrich, 2001). More recent views on the intersection between competition policy and intellectual property rights, however, suggest that the two are complementary. Both seek to promote innovation in the economy. Though intellectual property law may restrict access or use, in the short term, its purpose of stimulating innovation and research contributes over the long term to growth and development. Competition law in Canada, and its enforcement, reflect this complementary thinking (Trebilcock et al., 2002). By section 79 (5) of the Canadian Competition Act (1985), the exercise of intellectual property rights is not considered an anti-competitive act, and it exempts the creation of monopoly rights through copyright.

The Canadian Copyright Act (1988) specifically allows for the establishment of copyright cartels for the purpose of managing copyright for Canadian works. The 1988 amendment to the Act provides for the establishment of "collective societies" to administer and collect fees for groups of copyright owners. The collectives may also set the terms for access and use of the material they represent. The most familiar Canadian example of a copyright collective in the library environment is Access Copyright (formerly known as Cancopy). Access Copyright has negotiated licenses with educational institutions across Canada setting out permissions for reprographic uses of the materials it covers. Access Copyright also serves as the national agent for reprographic societies representing written materials published outside of Canada (there are some countries and many individual publishers and authors in other countries excluded from this).

Put in the language of buyers and sellers, copyright collectives operate as "seller cartels." The Copyright Act sets out the parameters for these cartels, defining how they will operate, how they will be monitored, and so on. The Copyright Act also provides exemptions for the collectives from certain provisions of the Competition Act. Section 70.5 (3) of the Copyright Act states that section 45 of the Competition Act (covers conspiracies) does not apply to collectives.

Yet, the Copyright Act makes no mention of, or provision for, any association or collective of users (i.e., of buyers) of copyright. What if there were collectives of buyers of copyright formed through an interest in purchasing access to and use of collections of copyrighted materials? Library consortia might be considered just such collectives. This raises the question, though, of whether, under current copyright law, library consortia, as buyer collectives, would be protected by any exemption from competition scrutiny.

The Competition Act prohibits anti-competitive action by buyers and sellers. Section 45(1) (c) on Conspiracies applies to both the *purchase* and the *sale* of products. Similarly, the definition of the term "business" for the Act includes *acquiring* or *supplying* products and *acquiring* or *supplying* services.

Buyer collectives must then presumably be covered by the Competition Act. Competition policy is based on maintaining a competitive market economy. From that perspective, the primary effect of library consortia may be to influence the market control of publishers by affecting the cost and control of the products supplied. Library consortia could be characterized as a direct competitive response by academic libraries (buyers) to counter the increasing monopolistic control of commercial publishers (sellers). Would this then be interpreted under Canadian competition policy as anti-competitive?

The Association of Research Libraries formed the *Information Access Alliance*[2] in 2004 (Case, 2004) to bring attention to their concerns over the increasing numbers of mergers of commercial academic publishers. The two main purposes of the *Alliance* were to investigate the possibilities of using economic and legal arguments that "would support an antitrust case against anticompetitive mergers and other practices such as bundling"[3] (p. 311) and to mobilize public policy debate on the increasing control of a few publishers over the scholarly record. In February, 2005, a conference of legal, economic, library, and public policy experts met in Washington, D.C., to explore anticompetitive issues in the scholarly publishing industry (Van Orsdel, 2005). One of the questions asked at the conference was whether a group of libraries (i.e., a library consortium) could band together to cancel all of a particular publisher's holdings. The answer given by legal attendees at the conference was that such an action, in the U.S. context, would be considered illegal. In discussing possible antitrust strategies, the overriding assumption made at the conference was that "publicly funded institutions and their libraries have become victims of the current market and need the protection of the state. There was also the argument made that U.S. states should protect their assets in the form of scholarly outputs created via public funding" (p. 376). The present research explores these issues in the Canadian context.

There have been several antitrust analyses of academic publishing centered on how the scholarly publishing market is defined and whether the practices publishers use, such as bundling, are in violation of U.S. competition law (Foer, 2004; McCabe, 2002; Edlin & Rubinfeld, 2004). Bundling of journal titles or the "Big Deal" as it is commonly known is a common practice currently used by publishers to sell full-text digital journal suites to academic library consortia. Foer (2004) discussed the negative effect of publisher mergers on the publishing options available to scholars and the subsequent negative implications for a society that believes in academic and intellectual freedom. He goes on to analyze the "Big Deal" publishers use in terms of U.S. antitrust law and suggests that an antitrust argument could and should be used to challenge publisher mergers. His closing argument makes a strong connection between publisher control and the erosion of access to information and support of democracy stating that the recent wave of mergers in the scholarly publishing industry and the Big Deal combine to push us all into "territory in which a small number of individuals, working through international corporations, may gain the power to control important aspects of the production and distribution of critically important information" (pp. 24–25).

The interesting point here is that this antitrust argument touches only very lightly on the role of academic library consortia in the scholarly publishing marketplace and seems to maintain the role of the library as a public institution requiring the protection of the state. The merger and selling practices of publishers are solidly tied to antitrust or anti-competitive activity and market control. What is less clear is the other side of the argument. What is the role of academic consortia with respect to competition and scholarly publishing?

Academic libraries, through the links and infrastructures they are building through consortia activities, are well placed to play a key role in any new scholarly publishing process. The academic library could take over the role of publisher, becoming a key player in organizing, publishing, disseminating, and archiving locally controlled scholarly information and, through consortia activity, could build a national or international infrastructure for scholarly communication that is in direct competition to commercial publishers.

Owen (2002) discusses the shift to institutions (and their libraries) taking on the role of publisher for their locally produced scholarly research as a possible response by libraries to the increasing consolidation of publishers' power. University presses, small departmental journals, self-publishing over the Internet, and open archives initiatives all are examples of institutions taking on the role of publisher to "take back" control of the scholarly product. There has been a growing call for changes in scholarly publishing systems that would take commercial publishers out of the scholarly communication cycle (Thompson, 1988). Wilkinson (2000) cites growing interest on the part of universities in regaining control of copyright for the works produced by their faculty members to increase the universities' bargaining position with commercial publishers with respect to purchasing scholarly output in the form of journals and other publications. She argues that Canadian universities should be becoming frustrated with their lack of control over the intellectual property created in their institutions. This should be particularly strongly felt with respect to copyright control of the scholarly record created at universities when it is lost to commercial, for-profit publishers.

Does consortia activity place Canadian academic libraries in a market economic framework that includes competition policy and anti-competitive practices scrutiny? The market economic perspective views academic library consortia as a direct attempt by participating libraries to affect the monopolistic control of commercial publishers over the scholarly publishing record. Library consortia would be principally identified as aggregations of buyers with the aim of influencing price and other elements of production and thereby achieving the acquisition of more and better products at lower cost. Consortia activity would serve the purpose of creating powerful buying cartels that can stand nose to nose with the publishers that have heretofore been able to raise prices and control content seemingly as they please. Even further, consortia, acting as publishers of scholarly information and research from member institutions, might be considered as direct competitors with publishers for product ownership and control.

CONSORTIA: A PUBLIC GOOD PERSPECTIVE

In contrast to these market-based effects of consortia activity, there could be another perspective that focuses consortia activity in a framework of supporting and strengthening academic libraries mandate of supporting the public good. Providing unhampered access to information has been a cornerstone of library service since its inception. Access to information has been the main argument of libraries and other public institutions for the maintenance of fair use or fair dealing[4] provisions in national copyright legislation. If, as Allen and Hirshon (1998) suggest, one of the main goals of academic library consortia is to influence current models of scholarly publication, then academic library consortia could be seen as an attempt by academic libraries to wield that influence through a more effective realization of the ideal of information as a public good. The goal of consortia activity may then be seen as one of ensuring that the control of commercial publishers does not expand to the point that information becomes entirely a commodity and access to that information is based totally on ability to pay.

The library, as an institution, has been and still is seen by librarians to be central to maintaining and supporting the public sphere and information as a public good. Many libraries provide access to information free to all within their purview and ideally operate free from political and economic interests. The Canadian Association of Research Libraries (2005) statement on Intellectual Freedom states that all persons in Canada have the right to "access expressions of knowledge, creativity and intellectual activity," and to that end, it is the responsibility of research libraries to facilitate access to that knowledge without censorship. In 2003, the Association of College and Research Libraries (American Library Association, 2003, p. 1) stated that "one of the fundamental characteristics of scholarly research is that it is created as a public good to facilitate inquiry and knowledge," and in 1988, the Association of Universities and Colleges of Canada (1988) placed the principles of intellectual freedom and university autonomy as "essential to the fulfillment of the role of universities in the context of a democratic society" (p. 2).

Lessig (2001) argues that it is critical to challenge the privatization of what *should* be public resources. Resources in the commons include those that are foundational to our participation in our society, and the values these foundational resources represent can be lost if they are moved out of the commons into a market where they can be bought or sold.

Benkler (2001) states that recent government policy decisions have favored large-scale commercial organizations over the small, independent firms or individual producers and that this has the effect of enclosing the public domain, of raising barriers for those who may freely contribute to the public domain in favor of increasing the economic advantage of large information production firms like commercial publishers. Librarians may view consortia activity as primarily and ultimately an effort to maintain scholarly information as a freely accessible public resource for the social good. From this perspective, although consortia activity affects economic outcomes such as price and supply, this market economy result is only a by-product to the goal of the responsibility of the librarian in maintaining equitable information access.

The library literature is also replete with references to the role of the library in support of the public good of access to information for all citizens. Stielow (2001), in an article titled "Reconsidering libraries as Arsenals of Democratic Culture," states that the library is the "most visible civic statement and monument to a democratic way of life" and that "the American library would come to serve as a powerful cultural symbol and visible goal for all democratic societies" (p. 12).

Gorman (2000, 2003) reiterates the belief that libraries are an important part of building, and maintaining democratic ideals and that the library's mission of providing unhampered free access to the world's information is part of how libraries fulfil that role.

According to Harris and Hannah (1993), many, if not most, members of the library profession set the purpose of libraries in the cultural and political sphere and not in the economic. They state that librarians feel that libraries support a democratic society by supporting the creation of an informed citizenry. Harris and Hannah note that this cultural view conflicts with the growing post-industrial view of information production and use and that librarians fear that "this tendency can only contribute to expanding the gap between the 'information rich' and 'information poor,' and contribute to the further erosion of citizen participation in the democratic process" (p. 50).

There have been calls to make research generated from the public purse freely accessible to everyone rather than allow it to be owned by publishers who control access based on the ability to pay. In Britain, a House of Commons committee made very strong recommendations that all UK higher education institutions establish institutional repositories in which their published output can be stored and that research councils and other government funders mandate that their funded researchers deposit a copy of all of their articles in the established repositories (Great Britain, House of Commons Science and Technology Committee, 2004). Reasons given for this recommendation were that the government "has an interest in ensuring that public money invested in scientific research is translated into outputs that benefit the public" (p. 5). In its response to this report, the British government rejected all of the main recommendations of the Committee stating that they [the government] were "not aware that there were major problems accessing scientific information and that the publishing industry is healthy and competitive" (Poynder, 2005, p. 1).

In September, 2007, the Canadian Institutes of Health Research published a policy on open access (CIHR, 2007), which argues for barrier-free access to CIHR research to promote further research and support the principles of scientific openness. The recommendations of the report make it clear that CIHR grant recipients are "required to make every effort to ensure that their peer-reviewed publications are freely accessible through publishers' websites or through online repositories as soon as possible and, in any event, within six months of publication" (pp. 3–5). The recommendations go on to state that before submitting their articles to a particular publisher, grant recipients may wish to choose a publisher that fully supports immediate open access or at least to be fully aware of a particular publisher's stand on open access, and that it conforms with CIHR's new open access mandate, before they submit their work.

In the United States, the National Institutes of Health recommended that all NIH-funded research be deposited in a database and made freely accessible to the public no longer than six months after publication (NIH, September 3, 2004). The NIH cited the public's need to know as a major reason for this recommendation. Significant lobbying by publishers against the NIH proposal resulted in the sixth month moratorium being changed to one year. The publishers argued that the six-month term would harm their profits and harm the "scientific enterprise they support" (Weiss, 2005). The extension was not well received by open access supporters who claimed that waiting a year to access publicly funded research was not acceptable. A more recent move to quash the NIH open access policy saw the introduction of the Fair Copyright in Research Works Act, legislation that would amend U.S. copyright law, overturn the NIH Public Access Policy, and effectively make it illegal for other U.S. federal agencies to enact similar policies (Library Journal Academic Newswire, 2008). The Association of American University Presses (AAUP), strong supporters of the Act, said the legislation would ensure that its members' ability to derive revenue from their copyrights was not diminished. The Act generated considerable and often heated discussion from open access advocates as well as those supporting publishers' views. It has been shelved until 2009.

Also, in 2007, the American Association of Publishers formed the Partnership for Research Integrity in Science and Medicine, or PRISM, to promote the publisher's role in scholarly publishing and to criticize the open access journal movement (Giles, 2007). The gist of the criticism is that open access publishing will mean the loss of peer review and cause a mass of junk science to be dumped into publication and also that government plans to mandate deposit of publicly funded research into publicly accessible repositories amounts to censorship and copyright theft (Giles, 2007).

The growing call for open access to publicly funded research supports a "public good" perspective that calls for governments to support and maintain a public sphere of information freely accessible to all citizens, rather than only available to the researchers who can pay for access. It can be seen, however, by the difficulties in gaining acceptance of the open access recommendations made in both the British Commons report and the U.S. NIH recommendation, that other policy objectives such as supporting industry and promoting innovation tied to economic gain give the upper hand to the economic side of the argument.

If librarians see consortia activity as primarily a means to develop and support a public good platform, how might that view affect academic libraries' abilities to lobby governments for information policy development or information policy change? Yet, if, on the contrary, librarians see consortia activity as primarily market economic based, this view may seemingly fly in the face of their own deeply held beliefs about the core values of librarianship and the core goals and objectives of libraries. Would this economic purpose be considered just? If consortia activity is viewed as an economic activity with the goal of achieving greater market power would this be interpreted as libraries taking a stronger role in the information economy rather than supporting long-held beliefs of information access and intellectual freedom?

It is important here to consider the definition and use of the term "public good." There are a number of terms such as "public sphere," "public domain," "public goods," and "commons" used by different disciplines to describe the same, or at least, very similar concepts.

The term "public domain" is used primarily in the legal literature in discussions of intellectual property and describes works that are free from copyright, or works, or portions of works, which cannot be owned by anyone and therefore are freely available for the public to use (Litman, 1990).

The term "public sphere" came into prominence in the work of the modern philosopher Jurgen Habermas and is described as a real or virtual space in which the public, the community, or the enlightened citizenry can discuss, criticize, and inform each other as to the government and economic policies of the day. For the public sphere to operate efficiently, it is important to make sure that all necessary information is available for use by the citizenry for them to fully participate in their community (Buschman, 2005, 2003).

"Public goods" is used predominantly in the economic literature and is based on economics and public policy. It assumes that the concepts of a market economy and private property are taken as given and describes goods or materials that cannot be commodified. Costs of manufacturing and maintaining resources under this economic public good definition must be borne by someone, and since there is usually no avenue for profit making associated with that manufacture and maintenance, it is often governments that must bear the cost of production (Callon & Bowker, 1994).

The term "commons" is used by social scientists to describe areas of society and culture, as well as resources, that should not be defined and managed by a market definition of resource development, commodification, and sale. Bollier (2002) includes both tangible and intangible assets in describing the commons and notes that in a "commons" definition of the public good things are not defined as "resources" or "goods." The philosophy of the commons does not "buy into" the economic definitions of markets and "non-commodifiable" resources that constitute the economic definition of public goods. Anton (2000) describes this "commons" non-market concept of the public good as a historical one pre-dating the enclosure movement and the move to a market economy. He uses a variation "commons," the term "commonstock" (p. 4), to define this historical public good concept and describes it as social property from which citizens have a right not to be excluded. The provision of commonstock is crucial to the democratic function of society and remains outside of the market economy.

For the research reported in this chapter, I use the term "public good" throughout, with the key distinction being made between public good based on market-based economic principles that will be referred to as an *economic public good* definition, and public good based on non-economic principles of supporting the commons and the public sphere, which will be referred to as a *cultural public good* definition. The interviews reported gather the views of federal government agencies and university librarians with respect to the "public good" purpose of academic library consortia activity, and it will be necessary to distinguish whether members of each group in professing a view that consortia support the "public good" is referring to the *cultural public good* view or the *economic public good* view. The difference between the two is important and this research will differentiate between the two "public good" views of the interviewees, both government and librarian, if members of either group view consortia activity from a "public good" perspective.

If academic librarians view consortia activity from the cultural public good perspective, and this differs from how others view consortia activity, it could also affect the views of others toward librarians. A disconnect between how librarians view information provision in the larger context of the scholarly publishing cycle and how governments and publics see information provision might impede attempts by academic libraries to influence policy development and to influence evolving models of scholarly publishing

If the cultural public good concept is perceived as the primary, overarching goal of academic library consortia, what are the implications for academic libraries and more broadly for information policy? Libraries, particularly academic libraries, have been doing extensive work in the open source arena, developing standards, technology, and policy around institutional repositories (the storage of institutional data or research on institutional servers) specifically and around open source initiatives, generally. Consortia, if viewed as a means to develop and maintain the public sphere as an information commons for the public good, feed directly into these initiatives. In apparent conflict with this view are government information policies that link university research to innovation and economic development. Universities and their libraries are encouraged to promote research that contributes to innovation and the growth of the Canadian economy. To promote the growth of the Canadian economy, it is perceived to be necessary to commodify innovation and information. This is traditionally done through copyright and patents. To extract value from the commodification of innovation and information, universities would need to engage in the market economy for patents and copyrights. Yet, universities are also seen as public institutions, supported by the public purse. There is a growing demand for university research to be freely available to the public (Association of Research Libraries, Association of American Universities, Pew Higher Education Roundtable, 1998; Great Britain, House of Commons Science and Technology Committee, 2004; Budapest Open Access Initiative, 2002). If academic library consortia activity provides a viable infrastructure for archiving and disseminating (i.e., publishing) scholarly research to meet the call for free public access, this outcome may run contrary to other policies, particularly government policies, that clearly support a market economic view.

CONSORTIA AS ORGANIZATIONS

As organizations, academic libraries are structured to acquire, store, and disseminate resources and provide service relating to those resources to their constituent communities. As such, they play the role described above to comprise the "library" part of the scholarly publishing cycle. Academic library consortia, from an organizational point of view, are themselves considered organizations, related to other organizations in the organizational group, that is, academic libraries.

Research from the sociological and other social sciences on consortia is often based on theoretical themes coming from the organizational literature about the function of consortia as organizations or the effects of consortia on member organizations. These theoretical models include (1) dyadic or resource dependence models, (2) network models, (3) ecological models, and (4) institutional models (Davis & Powell, 1990).

Dyadic models focus on the exchanges between organizations and on how inputs and outputs between two organizations affect structure and function. Research centers on how alliances can achieve economic advantage for the focal organization. Using the dyadic model, consortia formation is a means by which an organization responds to its environment by creating linkages with other organizations to reduce market uncertainty or increase market control.

Network models emphasize the embeddedness of organizations in interorganizational networks or domains and if and how they are empowered by the social ties inherent in those networks. A consortium is a type of network formed between organizations. The flow of resources, information, and social contacts between the members of the network or between members of an individual consortium is examined from the perspective of the strength of ties, the position of organizations relative to other organizations, and how information and resources flow between and within the organizations that are members of the network.

Ecological models focus on the organization of the environment and populations of organizations within that environment and on the selection processes that occur at the population level that contribute to organizational survival and success or, conversely, failure and death (Davis & Powell, 1990). From this perspective, consortia would be studied as a group, looking at the environmental factors that lead to consortia formation, growth, and death.

The institutional model emphasizes the wider social and cultural environment in which organizations are embedded (Scott, 1995). The environment is composed not only of resources and technical requirements but also of cultural elements, belief systems, and professional claims of knowledge and jurisdiction (DiMaggio & Powell, 1991). The institutional perspective goes beyond resource exchange and network models, which consider only those organizations that actually interact with each other, to consider the totality of the social, cultural, and economic realm in which an organization and the consortia to which it is linked operate (DiMaggio & Powell, 1991). Research on consortia from an institutional perspective investigates the social, political, and cultural factors that contribute to consortia formation and how member organizations of consortia and consortia themselves adapt their structures and processes to the influences that may flow from consortial ties.

Part of determining what roles university librarians see for academic library consortia is an examination of the types of organizations they perceive academic library consortia to be. Whether they see consortia as purely a means to acquire resources in a competitive environment or as an extension of the academic library's philosophy and goals, university librarians' views of consortia as organizations contribute to our knowledge of how academic library consortia may be affecting academic libraries' role in the scholarly publishing cycle. If consortia are seen as organizations that primarily serve a resource exchange function between publishers and academic libraries, then in the context of the scholarly publishing cycle, consortia activity could be viewed as an intermediary between publishers and academic libraries in the cycle (Fig. 3(a)). If consortia, though, are seen as organizations that are

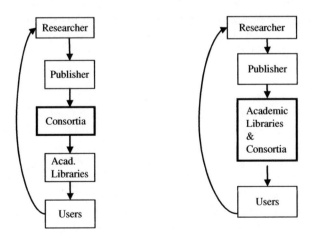

A: Consortia as Intermediary   B: Consortia as part of Academic Libraries

Fig. 3. Consortia as Organizations in the Scholarly Publishing Cycle.

extensions of the academic library, with the same philosophy as academic libraries, then consortia might be viewed as strengthening and supporting academic libraries' role in the scholarly publishing cycle (see Fig. 3(b)).

It may be that the librarians' answers will reflect a mental model that follows one of the models outlined above: dyadic, network, ecological, or institutional. However, as others investigating organization/environment interactions have discovered, it may also be that respondents' models of consortia activity reflect a blending of models.

CONSORTIA AND ACADEMIC LIBRARIANS AS PROFESSIONALS

As the university librarians discuss the purposes of academic library activity, their responses may also illuminate their views of how consortia activity affects the professional values of academic librarians.

Orientation toward a public good perspective that is not based on principles of the market economy has been an underlying theme not only in ideological discussions of the library as an institution but also as the mainstay for the profession of librarianship. Early trait theories of the professions focus on their special characteristics, one of which is an altruistic commitment to public and universal values connected with service (Evetts, 1999). More recent theories focus on how economic, social, and cultural devices are used by the professions to maintain their dominant position. One such cultural device is the claim to service in the public good and a higher social purpose, to claim that the professional's work is of critical importance to the good of the public as a whole or at least an important part of that public (Freidson, 1999).

Winter (1988) applies modern professions theory to librarianship discussing the link between librarianship and its broader cultural role and how the claim to that broader role is an integral part of librarians' claim to professionalism. Professional librarians control their work settings, and attempt to control the larger cultural sphere, because of their view that the library discharges a critical social and cultural function that cannot be left to chance or even worse, to market forces.

The role of the professional academic librarian develops from, and informs, the role of the academic library in the scholarly publishing cycle. In this research, as the discussions with university librarians illuminate their views about consortia activity as either from a market economic or a public good perspective, and their views about consortia as organizations, their conversations may also provide information about how consortia activity may be affecting the professional roles of academic librarians.

THE RESEARCH QUESTIONS

The research presented in this chapter explored Canadian academic library consortia, within the framework of the scholarly publishing cycle, to address the following research questions:

1. Do the attitudes of federal government agencies and of the Competition Bureau toward academic library consortia differ from those of university librarians?
2. Do federal government agency and Competition Bureau representatives see library consortia activity from a market economic or public good perspective?
3. If federal government agency and Competition Bureau representatives see consortia activity from a public good perspective, is it an *economic public good* perspective or a *cultural public good* perspective?
4. How do Canadian University Librarians see the purpose of academic library consortia activity? Does it serve primarily a market economic function or a public good function?
5. If university librarians see consortia as serving a public good function is that public good view based on a traditional *cultural public good* perspective (i.e., public good as serving social and democratic ideals) or an *economic public good* perspective based on the economic analysis of public good as a market value?
6. Do university librarians speak of consortia in a way that reveals their mental model of the organizational role of consortia, and if so, which model predominates?
7. Do university librarians' views reflect a relationship between consortia activity and professional roles, and if so, what is that relationship?

RESEARCH DESIGN AND METHODOLOGY

Semi-structured in-depth interviews were used to explore the research questions outlined above. Since there are significant national differences in academic library and university funding, information policy, and the government agencies involved, this research focused on Canadian academic libraries only. Furthermore, since the objective of the research was to examine questions involving national information policy (e.g., competition policy, the funding of the CNSLP), it was decided to pursue a national sample rather than a case study of a few institutions, or even a provincial or regional consortium group.

University librarians were selected as key informants, being directly responsible for, and representative of, their respective libraries' policies for consortia participation. For the federal government informants, the individuals selected were senior administrators within their respective agencies.

University Librarian Interview Group

The population studied was the university librarians of institutions involved in the CNSLP. The membership of the CNSLP was selected as the population of libraries being studied because it includes universities across Canada that are all involved in consortia initiatives since they are all at least involved in the CNSLP. Sampling was designed to achieve a representative national perspective by choosing institutions from each of the four regions defined by the CNSLP, and, within each region, by selecting institutions to include representations from small-, medium-, and large-sized universities. This selection of a variety of sizes of academic libraries from different geographic regions was designed to illuminate diversity in opinion and to provide for generalizability of the results (Bogdan & Biklen, 1992).

Across Canada, interviews were completed with a total of thirty university librarians. The questions asked of these university librarians explored the several points including why have academic library consortia formed?; what is their primary overarching purpose?; how has academic library consortia activity affected the relationship between academic librarians and publishers?; how has academic library consortia activity affected the position of academic libraries in the market for scholarly material?; and how successful have academic library consortia been in meeting their objectives? See Appendix A for the interview protocol used for this group.

Federal Government Agency Interview Group

Representatives from federal government agencies were asked, in their official capacity, to give their views of the purpose of academic library consortia and the publics those consortia serve. Only federal agencies were studied because it is at the federal level in Canada where there is a confluence of policy-making directly related to this research. Although Canadian information policy can be considered fragmented (Buchwald, 1995), the federal government has been central in producing policies directly aimed at access to and control of information. The federal government's innovation strategy (Industry Canada, 2001) identified knowledge creation and use as a key factor in increasing Canadian innovation and competitiveness. The subsequent creation of funding sources at the federal level (e.g., the Canada Foundation for Innovation, the Canada Research Chairs Programme, the Indirect Costs Programme) grew directly from this innovation strategy and invested millions of dollars in university research production and also forged stronger linkages between universities and corporate Canada. It is also at the federal level that the institutional responsibility for copyright policy and for competition policy lies.

The research questions centered on federal government agencies dealing with competition, intellectual property (especially copyright), and federal sources for university funding (especially academic library consortia funding). Using government web sites and directories that identify federal agencies dealing with competition and copyright, other research that examined federal information policy (Dorner, 2000), and my own knowledge of academic library consortia funding, agencies were identified for inclusion in the federal government interview cohort. The agencies selected were the *Canada Foundation for Innovation* (CFI);[5] from Industry Canada, the *Knowledge Infrastructure Directorate*, the *Canadian Intellectual Property Office* (CIPO), and the *Competition Bureau*;[6] from Heritage Canada, the *Copyright Policy Branch*;[7] and the *Copyright Board*.[8]

Six interviews were conducted. The same protocol was used for both the in-person and the telephone interviews. Representatives of the selected agencies were asked questions that examined their views about the purpose of academic library consortia activity. In addition, the representative of the Canada Competition Bureau, the regulatory body charged with enforcing the Competition Act, was asked questions focused on how academic library consortia activity is viewed in light of the Bureau's mandate. Questions were structured to elicit the participants' views about the purpose of academic library consortia generally (in the past, the present, and the future), how academic library consortia may affect the scholarly publishing cycle generally, and relationships within that cycle (such as the relationship between academic libraries and publishers) in particular. See Appendix B for the interview protocol used for the federal government agency group.

DATA SUMMARY

Federal Government Agencies

All but one of the interviewees were senior administrators within their department or branch. The representative from the Competition Bureau was a senior economist with the Bureau with in-depth experience with the intersection of competition policy and intellectual property generally and copyright specifically. The other federal government agency representatives interviewed were the Director of Programmes for the Canada Foundation for Innovation, the Head of Legal Services for the Copyright Board, the Director of the Knowledge Infrastructure Directorate, the Director of Trademarks and of Copyright and Industrial Design with the CIPO, and the Director General of Copyright Policy with the Copyright Policy Branch of Canadian Heritage.

Purpose of Consortia

Five of the government agency representatives identified the purpose of academic consortia activity primarily, though not exclusively, as maximizing the economic benefits consortia bring to academic libraries. The five were the representatives from the CFI, the Copyright Board, Canadian Heritage, CIPO, and the Competition Bureau. The specific economic benefits listed included achieving economies of scale, sharing costs, and leveling the playing field between academic libraries and publishers, to the effect that libraries could negotiate better prices and improved products.

The representative of the CFI described several economic purposes for the formation and current structure of academic library consortia but also included some non-economic purposes. He stated that in the late 1980s and early 1990s, academic library consortia were driven by two factors. One factor was trying to respond to the economic hardship libraries faced in their inability to deal with rapidly escalating costs. The other factor was to take advantage of new information technologies that allowed libraries to share collections that did not have to be physically located on their bookshelves. He described the overall purpose of academic library consortia as a "counterweight to corporate control." When asked if he thought consortia activity would still be of benefit if the economic factors diminished or disappeared, he stated that he believed that consortia have significant value beyond the economic, in helping academic libraries deal with a changing world of information. Overall, though he discussed some non-economic goals for consortia, he predominantly placed consortia activity in a market perspective of achieving economies of scale and gaining better prices.

The representative from the Copyright Board placed the cost sharing and resource sharing purposes of consortia in the context of efficiency, of creating synergies among institutions for reasons of cost or scarcity and getting together to create economies of scale.

The person from the CIPO also put the purpose of consortia in terms of efficiency, posing the question of whether the scholarly publishing cycle would work more efficiently through consortia than through individual libraries.

The participant from Canadian Heritage placed the value of consortia activity in the ability of consortia to negotiate better prices and related the purpose of consortia to Canadian intellectual property collectives, in that, like the collectives, the value of academic library consortia activity is that they are able to do as one voice what many cannot do on their own.

The Competition Bureau representative described the purpose of academic library consortia as providing another viable outlet for academic works, as providing efficiency, as being cost-effective, and, from more of a competition viewpoint, as giving academic libraries countervailing market power with publishers.

Who Benefits from Consortia?
When asked who ultimately benefited from academic library consortia activity, the representative from CIPO stated that his first reaction is that consortia benefit the people attending the institutions involved. The person from the Copyright Board put the staff of libraries and the users of libraries as the primary beneficiaries of consortia activity, but also went on to allocate some benefit to institutions (i.e., universities) in that through consortia activity they can do more with what they have, and to the funding agencies such as NSERC and SSHRC, in that consortia activity may result in financial savings in the research process.

The interviewee from the Knowledge Infrastructure Directorate described the benefits of consortia from a broad non-economic perspective focused on users. He stated that academic library consortia increase libraries' ability to support the research community. Through consortia activity, libraries give researchers the opportunity to keep pace with the knowledge generated in their field. He also discussed how smaller universities are also beneficiaries of academic library consortia activity. Since consortia provide equal access to a broad array of resources, smaller institutions can be more fully incorporated into the policy planning process of the government with respect to promoting and generating research.

The participants from Canadian Heritage and the Competition Bureau, on the contrary, put the benefit of consortia activity in economic terms from their respective policy areas, copyright (Canadian Heritage) and competition (Competition Bureau). The representative from Canadian Heritage considered how gaining control of copyright might provide some benefit to academic library consortia. If the consortia gain copyright ownership of the products they provide, then the benefit of that copyright accrues to the consortium and ultimately to the institution. If the consortial acquisitions function is more like buying a music CD, then the copyright stays with the publisher and the benefit of ownership of that copyright stays with the publisher. The representative of the Competition Bureau described the benefit of consortia activity from a competition perspective of market entry and market strength. If one considers consortia as buying clubs, then they gain the benefit of volume purchasing. Academic libraries are able to acquire more products at lower cost. Consortia could be considered as a new market entry in scholarly publishing and, as such, gains the benefit of that new market.

Relationships with Publishers and Competition
Again, except for the representative from the Canada Foundation for Innovation, the respondents were very clear that they could only speculate on the relationship between academic library consortia and publishers because of their lack of in-depth knowledge of academic library consortia structure and activity.

Similar to his comments on the purpose and benefits of consortia, the representative from the Canada Foundation for Innovation described consortia as giving academic libraries stronger purchasing power that "creates a more level playing field where you can have a true negotiation of not only price but also sort of a menu of possibilities." When asked to consider how consortia might affect the relationship between publishers and academic libraries in the future, he stated that currently consortia are collaborating to get the best deal, but it may be the case that in the future consortia will more fully realize the extent of their market power and, as a result, affect long-term changes in the marketplace such as using consortial decisions to purchase or not to purchase to influence the titles publishers choose to maintain.

The representative from the Copyright Board put the effect of consortia on the relationship with publishers in a more local context with, on the one hand, consortia freeing library staff to do other things, and, on the other hand, causing a degradation of the one-to-one relationship that may have existed between individual institutions and publishers. He posed the question of whether that institution–publisher relationship could be created at the consortial level. He felt that consortia do create more market power for libraries and make them less disadvantaged in their negotiations with publishers. Although stating that he had no idea about how consortia might unfold in the future, this respondent did propose structural questions that consortia might have to consider, such as whether their memberships are optimal, whether they are at their optimal size, and whether there might be different, more effective groupings of consortia members. When discussing whether academic library consortia could compete with publishers, as publishers, this respondent answered that he did not know if being a publisher would be included in the mandate of consortia, but that digitizing and sharing unique collections could be considered a type of publishing. However, if a project was one that a publisher would never have done in the first place, it could not be considered as any sort of competition with publishers.

The representative from the Knowledge Infrastructure Directorate stated that academic library consortia gave libraries more leveraging power with publishers. Libraries want cost-effective access and publishers want to make profits, and the two are not mutually consistent. Consortia activity pushes power to libraries to achieve the cost-benefit they are seeking. The respondent would not speculate on the future of academic library consortia or on how consortia might compete with publishers due to his unfamiliarity with the specifics of consortia activity.

The person from CIPO felt that consortia activity could give academic libraries a stronger bargaining position especially since libraries would be bargaining in an international market. He felt that academic library consortia are evening out the relationship between academic libraries and publishers. In discussing how academic library consortia could effect competition with publishers, the discussion turned to how copyright ownership might influence consortia as they compete with commercial publishers. Although this respondent's area of expertise was in the area of patents and the tie-in between consortia and copyright was not immediately apparent to him, he did wonder if consortia do become publishers and that includes the consortia retaining ownership of the relevant copyrights, what be the value in that result, and how the ownership of that copyright might feed back into the process of scholarship creation.

The Canadian Heritage representative considered the question of how consortia activity might be affecting relations with publishers from the perspective of how consortia may affect copyright. Although the link between consortia activity and copyright was not at first apparent to this respondent, the comparison between consortia and collectives was made. Consortia may give libraries, acting as buyers of resources, more power to negotiate royalties with other collectives acting as sellers of resources. Academic library consortia could affect publishers through negotiating different royalties with supplier collectives and ultimately affecting the dollars flowing back to publishers from those collectives. He went on to state that consortia activity does challenge the market position of publishers to some extent. Though consortia may be resisted by publishers as a negative impact on their business, this is offset by the publisher also realizing a bigger purchase in a more efficient manner. When asked if academic library consortia activity and its interaction with publishers might influence government policy, such as copyright policy, this respondent stated that how consortia interact with publishers is a function of the marketplace and would have little impact on government policy decisions.

The respondent from the Competition Bureau discussed the impact of consortia on libraries' relationship with publishers from a competition perspective of markets and market behavior. If consortia activity gave academic libraries countervailing power with publishers, the Competition Bureau would not consider this, in itself, as bad. Countervailing power is considered as a good outcome from a competition point of view. To consider whether academic library consortia might be considered anti-competitive, this respondent stated that the Bureau would have to first determine what markets are involved and then look at the specific activities consortia are undertaking within those markets. For example, they might look at whether there are market alternatives to publishing with consortia (or with a commercial publisher) and then look at what those alternatives would mean to the power of the market leaders such as the traditional commercially controlled journals. The Bureau would have to consider whether the success of consortia as publisher is due to better performance or due to other less reputable conduct. When asked if there would be any concern vis-à-vis the Competition Act if library consortia were to encourage scholars to publish with a consortium rather than with a commercial publisher, the respondent noted that it depended on the nature of the encouragement. If there was some exclusive dealing situation where it was stipulated an author had to publish everything with the consortium or that author would lose another service or some type of access to other resources, this might lead the Competition Bureau to look at the conditions involved.

Summary
It is clear from their responses that the federal government agency representatives defined academic library consortia activity as a market activity.

Overall, the respondents considered the goals of academic library consortia as economically based. When asked how consortia activity might be affecting the relationship between academic libraries and publishers, the most common response was that consortia have given academic libraries a stronger voice with publishers, that consortia have leveled the playing field between publishers and academic libraries with the "field" being the scholarly publishing market. The link between copyright and consortia activity was not immediately apparent to the representatives from CIPO and the Copyright Policy Branch of Canadian Heritage though, later in their conversations, they both did consider how that link might manifest itself. The Competition Bureau representative primarily framed his comments on consortia in terms of market structure and how academic library consortia activity might be considered in terms of anti-competitive behavior. Among the six interviewees, there were varying opinions about whether academic library consortia could compete with publishers. They all considered competition from the context of academic libraries having a stronger voice with publishers and not in terms of academic library consortia competing with publishers directly by becoming publishers. The respondents were, however, willing to consider the possibility of academic library consortia as publishers from a hypothetical viewpoint, relating it back to their respective agency's mandate or their respective areas of expertise.

The representative from the Competition Bureau discussed academic library consortia, as one might expect, from a competition perspective situating consortia in the existing market structure of scholarly publishing. He discussed the possibilities of consortia undertaking anti-competitive behavior in terms of how consortia activity may affect market entry of other competitors and how consortia activity may affect market control of the scholarly publishing product. One significant difference between the views of the Competition Bureau and the views of the other government agencies representatives was that the Competition Bureau participant had no difficulty accepting the viability of academic library consortia acting as publishers. He accepted the general premise that academic library consortia could directly compete with publishers and from that premise, therefore, academic libraries would be subject to competition policy scrutiny when warranted.

UNIVERSITY LIBRARIANS

Roles of Consortia

The context of modern consortia activity was set for the respondents through the question "if modern consortia activity is defined as consortia that formed in the early to mid-1990 what would you describe as the original purpose of those consortia." All of the university librarians responded that consortia were formed to deal with the major financial problems facing academic libraries at the time (i.e., in the early to mid-1990s). Consortia were described (a) as "buying clubs"; (b) as a response to exponentially rising resource costs, particularly with respect to serials; (c) as a response to stagnant or minimally increasing library budgets; and (d) as ways to push back at publishers (who were gouging academic libraries with double-digit annual price increases for serials) with a stronger negotiating stance. Although the financial imperative was listed by all the interviewees, there were several who felt that saving money was not the only reason academic library consortia were formed, that other factors, as well as the financial one were important goals in the formation of academic library consortia.

The interviewees were also asked to consider whether the goals of academic library consortia have changed from the original goals of ten or fifteen years ago. Twenty-six responded that consortia activity was now about collaborating on other projects or services as much, if not more, than it was about being cost-effective and realizing budgetary advantages. Evolving to be more than "buying clubs" was a common theme throughout the responses. While the financial benefit of consortia is still important, most of the university librarians felt that academic library consortia activity has matured to the point that the synergy of working together not only saves money but also enables libraries to realize new opportunities for change and innovation. Other current goals of academic library consortia included sharing staff expertise, collaborating on technology development, and developing new services such as interlibrary loan and virtual reference. The university librarians from the large institutions raised more reservations about the current goals of consortia activity even as they supported the majority view that consortia activity was evolving into other areas. The reservations they expressed primarily questioned the amount of consortia activity in which their libraries were involved and whether that activity was still of benefit.

When asked what the goals or purpose of consortia might be in fifteen or twenty years, all of respondents felt that there would be academic library consortia activity in some form in the future, although a few questioned whether consortia would be as prevalent as they are today and whether the consortia that exist today would be able to reinvent themselves to adjust to the changing landscape of academic libraries and the institutions they serve. The responses given about the future goals or purpose of consortia can be categorized in terms of four main issues: (1) the budget management aspects of future consortia activity, (2) "other projects" (other than acquisitions) that consortia could be involved in, (3) internal structural changes of consortia that need to be addressed, and (4) developing consortial roles in scholarly publishing. Every respondent listed more than one of these four issues, and all four of the issues were given in each of the regions and in each of the size categories. Overall, the budget management issues and the "other projects" were given most often as descriptive of the future roles of academic library consortia.

Budget Management Issues

Twenty-one cited financial issues such as saving money and leveraging budgets as important goals for the consortia of the future. However, the university librarians also identified specific problems they felt would have to be addressed by consortia in the future, including a re-examination of the financial models by which consortia will operate to address cost-sharing mechanisms between consortium members and the future viability of "Big Deal" types of consortium acquisitions. Taking a wider perspective than just the consideration of the effects of "Big Deal"-type acquisitions, several felt that academic libraries would need to re-consider the financial models on which academic library consortia are currently based. Although they felt that consortia activity would continue, they also saw a need to re-examine the current cost-sharing formulas in place and look at how institutions will be able to continue supporting consortial acquisitions in a future continuing environment of constrained budgets.

Other Projects (Other Than Acquisitions)

As was the case when discussing their views about the past and current roles for consortia, a majority (twenty of thirty) felt that consortia will continue to evolve, taking on non-economic-based projects. The range of projects they expect academic libraries to tackle in the future include digitization projects, the development of institutional repositories, technology development, the development of alternative licensing models for content and services, the development of local and consortial level archives, the sharing of staff expertise, and the provision of robust and secure access.

Internal Consortia Structural Issues
Fifteen listed internal consortia structural issues as a future issue for academic library consortia. These structural issues revolved around the question of whether the consortia of the future would be able to meet the goals set for them by their member libraries. Elements of future structural issues included examining the membership, goals and dynamics of future consortia, balancing local and consortial activity for member institutions, developing more focused or uniquely purposed consortia, clarifying the roles of regional consortia, and exploring the possibilities of expanding the scope of consortia by taking membership to a national or international level or by including members from other sectors such as governments or other libraries.

Developing Roles in Scholarly Publishing
When discussing the future, twelve of the librarians interviewed expressed the view that academic library consortia will be involved in a changing scholarly publishing paradigm in some manner. Although consortia activity and scholarly publishing were addressed in response to other questions, and will be discussed further below as those questions are reported, it is important to note here that the respondents felt that the future structure and future benefits of academic library consortia would depend, in part, on those consortia being involved in changing the way scholarly material is published and disseminated. Most felt that open source platforms and institutional repositories could play an important role in the development of a future scholarly information paradigm.

Some of the respondents felt that the current model of consortia with its "Big Deal," and heavy dependence on acquisitions, is standing in the way of a transition to a new scholarly publishing model and that academic library consortia may need to choose between the current model of publishing and a future one in which publishing will be under the purview of scholars, academic libraries, and academic institutions.

Consortia and Publishers, Competition and Scholarly Publishing

Consortia and Publishers

As the respondents were discussing their views on the past, present, and future roles of academic library consortia activity, their thoughts about academic libraries' relationships with publishers were explored.

As discussed previously, all of the university librarians listed financial factors as the main purpose of modern consortia activity (i.e., consortia activity originating in the early to mid-1990s). Saving money, making budgets stretch farther, being able to better cope with escalating materials costs, particularly the rapidly rising costs of journals, were all given as descriptors of the financial benefits of academic library consortia. Twenty-three said they felt that consortia activity (past, present, or future) gives academic libraries more power or a stronger voice with publishers, either through being able to demand better prices or demanding product changes. Consortia are seen as "leveling the playing field" between publishers and Canadian academic libraries because "in all cases people negotiate better deals with the publishers through a consortium than they can outside a consortium." Consortia activity is seen as a way to leverage how academic libraries interact with publishers to create a positive outcome for academic libraries. When broken down both by region and by institution size, the attitudes that consortia activity give academic libraries more power or a stronger voice were relatively evenly distributed across the regions and library sizes.

For the seven who responded "no," they did not feel consortia activity had given academic libraries more power or a stronger voice; their reasoning generally reflected the idea that the strength of the publishers has not been diminished through consortia activity. Although most of the respondents felt that consortia activity had positively affected libraries' position with publishers, sixteen also felt that consortia activity had positively benefited publishers. They felt some of the benefit to publishers resulted from consortia activity changing the structure of the scholarly publishing market in Canada by making the consortia, rather than the individual institution, the new customer. Consortia activity was perceived as stabilizing the Canadian market for publishers by giving publishers access to a larger number of institutions with fewer negotiations and was seen as making money for publishers by reducing their marketing and distribution costs and through accelerating publishers' switch to digital over print products.

Consortia and Competition
During the interviews, a further discussion point with respect to how consortia activity may be changing the relationship between academic libraries and publishers related to whether the university librarians felt that academic library consortia could be considered to be in competition with publishers. Almost all of the librarians expressed an opinion on academic libraries competing with publishers with only two indicating that they "did not know" or "could not guess." See Fig. 4 for a flowchart of the librarians' responses about competition.

Of the twenty-eight who did discuss competition, their responses reflected different interpretations of the meaning of "competition." Twenty-one discussed whether academic library consortia could, or should, compete with publishers by having the consortia themselves taking on the role of publisher of the scholarly research record. The remaining seven discussed competition either from a more abstract perspective of the concept of competition posing a question back to the interviewer about whether "competition" was a valid concept to use in a discussion about academic library consortia or in terms of academic library consortia competing by gaining a stronger voice with publishers and being able to achieve better prices, better products, and better customer service.

All of the twenty-one respondents who discussed competition from the standpoint of academic library consortia becoming publishers put their comments in terms of a future or potential goal of consortia rather than one that is being fulfilled currently. Consortial competition with publishers would grow out of the open source institutional repository initiatives that library consortia are developing and implementing.

Three of the eleven who expressed the view that consortia could compete with commercial publishers by having consortia become publishers felt that the competition would come through academic libraries developing open source initiatives such as institutional repositories that organize and archive institutional research. They also felt that open source initiatives were catching the attention of publishers and that publishers did feel that open source initiatives now and in the future were something they would have to address. Consortia might have a role to play in a changing scholarly publishing model by becoming publishers in niche markets in which the large commercial publishers are not interested. Consortia would not be directly competing with the commercial publishers but would be competing instead by providing alternative publishing avenues.

The view that academic library consortia could eventually compete directly with publishers, as publishers, was also tempered with some

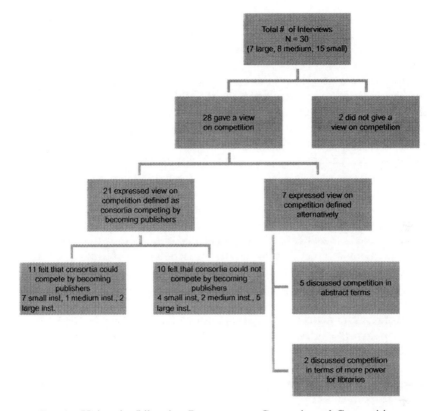

Fig. 4. University Librarian Responses on Consortia and Competition.

cautions that, in this future scenario, consortia will have to work to develop publications that are accepted by the academy and provide established value-added elements such as peer review, editorial services, and publication layout.

Ten felt that competing with the huge, well-established, international commercial publishers is a task beyond library consortia, particularly Canadian library consortia, because commercial publishers have a very strong hold on the market and also provide value-added services in the scholarly publishing process that library consortia could not effectively match.

It is important to note that respondents in both groups felt that open source platforms and institutional repositories would be a part of academic library consortia activity of the future. Both sides of the competition discussion felt that institutional repositories were an activity that academic libraries would and should be involved in through their consortia activity and that open source initiatives would be a means for academic libraries to continue to be able to obtain more content for their respective communities.

There were no regional differences between the groups who did and did not think consortia could compete with publishers, but there may be some differences by institution size. More librarians from small institutions tended to think that consortia could compete by becoming publishers, and more librarians from large institutions appeared to believe that consortia could not compete by becoming publishers (see Fig. 4).

Scholarly Publishing
Beyond the issue of consortia and competition, the respondents also discussed other aspects of how consortia may relate to scholarly publishing. Twenty-seven respondents felt that academic library consortia have a broad role in changing the current model of scholarly publishing. Of those, seventeen viewed it as a future role, while ten felt it was a role academic libraries are already fulfilling. See Fig. 5 for a flowchart of university librarians' responses about scholarly publishing.

Several respondents felt that library consortia would not be the leaders or primary drivers of change in scholarly publishing. They felt that academic libraries would more likely play a more normative role of partnering with other key players in the cycle, specifically scholars and the universities in which they work, to work together to affect changes in scholarly publishing. These respondents felt that academic libraries would probably play the role of educator, consciousness raiser, or technology developer with respect to how scholarly publishing will change and with respect to the viability of alternative models that may be considered.

Fourteen librarians felt that although changing the scholarly publishing model was a legitimate goal of academic libraries and academic library consortia, this goal has to be fulfilled in partnership with faculty and the universities. Their reasoning is that a new scholarly publishing paradigm might be challenging a well-established model controlled by commercial publishers, which provides a number of value-added services such as peer review, editorial review, and professional formatting. As a result, any new models in which academic libraries are involved must achieve the buy-in of faculty and the larger institutions along with preserving important process elements such as peer review.

Whether the respondents felt that academic library consortia could eventually compete with commercial publishers, as publishers (see section

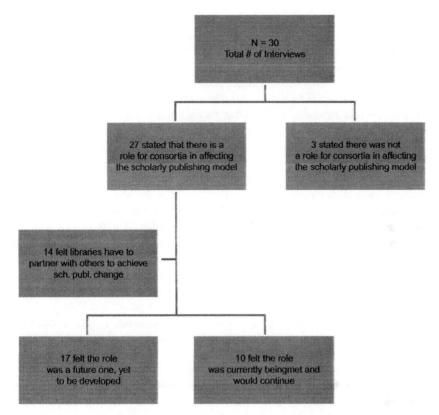

Fig. 5. University Librarian Responses about Scholarly Publishing.

Consortia and Competition), or felt that academic library consortia would be part of a changing scholarly publishing model through more moderate means, a common theme expressed by the respondents was that open source projects such as institutional repositories are important activities for academic library consortia. Looking at the responses to all of the questions about how academic library consortia activity affects the libraries' relationships with publishers, how consortia may affect libraries' competition with publishers, and how consortia may affect scholarly publishing, seventeen university librarians linked the development of open source platforms and institutional repositories to consortia activity. They felt that it is in the implementation and maintenance of open source projects such as institutional repositories that academic library consortia can play a leadership role. One respondent stated that academic library consortia are solving the technical problems of developing and maintaining open source infrastructures, and it is this expertise that academic libraries bring to scholarly publishing partnerships with faculty and with the larger institution.

Within the group of twenty-seven who felt academic library consortia did have some role to play in changing the scholarly publishing model, nine expressed reservations about how this involvement might unfold. Three felt that current consortial initiatives that focus on buying content, such as the "Big Deal"-type acquisitions, may impede libraries' abilities to participate in the transition to a new scholarly publishing paradigm and that academic libraries would have to address this conflict before they could fully participate in a new scholarly publishing regime. In their view, the "Big Deal" ensures publishers continue to have a market for their full suite of journal titles and may artificially support the continuing existence of those titles. They also perceive that faculty are become increasingly aware that signing over their copyright to a publisher may not be the best route to take in getting their research published. Respondents saw a conflict between library consortia continuing their current mode of operation that supports publishers through the "Big Deal"-type acquisitions and consortia supporting changes in the scholarly publishing cycle that will result in faculty moving their research publications from commercial publisher titles to consortia-controlled publications instead.

A few respondents felt that while libraries' implementation of institutional repositories is an important element of libraries' involvement in new models of scholarly publishing, faculty members have not "bought in" to the new type of scholarly publishing institutional repositories represent. These repositories are not seen by faculty to address their desire to publish in the most prestigious journals and they are uncertain about the review process.

There were also a few general reservations expressed wondering whether Canadian academic library consortia are too small and too immature to have much effect on changing scholarly publishing and wondering as well if Canadian libraries see themselves as publishers in any way and thus able to step in as part of a new model of scholarly publishing.

When asked who ultimately benefits from consortia activity, all but two of the university librarians stated that it was the students and faculty of their institutions who were the ultimate beneficiaries of consortia activity. Whether it was by increasingly available content, improving access, or a combination of factors, meeting the needs of academic library patrons is what the respondents felt academic library consortia activity is all about. Most of the respondents also went on to list other benefits including benefits to the library with respect to leveraging budgets to obtain more content and with respect to developing library staff, benefits across consortia in improved communication and a wider array of collaborative projects coming out of consortia activity, and benefits to publishers and scholarly publishing with respect to bringing the issues and problems of the current scholarly publishing model to the table and at least discussing, if not implementing, new publishing models. Generally, the comments about who ultimately benefits from consortia activity focused on non-economic factors such as skills development for library staff and access to more content for the user. Although the economic benefits of consortia activity were still "on the list" of benefits, they were not the main focus of the respondents' answers.

Relationship Effects

Among Academic Libraries

All but four university librarians stated that academic library consortia activity has positively affected the relationship amongst academic libraries. The most common effects noted were that consortia activity brings academic libraries closer together; it lets them know each other better with respect to each other's goals, operations, and problems; and it increases opportunities for dialog and shared projects. The respondents felt that academic consortia activity has increased the trust between academic libraries, made academic libraries think beyond their individual institutions to the consortia level, and led to academic libraries learning to "think consortially" as a part of their daily operations. They also felt that consortia activity has led to other librarians at their institution becoming involved in extra-institutional consortial activities and, as a result, has increased those librarians' knowledge and skills. Six mentioned that there can be tensions between consortium members with respect to cost sharing and other equity issues among large, medium, and small institutions but that this did not detract from the overall value consortia activity brings to the relationship amongst academic libraries.

Of the four who felt that consortial activity had not positively affected the relationship amongst libraries, one felt that the realization of huge increases in digital content had made it more difficult for libraries to get material they did not have (because licensing agreements restricted interlibrary loan), and one felt that if an institution does not participate in consortia activity, it is seen as "the bad kid"; yet, if an institution does participate, there is often no recognition by the other members of that participation.

Parent Institution
Twenty-five of the university librarians felt that their library's consortia activity had positively affected the library's relationship with its parent institution. Several respondents stated that the benefit gained for libraries is that senior university administrators have increased knowledge of what library consortia activity is and how it benefits the institution. Another commented that consortia activity has provided better benchmarks for university administrators to judge library performance. One described the effect of consortia activity as raising librarians' image as managers and professionals and giving librarians and giving the library more respect from the larger institution.

Though generally viewing consortia activity as benefiting the library's relationship with the campus, a few respondents noted that, at times, their library's consortia activity has caused tensions on campus because faculty and students perceive differential treatment in library consortial acquisitions amongst faculties and units, with science, medicine, and engineering realizing the lion's share of the benefit of consortial purchases and the social sciences and humanities obtaining less content through consortial acquisitions.

The comments on the budgetary gains consortia activity brings to libraries within their own institutions came from a few respondents who felt that the library had actually received more budget dollars or at least made their budget arguments more persuasive.

One respondent stated that consortia activity has made his/her role as university librarian more powerful within his/her library, and another respondent noted that his/her library's links to other academic libraries, through consortia, has given the library quasi-autonomy from its parent institution with respect to its acquisitions and performance decisions.

Relationship with Governments
Twenty-five of the university librarians felt that consortia activity has raised the profile of academic libraries in Canada. Although most spoke of a raised profile, half qualified their response by noting that government attention shifts quickly, and since governments come and go, what may have been important may quickly fade from notice.

Five respondents discussed the longer term effects of consortia activity on academic libraries' relationships with governments. One stated that consortia activity has shown governments that academic libraries are about research and not just dollars, and another stated that consortia activity has put pressure on governments to listen to academic libraries and has put academic libraries on governments' policy planning radar. Another felt that consortia activity has shown governments that libraries can rationalize collections regionally or even nationally to avoid unnecessary duplication and has proven that academic libraries can build shared collections to support Canadian research. This respondent went on to state that consortia activity may have been successful in making some government agencies more knowledgeable about the "exploitation" underway in the scholarly publishing market but that knowledge does not necessarily translate into academic libraries getting something they want because often "politics gets in the way." Consortia activity has given academic libraries the opportunity to advance social and political agendas with governments, but this does not necessarily mean that governments respect libraries more or less. In the respondent's view, consortia activity is business with governments and provides a common language that governments and academic libraries can use to talk to each other to achieve common goals.

Effects on Professional Values
When asked whether they felt that consortia activity has affected the core values of librarianship, seventeen respondents replied that consortia activity has strengthened librarians' core beliefs about sharing to provide resources and access and has contributed to the evolution of librarians' roles. One librarian noted that librarians' core values have been strengthened by the additional voices consortia activity brings. Five felt that individual academic libraries bring local issues, problems, and processes to the larger consortial table, and they consider this larger professional audience to be a positive factor in the evolution of academic librarians' roles and the profession of librarianship generally. These respondents felt that academic libraries, and the librarians who manage them, must integrate consortia standards and consortial goals into their institutional operations and that academic librarians are now operating in an environment where the other institutions in their consortial groups are more knowledgeable about what their library is doing and how they are doing it. They also felt that consortia activity has promoted an involvement with other groups on campus and other academic libraries and thereby engendered new and evolving roles for academic librarians.

Nine respondents felt that consortia activity has not affected academic librarians' professional values either positively or negatively, but rather viewed consortia activity as an expression of librarians' core values and did not see consortia activity changing those values.

The four respondents who felt that consortia activity may be having a negative effect on librarians' values were concerned about the buying or acquisition role of consortia. They noted that some librarians feel that consortial acquisitions have decreased the individual academic library's ability to choose resources tailored to its faculty and student needs, and they see this as having a negative impact on librarians' professional values. Consortia activity may be maintaining the construct of information as a commodity and causing librarians to lose sight of their long-held belief in information as a public good and that consortial buying may take on a "bandwagon" effect and cause academic libraries to lose sight of the needs of their patrons.

In summary, there was a diverse range of opinions of whether consortia activity has affected librarians' professional values. Seventeen respondents felt that academic library consortia activity has positively affected academic librarians' values by expanding librarians' expertise and providing opportunities to broaden individual library activities to a larger professional group. Nine felt that consortia activity has not affected librarians' core values either positively or negatively, and four felt that consortia activity has negatively impacted academic librarians' values.

DATA ANALYSIS, FUTURE RESEARCH, AND CONCLUSION

Government Attitudes toward Library Consortia

The comments from the government agency representatives about the purpose and benefits of academic library consortia activity were based in a market economic framework of efficiency and cost-benefit that places consortia within a framework of Canadian university research production and the existing system of scholarly publishing. The views of the representative from the CFI were exceptional in that he cited both market economic and public good benefits for library consortia activity. Overall, though, his comments were more economically based, with consortia activity increasing the university's "ability to draw on intellectual capital."

In reviewing the responses from the government agencies, it was clear that most of the government respondents had no in-depth understanding of what academic library consortia do or how they operate. Given that the Canada Foundation for Innovation funded the CNSLP, it may not be surprising that the CFI respondent knew the most about academic library consortia.

The other respondents qualified several of their responses about academic library consortia with introductory phrases such as "I can't really say because I don't know about consortia ..." When considering the relationship between academic library consortia and publishers, other than the CFI, the respondents had trouble placing consortia in the scholarly publishing picture as a direct competitor to publishers: they did eventually suggest, on the contrary, that, though they did not know any details about academic library consortia activity, they thought consortia activity would give academic libraries more power with publishers as buyer collectives.

Their answers about the goals, benefits, and inter-relationships among stakeholders of library consortia activity at times reflected an uncertain understanding of academic libraries. On the one hand, their views described the clear economic benefits of consortia, interpreting library consortia activity in terms of their agency's specific mandate and how consortia activity generally provides greater market power and advantage. On the other hand, though, they seemed to pair this view with a traditional view of academic libraries and what it is that academic libraries do. The respondents know consortia activity generally has economic value and accomplishes economic efficiencies. Yet, what was also apparent was that the respondents' interpretations of the questions about *academic library* consortia activity were also based on traditional institutional views of the role of academic libraries in Canadian universities. Some of the respondents' answers particularly demonstrated this orientation toward a traditional view of academic libraries. For example, the person interviewed from the Copyright Board emphasized the Board's mandate of issuing copyright licenses to organizations such as libraries, if original rights owners could not be found, as particularly relevant to this research. He also described the Board's possible involvement with academic library consortia as licensing use rights to library consortia (such as the Canadian Institute for Historical Microreproductions) and helping library consortia understand their use rights. This demonstrates his characterization of libraries as intermediaries of information. The representative from the Copyright Policy Branch of Heritage Canada described his agency's mandate as ensuring the rights of creators and ensuring fair access for institutions such as libraries (in their traditional role of users of copyright materials) and went on to consistently define academic library consortia activity purely in terms of their activity as collectives of copyright users. The person interviewed from the Knowledge Infrastructure Directorate placed academic library consortia activity as part of the success of universities in the context of a very traditional description of the library supporting university research.

Overall, the government respondents viewed academic library consortia activity from a market economic perspective, looking at consortia as giving academic libraries more power to achieve cost reductions and better products. Their views in this respect contrasted with the views of the university librarians discussed further below. The government interviewees consistently placed consortia in the role of a user (or buyer) collective for scholarly publications. For example, they identified the chief benefits of consortia activity as giving academic library consortia the power to negotiate better fees for accessing or using copyright material.

How do these federal government views on library consortia activity relate to information policy? If consortia are properly characterized as they are currently seen by the government, as buyer collectives, there is no provision in the Copyright Act that deals with the establishment of such collectives (whereas seller collectives, since 1988, have been provided for in the Copyright Act). Because there is no protection for buyer collectives in the Copyright Act, they are left entirely to the regime established in the Competition Act. This Act generally prohibits the creation of buyer or seller cartels. There is also no provision in the Competition Act to protect consortia, as buyer collectives, from any action that may claim those consortia are anti-competitive. Geist (2005) suggests that, under the new C-60,[9] the Competition Bureau's ability to challenge IP management as anti-competitive, at least from the perspective of seller collectives, would be further weakened.

One of the best defenses to a challenge that consortia activity is anti-competitive may be that, whatever the views of government players, the librarians and libraries who drive Canadian academic consortia do so, at present, overwhelmingly from a perspective of participation in a public good environment, not an economic market. Competition policy is meant to control only economic activity and would have no relevance with respect to the support and maintenance of the public good. If academic librarians can clearly demonstrate that consortia activity supports the public good and is not intended to be considered a market-based activity, academic library consortia should not face competition scrutiny.

This perspective of academic library consortia activity as a public good, not subject to competition policy, is supported by the recent work by the *Information Access Alliance* (Case, 2004) exploring the use of American antitrust law to counteract the increasing dominance of the scholarly publishing market by a few huge commercial publishers. The antitrust view of the Alliance is focused on the commercial publishers and not the activities of libraries or library consortia. Other articles discussing publishers' mergers (Foer, 2004; McCabe, 2002) make the case that libraries and the information resources libraries provide should be protected in the name of public good and the principle of unhampered access to resources, from the machinations of publishers.

The findings in the present research show that Canadian academic library consortia are viewed by university librarians as firmly supporting a public good philosophy. As previously described, in contrast to the university librarians' views, the research also suggests that the federal government sees consortia activity as primarily relevant to a market economic perspective focussed on the current activity of academic library consortia as buyer collectives. Yet, at the same time, the responses of the federal government agencies also reflected their placement of academic library consortia *with* academic libraries in a traditional view of providing service and resources to support Canadian research.

This complex interaction between federal government agencies' views of academic library consortia activity and university librarians' views of consortia activity suggests that Canadian academic libraries need to be clearer about the overall role of academic library consortia. Since the view of academic librarians is that consortia continue to remain part of the traditional public good framework of academic library service, libraries need to pay attention to the perspective on consortia held by government, as demonstrated in this research, and work to inculcate an acceptance of the public good perspective amongst government players, whether academic library consortia continue as either buyer or seller collectives.

University Librarians' Attitudes

Overall, the university librarians' views on the purposes of consortia activity universally reflected a strong public good perspective. Whether they were referring to past, current, or future purposes of consortia activity or how consortia activity might change relationships between players in the scholarly publishing system, the respondents consistently placed their comments in a framework in which consortia activity is seen as a means for libraries to continue to meet their traditional mandate of collecting and disseminating scholarly material. This relates to the definition of the public good provided above in that, although the respondents' comments referenced a number of financial issues and used a lot of financial language, their economic discussions were all explicitly in the context of their view that the overall goal of consortia is to achieve increased access to scholarly information and provide that information to the academic community. The respondents' comments did not define consortia activity from a market economic perspective, that is, as primarily a means to increase libraries' control vis-à-vis publishers in the context of the scholarly publishing market.

Espousing a public good perspective does not mean that these librarians never used financial vocabulary. When asked about early, current, and future goals of academic library consortia activity, all of the respondents identified financial issues as a key part of why consortia activity "took off" in the early to mid-1990s. They stated that academic libraries used developing technologies to launch consortial deals that helped each individual library gain more products at less overall cost. The respondents felt that consortia helped academic libraries deal with a huge increase in the number of scholarly journals available, with annual increases in serials costs that were often above 10%, and with stagnating library budgets. Their views that financial issues were the primary drivers of modern consortia formation were, however, within their conversation focusing on the context of the traditional role of academic libraries in acquiring and disseminating scholarly material for their patrons. With respect to the scholarly publishing cycle, the respondents' views of the initial formation of modern consortia reflected their perception that academic libraries were playing a traditional role, albeit one that was being severely hindered by the financial conditions of the day. The unanimous view of the respondents that consortia were developed because of financial conditions was anchored in a traditional public good view that libraries should acquire all the information patrons need. When that role was negatively affected by economic conditions such as double-digit inflation of serials costs and stagnating budgets, libraries reacted by developing consortia. This is not a market economic perspective even though financial language is being used because the respondents viewed the underlying premise of consortia activity as allowing libraries to increase their ability to obtain the scholarly resources needed by their faculty and students rather than achieving long-term economic gains at the expense of publishers. This same analysis applies when considering the respondents' views on current and future purposes of consortia activity: the economic purposes the respondents gave for consortia activity were within a public good viewpoint of that consortia activity.

That the respondents also saw past, current, and future consortia activity as *more* than just involving financial issues further corroborates the finding that the librarians' perspective was consistently one built on the notion of the public good. When discussing the past, current, and future goals of modern consortia activity, most respondents linked financial issues with other issues such as improved skills for library staff or developing new, shared services. When discussing how consortia activity affects the relationships amongst academic libraries, between academic libraries and their parent institutions, between academic libraries and governments, and between academic libraries and publishers, the respondents' views again reflected a public good perspective. Their comments on these relationships did not place the consortial activity of academic libraries in a market relationship in the scholarly publishing cycle. Many of their comments reflected a view that consortia activity strengthened the libraries' traditional roles in their academic communities with the outcome that libraries are better able to do, with the additional strength of consortia, what they do best: collect and disseminate information.

The librarians' views on how consortia activity affects scholarly publishing mostly reflected a public good perspective. Their responses most often linked consortia activity to scholarly publishing through affecting changes that enhance academic libraries' ability to provide information. Many of the respondents discussed partnering with faculty to affect change, or the libraries' role in educating faculty and others about the need for change in the scholarly publishing cycle. Fourteen of twenty-seven respondents who felt consortia did have a role to play in scholarly publishing felt that this role was one of educating faculty and other stakeholders on the need for change in the current scholarly publishing cycle and one of partnership (not leadership) with faculty and universities to affect those changes. This reflects a public good viewpoint of libraries as service providers and partners with other academic stakeholders in providing the scholarly resources required for their communities. The respondents' comments that consortia "increase libraries' power with publishers" or "give libraries a stronger voice with publishers" did not reflect an underlying premise that this increased power or stronger voice was due to consortial membership in the market economy but rather that the stronger voice enhanced academic libraries' abilities to obtain and provide more information. Nine of the fourteen who felt that consortia did have a role to play in scholarly publishing did not feel this role was one of competition with publishers but rather a means for libraries to develop more resources for their users (a public good perspective).

Similarly, in their responses to questions about how academic library consortia activity has affected relationships amongst academic libraries, between academic libraries and their parent institutions, and between academic libraries and governments, librarians consistently viewed consortia activity in terms of supporting academic libraries' role of collecting and providing information. Their answers to these *relationship* questions showed no linking of consortia activity to gaining market control or to acquiring information resources in a market defined "efficient" manner.

The university librarians see the commercial necessities of consortia activity as a lesser role for consortia, subservient to the role of providing access and serving the user community. The results suggest that academic library consortia are an extension of the cultural and social role of academic libraries and academic librarians. The respondents consistently positioned the benefits of consortia activity as sharing among libraries, gaining expertise to deliver better services and resources, and increasing or expanding academic librarians' expertise rather than diminishing it.

The public good role the library respondents felt that consortia fill is one based on a non-economic cultural definition of public good. Many times the respondents spoke of consortia activity from a cultural service perspective with phrases such as "this is what we do" or "this is our role." Even if they spoke of tensions between consortial members, they noted the benefits of consortia activity in providing more content and more services outweighed the tensions that might exist. The university librarians consistently spoke of consortia activity in non-economic terms of provision of equitable and increased access rather than as part of a market economic model that could have defined consortia in the economic framework still as public good, but from the perspective of focus on the non-commodifiable role they would play in the market economy of scholarly publishing. The librarians overwhelmingly stated that the ultimate purpose of consortia activity is to serve the user and to provide information users need, whatever that information might be. Their views on past, current, and future consortia activity consistently listed words such as "sharing," "collaboration," and "service." Consortia activity was not seen as primarily an economic advantage to libraries but rather as a way to do more of what academic libraries have always been charged to do, provide the information users need, when they need it to participate in the democratic process, to participate in the new information society fully, and to preserve intellectual freedom.

Consortia as Organizations

The respondents' views reflected an institutional organization model in which consortia, as organizations, are a reflection of the values and goals of academic librarians. The university librarians' views on the past, current, and future roles of consortia activity reflected strong institutional elements. In answering those questions, they put consortia activity in a broader concept of librarianship that values sharing and collaboration. Though all the respondents listed financial factors are drivers in the formation of modern consortia, almost half also listed non-financial factors as key determinants in the development of modern consortia. The emphasis on non-financial consortial goals was even stronger in respondents' views on current and future consortial activity. Though financial factors were important, it was apparent that the university librarians viewed non-financial goals such as sharing expertise and the collaborative development of services as being equally or even more important. These views reflected an organizational view of consortia that develops directly from the normative values of academic librarians that hold service, sharing, and collaboration as more fundamental to the profession than the economics of information. The institutional framework was also evident in the respondents' discussions about how consortia have affected relationships with publishers. A majority of librarians felt that consortia activity has given academic libraries a stronger voice with publishers to the extent that libraries are now able to obtain more scholarly product for their users within existing budgets. Placing these views in the institutional framework, the respondents see consortia as extending and improving on a key goal of academic libraries, collecting as much of the scholarly record as users may need. The view of more than half of the librarians, that academic library consortia would play more of a collaborative partnership role with other players in the scholarly publishing cycle rather than openly lead in changing the cycle, supports a conclusion that university librarians hold an institutional model of consortia as organizations in their view. Consortia exemplify education and partnership, two normative beliefs that define the role of academic libraries and academic librarians as educators and partners rather than as leaders or competitors. Finally, the majority of respondents expressed a view that consortia activity has positively affected libraries' relationships with each other through the development of shared services and the sharing of expertise that again reflects a view of consortia as organizational extensions of the academic library.

The university librarians' views set consortia activity in the normative institutional space of academic librarianship. The attitudes of these university librarians support the view that academic libraries achieve results through sharing and collaboration and not through competition with each other. Consortia activity achieves this same benefit at the consortial level through the interaction of libraries with each other in the shared consortial environment.

The institutional model of organizational action is an iterative one in which shared norms and beliefs drive planning and process, but, as well, one in which the daily implementation of shared norms informs the continuation and moderation of those norms at an institutional level (Scott, 1995). The results of this research show that university librarians see consortia as strengthening the traditional public good role of academic libraries and as reinforcing libraries as players in the scholarly publishing cycle. There were some indications, however, that a number of university librarians also see a future role for consortia as competitors with publishers by becoming publishers themselves. If this future scenario develops, then the role of academic libraries in scholarly publishing becomes twofold: one of collector and disseminator of the scholarly record and one of publisher of the scholarly record. Currently, consortia as organizations are embedded in the normative public good framework of academic libraries. If consortia develop a publisher role, it may be that through the iterative nature of the institutional model, consortia will eventually influence the traditional cultural public good philosophy of academic librarianship, introducing either more of an economic public good philosophy or a market economic framework. It is important to recognize this potential for librarians to successfully maintain a public good perspective on future consortial endeavors and then ultimately on the role of the academic library itself.

Though the respondents' mental model of consortia activity reflected an institutional view, this does not mean that all of the respondents felt that consortia were successful in every respect or every endeavor. There were some university librarians who felt that consortia were facing challenges due to the problems presented by the "Big Deal" and by other structural and functional issues such as cost-sharing mechanisms. One respondent was almost completely negative about consortia activity, feeling that consortial obligations did not allow his/her library to meet the needs of its user community. The concerns and negative views that were expressed by the respondents, however, are still consistent with the finding that university librarians hold an institutional organization model of consortia. Problems identified, and negative consequences of consortia activity reported, were an evaluation of consortia actions rather than a negation of the institutional organization model held by the interviewees.

Consortia and the Professional Roles of Academic Librarians

Finally, in relation to the research question asking how university librarians viewed consortia as affecting academic librarians' professional values, the respondents answers showed that they viewed consortia activity as a positive impact on the profession. Across all the questions, and specifically the questions asking about their views on how consortia activity affects the relationship between academic libraries, and about how consortia affects professional values, the respondents' comments reflected positive effects through consortia encouraging extra-institutional responsibilities for librarians.

The university librarians' language in discussing consortia is reflective of a strong view that academic library consortia have not contributed to any de-skilling or de-professionalization of academic librarians' work. Their views that consortia contribute to, or even strengthen, academic libraries' abilities to meet their mandates of providing information and service in the public good support a conclusion that consortia are part of the librarians' professional role of resource and service provision. Throughout their conversations, the university librarians referred to consortia as providing resources for the user and allowing libraries to do what they do better (i.e., resource and service provision). The questions about how consortia activity affected the interrelationships amongst libraries, who were ultimate beneficiaries of consortia activity, and whether consortia activity has affected librarians' professional values all showed that the respondents felt that consortia activity has increased the professional opportunities for academic librarians. Though some comments touched on consortia activity as negatively affecting individual institutional autonomy with respect to resource and service provision, the respondents in this research overwhelmingly viewed consortia activity as providing the same choices though on a consortial scale, and moving the professional work of collections and service provision to a consortial level. What may be seen as lost at the individual institutional level is seen as more than made up for at the consortial level.

The responses of the university librarians in this study reflected their views that consortia activity has greatly expanded the role of academic libraries. Some of the elements of this role include leadership, representing their library and institution, planning consortial directions, and seeking out and initiating consortial opportunities. The respondents also stated that a major challenge for university librarians today was balancing competing consortial activities and managing the impacts of increasing consortial involvement on their libraries. The university librarians felt that consortia activity is no longer the sole purview of the Chief Administrator of the library, as many rank and file librarians were reported to be also now involved in consortial initiatives. They also felt that this extra-institutional involvement of librarians was a positive benefit for academic librarianship and did not diminish librarians' authority or expertise but rather provides opportunities to increase or expand their professional abilities. The university librarians in this study saw the benefits of consortia activity to include major increases in content, developing shared resources and services, and developing shared infrastructures to support consortium-wide access.

An Integration of Consortia into the Scholarly Publishing Cycle

Combining the responses of all participants into an integrated view of the way in which consortia may affect the traditional model of scholarly publishing, the conclusion of this research places Canadian academic library consortia as augmenting and strengthening academic libraries' traditional role.

The majority of the librarians felt that consortia activity was focused on developing and delivering content and services to patrons (meeting a public good mandate). They felt that consortia activity reflects the traditional collection and dissemination role for academic libraries and, in fact, strengthens academic libraries' abilities in that respect. This view can be interpreted as consistent with government views once governments become more familiar with the consortial environment. The university librarians also saw consortia, as organizations, from an institutional perspective wherein they are extensions of academic libraries reflecting normative values of provision of service and access to information. As well, the librarians' view consortia as affecting the professional roles of academic librarians in a way that supports and enhances the role of the academic librarian and ultimately, therefore, supports and enhances the academic library.

With respect to scholarly publishing, academic library consortia activity is seen by librarians as serving the purpose of strengthening the role of academic libraries by more firmly establishing their role in collecting and distributing the research record. Consortia activity is viewed as continuing the academic library's role in being the best avenue for collecting and disseminating the scholarly research record and as reaffirming the academic librarian's role as service provider and professional.

Some of the respondents' views (both government representatives and librarians) suggest some interesting future scenarios for academic library consortia activity and how that activity might affect the academic library's role in the scholarly publishing cycle. More than half of the librarians felt that consortia activity has not only strengthened the academic library's role but also that of the publisher. These university librarians felt that consortia activity has worked to the benefit of publishers by expanding their markets and by making it easier for publishers to sell, distribute, and maintain their products. One respondent indicated that consortia activity has made consortia the new customer rather than the individual libraries. Several respondents also felt that consortia activity is propping up the existing scholarly publishing model by giving publishers opportunities to make "Big Deal"-type acquisitions with academic libraries and to push publisher's entire suite of titles to all consortia members whether the content is valid for those libraries or not. Several librarian respondents also felt that consortia have resulted in some loss of autonomy for individual libraries because consortial deals may mean less money for unique collections and also that libraries often have to accept more content through consortial deals to get the part of the deal they actually wanted. Putting these views in the broader perspective of the scholarly publishing cycle, academic library consortia might be considered not as augmenting and strengthening the role of academic libraries in the scholarly publishing cycle but rather becoming an increasingly powerful intermediary between the publisher and the academic library. The scholarly publishing diagram would then look more like the one shown in Fig. 6.

This possible future scenario is suggested only by the librarians' responses and was not suggested by the government agency representatives.

The intermediary position of consortia in Fig. 6, if it becomes the reality of the future, may lead to consortia developing mandates, goals, and objectives, including market economic–based objectives, independent of the control of university librarians and thus independent of academic libraries. Consortia, as new players in the cycle, might then develop as part of the supply chain to libraries in the same chain as publishers are now suppliers. In this possible future scenario, consortia as organizations may become more a means of input and output for academic libraries, moving to more of a dyadic "resource in/resource out" exchange relationship rather than reflecting and integrating the values of academic libraries into their structure and operations (i.e., rather than reflecting the institutional mental model that this research shows is the model of consortial organizations university librarians currently hold). The academic library in this future scenario would become, in fact, a customer of the consortia and would lose its direct connection to the research record publication process and, possibly, the

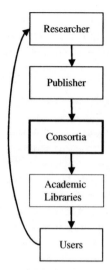

Fig. 6. Hypothetical Future Scenario: Consortia as Intermediary in the Scholarly
Publishing Cycle.

limited ability it has had to influence the maintenance of the scholarly
research record. The concerns expressed by the university librarians about
the Big Deal, about losing individual autonomy to support consortial
acquisitions, and about consortia supporting the current scholarly publishing model all contribute to this more disadvantageous future view of the
possible impacts of consortia activity on the scholarly publishing cycle.

    Another future scenario suggested by this research relates to academic
library consortia competing with publishers by becoming publishers. One-
third of the librarians thought that academic library consortia could become
publishers. Coupling that response with the view of the majority of
university librarians who felt that academic library consortia would have a
role to play in changing scholarly publishing through the development of
open source initiatives, academic library consortia may also have the
potential to create a new role for academic libraries in the scholarly
publishing cycle as shown in Fig. 7.

    Consortia would both become publishers (and thereby a supplier to
academic libraries) and remain a consumer or user of published materials.
The university librarians' responses about consortia competing with
publishers reflected the widest diversity of opinion amongst the respondents
in this study and also brought forward some respondents' discomfort with
the idea of academic library consortia competing with commercial

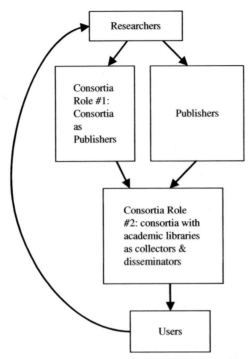

Fig. 7. Hypothetical Future Scenario: Consortia as Publishers in the Scholarly Publishing Cycle.

publishers by themselves becoming publishers. Nevertheless, a majority of university librarians felt that open source initiatives such as institutional repositories *were* areas where academic library consortia could take a leadership role and make significant contributions to a new scholarly communication model. Taken together, this suggests that there are a number of university librarians who view consortia activity as a means to challenge the current scholarly publishing paradigm and move academic libraries into a publisher role. This would have a significant effect on the existing scholarly publishing model and engender significant policy questions for academic libraries and significant public policy questions in the broader context.

Most interestingly, this would raise a new scenario for the relationships between consortia and competition policy. Consortia as publishers, or as seller collectives, would be covered by the Canadian Copyright Act exception to the Competition Act, and, as such, protected from competition policy scrutiny as are all other copyright "seller" collectives. Consortia as publishers would be one of many publishers in the scholarly publishing market, however, and as such would not be considered monopolies (as current consortia as buyer collectives may be considered) and therefore would be considered as a proper player in the scholarly publishing market posing no cartel threat to the market. In this scenario, consortia might be firmly placed in the market economic environment publishing "market" and no longer considered as in the public good, invisible to competition and copyright policies.

The librarians' discussions about consortia activity reflects current debates in academic librarianship and in the wider information policy sector on the current, and possible future, structure of the scholarly publishing cycle. In 2005, a report was presented to the Canadian Association of Research Libraries (CARL)[10] (Birdsall et al., 2005) that discusses the Canadian scholarly research environment and supports a strong government invest-ment in dissemination strategies for Canadian research. The report recognizes that Canadian government policy to date has been focused on the creation of research to support economic innovation, but it stresses that Canadian government policy should also support a social agenda of disseminating and archiving research so that it is, as much as possible, available for others to access and use. The report focuses on developing a national strategy for disseminating Canadian research with the CARL taking a leadership role because they "manage much of the existing infrastructure for scholarly communication in Canada and have the expertise and resources critical to the implementation of the infrastructure that may be required" (p. 136). The report does not suggest a dismantling of the scholarly publishing market but rather reflects a diversity of opinion similar to the findings in this research. There are a wide variety of views on the problems facing scholarly communication and no one solution is seen as the answer to those problems.

Similarly, the Scholarly Publishing and Academic Resources Coalition (SPARC) places the reintroduction of competition into scholarly publishing as a cornerstone of its activities. SPARC does not advocate abolishing commercial publishing so that academic libraries can take over that role but rather proposes different models of scholarly publishing to re-establish wider competition into the process. SPARC's published mission is to restore a "competitive balance" (Case, 2002) to science, technology, and medical publishing by encouraging alternative journal publications that can directly compete with established commercial publisher titles. One of the first decisions made by SPARC was that it would not be the "publisher" of the journals it helped create but rather would partner with existing publishers ready to participate in the SPARC vision. SPARC's goal is not to become publisher but to counter the monopolistic hold that some commercial publishers have on specific subject areas by introducing journals in the same subject, but at a lower cost. Yet, SPARC also argues that libraries should take a leadership role in re-establishing academic control over academic scholarship through various projects such as institutional repositories.

Finally, faculty have also been adding their voice to calls for changes in scholarly communication. Canadian scholar Jean-Claude Guédon (2001) focuses on the development of open source platforms to archive and disseminate Canadian research. In this role, his focus is not unlike that of SPARC and not inconsistent with the CARL report. However, Guédon questions the value of current academic library consortia activity, and Guédon suggests that consortia activity, though providing some short-term economic benefit to academic libraries, may only serve to support continuing publisher control of the scholarly publishing market. The majority of the librarians in the present study, on the contrary, reflect acceptance of the existing publisher control, at least for the present. However, since one-third of the university librarians in this study saw a possible future role for academic library consortia as direct competitors with publishers, if these future competitive consortia do develop, Guédon's view of academic consortia may change.

The complexity of the range of views on the interaction among publishers, libraries, scholars, and information policy in Birdsall et al. (2005), Case (2002), and Guédon (2001) is mirrored in the interviews with the thirty university librarians and the six government agency representatives who participated in this study. Their responses reflected mixed views on whether academic libraries can compete with publishers as publishers, blended with a stronger view that Canadian academic libraries will play a role in developing alternative scholarly publishing models.

The range of responses from the university librarians and the lack of specific knowledge about consortia demonstrated by the government participants suggest that a major focus of Canadian academic libraries should be to clarify and widely communicate what Canadian academic libraries see as their role with respect to evolving models of scholarly communication and how academic library consortia will play a part in that role. The present research shows that the regional groups are the major spheres of consortial activity in Canada, and so the question of how Canadian consortia view their roles with respect to scholarly publishing could begin at the regional level and then, perhaps, move to a coordinated national response. The results of this research show that some of the respondents see CARL as a strong national voice for libraries. Coordinating a national view of how Canadian academic library consortia will be involved in scholarly publishing with the regional views could be a reasonable next step for CARL.

Future Research

This research has brought together themes from organizational behavior, from the professional literature of librarianship, from competition policy, and from information policy generally in a way that had not been done before in any of these literatures. Because the work was in this sense exploratory, it was necessarily to limit its scope in various ways. For example, the examination of organizational models was limited to a reflection of the mental models that the subjects held about the organizations upon which they had been asked to reflect. The government officials involved were those working at the federal level in Canada because the areas of copyright, competition, and innovation funding involved were the responsibility of federal agencies. In Canada, provincial officials are frequently involved in other aspects of information policy and the lives of colleges and universities. Participation by libraries in consortia activity involves many other librarians besides the university librarians. However, the focus of this study required that university librarians be interviewed, and thus, the perspective of others will have to await further studies.

The results of this research suggest future research avenues to further explore consortia activity in academic libraries or to gain insight into consortia activity across other library sectors. The libraries studied in this research were academic libraries, because academic libraries as a group demonstrate the most advanced and most in-depth consortia activity amongst library sectors, and it seemed useful to begin with the most developed sector. College libraries have less consortial activity than do academic libraries, and public libraries even less than college libraries. Examining the questions posed in this research in other library sectors such as the college library and public library sector would be useful.

Furthermore, the academic libraries in this study were Canadian academic libraries, because both the competition environment in each nation is unique and the researcher is situated in Canada but also because the Canadian government created a unique opportunity for these questions when it funded the national CNSLP in 1999. Comparative studies for other jurisdictions would be most illuminating.

The data for this research was collected in 2003 and 2004. Since that time, Canadian academic library consortia have continued to grow in complexity and influence. Replicating this research in 2007 would illuminate whether university librarians' and government agencies' views on academic library consortia activity have undergone any change. Of particular interest would be an investigation of structural changes within and between national level Canadian consortia (i.e., the CNSLP) and the regional or provincial consortia. Because of these consortial developments, it may also now be more propitious to directly undertake study of the organization behavior of the consortia themselves, rather than relying, as I did, on the perceptions of the university librarians who initially guided them. Some of the librarians' responses in this research suggested that future Canadian academic library consortia would need to address structural changes at both the provincial/ regional level and the national level. An in-depth examination and comparison of the structure and function of these consortia could prove interesting.

This research concentrated on the views of librarians and the views of federal government agencies involved in information policy. To complete the picture of consortia activity as it relates to the scholarly publishing cycle, future research could examine how publishers view consortia and what their views may be about the past, present, and future roles of academic library consortia and how those consortia may impact scholarly publishing. Indeed, within the interview data gathered for this research, there was considerable evidence of librarians' views on ways consortia might be competitive in the future, and this data might be fruitfully plumbed more deeply in future.

Finally, a more in-depth look at how consortia activity is affecting the professional roles of academic librarians would provide additional information on the impact of consortia activity on academic libraries and academic librarianship. Carson's research (2002) explored, in part, how consortia activity may be affecting the professional roles of rank and file librarians. Her findings suggested that consortia activity contributes to a loss of power and control for academic librarians in the fulfillment of their role as academic librarians. My research found that university librarians (i.e., directors of academic libraries) felt that consortia activity does not negatively affect the professional values of academic librarians. These university librarians' views suggest that consortia activity does not contribute to de-skilling of academic librarians but rather enhances librarians' skills and expertise. A more in-depth investigation into the views of university librarians and the rank and file librarians working in their organizations about how consortia activity affects both the roles and the professional values of academic librarians would add to our knowledge of modern academic librarianship and academic libraries.

CONCLUSION

The focus of this research was to place Canadian consortia activity in the wider sphere of the scholarly information cycle and from that determine the following:

1. How consortia activity may be affecting federal government attitudes toward academic libraries;
2. How consortia activity may be affecting the role of academic libraries in the cycle from the competing perspectives of market economic versus public good;
3. How consortia as organizations may relate to their role in the scholarly publishing cycle; and
4. How consortia may be affecting the professional role of academic librarians within the cycle.

Findings from this research suggest that, from the perspective of various federal government agencies involved in information policy and competition policy, academic library consortia are primarily seen in economic terms and may in future interact more directly with competition policy and copyright policy in their roles as buyer collective. There is an apparent need to educate the government about what academic library consortia are and the benefits they bring, but this needs to be done within the context of a clear vision on the part of academic librarians about what they think consortia are now and what roles consortia might play in the future. Currently, Canadian University Librarians see consortia as strengthening libraries' traditional public good role in the scholarly publishing cycle. If this remains the dominant view, academic libraries could promote the public good purposes of consortia activity with governments and other funders to continue to achieve their goals for resource and service provision while remaining appropriately outside the purview of competition policy. If, however, academic librarians move to seeing consortia as predominantly as a market tool to push back at publishers, then the implications for possible anti-competitive scrutiny should be considered.

The results of this research provide a rich in-depth view of Canadian academic library consortia activity. Though seen by librarians as strengthening academic libraries' traditional public good role, there is some evidence to suggest that consortia may develop into avenues such as publishing, which will involve either a re-evaluation of that public good perspective or a re-focussing of it. Academic library consortia, a type of collective, have the potential to generate information policy questions at the federal government level. For Canadian academic libraries, the objectives of academic library consortia and whether those objectives are truly in line with what academic libraries do bear constant evaluation and monitoring, and the role of the consortia needs to be more clearly communicated to all relevant stakeholders. This research suggests that consortia activity is not just "something that libraries do" but rather an important facet of how academic libraries and academic librarians function within the scholarly publishing cycle.

NOTES

1. The Canadian National Site Licensing Project is a consortium of sixty-four Canadian academic libraries that came together through their provincial or regional consortial groups in 2000/2001 to successfully apply for funding to acquire science, technology, and medical digital resources (i.e., full-text online journals and indexes and abstracts). Now fully incorporated, the CNSLP, now called CRKN (Canadian Research Knowledge Network), has expanded its mandate to also provide content in the social sciences and humanities. For consistency throughout this chapter, I will use the acronym CNSLP.

2. The Information Access Alliance includes the American Library Association, the Association of College and Research Libraries, the American Association of Law Libraries, the Medical Library Association, the Association of Research Libraries, the Scholarly Publishing and Academic Resources Coalition or SPARC, and the Special Libraries Association. For more information, see the article by Case (2004).

3. Antitrust is the U.S. term used to describe competition policy and anti-competitive regulation.

4. Fair use is the term applied to the exemptions allowed under the United States Copyright Act of 1976 (section 107 of the U.S. Act) for purposes of criticism, comment, news reporting, teaching (including multiple copies for classroom use), scholarship, or research. For more information, see the American Library Association (2005) document "What is fair use? Fair use and guidelines" at http://www.ala.org/ala/washoff/WOissues/copyrightb/copyrightarticle/whatfairuse.htm. Fair dealing is the term used in the Canadian Copyright Act (Section 29 of the Canadian Act) for the same type of exemptions. For more information, see Canadian Association of Research Libraries (2002). *Copying Right* at http://www.carl-abrc.ca/projects/copyright/copyingright_2002-e.html

5. The CFI was created in 1997 as an independent, non-profit organization with the goal of strengthening the research capacity of Canadian universities, colleges, research hospitals, and non-profit research institutions. The CFI has been a major source of federal funding for university research and in fact funded the CNSLP.

6. Industry Canada is a key player in developing Canadian information policy, copyright policy, and competition policy. Three agencies attached to Industry Canada were included in the study: (1) The Knowledge Infrastructure Directorate of the Innovation Policy Branch of Industry Canada (liaises with the university community and the federal granting councils); (2) The CIPO (responsible for the administration and processing of intellectual property in Canada); and (3) The Competition Bureau (independent administrative agency overseeing the administration and enforcement of the Competition Act). The Commissioner of the Bureau reports to the Deputy Minister of Industry with respect to administrative and financial matters and to Parliament through the Minister of Industry in respect of its independent law enforcement role.

7. The Copyright Policy Branch (attached to the Ministry of Canadian Heritage), in co-operation with the Intellectual Property Policy Directorate of Industry Canada, is responsible for formulating and implementing Canadian copyright policy.

8. The Copyright Board (established under the Copyright Act) is a regulatory body responsible for setting and monitoring royalties paid to copyright collectives. The Board may also supervise agreements between licensing bodies and users and issue licenses for copyright use when the copyright owner cannot be located.

9. C-60 was under consideration by the federal government until the government was dissolved in December, 2005.

10. The CARL is an association representing twenty-seven university libraries plus the Library and Archives Canada, Canada Institute for Scientific and Technical Information (CISTI), and the Library of Parliament. Membership is institutional, and is open primarily to libraries of Canadian universities that have doctoral graduates in both the arts and the sciences.

REFERENCES

Alexander, A. W. (1999). Toward "The perfection of work": Library consortia in the digital age. *Journal of Library Administration, 28*(2), 1–14.

Allen, B. M., & Hirshon, A. (1998). Hanging together to avoid hanging separately: Opportunities for academic libraries and consortia [electronic version]. *Information Technology and Libraries, 17*(1), 36–44.

American Library Association. (2003). Principles and strategies for the reform of scholarly communication. Retrieved Sept. 16, 2005 from http://www.ala.org/ala/mgrps/divs/acrl/publications/whitepapers/principlesstrategies.cfm

American Library Association. (2005). What is fair use? Retrieved December 12, 2005 from http://www.ala.org/Template.cfm?Section = copyrightarticle&Template = /ContentManagement/ContentDisplay.cfm&ContentID = 26700

Anton, A. (2000). Public goods as common stock: Notes on the receding commons. In: A. Anton, M. Fisk & N. Halstrom (Eds), *Not for sale: In defense of public goods* (pp. 4–40). Boulder, CO: Westview Press.

Association of Research Libraries, Association of American Universities & Pew Higher Education Roundtable. (1998). To publish and perish. *Policy Perspectives, 7*(4). Retrieved on September 16, 2005. Available at http://www.thelearningalliance.info/Docs/Jun2003/DOC-2003Jun13.1055537929.pdf

Association of Universities and Colleges of Canada. (1988). Statement of academic freedom and institutional autonomy. Retrieved September 16, 2005 from http://www.aucc.ca/_pdf/english/statements/1988/aucc_academic_freedom_e.pdf

Baker, A., & Sanville, T. (2000). Consortia, networks, and publishing in 1999. In: *Bowker annual library and book trade almanac* (45th ed., pp. 219–226). New York, NY: R.R. Bowker.

Ball, D., & Pye, J. (1998). Library purchasing consortia: Achieving value for money and shaping the emerging electronic marketplace [electronic version]. In: *The Challenge to be relevant in the 21st century: Abstracts and fulltext documents of papers and demos given at the [International Association of Technological University Libraries] IATUL Conference*, Pretoria, South Africa, June 10–15, ERIC document no. ED 434663.

Benkler, Y. (2001). A political economy of the public domain: Markets in information goods versus the marketplace of ideas. In: R. C. Dreyfuss, D. L. Zimmerman & H. First (Eds), *Expanding the boundaries of intellectual property: Innovation policy for the knowledge society*. New York: Oxford University Press.

Birdsall, W. F. et al. (2005). Towards an integrated knowledge ecosystem: A Canadian research strategy (a report submitted to the Canadian Association of Research Libraries/ L'Association des bibliotheques de recherché du Canada (CARL/ABRC)). Available at http://kdstudy.ca/2005/finalreport.pdf. Retrieved on September 16, 2005.

Bogdan, R. C., & Biklen, S. K. (1992). *Qualitative research for education: An introduction to theory and methods*. Toronto: Allyn and Bacon.

Bollier, D. (2002). *Silent theft: The private plunder of our common wealth*. New York, NY: Routledge.

Bostick, S. (2001). The history and development of academic library consortia in the United States: An overview [electronic version]. *Journal of Academic Librarianship, 27*(2), 128–130.

Buchwald, C. (1995). Canada in context: An overview of information policies in four industrialized countries. *Canadian Journal of Information and Library Science, 20*(September/December), 5–33.

Budapest Open Access Initiative. (2002). Budapest, Hungary. Retrieved September 16, 2005 from http://www.soros.org/openaccess/read.shtml

Buschman, J. (2003). *Dismantling the public sphere*. Westport, CT: Libraries Unlimited.

Buschman, J. (2005). On libraries and the public sphere. *Libraries, Philosophy and Practice, 7*(2)Retrieved on September 16, 2005. Available at http://www.webpages.uidaho.edu/~mbolin/buschman.pdf

Callon, M., & Bowker, G. (1994). Is science a public good? (Fifth Mullins lecture, Virginia Polytechnique Institute, 23 March 1993) [electronic version]. *Science, Technology, & Human Values, 19*(4), 395–424.

Canadian Association of Research Libraries. (2002). Copying right: A guide for Canada's universities to copyright, fair dealing and collective licensing. Retrieved December 12, 2005 from http://www.carl-abrc.ca/projects/copyright/copyingright_2002-e.html

Canadian Association of Research Libraries. (2005). CARL policy statement on Freedom of Expression. Retrieved December 5, 2005 from http://www.carl-abrc.ca/about/freedom_of_expression-e.html

Canadian Institutes of Health Research (CIHR). (2007). Policy on access to research outputs. Available at http://www.cihr-irsc.gc.ca/e/34846.html

146   CATHERINE MASKELL

Case, M. M. (2002). Capitalizing on competition: The economic underpinnings of SPARC. Retrieved September, 26, 2005 from http://www.arl.org/sparc/publications/papers/case_capitalizing_2002.shtml

Case, M. M. (2004). Information Access Alliance: Challenging anticompetitive behaviour in academic publishing [electronic version]. *College & Research Library News*, *65*(6), 310–326.

Competition Act. (1985). *Revised statutes of Canada, 1985. Chapter C-34*. Ottawa: Queen's Printer.

Copyright Act. (1988). *Revised statutes of Canada, 1985, Chapter C-42*. Ottawa: Queen's Printer.

Davis, G. F., & Powell, W. W. (1990). Organization-environment relations. In: M. D. Dunnette & L. M. Hough (Eds), *Handbook of industrial and organizational psychology* (2nd ed., Vol. 3, pp. 315–375). Palo Alto, CA: Consulting Psychologists Press.

DiMaggio, P. J., & Powell, W. W. (1991). The Iron cage revisited: Institutional isomorphism and collective rationality in organizational fields. In: W. W. Powell & P. J. DiMaggio (Eds), *The New institutionalism in organizational analysis*. Chicago, IL: University of Chicago Press.

Director of Investigation and Research. (1995). Strategic alliances under the "Competition Act" *Information Bulletin*. Minister of Supply and Services Canada Catalogue No. RG 52-2711995 Industry Canada IC5029OB95-10. Retrieved September 6, 2005 from http://www.apeccp.org.tw/doc/Canada/Decision/5d.htm

Doern, G. B. (1996). Canadian competition policy institutions and decision processes. In: G. B. Doern & S. Wilks (Eds), *Comparative competition policy: National institutions in a global market*. Oxford: Clarendon Press.

Dorner, D. (2000). *Determining essential services on the Canadian Information Highway: An exploratory study of the public policy process*. Doctoral Dissertation, University of Western Ontario. *ProQuest Digital Dissertations* (AAT NQ58126).

Edlin, A. S., & Rubinfeld, D. L. (2004). Exclusion of efficient pricing [electronic version]? The "big deal" bundling of academic journals. *Antitrust Law Journal*, *72*(1), 119–157.

Evetts, J. (1999). Professions: Changes and continuities. *International Review of Sociology*, *9*(1), 75–85.

Foer, A. A. (2004). *Can antitrust save academic publishing?* Orlando, Florida: American Library Association Annual Meeting. June 28, 2004 (revised July 20, 2004). Retrieved on November 25, 2005. Available at http://www.informationaccess.org/bm~doc/Bert.pdf

Freidson, E. (1999). Theory of professionalism: Method and substance. *International Review of Sociology*, *9*(1), 117–129.

Garvey, W. D. (1978). *Communication, the essence of science: Facilitating information exchange among librarians, scientists, engineers and students*. New York: Pergamon Press.

Geist, M. (2005). Anti-circumvention legislation and competition policy: Defining a Canadian way. In: M. Geist (Ed.), *In the public interest: The Future of Canadian copyright law*. Toronto: Ontario. Irwin Law608p. Retrieved on October 17, 2005. Available at http://www.irwinlaw.com/pages/content-commons/anti-circumvention-legislation-and-competition-policy–defining-a-canadian-way——michael-geist

Giles, J. (2007). Information wants to be free. *New Scientist*, *195*(2622), p. 22.

Gorman, M. (2000). *Our enduring values: Librarianship in the 21ˢᵗ century*. Chicago: American Library Association.

Gorman, M. (2003). *The enduring library: Technology, tradition, and the quest for balance.* Chicago: American Library Association.

Great Britain, House of Commons Science and Technology Committee. (2004). *Scientific publications: Free for all?* (tenth report of Session 2003–04, Volume 1: Report, printed July 7, 2004). London: The Stationary OfficeAvailable at http://www.publications. parliament.uk/pa/cm200304/cmselect/cmsctech/399/399.pdf.

Guédon, J.-C. (2001). *Beyond core journals and licenses: The paths to reform scientific publishing.* ARL Bimonthly Report, #218. Available at http://old.arl.org/newsltr/218/guedon.html. Retrieved on September 6, 2005.

Harris, M. H., & Hannah, S. A. (1993). *Into the future: The foundations of library and information services in the post-industrial era.* Norwood, New Jersey: Ablex Publishing.

Helmer, J. F. (2002). Editorial: Inhaling the spore [electronic version]. *Information Technology and Libraries, 17*(1), p. 5.

Hirshon, A. (1999). Libraries, consortia and change management [electronic version]. *Journal of Academic Librarianship, 25*(2), 124–126.

Industry Canada. (2001). *Achieving excellence: Investing in people, knowledge and opportunity.* Ottawa: Government of Canada.

Kopp, J. J. (1998). Library consortia and information technology: The past, the present, the promise [electronic version]. *Information Technology and Libraries, 17*(1), 7–12.

Lancaster, F. W., & Smith, L. C. (1978). Science, scholarship and the communication of knowledge. *Library Trends, 27*(3), 367–388.

Lessig, L. (2001). *The future of ideas: The fate of the commons in a connected world.* New York: Random House.

Library Journal Academic Newswire (2008). This Week's News-After Hearing, Sweeping Anti-NIH Bill To Be Shelved—for Now, September 16. Accessed October 1, 2008 at http:// www.libraryjournal.com/info/CA6596784.html#news1

Litman, J. (1990). The public domain [electronic version]. *Emory Law Journal, 39*(4), 966–1023.

McCabe, M. (2002). Journal pricing and mergers: A portfolio approach. *American Economic Review, 92*(1), 259–269.

National Institutes of Health (NIH). (2004). *Notice: Enhanced public access to NIH research information.* Notice Number: NOT-OD-04-064, release date: September 3, 2004. Retrieved September 6, 2005 from: http://grants1.nih.gov/grants/guide/notice-files/ NOT-OD-04-064.html

Oppenheim, C., Greenlaugh, C., & Rowland, F. (2000). The future of scholarly journal publishing [electronic version]. *Journal of Documentation, 56*(4), 361–398.

Owen, J. M. (2002). The new dissemination of knowledge: Digital libraries and institutional roles in scholarly publishing. *Journal of Economic Methodology, 9*(3), 275–288.

Owen, J. M., & van Halm, J. (1989). *Innovation in the information chain: The effects of technological development on the provision of scientific and technical innovation.* New York: Routledge.

Patrick, R. J. (1972). *Guidelines for library cooperation: Development of academic library consortia.* Santa Monica, CA: Systems Development Corporation.

Poynder, R. (2005). U.K. Government rejects call to support open access. Retrieved September 6, 2005 from http://www.infotoday.com/newsbreaks/nb041115-1.shtml

Rowse, M. (2003). The consortium site license: A sustainable model [electronic version]? *Libri*, *53*(1), 1–10.

Scott, W. R. (1995). Introduction: Institutional theory and organizations. In: W. R. Scott & S. Christensen (Eds), *The institutional construction of organizations: International and longitudinal studies*. Thousand Oaks, CA: Sage Publications.

Stielow, F. (2001). Reconsidering arsenals of a democratic culture. In: N. Kranich (Ed.), *Libraries & democracy: The cornerstones of liberty* (pp. 3–14). Chicago: American Library Association.

Thompson, J. C. (1988). Guest editorial: Journal costs: perception and reality in the dialogue. *College & Research Libraries*, *49*(6), 481–482.

Trebilcock, M., Winter, R. A., Collins, P., & Iacobucci, E. M. (2002). *The law and economics of Canadian competition policy*. Toronto: University of Toronto Press.

Ullrich, H. (2001). Intellectual property, access to information, and antitrust: Harmony, disharmony, and international harmonization. In: R. C. Dreyfuss, D. L. Zimmerman & H. First (Eds), *Expanding the boundaries of intellectual property: Innovation policy for the knowledge society*. New York: Oxford University Press.

Van Orsdel, L. C. (2005). Antitrust issues in scholarly and legal publishing [electronic version]. *College & Research Libraries News*, *66*(5), 374–377.

Weber, D. C. (1976). A century of cooperative programs among academic libraries. *College & Research Libraries* (May), 205–221.

Weiss, R. (2005). Plan postpones public access to research: Science publishers prevailed against 1st NIH proposal. *Boston Globe*, January 19, 2005. Available at Boston.com. Retrieved on September 6, 2005.

Wilkinson, M. A. (1996). Anticipating the impact of intellectual property. *Canadian Journal of Information and Library Science*, *21*(2), 23–42.

Wilkinson, M. A. (2000). Copyright in the context of intellectual property: A survey of Canadian university policies. *Intellectual Property Journal*, *14*(2), 141–184.

Winter, M. F. (1988). *The culture and control of expertise: Toward a sociological understanding of Librarianship*. New York: Greenwood Press.

APPENDIX A. INTERVIEW PROTOCOL FOR UNIVERSITY LIBRARIANS

First give a short outline of the project and the interview:

- I am interviewing university librarians across Canada as well as federal level information policy makers
- I am looking at the dynamics of academic library consortia activity
- The general format of interview will be an introductory part describing your position, your institution, your institution's consortia activity followed by your views on academic library consortia activity – how they work, how they have changed, and so on.

Questions:

1. How long have you been university librarian?
   Prompt: for previous position if in UL position less than two years

2. Describe your library's involvement in consortia

3. As university librarian, what is your role with respect to consortia activity?

4. To what level has your library become involved in consortia? Why? Have consortia been successful for your library?

5. (RQ 4,5,6) How have academic library consortia changed from say ten to fifteen years ago?
   Why were they formed initially? Has their purpose changed?
   Prompt: look for public good vs. economic

6. (RQ 4,5,6) How do you think academic library consortia will change in the next ten to fifteen years?
   Prompt: look for public good vs. economic

7. (RQ 4,5,6) If academic libraries are one of the major players in consortia activity, who would be the other major players?
   Prompt: for other institutional players-public, private, government

8. (RQ 4,5,6,7) What are the relationships between the players? How do they interact?
   • among the academic libraries in the consortium
   • between the academic libraries and the government
   • between the academic libraries and publishers

9. (RQ 4,5,6) If you think about how academic library consortia activity might change in the future, how do you think the relationship between libraries and publishers might change? Who will benefit from this change?
   Prompt: watch for cues to further discuss who ultimately benefits
   Prompt: watch for cues to further discuss public vs. economic good

10. (RQ 4,5, 6, 7) What do you think are the value of academic library consortia? To your library specifically? To academic libraries generally? To scholarly publishing?

11. (RQ 7) Is consortia activity affecting librarians' professionalism – are they core to librarianship?

12. *(conditional)* (RQ 4,5) Do you think consortia activity is a means to directly compete with commercial publishers?

APPENDIX B. INTERVIEW PROTOCOL FOR FEDERAL GOVERNMENT AGENCIES

First give a short outline of the project and the interview:

– I am interviewing librarians across Canada as well as federal level information policy makers
– I am looking at the dynamics of academic library consortia activity (may need to define academic library consortia and give a few examples)
– The general format of interview will be an introductory part describing your position, your agency, followed by questions on your views on academic library consortia activity, and so on.

Questions:

1. How long have you been at your position?
   Prompt: for previous position if in current position less than two years

2. Describe your agency's primary activities.
   Prompt: for relationship to university sector, academic libraries, publishing

3. How much of your work is involved with consortia of any type (i.e., other research consortia, corporate consortia)?

4. How much of your work is specifically with academic library consortia?

5. (RQ 1,2,3) Why do you think academic library consortia have formed?

6. (RQ 1,2,3) What do you think are the main benefits of academic library consortia?
   Prompt: explore points that come up around economic or public good benefits

7. (RQ 1,2,3) If you consider academic libraries and publishers as the main players in consortia activity how do you see this relationship working (is it equitable, who benefits more)?

8. (RQ 1,2,3) How do you think academic library consortia may change, how might they work say twenty years from now?

9. (RQ 1,2,3) Thinking about how academic library consortia activity might change in the future, how do you think the relationship between libraries and publishers might change?
   Prompt: watch for cues to further discuss who ultimately benefits
   Prompt: watch for cues to further discuss public vs. economic good

10. *(conditional)* (RQ 1,2,3) Do you think consortia activity is a means to directly compete with commercial publishers?

11. Are there other policy makers within your own agency or other government agencies who could provide useful feedback on this topic?

WHY LIBRARIANSHIP? AN EXPLORATION OF THE MOTIVATIONS OF ETHNIC MINORITIES TO CHOOSE LIBRARY AND INFORMATION SCIENCE AS A CAREER

Lisa K. Hussey

ABSTRACT

Although there is great potential for diversity, library and information science (LIS) is a relatively homogenous profession. Increasing the presence of librarians of color may help to improve diversity within LIS. However, recruiting ethnic minorities into LIS has proven to be difficult despite various initiative including scholarships, fellowships, and locally focused programs. The central questions explored in this research can be divided into two parts: (1) Why do ethnic minorities choose librarianship as a profession? (2) What would motivate members of minority groups to join a profession in which they cannot see themselves?

The research was conducted through semi-structured, qualitative interviews of 32 ethnic minority students from one of four ethnic minority groups (African American, Asian American, Hispanic/Latino, and Native American) currently enrolled in an LIS graduate program. Eleven themes

Advances in Library Administration and Organization, Volume 28, 153–217
ISSN: 0732-0671/doi:10.1108/S0732-0671(2009)0000028007

emerged from the data: libraries, librarians, library work experience, LIS graduate program, career plans and goals, education and family, support, mentors, ethnicity and community, acculturation, and views of diversity.

The findings seem to support many assumptions regarding expectations and career goals. The findings related to libraries, librarians, mentors, and support illustrate that many recruitment initiatives are starting in the right place. However, the most noteworthy findings were those that centered on identity, acculturation, and diversity because they dealt with issues that are not often considered or discussed by many in the profession outside of ethnic minority organizations.

INTRODUCTION

The United States is a diverse society, but it has not always acknowledged itself as such. Since the Civil Rights Movements, the acceptance or recognition of difference has become part of mainstream society. Ethnic and racial identity, religious background, and gender identification are just a few of the characteristics used to identify difference in the population. As society becomes more conscious of diversity, issues regarding equitable treatment and representation have become recognized concerns in various fields such as education, management, and psychology. As a result, there is a growing body of literature that discusses the need for diversity in all aspects of social life, especially with regard to public institutions such as libraries. A commonly stated goal for diversity is for these institutions to reflect the wider population to better serve their constituents.

Libraries are service-oriented organizations that serve various populations, and there is great potential within the Library and Information Science (LIS) professions for diversity. LIS is an interdisciplinary field. For most professional positions within LIS, individuals are required to have a bachelor's degree and a master's dregree preferably in library science (MLIS). However, there is no preferred undergraduate major. Although the majority of LIS students have undergraduate degrees in education, the humanities, and liberal arts (Moen, 1988; McClenney, 1989; O'Brien, 2002), there is potential for a rich and varied educational backgrounds within the profession. The only common thread is an interest in information.

However, librarianship tends to be homogenous. Librarians are traditionally white and female, even now when the information professions are expanding. In the 2000 census, the ethnic breakdown of the U.S.

population is approximately 61% white (U.S. Census Bureau, 2000), whereas approximately 85.3% of librarians are white (U.S. Department of Labor, 2004). This is a noteworthy difference when compared to overall breakdown of management, professional, and related occupations where ethnic minorities make up 20.1% of the workforce (U.S. Department of Labor, 2004), and almost 20% of all K-12 teachers, instructors, and teacher assistants identify themselves as members of an ethnic minority group. In community and social services occupations, the ethnic break down is a closer reflection of the wider population with 31.3% of the workers identified as members of ethnic minority groups (U.S. Department of Labor, 2004). These professions, like librarianship, deal with ethnically and culturally diverse communities. One of the best ways to address the needs of these communities is to include members of the ethnic and cultural groups in the professions who can reach out to minorities and help us to understand what the specific needs are. While almost all these professional or management groups need to improve minority representation, LIS has even more ground to cover than most.

A lack of diversity can be seen in all areas of LIS. Over the past 40 years, as the number of individuals pursuing a bachelor's degree has increased and as high schools have made a more conscious effort to prepare students for college, minority student populations on college campuses have grown as has the percentage of ethnic minorities who have completed at least a Bachelor's degree. As a result, university and college campuses are more diverse (U.S. Census Bureau, 1980, 2000; ASHE, 2005). Ethnic groups such as Hispanic/Latino, Asian American, and African American make up a more visible part of the general student body on college campuses, but they do not have a significant presence in LIS programs or as LIS professionals.

According to the *Association for Library and Information Science Education 2004 Statistical Report*, 11.9% of MLIS students are from ethnic minority groups, and 10.6% of those who graduate with American Library Association (ALA) accredited master's degrees are classed as members of ethnic minorities (ALISE, 2004). Through recruitment and training programs, public libraries tend to have a more diverse staff (Lynch, 2004; Winston, 1998), but the majority of professional positions are still held by white librarians (U.S. Department of Labor, 2004; Lynch, 2004). Public libraries have instituted programs to improve recruitment by targeting library staff using programs such as the "Grow Your Own" initiative, which was started at the Broward County Library system (McConnell, 2004) and has since been adopted by the Public Library Association and the Page Fellows program at the Queens Borough Public Library. Despite these efforts, public libraries' professional staffs still fail to reflect their communities' make-up. According to the most recent Census (2000) data, ethnic minorities constitute approximately 39% of the population, yet only 13.45% of all public librarians are ethnic minorities (Lynch, 2004).

Academic libraries have also tried to improve the staff diversity. The Association of Research Libraries (ARL) offers financial assistance to academic libraries for scholarships and residency programs (ARL, 2006a, 2006b). ARL also provides a database of internship opportunities and residency programs for students and professionals (ARL, 2006a, 2006b). Some academic libraries have established residency or fellowship programs that offer one- or two-year positions to qualified ethnic minority LIS graduates. The intent of these programs is to provide recent MLIS graduates with an opportunity to gain valuable work experience while introducing them to "all aspects of their [LIS] careers" (Hepburn, 2001, p. 143). The underlying concept is that the residency programs will help increase diversity as these individuals take the skills learned to another library, preferably an academic setting (Brewer & Winston, 2001). Those residents of these programs who consider them to be successes report positive experiences, and most are still employed in academic libraries (Cogell & Grunwell, 2001). However, although they are well intentioned, other residency programs have sometimes "become examples of what not to do" (Hankins, Sanders, & Situ, 2003, p. 309) by inserting a new librarian into alien environments and expecting this inexperienced individual to foster change with little to no authority or administrative support. Some residents have mentioned the emphasis on minority status and how that "led to perceptions [by library staff] that these residents were substandard" (Weissinger, 2003). Although created with the best of intentions, some diversity initiatives are quota based or put together in reaction to diversity mandates with too little attention to fostering a spirit of inclusion and diversity.

Theoretical Framework

The need for diversity is inherent in our society. Most publicly supported libraries are social institutions funded through municipal or shared funds and cannot exist independently or outside of a social framework. As a result, it is difficult to study or analyze libraries or LIS as a profession outside of the context of social interactions or society as a whole. Libraries often act as community centers and/or cultural repositories (Wiegand, 1999). As such, issues in the larger society, including tensions involving race, sex, and socioeconomic status, can be and, often are, reproduced within these institutions. The individuals who work within LIS in leading and staffing these organizations affect how the library is presented to and received by various communities and society. Decisions regarding library collections, community programming, building locations, and institutional preservation are made by those who work in the institution, as well as those who fund libraries. How these decisions are made and what influences them are central to understanding the libraries' position in society. The theories of cultural hegemony and discursive formation can help explain how libraries are influenced by communities and governments and illustrate how these public institutions exert influence on the larger society.

Cultural hegemony is a concept first introduced by the Italian Marxist Antonio Gramsci who defined it as the creation and maintenance of a dominant culture by the ruling class that is accepted, either consciously or unconsciously, by the subordinate and/or oppressed classes through complicity and coercion (Lears, 1985). In other words, cultural hegemony is the process of providing and institutionalizing accepted standards and policies in society based on one powerful group's idea of what is correct and incorrect. This powerful group is united under particular characteristics such as economic factors and ethnic identity, which provide the source of their authority. The influence of a powerful group, which forms the basis of cultural hegemony, is preserved and advanced in society through the utilization of intellectuals. Gramsci divides intellectuals into two groups, traditional and organic. Traditional intellectuals are the scholars and philosophers. Organic intellectuals, however, occupy a "whole range of positions...from the lowest state official...to the highest civil servant" (Sassoon, 1987, p. 138), including teachers and librarians. They are the individuals who create a connection between various levels of the social hierarchy and who legitimate and reinforce the dominant cultural hegemony (Raber, 2003). In LIS, librarians, acting as organic intellectuals, are the individuals who handle the technical and organizational needs of the profession by performing "ideological and organizational functions based on practical intervention to change the real world" (Sassoon, 1987, p. 140), and they provide a basis for institutionalizing the current cultural hegemony. This explanation simplifies the concept and the processes of a hegemonic culture but provides a starting point for examining the impacts and implications within libraries as public institutions.

Although cultural hegemony helps to explain the position of the library and the role of librarians in society, it is a theory that focuses mainly on class structure and can be used to view social structures, which are generally, but not always, formed around issues relating to class. Although the concepts of class and social structures are often tied with ethnic breakdowns in society, they also exist outside of ethnic and racial lines. Hence, the concept of cultural hegemony does not sufficiently explain the influences and structure of social and public institutions.

Although hierarchies and class structures are important to understand social orders within LIS, a consideration of individual and community socialization is also essential to create a comprehensive picture of LIS and the role of diversity within the profession. In addition to the concept of cultural hegemony, discursive formations, as defined by Michel Foucault (1972), provide a power base for the dominant groups through the teaching of values and norms. The power described here is not a matter of overt control, but rather an unspoken acceptance of policies and procedures reflected in unconscious actions within social settings and reactions to society. It is how and why we as individuals take certain actions or make specific decisions. The actual knowledge of an individual or organization is created in part through concepts presented as knowledge that are used to explain knowledge by influential entities such as one's culture or class status. Libraries can act as a tool to reinforce and legitimize or to belittle and discredit the knowledge presented by these entities. Both cultural hegemony and discursive formations influence an individual's identity, knowledge base, and perception of reality. However, each theory holds a different place in social structures. Cultural hegemony comes from the top of a social hierarchy, whereas discursive formations evolve at the individual's level in the hierarchy. Cultural hegemony provides the "acceptable" responses to events, whereas discursive formations inform the individual's reaction.

Although the two reactions may be similar, they are configured with different levels of influence and power. The power base and structure of discursive formations manifest themselves in the discourse and discursive practices of many public institutions, to include libraries. In Foucault's (1972, p. 200) view, discourse is a means used "to reveal, in the density of verbal performances, the diversity of the possible levels of analysis, to show that in addition to methods of linguistic structuration (or interpretation), one could draw up a specific description of statements, of their formation, and of the regularities proper to discourse." How we speak and what we say is one part of discursive formations. An example of this is story time, a common service offered by public libraries. The language that is used and which stories are told can reflect the influence of local community on the practices of the library. The language and terminology used in written policies may also reflect local influences or it may be completely the product of the larger organization, but it is still an important measure of the capacity and willingness of the library to enter in to real discourse with its community. Discursive formations create and reinforce the foundation for both individual and community values and reveal how those in authority view society, individual cultures, and the people within both. As each individual is unique, each discursive formation is also unique, but still connected to its original influences. Everyone who is a part of the LIS community brings a part of his or her own experience into the community's larger experience. However, the extent to which this experience is used depends on the larger institution and the individual's ability to adapt and act within the institution and its environment.

The two theories provide possible explanations for why diversity is often absent in libraries and why it is so important to the profession to change that. From this point of view, cultural hegemony can be perceived as a tool that has helped maintain such a homogenous profession by perpetuating unconscious and unrecognized policies and attitudes. These policies and attitudes support racism and maintain discriminatory practices, thereby reducing the influence and visibility of professionals and staff members from outside of the majority culture. The potential influences of discursive formations, both individual and institutional, are frequently subsumed or minimized by the dominant cultural hegemony. For example, despite achievements brought to the LIS profession since the Civil Rights Act of 1964, many libraries and information organizations still maintain policies of subtle discrimination which "institutionalize discriminatory practices within the organization's policies and structures, even as those policies seem to emphasize equal treatment with both the formal and informal social systems of the organization" (Josey, 1999, p. 192).

In academic settings, ethnic minorities are often over-assigned, expected to be the minority representative on committees, and to be part of various diversity initiatives, all in addition to their other commitments (Alire, 2001; Allen, 1998; Niemann, 2003). This workload often results in lower productivity and fewer publications. However, they are still measured by the same standards as their white counter-parts (Allen, 1998; Niemann, 2003). Additionally when acting as the ethnic minority representative on a committee, the individual may feel if they are separate from others while being held to high expectations. Many white librarians feel racial discrimination does not exist in LIS, whereas many ethnic minorities have actually experienced racism (St. Lifer & Nelson, 1997; Josey, 1999). The term *minority* has "racist overtones and implies that a particular groups has been and continues to be the victim of collective discrimination" (Trimble, Helms, & Root, 2003, p. 243).

Academic requirements, like standardized tests, can create barriers, especially if the student is not a native English speaker (St. Lifer & Nelson, 1997). Although graduate programs do need to set academic standards for admittance, inherent racism and unfairly restrictive policies can be utilized to legitimately limit ethnic minority admissions. Those in power can point to ethnic minority students' inability to meet requirements as a legitimate way to exclude them from the profession. For those who are able to enter LIS programs, inherent racism and implicit stereotyping can create an atmosphere where failure is expected and success is seen as an aberration (Niemann, 2003). When ethnic minority groups fail to achieve as students or as professionals, it is often attributed to an inability to conform to or meet standards rather than the lack of opportunities available. These issues stem from the dominant cultural hegemony.

Libraries, if they are to reflect their communities, should do so both visually and culturally. Visual diversity can be achieved by hiring a pool of librarians that reflects the ethnic make up of the community so that when patrons enter the library, it appears to be a part of the neighborhood. However, visual diversity does very little to improve overall diversity within the organization unless the kind of cultural diversity that includes the recognition and inclusion of various discursive formations extant within the staff and the patrons is addressed.

LITERATURE REVIEW

Before directly addressing the need for diversity, it is important to first try to define it. Regardless of the discipline, diversity is a frequently discussed and often misunderstood concept. Many authors point to the changing demographics of various communities as a way to justify diversity (Josey & Abdullahi, 2002; St. Lifer & Nelson, 1997; Gomez, 2000; McCook & Lippincott, 1997a, 1997b) without clearly defining it. In addition, the concept of power is rarely included in the discussion. It is a nebulous, vague, and extensive idea, and in fact, it may not be possible to definitely define it given the fact that it is such a broad and encompassing notion. Yet, within the LIS literature, there are some common ideas of what it means.

Many in LIS refer specifically to cultural diversity, but do not explain their definition of culture. Culture, according to the *American Heritage Dictionary* (2004), is "the totality of socially transmitted behavior patterns, arts, beliefs, institutions, and all other productions of human work and thought...[and] the predominating attitudes that characterize the functioning of a group or organization." This is a very broad concept because any socially constructed group exhibits its own culture and what one visualizes as culture is dependent on his own discursive formation. The underlying intention of most of the authors of LIS literature is to use diversity as a method for acknowledging differences among people and to include a "representation of multiple (ideally all) groups within a prescribed environment, such as a university or a workplace" (Diversity Dictionary, 2000). Diversity implies that differences exist, but how is this explained or addressed within LIS?

Within the LIS profession, considerations of diversity are often limited to ethnic background and ethnic minority representation. Although various underserved groups are mentioned, there seems to be an implicit understanding in much of the LIS literature that diversity refers to the inclusion of librarians of color (Gomez, 2000; Hankins et al., 2003; Weissinger, 2003; Watkins, 1999b; Berry, 2004), especially of the "four protected minority categories recognized by the U.S. Equal Opportunity Act: African American, Hispanic/Latino, Asian American, and Native American" (Adkins & Espinal, 2004, p. 53). This implicit understanding seems to be based on the idea that, by providing a diverse library staff, the library can better serve diverse communities. The authors are not claiming that only librarians of color can effectively serve a diverse population, "but institutions that reflect their community [visually] are generally more effective, responsive, and accountable to those communities" (Watkins, 1999b, p. 64). Although there are not any empirical studies to back up this claim, it is supported by anecdotal evidence from librarians in diverse communities who notice the reaction of patrons to librarians of color (Watkins, 1999a). The underlying idea suggests that, if patrons can see themselves in the library through "the displays, collections, websites, and staff," they will feel more comfortable and have a sense of belonging (ALA, 2005a, 2005b). Creating a truly diverse organization is a complicated and difficult process. Hiring librarians of color is only one step along that path.

When looking at diversity in libraries, it is important to consider how the educational process influences the profession. Library staff is made up of professional librarians, paraprofessionals, and clerical staff. Professionals are at the top of the organizational hierarchy, paraprofessionals in the middle, and clerical staff at the bottom. In most libraries, professionals have larger salaries and more influential positions, including administration. To be considered a professional in LIS, one is generally required to have MLIS.

Although this is an important distinction in all libraries, this is particularly important in academic libraries because they may employ paraprofessionals who have Master's degrees in other disciplines. Hence, the majority of those in positions of power and influence have received an LIS education, and the LIS professionals are those who are most likely to influence and encourage the changes inherent in diversity.

As a MLIS is generally required for professional status, LIS education is the first step in preparing professionals to enter librarianship. The ethnic makeup of the LIS student body is one reflection of the potential diversity of the profession. Looking at LIS education provides an important component of the issues of diversity in librarianship.

Over the past 10 years, the ALA and other educational and professional organizations have been exploring ways to recruit and retain ethnic minorities in LIS (Patterson, 2000; Guerena & Erazo, 2000; Totten, 2000; McCook & Lippincott, 1997a, 1997b; Neely, 1999a; Buttlar & Caynon, 1992). The focus is often on educating more ethnic minorities for professional positions in libraries. As a result, the main tool of recruitment has been providing scholarships for LIS education. ALA, universities, and LIS programs have all established scholarships and grants aimed at minority students. Yet, the number of ethnic minorities enrolled in LIS programs has shown little increase (Josey & Abdullahi, 2002; Totten, 2000; Adkins & Espinal, 2004). According to the *2004 ALISE Statistical Report*, ethnic minorities make up only 11.9% of students pursuing the MLIS. This is a small increase over previous years, but it still does not reflect the larger general population. "[A] graduating class of 5000 MLIS students would need to include 1,535 students of color to equal their representation in the general population as of 2001" (Adkins & Espinal, 2004).

McCook & Lippincott's (1997b) survey of LIS deans and directors highlights the sundry and sometime chaotic plans and methods used to recruit ethnic minorities. The chaotic nature of these plans is due, in part, to a failure by the profession to clearly define ethnic or cultural diversity. Across LIS programs, there is little agreement regarding methods to encourage ethnic minorities into librarianship. The focus is primarily on students with little attention paid to the diversity of faculty and staff within LIS programs. Strategies include mentoring programs, distance education including specialized local classes, increased funding, advertising, and targeted recruitment (McCook & Lippincott, 1997a, 1997b). Although common themes and ideas exist, there are not proven or established methods of ethnic minority recruitment and retention within the LIS community. Some initiatives are proactive and work toward a larger understanding of cultural and ethnic issues. However, many are simply reacting to community pressure and institutional mandates, which only serves to illustrate the absence of a unified definition of and goal for diversity in LIS.

While recruiting students for program, diversity starts with identifying and attaching minority students into graduate programs and then graduating them with the MLIS required to make them full members of the profession. However, there has been relatively little discussion in the LIS literature regarding what motivates students to pursue the MLIS. The studies that have been done are quantitative and focus on the general student population without considerations of ethnic background (Van House, 1988; McClenney, 1989; Gordon & Nesbeitt, 1999; Ard et al., 2006) or informal research of professionals that focused on people performing specific job responsibilities (Weihs, 1999; O'Brien, 2002). Consistent trends in this research include library use, love of reading, previous library work experience, and an influential librarian as factors (Ard et al., 2006). The importance of salary and "liking" the profession are also acknowledged (Van House, 1988; McClenney, 1989). Rather than center on students, some researchers have focused on personal experiences of librarians from ethnic minority groups (Adkins, 2004; Neely, 1998; Neely & Abif, 1996; Patterson, 2000; Peterson, 1999; Vang, 2002; Watkins, 1999b), but despite the available information on the general motivations of students to pursue the MLIS, there is very little focus on the individual. The reasons that individual librarians offer as to why they entered the profession are often glossed over in favor of generalizable findings resulting from surveys and statistical data. When looking at all LIS students, the individual point of view, while interesting, may not be dissimilar to the generalizations because of the homogenous nature of LIS professionals. The majority of students fit within a specific demographic, often have had similar life experiences and backgrounds, and do not generally have concerns regarding ethnicity.

For ethnic minorities, the experience is usually different. As a result, the individual point of view is important when looking at minority students who are often automatically viewed or view themselves as "different" or an "other," individuals who do not blend in with the larger student population. These students usually do not have the same educational experiences as white students. When looking at underrepresented groups, it is the unique or unusual experience that can lend insight into entering a situation where one does not fit within the majority. Their point of view is different, and their motivations and the decisions they make are often based on factors relevant to their culture or discursive formation that has to be reconciled with or set up in opposition to the dominant culture.

How one identifies his or her ethnic heritage can influence how he or she select careers. Ethnic identity is a complex process that can "include personal identity, notions of belonging, knowledge of the reference [ethnic] group, and shared values" (Trimble et al., 2003, p. 240). Identity is not private process, but requires acknowledgement of others. The concepts of self and other are tightly woven together to the point that "one cannot be thought of without the other, that instead one passes into the other" (Ricoeur, 1992, p. 3). To identify oneself, an individual must also identify "other." The process of self-identification can also be influenced by the "sociocultural context in which one is reared, socialized and educated" (Trimble et al., 2003, p. 249). As a result, how one self-identifies and how one views "others" can have a strong impact on how that person recognizes career options.

There are several reasons that individuals choose to enter any career or profession. The choice is often based on their cultural and economic background and their parents' educational levels (Durodoye & Bodley, 1997; Brown, 2002; Garrison, 1993). How a person views his/her abilities to handle the responsibilities of a job can also either encourage or discourage the individual to pursue a profession (Bandura, 2001), as will the information that is available to them about the career path and what is expected of the individual by their family and/or community (Durodoye & Bodley, 1997; Hawley, 2001).

Ethnic minorities are at a disadvantage when considering a career in a professional field such as LIS because of limited resources, lack of information, and the scarcity of role models or mentors (Vang, 2002; Josey & Abdullahi, 2002; Durodoye & Bodley, 1997; Brown, 2002). The perception of the library as part of the dominant culture may also act as a deterrent as will the lack of prominent librarians of color. If there are few ethnic minorities within a profession or if the social standing of the profession is perceived to be outside of an individual's culture, it fails to become an option (Durodoye & Bodley, 1997; Mosley, 1999).

The career-counseling model is framed on the white, western European outlook (Siann & Knox, 1992; Brown, 2002), which is based on assumptions of individuality and desired independence from family. These impetuses may be very different from aspirations and motivations of many who are not white. Unlike the better understood sense of individualism of the white students (Siann & Knox, 1992), many ethnic minority students make choices based on family influence (Brown, 2002). What is best for the family is the primary consideration and comes before thinking about what is best for the individual. Although this simplifies both points of view, it is an important criterion to consider when examining the career choices of both white and ethnic minority students.

Most of the research results on the motivations of minorities to enter LIS have come from broad quantitative studies (Buttlar & Caynon, 1992; St. Lifer & Nelson, 1997; Moen, 1988) or personal accounts of librarians and their career histories (Neely & Abif, 1996; Vang, 2002). Most of these studies center on the individual experience within the profession after receiving the MLIS. Among the problems discussed are heightened expectations from their supervisors (Vang, 2002), lack of actual opportunity (St. Lifer & Nelson, 1997; Neely & Abif, 1996), and insufficient support systems (St. Lifer & Nelson, 1997; Knowles & Jolivet, 1991). Although these issues are not limited to ethnic minorities, they represent reoccurring themes within the literature and identified problems in literature regarding recruitment and retention. These problems can be perceived as the influence of the dominant culture and the impact of cultural hegemony as they identify barriers for ethnic minorities constructed by those in power within the profession. Discussion of the original decision to enter LIS is usually given very little attention and is quickly glossed over. Even studies that focus on the impact of mentors pay scant attention to the personal motivation and ultimate decision to enter LIS (Buttlar & Caynon, 1992; St. Lifer & Nelson, 1997), and studies that focus on the impact of cultural heritage barely touch on why individuals apply to and attend a graduate LIS program (Neely & Abif, 1996; Vang, 2002). When issues of racism and discrimination in LIS education are addressed, it is done in the context of current students, not potential applicants (Williams, 1987; Neely, 1999a, 1999b). Some research centers on the current ethnic make up of the LIS student body and recruitment strategies, but it does not address the motivations that encouraged students to enter MLIS programs (McCook & Lippincott, 1997b; Adkins & Espinal, 2004). In the few studies that do discuss why ethnic minorities have considered LIS education, the focus is on Ph.D. studies (Adkins, 2004; Gollop, 1999), and most often the quantitative nature of the research is too broad to provide any insight into personal decisions (Moen, 1988; Buttlar & Caynon, 1992; Grover, 1983).

Inherent in most of the LIS literature is the isolation of ethnic minority students in the educational process. Despite this, very few authors directly address issues of racism, tokenism, stereotyping, and discrimination. In addition, the concepts of power relationships and conflict are rarely included in the diversity discussion. Instead, much of the literature, even when dealing with these issues, is couched in broader, less charged language, as many in LIS either do not believe that racism or discrimination exist within the profession or are uncomfortable raising these issues. In contrast, many ethnic minority librarians report having experienced racism or discrimination in their library experiences (St. Lifer & Nelson, 1997). Yet racism and discrimination are not often seen or discussed as possible reasons for the lack of ethnic minorities in LIS. Rather, the focus is on problems such as the scarcity of "students who look like me" (Totten, 2000) or the need for mentors (McCook & Lippincott, 1997b; Knowles & Jolivet, 1991). Outside of the dialogue of recruitment, these subjects are raised and openly discussed (Josey, 1999; Peterson, 1999; Neely, 1998; Howland, 1998), but generally only by ethnic minority authors. While given scant attention, these may very well be two of the most important issues in the recruitment of ethnic minorities to LIS programs. Isolation from the student body, a lack of professional role models, and feeling unwelcome or discriminated against in libraries from an early age can impact and shape the decision whether or not to pursue LIS as a career.

Research Question

Increasing the presence of librarians of color may help to improve diversity within LIS. As more individuals with diverse experiences and worldviews join the profession, librarianship possibly will diversify its point of view and its presentation to society. However, recruiting ethnic minorities into LIS has proven to be difficult. This may be the result of issues with diversity or the white ethnocentric view of libraries. The first step to improve diversity within LIS is to understand the motivations and decision process of students and professionals who have already entered the profession. The central questions explored here can be divided into two parts: (1) Why do ethnic minorities choose librarianship as a profession? (2) What would motivate members of minority groups to join a profession in which they cannot see themselves?

METHODOLOGY

There are many ways for researchers to discover the motivation of individuals to choose a career path. Quantitative measures such as surveys can provide insight into this process on a large scale, but they do not show the underlying incentive or drive for certain persons to pursue a specific opportunity. Data that are collected from individuals and generalized yield results about the larger population to explain the phenomena, but unique experiences tend to get submerged in the aggregate data. Qualitative measures can illustrate the underlying reasons for an individual's actions and allow researchers to approach a study with few or no preconceived expectations of results.

Given the focus on *why* and personal histories, I conducted interviews using open-ended questions to collect the data. To formulate questions, it was necessary to identify certain possible commonalities. The interviewee controlled the flow of the conversation because he/she influenced the interview based on how he/she answered the questions. The participants' words provide an insight into their own discursive formations and the cultural hegemony of their environment and how both have influenced their decisions and motivations. In the context of this research, cultural hegemony and discursive formations are seen as influences on the participants, not theories to be proven. The participants' responses are in their own words, based on their perception of the questions and their experience, which are influenced by cultural hegemony and discursive formations. Both concepts help identify and explain the basic social processes that are used to create reality for the students.

By engaging in a conversation with an individual or group, the researcher worked with the participants to develop answers based on their own understanding of the questions asked using a negotiation between the interviewer and interviewee. Follow-up questions were used to clarify answers and to verify that researcher's understandings reflected the jist of the participants' responses. These interviews provided an opportunity for open discussion where the researcher and the participant jointly "constructed meanings" (Rossman & Rallis, 1998, p. 124). The discussions proved "essential for the understanding of how participants view their world" (Rossman & Rallis, 1998, p. 124), helping the researcher understand *why* or *how* these individuals made the decisions to enter the LIS field and followed through on those decisions.

In this research, two theories, phenomenology and grounded theory, were used to allow themes and theories to emerge and to develop an understanding of the concept being examined. The first theory, phenomenology is "the investigation of the way that things – objects, images, ideas, emotions – appear or are present in our consciousness" (Horrocks, 2001, p. 64). It is a theory that looks at how we, as individuals, experience phenomena in the world around us, without "reference to the status of the object outside our consciousness" (Horrocks, 2001, p. 64). In other words, what is important is the individual's perception of events, emotions, ideas, and images, not the actual "reality" of those items. The goal is not explanation, but to understand the immediate experience of the individual. One of the objectives of the theory is to "perceive phenomena with as few barriers as possible between the thing and the perceiver" (Budd, 2001, p. 249). While interviewing still introduces some barriers, including the interpretation of the answers, it provides an opportunity for participants to describe their perceptions in their own words.

Grounded theory was originally developed as a way to combine "a set of ideas and hypotheses in an integrated theory that accounts for behaviour in any substantive area" (Lowe, 1996, p. 1). In other words, it allows a researcher to examine phenomena or experiences without preconceived answers or expectations. Rather than approach research with the purpose of fitting results to a theory, the researcher is able to build the theory based on the results. It is "theory as a process" (Glaser & Strauss, 1967, p. 9), using induction rather than deduction. The inductive process allows a researcher to go from a broad view to a narrow point without having to define the exact point before collecting data. There are two purposes to grounded theory; "[f]irst to discover which patterns of behaviour exist, and second how these processes of socialization are sustained" (Lowe, 1996, p. 2). This theory allows the researcher to collect the data without expectations of fitting that data into a certain pattern, allowing the data to direct the research through emerging categories and ideas.

The method and the theories permitted themes to emerge. Although the participants were asked open-ended questions, it is important to maintain a level of consistency among the data. The idea was to possibly find common threads among the participants' answers, rather than to identify many completely unique stories. Hence, the interviews were semi-structured. For purposes of consistency in the data, all participants were asked the following questions.

- How did you get interested in library science? Why did you decide to pursue the MLIS?
- What role has the library played in your life? How were you introduced to the library?
- Were you mentored at any point in your education or career? By whom?
- How important was education in your family?
- How does your family view your decision to enter LIS? What was your family's socio-economic background?

- How do you view diversity?
- What do you plan to do once you graduate? Why?

The intent of the questions was both to provide some structure to the interviews and to uncover the influence of discursive formations and cultural hegemony on the motivations to pursue LIS as a career. Questions focused on family and cultural background generally dealt with the influence of discursive formations. Discussions of education and socio-economic background often brought up issues related to cultural hegemony. Comments about the library, career plans, and diversity reflected both elements. Combined these three sets of questions provided insight into what influenced the participants' decision to enter LIS.

In this research, the "particular concern is with *lived experience*" (Silverman, 2001, p. 90). The idea is that the participants described their perception of reality. Both the participant and the interviewer participated in the process, working together to construct meaning and to find a mutual understanding of the concepts. In the interviews, I listened for terms or phrases that seemed unique to the student and followed up with questions. Rather than ask for clarification, I requested a broader explanation or asked additional questions related to the topic. Although the information provided was not always directly connected to the research, it did create some insight into the participant and his or her thought process, which shed light on the individual's discursive formation. The process also identified their understanding and acceptance of cultural hegemony.

Participants

To learn about the initial influences and motivations that influenced this decision making, I interviewed current LIS students rather than established library professionals. The participants were ethnic minority students currently enrolled in LIS programs in the United States. As of 2005, there are LIS programs in 32 states, ranging from Massachusetts to California, and Puerto Rico (ALA, 2004). Owing to the vast geographical area and travel limitations, I decided to interview students in six schools located in different geographical regions and in diverse communities: Queens College (NY), Pratt Institute (NY), San Jose State University (CA), the University of Arizona, Wayne State University (MI), and the University of South Florida. Enrollment of the four federally protected ethnic groups (African Americans, Asian Americans, Hispanic/Latinos, and Native Americans) is well represented in each of these programs. The Knowledge River program aimed at recruiting Hispanic/Latino and Native American students is located at the University of Arizona. These ethnic groups make up 16.75% of its student population. San Jose State University's student body includes over 20% ethnic minority students, and the ethnic minority population at both Queens College and the University of South Florida are over 14% of the total student population. Wayne State University has an African-American student population that is almost twice the national average for LIS programs (8.88%) and is in the inaugural year of an Institute of Museum and Library Services (IMLS) scholarship program aimed at attracting ethnic minorities to work with digital libraries (ALISE, 2004). Pratt Institute's student body is made up of 22% ethnic minorities (ALISE, 2004).

The participants were recruited through student listservs from their LIS programs or through faculty or from both. There was one exception where a faculty member arranged all of the meetings with the students she identified. The faculty member is an ethnic minority and the advisor of many ethnic minority students, as well as her institution's contact person for ALA's Spectrum Initiative. She personally asked students to participate, and, although this resulted in less work for the researcher, it further limited and potentially biased the participant pool as students who did not have direct contact with this person did not have the opportunity to participate. Additionally, the students who did take part in the research may not have actually volunteered, but rather might have felt an obligation to participate after being asked by this individual.

There were a total of 33 participants, all of whom were current students in an ALA-accredited LIS program. They came from various backgrounds and locations. There were 6 males[1] and 27 females ranging in age from the early twenties to the mid-fifties. The ethnic breakdown was 8 Hispanic/Latino students [Alanna, Jamie (M), Jill, Luisa, Lydia, Marta, Rita, and Serena[2]], 13 African-American students [Amanda, Karen, Kelly, Lynn, Martha, Mary, Mike (M), Rick (M), Ruth, Sadie, Sally, Sondra, and Tami], 9 Asian-American students [Dean (M), Iris, Josephine, Ken (M), Maggie, Molly, Olga, and Seta], and 3 Native American students [Derek (M), Nathan (M), and Steve (M)].[3]

Although there was no intent to develop a representative or stratified sample, the percentages of Asian American and African American was proportionate to their representation among ethnic minority LIS students. Asian Americans comprised 27% of the participants, and 26% of all ethnic minority students (ALISE, 2005). African-American students make up 39%

of the research participants, and 37% of the ethnic minority LIS population (ALISE, 2005). However, Hispanic/Latino participants had a smaller presence in this research, representing 24%, of those interviewed even though they make up 33% of the minority students in studying in LIS programs (ALISE, 2005). Native American representation was the opposite, with 9% of the participants identifying with this ethnic background though only 4% of the total ethnic minority student base comes from a Native American background (ALISE, 2005).

Over half of students felt they were from a middle-class family or felt that middle class status had been reached at some point during their childhood. Participants who stated that they came from lower socioeconomic families still felt they had advantages. The concept of "not wanting" was mentioned by more than one student. Their families may not have had extensive financial resources, but these students felt they had not been disadvantaged or that their needs had not been neglected. There were three distinct exceptions – two students came out of the foster care system (Sadie and Ruth) and a third was the child of migrant workers (Steve).

Setting

The interviews were conducted in a face-to-face setting at the student's location, either at the site of the LIS program or at another location of the student's choosing. This allowed a certain comfort level for each student because he or she was in a familiar setting. All the interviews took place between October 2005 and January 2006. As noted earlier, the interview questions were semi-structured and open-ended (Cresswell, 2003; Bogdan & Bilken, 2003; Anderson & Jack, 1991) starting with an inquiry into each student's initial interest in LIS and the decision to apply to an LIS program. Follow-up probes were based on the responses provided by the participant. As already noted, similar issues were addressed with all the participants to maintain a level of consistency and allow for comparisons across the interviews.

Analysis

The interviews were all recorded for transcription and analysis at a later time. Recording the interviews provided detailed resources of the participants' conduct for analysis through "listening to the tape[s] and the investigation of the subsequent transcript[s]" (Wetherell, Taylor, & Yates, 2001, p. 51). When reviewing the interviews, attention was paid to both *what* was said and *how* it was said (Silverman, 2001). The purpose of using interviewing as a research method is to allow the participants to use their own words to describe their experience, and, in this case, the method allowed "interviewer and interviewee [to] rely on their conversational skills and common-sense knowledge of social structures in order to produce locally 'adequate' utterances" (Silverman, 2001, p. 101). This, in turn, ties back to their individual discursive formations. Whether or not the information presented was true or false was irrelevant as the focus was on what was said, how it was said, and what it meant as it related to the participants' perception of their experience (Wetherell, et al., 2001).

Once the interviews were transcribed, the data were coded. This process involved several steps. First, each interview was read twice before highlighting any interesting passages or comments. I consulted my observations during the initial readings of the interviews to reacquaint myself with the participants (Bogdan & Biklen, 2003; Rossman & Rallis, 1998). After reading through the transcripts, I highlighted or marked any passages that caught my attention (Rossman & Rallis, 1998), repeating this process three times, each after a short break of one to two days from the data. Going through the data, I looked for "instances of a specific phenomena...considered to be worthy of detailed analysis to discover how its features were interactionally produced by the participants" (Wetherell et al., 2001, p. 73). A list of topics or themes in the data was identified as a result, and then the interviews were reread to see how well the topics and themes fit within the data (Cresswell, 2003). As a result, the list of themes was revised based on my interpretation of the data and the 11 themes that emerged were used as coding categories. These were

- Libraries
- Librarians
- Library Work Experience
- LIS Graduate Program
- Career Plans and Goals
- Education and Family
- Support
- Mentors
- Ethnicity and Community
- Acculturation
- Views of Diversity

Within the 11 coding categories, there are two with sub-topics within the groupings: *Libraries* and *Ethnicity and Community*. *Libraries* includes information on Library Use, Introduction to the Library, and Libraries as a Place. Each sub-topic is tied with comments about the library as an institution and how it affected the participants' decisions. *Ethnicity and Community* was initially two separate coding categories (*Ethnic Identity* and *Role of the Community*), but after further review, the two concepts were found to be tightly connected in most of the participants' discussion. Hence, Ethnic Identity and the Role of the Community were combined into one coding category, *Ethnicity and Community*, with sub-topics, Ethnic Identity and Community.

Once the coding categories were identified, I went back through the interviews and assigned the highlighted passages to a category. Using MS Word, I cut and pasted the quotes into lists for each coding category. If a particular quote seemed to fit more than one category, I placed it in multiple lists for further review. Once the lists were completed, I reviewed the coding categories as I had reviewed the interviews, making changes and revising assignments of the quotes where needed. I reviewed the lists multiple times, taking short breaks each time to step away from the data and refresh my point of view.

FINDINGS

The participants in the study all had their individual reasons for pursuing the MLIS, but several distinct themes did emerge from the data. When asked why they had decided to enter an LIS program, approximately one-third of the students answered with direct answers regarding their graduate work. The others immediately tied the decision back to their library use throughout their lives. Libraries and their uses were central to almost all of the students' responses. Librarians, while still influential, were not mentioned as often as the library itself. More than three quarters of the students were entering LIS as a second career, which is similar to the general LIS student body. Ethnic identity and ties to community were important to the majority of students, and many had definite plans for their career in LIS. The importance of education to themselves and to family, as well as support for their goals, was frequently mentioned in the interviews. The students also discussed the diversity of their primary education and childhood neighborhoods, which often involved functioning in Caucasian communities. All of these factors influenced their decisions to pursue the MLIS.

When asked why they decided to enter an LIS program, most of the students immediately tied their decision to their love of libraries. At the same time, almost all the participants followed this comment with the observation that they considered librarianship only after their initial career path disappointed them. It usually took someone pointing out that librarianship was a possible career before they even considered it. Iris spent seven years as a lawyer, but never quite felt satisfied by her work. When she started law school, she took a battery of tests to see what career would be most appropriate.

> They gave me a series of tests, fill in the bubble tests and one of those things spat out, you should look into library science, you know…I like research, I'm very sort of intellectual that way. So that, I mean that, that kind of planted the idea initially.

Although it took several years before she decided to leave the legal profession, Iris mentioned that every time she met with a law librarian, she would think about the test results. It was not an immediate response, but Iris' decision was based on the results of the aptitude tests. As she put it, "until computer told me, I had never thought of it as a career for myself."

Several of the students mentioned an individual who encouraged them to look at pursuing a MLIS degree. Karen, Nancy, Olga, and Seta all commented on friends or co-workers who told them they should be librarians because of their organizational abilities and people skills.

> [I] was talking with a friend who told me, who has told me frequently over the years, you know you should be a teacher, and he's not the only person I have encountered in life who has mentioned about teaching, but he has also mentioned librarianship… I've heard that kind of descriptor for me for a long time and always wondered why do people who don't know me, could come up with this particular assessment, just based on either non-verbal communication or me saying or you know, very, very brief conversations and it comes up, are you a teacher, are you librarian, do you work in that field of knowledge and sharing information.

Dean, Jill, Luisa, Marta, Martha, Rita, and Tami all mentioned a supervisor who told them about library school and explained why they should pursue the degree. Amanda, Kelly, Maggie, Ruth, Sadie, and Sondra did research in a library to try to figure out a suitable career.

Most of the participants came to the decision gradually, but four of the students went straight from their undergraduate work into an LIS program. These students discussed the comfort of the library and how they saw it as part of their future. Alanna mentioned wanting to be a librarian since the age of 7. As she explained, she realized that what she "wanted to do in life was to be immersed in books, to be immersed in this wealth of knowledge, wealth of information surrounding me."

Libraries

When asked why they were interested in library science, almost all the students responded with some comments about their love of and experiences in libraries. Lynn summed it up when she stated that "[m]y experience in libraries was absolutely seminal to who I became, and it was later that I realized, hey, I can do that." The participants often said that the role of the library in society was one of the motivators for their pursuit of the MLIS. "I think [libraries are] a part of everyone's life. Some people are just more aware of it than others, and people like myself, chose to become librarians and continue the work" (Molly).

All the students made some kind of connection between libraries and their decision to pursue an MLIS. The remarks mainly focused on library use, how they were introduced to the library, and the library as a place.

Library Use

The students are all library users, but they came to the library at different times in their lives. For some, the library was a haven in childhood, whereas other discovered the joys of learning and the connection to the library in high school or college. Yet, once the students found the library, it became a central part of their lives. Amanda discussed how becoming a librarian seemed to just be the next step.

> I was a total library geek. I lived in the library... I spent my whole life hanging out in libraries, so it seems natural to move in that direction.

The participants who were library users from an early age tended to speak of the library in exalted terms, as if referring to a place of worship. Mike described this feeling when he commented "I see the library as a refuge in the world, and coming from a small town, that's where I learned about the world. I could go to books and read and that type of thing." Almost all the participants spoke of the accessibility of information and the ability to gain knowledge as key components of what the library represented to them. Mary described the library as a place where the "information is very organized and that I could step in to an aisle and pick up a book and learn about something." She expounded on this again when she described the connection between reading and learning.

I grew up and realized that there was a direct relationship between my interest in reading and my comprehension level at school. And because I knew that, it made me feel good, that kept me going back to the library… it was like a comforting place for me because it was a place where I was successful, so I guess I always go back.

The library was also referred to as a place of privilege, a right to be earned. It was a place that offered learning and comfort. Karen spoke about the privilege attached to the library:

The way it was presented to us, it was a treat and so it was like 'ooh, you get to go to the library…And, I remember my older sister taking me to the bookmobile to get my first library card. I would have had to accomplish a couple of thing before I could do that…this was like a big deal.

The library was also a day-care resource for many families. Several participants discussed the library as their unofficial after-school program, where they waited for their parents to finish work. Alanna, Jamie, Lydia, and Lynn all mentioned the library as a replacement for daycare or the safe locale where they would wait for their parents to finish work.

So I would go there and do my homework, look at the fish tanks…you know, they had the story time…I mean, it was kind of more or less my babysitter for the 3 or 4 hours I had after school. (Lydia)

The library was a place where the participants could learn and enjoy themselves, and it was perceived as a safe place for kids to hang out until parents were done with work.

Introduction to the Library
More than half of the students were introduced to the library by a parent or a teacher. Several mentioned having classes in the library to learn how to conduct searches properly and to learn the classification system. Derek, Karen, Lynn, and Sondra all talked about classes in the library when they were in elementary school.

When I was younger, they didn't have that much in terms of programming, but when I was younger we had library as a class in elementary school… It was a big deal to be able to go to, uh, outside, to a public library and go in and um, you know, pull your own, find your own information. (Sondra)

Those who were introduced by their parents spoke of family trips for reading, often as a regular habit. They discussed special days spent with family going to the library, either as just a library trip or as part of a larger day.

> We used the library a lot, even as um, young children, we always went to the library...we
> didn't have a lot of money, but we always went to the library...it was something we did,
> our whole family. (Serena)

Two of the participants located the library by themselves. Sally and Sadie were not encouraged to go to the library as children for different reasons. Sally's parents felt her love of reading interfered with their family. Sadie, on the contrary, did not have a stable family in her life and mainly pushed herself in school. It was not until her undergraduate studies that she discovered the library.

> I started going to the library when I started in undergrad and I was like, wow, there are
> all these books and when I would come home, that's when I would start going to the
> library a lot. [Before college] I just didn't realize what the library was.

As with the other students, as soon as they did discover the library, it became an important part of their lives.

Library as Place

When discussing the library, the majority of the students referred to characteristics of the environment or the atmosphere of the place. Several of the students spoke of the library being a safe place, a comfortable spot, somewhere to learn and to enjoy. For some it was a refuge or a sanctuary. Lynn and Steve mentioned how the library protected them, provided a comfortable space to grow and learn. Lynn's public library acted a safe haven from the rough neighborhood she lived in and gave her the tools to learn as she was protected.

> I would run to the library every day after school to beat the junior high school kids.
> I was scared...I would run from the bus stop, knowing when I hit the library doors,
> I was okay, I would be safe until [my parents] took me home.

Steve, on the contrary, was not as concerned with physical safety as he was with surviving the system. As a troubled youth, he dealt with discipline and academic problems, but the library was

> a place that I could be myself in. It was just me and the assistant librarian and couple of
> other aids. We had a good time. You know, we got to talk, we got to share a lot. I was in
> there with a few other 'at-risk' students, so I knew that other kids had problems too.
> It wasn't just me, you know. So I realized, that part of the reason that we graduated
> was this.

The atmosphere of the library was a common comment among the participants. It was a welcoming and comforting place to many students. For some students, however, it was more than just the physical trappings of the library; it was a more nebulous concept. Mary recognized the role of feelings of belonging in creating a comfortable environment.

It's really important that people feel welcome and warm about their local library or whatever it is, a sense of ownership...But that whole customer service and actually feeling as if you *know* your librarian as opposed to just a person behind a desk or just a person standing behind a counter.

Librarians

The role of librarians in the library experience was not as profound, but still influential. At least a third of the participants could not think of a particular librarian despite having spent large amounts of time in the library. However, no one spoke negatively about librarians in general. It seemed as if the students considered librarians as part of the scenery, an important contribution to the overall organization, helpful when needed, but they did not play a central role in their overall decision to become a librarian.

I loved the environment and I loved literature and I loved books, but I never really saw it as a career or even looked up to librarians. They were very helpful people, but you know, they weren't really what I wanted to be. (Jamie)

Despite this lack of direct recognition, some students did realize that the librarians played an integral role in their love of the library. Although she could not remember any librarian before high school, Jill appreciated that they were still central to her love of the library.

I would really say that, I really feel like every librarian I've come in contact with has been a really great person, really excited to help me. I feel that if I had not had such good experience in the library when I was little, it wouldn't be the same, I wouldn't have wanted to volunteer at the library in the first place.

Just over a third of the students could point to a specific librarian who was influential. The role of these individuals varied; some acted as a mentor, whereas others were the student's supervisor or a family member. Luisa, Alanna, Karen, Sadie, and Tami all spoke about their school librarians as people who introduced them to new learning experiences and awaking an enthusiasm for knowledge.

As a teacher, you kind of know what your students are capable of doing, so, um [the librarian] guided me towards some material probably I never would have experienced without her...that just kind of just opened up a whole slew of things for me. (Karen)

Steve also spoke fondly of his high school librarian, but in his case, it was not suggested reading or learning that was important. It was the encouragement and attention provided that made the difference in his life. The librarian encouraged Steve to reach beyond his limitations and to strive for more than what others expected of him.

> It wasn't so much [the librarian] showed me the ins and outs of librarianship. I just think he, he kind of sensed that I came from a troubled family and that the fact that I was in alternative education and maybe he felt like, you know, that I was just getting put through the system... He just wanted me to get through...he just seemed to be interested in me in a certain sense, you know, 'how are things going?'...You know, he just kept telling me 'don't give up on yourself, don't sell yourself short.'...he was one of the few people who reached out to me in high school in some sort of way, human sort of way.

The ethnicity of librarians, while not perceived as influential or important by the majority of the students, was noted by several participants. Most of the librarians the students had worked with, either as a patron or in a job, were white. Maggie was surprised when she realized all the librarians she had interacted with were white. Marta reflected that she did not "remember any Latinas behind the desk. There were no role models." A few could point to ethnic librarians, but often not until they were in college, generally at a traditionally black institution or an ethnic studies library, or as a co-worker or supervisor. Only two mentioned interacting with an ethnic librarian in their K-12 years.

Three students noticed the role of the Young Adult (YA) and Children's librarian, especially in terms of community outreach. Alanna discussed how the Children's librarian at her childhood library was partially responsible for her decision to pursue a career in librarianship. Marta commented on observing a YA librarian speaking with teens and wondered why she never had this interaction as it may have helped to pursue a career in LIS earlier. Sadie noted that it was the YA librarian at her branch who interacted with the public. She was a popular figure because she knew how to relate to the community.

> The YA librarian in our library is young, African American, hip to everything. She knows the music and the dances and everything, um, tons of children come in, teens come in...she knows how to talk to them...I'm always monitoring librarians because I'm big into service, very big into service.

Library Work Experience

Fifteen of the thirty-three participants had previous library work experience. The actual level of experience varied, ranging from working as a student shelver to volunteering at a local library, to working in their college library, to holding a professional positions without the degree. When asked why they were pursuing the MLIS, two students immediately referred to their work experience. Molly discussed how she felt comfortable and that she "like[d] the environment and...could picture [herself] working in that environment, that atmosphere for the rest of her life." Jamie pointed out that despite spending his youth in libraries,

> the initial interest came from working at the library. I believe I was an associate librarian 2 at a public library...my administrators and supervisors, and from attending conferences, and interacting with other colleagues, encouraged me to attend library school.

Of those working in libraries, the idea of improving their pay and benefits was also important. Serena also talked about working as a school librarian without the benefits of having the MLIS. She would read job ads and realize that she was already doing the work without the pay.

> I worked in libraries for many, many years, like since high school and...I belong to...a [library professionals'] listserv, and...from reading the entries of other people, I would think, oh, I'm already doing that now, but of course, I don't have the pay or benefits, I should get the degree.

Three students mentioned volunteer work in libraries. Jill and Luisa volunteered before deciding to apply to an LIS program, and Lynn began volunteering after beginning her MLIS studies. Jill did her high school community service requirement at her local public library. Luisa volunteered at several libraries in her city while she was trying to decide what to do after leaving journalism. After speaking with a business librarian at a real estate firm, she learned the depth of the profession and began volunteering at a local museum library. Central to her decision, however, was the idea that she was doing commendable work.

> Then I went into the [museum] and I started volunteering in their library and I was working with their special collections and I really like it, I liked it a lot and I wasn't getting it paid. I was working from 10 to 5 everyday and...I liked it because it was really commendable...I didn't choose it because of my background...I wanted something that would make me happy when my alarm clock went off in the morning.

Other students mentioned learning about how libraries worked and the central role of information in libraries as reasons why they wanted to enter LIS as a career. While working for a communications company, Nathan was contracted out to his local library, and he was quickly "intrigued at how everything worked out there, just the amount of information around." Rick quickly recognized how his art background would integrate with digital archiving and preservation after working with the public library on a weeding and preservation project.

LIS Graduate Program

I also asked about how each participant selected his or her LIS program. While scholarships were mentioned, more often than not, the decision was based on location, availability of classes, flexibility of schedule, and actual cost of the program, the same factors that influence the majority of LIS students (McCook & Moen, 1992). However, several of the participants who pointed to these factors as the reason for selecting a particular program quickly followed up with a comment about the good reputation of the LIS program they chose.

> When I looked into the other programs, I had heard about [this LIS program], if you come here, they will make you work until you sweat blood. I have heard this from people who got their master's, their MLIS 10 to 20 years ago. The reputation was the same, it hasn't changed...I've actually learned more through doing all those things... (Seta)

Only a few students mentioned recruitment by the LIS program. The overtures from the LIS program were mostly connected to diversity-based scholarship and fellowship programs. These opportunities were central to some of the students' final decision. Mike mentioned how he had always wanted to be a librarian, but "when [he] came out of high school...there weren't a lot of scholarships, monies for that type, for college." He spent 20 years in computers before returning for his MLIS. Derek had just completed his first master's when the possibility for studying toward an MLIS came up. He had not really considered looking at librarianship, but decided to study LIS once he realized that his scholarship "would pay for a whole year's tuition. And I love the school," so it seemed like too good of an opportunity to pass up. Jamie, Nathan, and Steve all mentioned pursuing the degree based on the ability to get funding.

The lack of diversity within LIS programs was noted by a few students. Amanda mentioned that she was one of a few ethnic minorities in her cohort. Lynn stated that she was the only ethnic minority in most of her classes. Marta and Maggie commented on the scarcity of other ethnic minorities in their class. Marta remarked on how she knew a few other ethnic minority students from shared classes. Once they met, Marta and the other students began to look for each other in other courses. Maggie was surprised by the lack of diversity in LIS. Until she started her LIS program,

Maggie was unaware of the diversity issues in librarianship. She explained it in the larger context of the profession.

> I think it's important to get a different kind of, even on a superficial level, more of a librarian population that's more reflective of the general population. And I really didn't see it as an issue before I started library school actually. It never occurred to me that all the librarians...I've interacted with are all white women. The ones that are around me, that I've spoken with or gotten ideas from before library school, they were all white women. It was interesting when I figured that out, I'd look around in class.

Career Plans and Goals

The students had various career goals for jobs after they completed their MLIS degrees to include working in public, academic, school, or special libraries. In my experience in LIS education, this is similar to the career aspirations of the general student population. However, many students mentioned wanting to work within their own communities or communities that reflected their own ethnic heritage, often to act as role models or to just be able to serve their community to the best of their abilities. Some of this came from a recognition that they themselves had not had this resource, some from a desire to give back and to improve their own communities.

> When I left the corporate world, my personal mission was to take, take whatever skills or talents I had and apply them to someone else, apply to another arena that I though could use it more than the corporate world...it was time for me to do something that was more personally and professionally, um, in line with what I think life should be like...I mean it should be more pleasing for me, work should be fun. It can be challenging, it can drive you crazy, but at the end of the day, did you have a good time, did you learn something, did you take care of someone, did they learn something from you? (Karen)

Over two-thirds of the participants wanted to work with patrons, mostly as public or school librarians, because they enjoyed the interaction with people and felt they could have a stronger impact in a public role. They also discussed the atmosphere of public and school libraries as more enjoyable and relaxed, as places that patrons wanted to come. Alanna explained her attachment to public libraries based on her own experience.

> [Public libraries] that's the experience I've always had. In a crazy way, I've always been intimidated by the academic libraries because I grew up in the public libraries where...there is no librarian with the finger over the mouth saying 'shush', I mean, there's talking and running and just being kind of carefree in the public library whereas in the academic library it's more traditional rigid feel of the library, you know, silence, study, meditation

The reasons for focusing on the public library extended beyond atmosphere and comfort. Four students specifically referred to the library as a social or public institution. Their comments reflected a vision of the library as part of the larger community. When Jamie worked in outreach in the library, he was focused on reaching the community because he perceived the library as a part of the community. This did not come from his job, but rather because he "grew up in libraries...[he] practically lived in libraries when he was a kid...[so he] was aware of the library as a public institution.". Maggie and Jill also recognized public libraries as social institutions and commented on how libraries serve their communities.

> You don't need money to come in [to the library], it provides information to anybody regardless of fees, the concept is universal access to information...libraries are all about sharing... (Maggie)

Sondra took the concept of the public library as a social institution a step farther. The library is not only a resource for all; it is also a place where social wrongs can be addressed.

> Those are the things that we have to fight for...we need to create programming, we have to meet them...to really find people where they are, we have to empower, I know that my empowerment came from that knowledge I gained, so we need to try to empower that same way. And not hiding that knowledge...that's a really big part of being diverse. Being able...to make all types of information accessible to all types of people.

Not everyone wanted a career working with the general public. There were also participants who were focused on careers in academic or special libraries. Marta had a scholarship that required her to work in an academic library for at least two years after graduation. Molly and Ken expressed the desire to work in an academic library because of the connection to education and learning. Tami actually wanted to be in a library away from the general public after working several years in an urban public library. She wanted to work in a business or special library:

> Because the public's not nice, in general. It's hard working with the public. It's really hard. I see, on a daily basis, the librarians working with different people, all kind of people. You don't have a real set kind of clientele that comes in and...I'm not interested.

Although she loved research and helping people with challenging reference questions, Tami did not like dealing with the general public.

Education and Family

Education was important to all the participants. There were seven students with multiple degrees, including one Ph.D., two Juris Doctorates (JD), and five master's degrees. In addition to her Ph.D. in education, Lynn held a Master's degree in psychology. Olga completed a Master's of Science in chemistry before switching to LIS. Lydia and Derek completed their first Masters degrees in education and Ken's was in philosophy. Iris and Amanda both completed the JD and worked in the legal profession for several years. Although it was clear that the students were ambitious in their educational goals, at least three quarters of the students pointed to their families as the source of their educational drive, the fact that education was stressed as important in the home motivated them, even if most of the members of their families did not have much education past high school.

About half of the students are the first member of their immediate or extended family to receive a bachelor's degree and approximately two-thirds are the first to pursue graduate education. Despite being from a rather large extended family, Derek was the first one in the family to earn a college degree.

> Among my family that lives on the Reservation, yes I was the first one to go. And, of all the grandchildren, I was the first one to earn a bachelor's degree...I was the first one from the Reservation. And I was the first one to actually earn a master's degree...in my family, there are only, from my parent's generation, my grandparent's generation and my generation, there are only 3 of us who hold any kind of degree, my cousin in [another state], myself and my sister.

Mary focused on her mother's encouragement and discipline regarding education. Mary's mother had high expectations, and Mary partially credited her own drive to her mother's influence.

> My mother, she's always been a worker and she has very strong ethics. So, although she wasn't sitting down at the table saying 'let me help you with this math problem' she did make sure that the TV was off and that we were studying. So, um, she did go to college. She didn't finish college. So it was very important to her that all of us, including myself, got up to college level and graduated.

Some students discussed how their families sacrificed for their education. Their families would make financial sacrifices such as no family vacations to ensure a good education for their children. This was not tied to a specific ethnic group. Jill's father told her the only thing they could guarantee was that she would get a good education.

He and my mother would tell us, "we're not wealthy so the only thing we can give you is to ensure that you have a good education so that you can support yourself through life...Both of my parents, actually, you know, they felt that education was extremely important...when I was in 4th grade I remember thinking, I have to plan so I can get into a really good high school and a really good college." Nathan's mother sent him to a private school because "[i]t was what my father wanted. He never got to graduate from college...[h]is whole purpose was for me to go to college and to get a degree." Serena's family had very little, forgoing vacations and other luxuries so that she and her siblings were able to attend Roman Catholic school.

> My parents just really believed...that's the way to succeed, you go to a catholic school and then you go to college and then you'll have a chance at a better job.

Derek discussed how his family spent precious time and money to get him to and from his summer programs. The participants did not see a connection between the efforts for a better education and their ethnic culture. In fact, Jill and Serena both commented that they perceived their parents' encouragement as unusual in the Hispanic/Latino culture.

In a few cases, the family support for education extended only toward certain professions, not including librarianship. Kelly always felt pressure from her family to excel academically and to enter a "prestigious career" with a high salary. This pressure was most pronounced among the Asian-American students. Iris, Dean, Josephine, Ken, Nancy, Molly, Olga, and Seta all talked about their family's expectations for them to attend college. A few were more specific about the degree expectations. Olga's father continues to ask her when she plans to return to her chemistry degree. Seta knew her family wanted her to pursue a business degree and the internal struggle over what she wanted to do and what her family wanted. Dean discussed the educational expectations he perceived in his family and in the wider Asian communities:

> I'd say education was stressed. Education was stressed, but a certain type of education...a certain type of profession...[n]ot professions that deal with arts & sciences or the humanities, but more so, technical, technical profession like dealing with computers, medicine, um, engineering... I think, there is that connotation when you say 'my son is an engineer' or 'my son is a doctor' it's like, you know, it's like all the other, whichever group you want to chose, be it Korean, Asian Indian, Japanese, Chinese.

Despite this pressure, these students expressed a belief that their families, while a bit reserved or initially disappointed, are now pleased with their choice to pursue the MLIS.

Although family was central to most of the students' comments about education, a few of the participants' educational drive was more internal, with little encouragement from parents or other authority figures. Some of the participants saw education as a way to move forward in life, as their ticket to a better life. Others were simply driven individuals. Luisa commented that she did not feel that education was stressed in her culture. Instead, it was her family "taught me to be very independent…to motivate myself," which she did through her bachelor's degree and career in journalism. Steve's father did not encourage education in any way, including belittling his status as a graduate student. However, both Luisa and Steve pointed to siblings that encouraged them in their educational endeavors.

Two students, Ruth and Sadie, grew up in the foster care system. Both recognized how education was the way to improve their lives from an early age. However, neither one could remember how they came about this knowledge. Ruth discussed the fact that in every school she attended, it was assumed that the students would go to college, so she simply perceived college as the next step out of high school. Sadie realized that she only had herself to depend on and she had to secure her future.

> I started working to take care of myself at 14. When you start learning about finances and about how important it is to do right by your money and stuff like that, I think automatically education becomes kind of a part of that, you know that, how do I get more money, that was my whole thing, how do I get more money…I had to have an education. I was not in any, nobody was giving me anything, you…had to go to work and make the dollars.

However, despite their lack of biological family, both of these participants mentioned how they built support structures around themselves. Ruth discussed how she and her "immediate friends…always pushed each other…It was just my friends, we pushed each other." Sadie also commented on her community of friends, but also remarked on how she looked to her culture and its history to stand in place of her actual family. As she did not have a family history to pass on to her children, Sadie "adopted the history of my ancestors" to fill that void and provide her with a sense of belonging.

Support

Support was another concept mentioned by the majority of participants. Over half of the participants remarked on family or friends who provided encouragement during their education. Family is important to most of the students. About half of the students spoke of unconditional support and encouragement from family. A little more than a third mentioned a lack of understanding of their choice, but they still received some level of support.

Several of the students are working mothers. In these cases, all the participants mentioned being encouraged by their husbands and also by their children, if the children were old enough to understand. Support was not always voiced or even overt. Instead, the students mentioned little things that their families did to allow them to attend classes. Serena compared her experience with a friend's:

> One of my friends that I was working with at the school, she doesn't have her [Associates of Arts] and she was going back to school to get it now...[h]er husband doesn't support it all, he just thinks it's a waste of time and a waste of money...my family, just talking to my siblings, but especially my husband being supportive and my kids. Because when you go back to school and you have a family, things really do suffer, you're not there for dinner, you don't clean the house (laughs). Things really do suffer. And I can't say they pitch in and help because they really don't, but at least they don't complain.

Lynn remarked on her husband's support in taking care of her two children when she has to study or attend classes on the weekend. Rather than expecting her to handle everything, Sadie and her husband coordinate their schedules to ensure that the family is taken care of and both of them can manage their schoolwork.

Two students credited their husbands for pointing them toward their LIS studies. Seta commented on how her husband helped her to realize that she could choose her career rather than just following family expectations. Marta's husband reminded her of how much she loved working in libraries and encouraged her to apply to her LIS program.

> I would complain about [my job] and [my husband] would wrack his brain and was like, you love research...he would come see me in the library [when we were both at college] and he was like, you used loved that job, you thought it was great, so I thought okay I'll go back.

Not all the discussion of family was about positive encouragement. Alanna, Dean, Iris, Maggie, Molly, Nancy, and Olga all remarked on how they had to explain or "sell" their decision to family members. Iris mentioned how her parents were supportive of her decision to leave the legal profession, but they did not understand why she needed to go back to school.

> [T]hey're very supportive, but their attitude is that you're obviously qualified to do whatever you want, so why do you feel you have to [go back to school]...but once I explained to them that the library, that the library degree is a real thing and there are

> jobs that require it for what I want to do...once I explained that, they were very
> supportive. Yeah, there was that initial sort of, huh?

Olga's mother is very supportive of her educational choices, but "I don't [think] my Dad's completely gotten over [me not completing a doctorate in chemistry]...[b]ecause to this day he's like, so when are you going to do something in chemistry?" Alanna's father originally wanted her to get an MBA, but was eventually convinced that becoming a librarian was the best decision for her. Molly's and Nancy's parents had financial concerns. Both students mentioned that their parents would have preferred they find a job instead of going to graduate school.

> At first they were kind of against it because they really wanted me to get a job, to start
> getting money and supporting myself and all that. And the program I'm in provides for
> tuition and all that, living expenses, so they're up for it. As long as I don't have to pay
> out of pocket money, they're fine with it. That was one of their worries, having to go into
> debt to go to school. (Molly)

A few students discussed the lack of support from family. Ken did not discuss his academic plans with his family, stating, "I'll tell them when I finish, I supposed. In a lot of ways, I'm really independent." Kelly and Sally both discussed the lack of understanding and support from their parents in regards to their MLIS studies. Kelly is still dealing with negative comments from her family and friends.

> They still, they still feel that somehow, after I finish with the degree, that somehow I'll
> change my mind, that I'll realize, that I'll finally see the light and they think that I'm
> going to change my mind...from library [and information science] to some other field.

Steve received a great deal of support and encouragement from his brother, but nothing from his father.

> My father, I really don't get any support from him. It's like, I don't know if it's
> intentional criticism, but the fact that I've been in school for 7 years, he says "oh, when
> are you going to graduate and do something?" And that's kind of not what I want to
> hear, like "good job" and "I'm proud of you." I attribute that to the fact that he's never
> been through the system. So he doesn't know the value.

Support mechanisms and structures in LIS programs were also mentioned. Eight students commented on support from their LIS programs, but the level of support differed. Five of the students who were part of a fellowship or scholarship program were positive when they discussed various support systems available. Amanda, Jamie, Karen, and Sondra all mentioned the importance of their cohort and how they worked together to provide support and encouragement for each other. Their faculty advisors also provided encouragement and opportunities to meet with other LIS professionals.

> in this [scholarship program], they invite guests from different disciplines from within library and information services so you can learn about options in museums and special collections and that kind of thing... (Jamie)

Lydia raved about the concern and support mechanisms provided by the program.

> Here, it's like, you know, you have so many people to turn to if you're having a great day or you're having a not so great day or you feel like you should be doing something else. They're very, very open. They want this program to work.

Lydia appreciated the support system provided by the faculty and fellow students in the program and the opportunity to discuss problems and ask questions. This is very different from her experience with the teaching program where she felt she was thrown into the classroom and expected to know everything. Rather than feeling lost, Lydia knows she has resources available to her in her fellowship program.

However, some of the comments focused on the lack of support available from the LIS program. Three of the participants remarked on feeling isolated from the program. Derek, Lynn, and Olga all commented on minimal support or alienation from their LIS program. Lynn was discouraged by the lack of support systems available for her. Olga received very little information from her LIS program. Instead, she created opportunities by arranging an internship at a prestigious engineering school and volunteering at her local public library. These institutions provided her with the support systems she wanted. Derek felt alienated from his scholarship program. This was partially because his academic focus diverged from the goals of the program.

> This program seems to be aimed at those with administrative goals and I don't want to do that...I'm trying to take what I can from this and certainly it will all be valuable and I know wherever I am, I will be a change agent and if that means sitting behind a desk for a while, I will. But I don't want to be there, I want to be on the forefront working with kids, individually on a one to one basis.

Another student addressed issues faced by ethnic minorities in programs and within the profession in regard to support. Martha recognized the importance of having members of her own ethnic minority group as part of the support structure.

> It's hard to explain when you see someone walk through halls that they know the history and pride of who they are, they look like you and whatever you're going through, you

know you can say, my sister, can I talk to you, how should I maneuver through this course...they are able break it down for you and they can relate to you.

Support also came from co-workers and supervisors, especially those who had recently, or were currently, working in libraries. Library staff were often described as encouraging. Both Molly and Tami mentioned how, once they expressed an interest in librarianship, the staff at the library provided them with information and suggested LIS programs that they might consider.

I was really close with the [library] staff, but they really didn't push me. Once they found out I was interested, they gave me all the resources, pointed me to where, things I should do, how I should go about it, that was about it. They were very supportive, but they never pushed me into it. (Molly)

Mentors

Support also came from individuals who had a strong influence on the participants. About a third of the students could point to a person who had mentored them at some point in their life. These mentors played a role in their ultimate decision to enter LIS. Yet not all of them recognized or referred to them as mentors. Instead, the students would mention terms such as "influential" or describe how this person pushed them to achieve.

The influence these mentors had varied. Some were simply individuals who introduced the student to reading, while others were credited with the student's success. In a few cases, the students did not realize the impact the mentor had on them until later, when they traced back their love of reading to a particular teacher or thought about a supervisor who encouraged them to pursue a degree:

There were many occasions when...she would go "there's this conference going on for library assistants, this seminar for library assistants." And then she would go, "you know you could be an academic librarian, there's a large need for people of color in the academic librarianship field" and you know, she'd throw things out there like that and it didn't really hit me until a few years later... (Dean)

The students who had mentors who were also ethnic minorities spoke of the importance of this shared understanding of their experience in LIS. These mentors were not always members of the same ethnic groups as the students, but they were perceived as influential and knowledgeable simply because of shared experience. Marta was assigned a mentor as part of her scholarship. Although she is not of the same ethnic heritage, Marta described her mentor as "wonderful and she's really great." Sadie also discussed the impact of having an ethnic minority as a mentor.

> There's an African American woman that has, you know, she's really wonderful to me. She's like, "I'm going to teach you the ropes, I'm going to show you this, show you that." I guess you can kind of say she's been my mentor, she's been really good...part of mentoring is also showing you the bad side of things and teaching you how to get around all that. And that's what she's done. Everybody else kind of tells you the good stuff, but she [tells me about]...the reality of dealing with it.

Not all attempts at mentoring were positive. Sadie discussed the attempt of one librarian to mentor her, but with outdated and irrelevant information. Lynn, while crediting her mentor with an abundance of support and for alerting her to opportunities, also recognized his limits of understanding her position.

> I really had to say to him, my reality as a woman of color, as a single mom, is really different from your reality as a white European academic, with a good reputation behind you...but he kept encouraging me.

Ethnicity and Community

Ethnic Identity

Ethnic identity was unique to each participant. Over half of the student had strong ties to their ethnic heritage and community. Their career plans and goals were based on these connections to their communities. However, a small number of students downplayed their ethnic background, stating that it had little to no impact on their careers or decisions. When asked directly about how she might feel being the sole ethnic librarian on staff, Olga did not seem to consider it an issue, as she explained "in my professional life, in my educational life, I don't see myself as Asian/Pacific Islander. It's just one of those, it's like I'm just that at home." Others did not necessarily see themselves as "ethnic," but recognized the role they could play in libraries.

The impact of ethnic identity was highly individualized and varied across the four ethnic groups. The three Native American students were very aware of their ethnic background. Although they each had different experiences with their tribes and their cultures, they identified themselves as Native Americans. Most of the African-American students were similar in their identification and awareness of their ethnic heritage. However, there were students who did not have strong ties to the African-American culture or communities. The Asian-American students identified with the Asian country with which they were associated, self-identifying as Filipina, Japanese, Taiwanese, Chinese, Cambodian, Bengalese, and Vietnamese rather than as Asian. It is important to the participants for the specific Asian country be recognized.

> Instead of saying I'm Asian American, I specifically say I'm Cambodian American, I think that makes a big different to show other people who aren't as familiar with Asia as I am, that there's a lot out there. That you can't just classify one thing as one group.

The Asian-American participants perceived the broad terminology as limiting because it removed the unique characteristics of their ethnic heritage.

There were also differences among the Asian-American participants based on geographical location. The students from the East Coast were more aware of their ethnic background, whereas those from the West Coast seemed to see it as secondary to their professional image. Part of this may be tied to the more established Asian communities on the West Coast. Both Dean and Josephine noted the differences in the Asian communities on the East Coast. They both felt there was less recognition of their culture and background than did Asian Americans from the Western States.

> Everyone's aware of the immigration act of the 60s, the numbers did explode and...the face of Asian Americans is from post 60s, but there are those of us that grew up before then...Hawaiians and the ones from San Francisco, they pre-date us. They deserve it, because of numbers, they assimilated much more quickly than the ones on the East Coast, we had a harder time. (Josephine)

Both Dean and Josephine felt Asian immigrants to the West Coast were able to fit into society faster because of the established communities, which provided shelter and opportunities to new arrivals. Both felt that the East Coast did not provide the same support structure for Asian Americans.

Most of the Hispanic/Latino students felt some ties to their ethnic heritage, but the depth depended on how acculturated their parents were to American culture. Serena, Jill, Jamie, Luisa, and Rita all discussed how they still considered themselves very closely tied to their Hispanic/Latino roots. Alanna, Lydia, and Marta, while still self-identifying as Hispanic/Latino, felt removed from their culture because their parents were more focused on fitting in with American culture.

> So my dad is completely Americanized. He sounds like someone from Fargo, ND, you know. I try to speak Spanish with him, he won't, he ignores it. It's really hard, I'm like, this is your language, but... (Lydia)

The concepts of language and fluency were mentioned as important cultural characteristics by members of all four ethnic groups. The ability to speak the language lent some level of legitimacy to the effort and established an important connection with the larger ethnic community. Derek discussed the importance of retaining his Native American heritage through literacy and fluency in the language. Sadie remarked on the importance of being able to speak "slang" to younger patrons in her community in order to show her understanding of their information needs. Jill's mother taught her Spanish from infancy despite the family's concern that it might create problems for her.

[My uncle] would often tell [my mother] that he was worried that I wouldn't pick up English and she'd tell him it was everywhere, I was going to get English, but [I] might not get Spanish.

Others recognized their culture, but did not see it as an overly strong influence on their lives. Ken and Olga spoke about their ethnic background and the fact that they did feel it was a part of their identity, but did not see how it affected their professional careers. Although she clearly stated that she was Filipina, Olga believed that her ethnic identity was something she was at home, not at work. Ken tended to distance himself from his ethnic background. Unlike Olga, he did not want to connect himself to his ethnic heritage at all.

I'm not a normal, minority or whatever you call it. I don't see myself in that way. I see myself as an individual. I don't seek out other Vietnamese people to be friends with or whatever. I've happened to have Vietnamese friends in the past and so forth, not because of that, just because I've met people at different locations and things like.

Three of the African-American participants also distanced themselves from their ethnic heritage. Amanda identified as an African American, but did not have strong ties to this culture or any African-American community. Amanda lived in a primarily white community until junior high school when her family moved to a more diverse neighborhood.

Unfortunately I wasn't around a lot of black people at school, I think there were may be three other black kids in class. So, I really didn't know how to fit in because I noticed the difference between the kids I grew up with…I got into a lot of fights because I was the kid who came from white [community] and spoke properly and um had real long hair and they thought, "she's too good, she thinks she's too good." So I had to learn to adapt and I did, but I hated it.

Although Amanda identified as an African American, she was comfortable being "the only little black girl [laughs] in the program because essentially I am. I don't have a problem with that at all."

A couple of students stated that they simply did not feel like minorities. The reasons for this perception varied. Sally and Kelly both came from Caribbean ethnic backgrounds where the focus is more on class than race. Both students commented on the fact that they tended to pay more attention to class structures. Neither identified as African American, but rather considered themselves Black. Sally discussed the difference between herself and African American students.

> Diversity is hard for me because I don't think that way... I see more, maybe in a class, more of a class system, if anything...it's hard for me to tell a black person that... because they don't see it that way.

Kelly discussed similar perceptions of African American culture. Kelly was very proud of her Jamaican heritage, but like Sally, she was more concerned with class than race. Both Sally and Kelly wanted to work in public libraries and were more concerned with available resources than the ethnic demographics of the community.

Ethnic heritage did have some influence on their decisions to enter LIS. Some students felt they could play an important role in improving diversity within LIS that their presence was an encouragement for diversity. Sadie, Marta, Molly, Jill, Nancy, and Rita all mentioned that one of their motivations for pursuing the MLIS was to improve the diversity of the profession by their presence and by the example they could be for other minorities. Ruth perceived librarianship as a profession where she could make a difference, but she was also pursuing the profession because, as she said, "... I really, really want to become a librarian because I feel the field is really underrepresented with minorities. And, you know, specifically black..." Rita also reflected on the role she could play in improving the library for the Hispanic/Latino community. While she was primarily focused on technical services and behind the scenes work, Rita realized she could help improve outreach to the community, even if it was a few patrons at a time. Like Ruth, she wanted to help create a library for all, but Rita's focus is to "reach those populations, the Latino populations, that was specifically, you know, [my] goal."

Community
The majority of the students mentioned wanting to work in an ethnic minority community when they graduate. Concepts related to 'giving back'

and 'working for the greater good' were discussed by many students. Most were focused on working within communities of their own ethnic background, but a few simply wanted to work in underprivileged areas regardless of the demographic breakdown. These students see librarianship as a way to work to improve their communities, as well as to give back some of what they have received. Several of the participants also recognize their potential as role models to whatever community they serve.

Karen and Sondra want to make libraries the wonderful resources they remembered from their youth, regardless of the ethnic make-up of the patron base. Nathan recognized how he could be effective in a variety of communities because "most of the time people can't figure out what my nationality is, so I think I can help out a lot, a lot of different groups because a lot of groups accept me as their own." Mike discussed the problems with underserved communities, the Digital Divide, and how, as a librarian, he could help contribute to solutions for the information 'have-nots', regardless of ethnic or cultural background.

> I really recognize the Digital Divide in this country and how it is growing. And, not just between black and white, but between the haves and have-nots. And, I really want to work towards closing that gap, or doing what I can to make as many people on the other side, on the positive side of using technology and the Internet as possible.

Ruth had similar career goals, but she was focused on schools. Initially she wanted to work in a privileged community, one with a majority Caucasian demographic because of the resources and opportunities at such an institution. However, after a practicum at a school for the children of migrant workers, Ruth realized she could contribute more to a school in an underprivileged area.

> I think I would prefer to be in an inner-city school because I feel like, I feel like I could touch more lives that way. I know that inner-city schools tend to have more, a larger amount of minorities and I feel like I could be an inspiration to one of them. Plus...it's a challenge that most people don't want to do, they don't want to do inner-city because it is a challenge, but they need love too, they need to know that somebody cares.

Some students were focused on communities whose demographics reflected their own ethnic identity. Jill and Alanna are focused on serving Hispanic/ Latino populations because of their ethnic background and their Spanish language skills. Both students felt they could contribute more to these communities than to others. Alanna mentioned "I've really strengthened my Spanish language skills, I really want to use that to benefit the public and be able to communicate with the population." Jill also commented that while she believes she has the skills and ability to serve any community, she would be most comfortable working within a Hispanic/Latino community. Serena was more focused specifically on her own community. She felt she could make a stronger contribution there than anywhere else.

> I think if you work and live in your community, you make it stronger…just the idea that it's my community and I want to work for its betterment. And, of course, you can go to any community and work for its betterment, you know, that's certainly a worthy thing to do; anywhere you go you should be working for the community's betterment. But just the idea that this is where I live this is where I work.

Derek and Steve are both focused on returning to the Reservation once they have finished their education. Both students planned to get additional degrees after the MLIS, with an eye toward using them to improve life for their Nations. Steve planned to eventually work his way into Tribal Governance, starting with the library and community center. He felt he could make a contribution to his tribe by increasing awareness of tribal history and bringing people into the community center.

> I'd like to eventually get to the tribe…work my way into the government, tribal government system. You know, it's not about money or anything, it's about giving back to the community… (Steve)

Derek was focused on education and literacy in the Native American languages. He saw his MLIS complementing his educational degrees so that he could work as a teacher librarian. His only focus was to return to the Reservation.

> I would not dream of moving beyond [the Reservation]. Because home is where my heart is and I'm one of those people, I'm going to return home no matter what. I don't care how much money I'll be paid to go elsewhere, I know I'm going to go home.

Many African-American students had similar goals of working within their ethnic community. Sadie was already employed at her local public library and felt she provided a good example for those who came into the library. However, she perceived that it should extend beyond just other African Americans.

> I want to provide an example for who's ever coming in, if the child is white or black or whatever. Of course, I do want to something specifically for African Americans. I want to be someone to look up to and see a face there. I want my face to be seen because I think it's important that um, that we should be everywhere, not just in the library, but everywhere. I think it's important, they might say, "hey, can I do that too."

Martha had similar goals and ideas. Growing up in an educational system with few teachers of color and no librarians of color, she felt it was important to present a positive image to children in ethnic communities.

For me growing up around your people and to be educated by them…you become empowered and when you can empower children, you don't have any problems out there, they are confident in the skin they are in. And then in this society, regardless of your ethnic background, for all children to be important and feel confident, you know, in the skin the Creator put you in. And if you don't see anybody that looks like throughout your life, how will you respond to them when you do see them? (Martha)

Acculturation

Regardless of their ties to an ethnic community or the depth of their ethnic identity, almost all of the participants experienced the need on some level to fit into majority or Caucasian culture. Even if they lived in ethnic neighborhoods, the participants each had some level of experience in schools with primarily Caucasian student populations, through bussing, special programs, or private schools. Some students lived in Caucasian communities. It was common for the participants to remark that they were one of, for instance, three Asian students in the school or that they were the only Hispanic family in the neighborhood. As a result, these are individuals who were acculturated into the majority culture. Alanna explained it well when she described how she and her sister regarded themselves.

You know, we've been so integrated into the culture since birth, at least my sister and I, we don't see that we stand apart. We don't see ourselves as a minority, until we have to bubble it in on a standardized test. So, it's never been a factor of, you know, oh, I'm a minority. It's more like, wow, I'm one of these people who has the unique situation where I do speak another language, you know and I want to be able to use that. But not because I am Hispanic because. I don't think that makes a difference.

The depth of acculturation varied among the students. At least half of the participants wanted to work in ethnic communities. Although they recognized their ability to function well within the majority culture, they did not feel they had to be integrated into or subsumed by it. However, a few participants were actually more comfortable within Caucasian communities than ethnic minority neighborhoods. Amanda commented on her comfort level in a Caucasian neighborhood in comparison with an African-American neighborhood. When discussing her career goals, Sally mentioned wanting to work in a public library, but was very specific about the community she wanted to work in.

I want to work at a library where I feel like, you know, as a patron, I was going there, that I was getting help, I was being supported, you know, getting good customer service. So, I guess, to answer your question, I think I would prefer a White community because of the level of, um, this is a judgment here, because there is a sense, to me, that they have more resources, which is so important, and the level of service is better.

There were only two participants who did not attend school or live in a primarily Caucasian area. Karen and Sondra are African-American students who lived through the Civil Rights movement in a major northern city. Both students were very aware of and comfortable with their ethnic heritage and had very open and accepting views of diversity and ethnicity based on their own experiences. Karen discussed how everyone worked together during the Civil Rights movement.

It was more of a blended kind of message, there's this issue and this issue and this issue, but we're all here and we need to just let people know these are the things that are going on, we had concerns about them.

Sondra commented on how learning about those involved in the Civil Right movement, such as Martin Luther King Jr. and Rosa Parks, helped her to be more accepting and open to others.

As I began to learn more and more about these people, and that's 30, 40 years ago now, I became an empowered person and very centered in who I am. Very easy to deal with, it just increased my ability to see thing for what they were and not really get caught up in the whole drama of, "no, this is a black/white issue and da, da, da." I just began to see things…but that comes with age and maturity.

Luisa and Lynn both discussed issues of being an ethnic minority within a predominately Caucasian field. Luisa had experienced problems related to discrimination while working in journalism, which she found to be "very white dominated. There's…not much of a minority presence…I was getting all these doors shut in my face, and I could tell, you just knew." Luisa was unhappy about the homogenous nature of librarianship, but she also believed that there were two sides to the issue.

It bothers me that there's not enough [minorities], regardless that's there's no welcome mat…but at the same time it's up to the minorities because there's always a struggle, you have to push more.

Acculturation dealt with more than just understanding how to live and work within majority culture. For some participants, there was also a realization of being an "other" and how that affects career choices and work productivity. Lynn discussed the issues of being an ethnic minority in a Caucasian profession. Rather than try to stand out and be an example, she finds it easier to maintain a low profile and, at the same time, continue to excel.

I've learned to cultivate silence and I think a lot of people of color learn to hide their light that way and the profession doesn't benefit I think from those who are in it... I would I think, fare a lot better if I didn't and I was one of those needy minority students, if I needed to find my way through and there was sort of a white man's burden fulfillment they could have with me and what do you do with someone like me. And so, I question, what do we do with people of color that really are stellar? Do we really allow them to bring what they could to the profession? Or do, again as I feel I've been, um, put into a position where they're sort of trapped into a subservient role or into, you know, a conspiracy of silence, or what I've decided to do, not [care] and shoulder really difficult moments.

Steve also recognized the stress inherent in being an ethnic minority in a majority dominated culture. He specifically addressed what he saw as the main causes of failure among Native American students and the problem of trying to work within majority culture.

It's that feeling of acceptance. I don't know, you're always going to feel less than, I think that's the reason why a lot of kids drop out. They have these high [expectations], whether they put them on themselves or it's perceived or it's really reality, it's just, they just, they don't want to lived underneath that microscope, the feeling 'oh, I can't make a mistake.' Otherwise people are going to scrutinize me more because they attribute it to their personality.

Views of Diversity

The definition assigned to diversity differed from individual to individual participant. However, there was a common theme – the acceptance of difference. Not the tolerance of or the assimilation into but the acknowledgement and acceptance of existing difference.

The first thing we need to do is to say "we are different and we're okay with that. We make an effort to understand other people and not that we have to be the same...I think that should be what diversity is, that we acknowledge that we're different and we're not afraid to be different, we make an effort to understand other people." (Jill)Sadie also acknowledged the need for individuals to recognize their personal role in encouraging diversity. It is not enough to perceive diversity, but one must also "understanding yourself sometimes, it's very important to keep your mind open to other people...You don't live in this world by yourself, you don't live in a box."

Several of the students recognized that diversity involves dealing with uncomfortable situations and conflict. Lynn, as a professor, deals with diversity and multicultural issues.

> That I see these issues not as something we solve, but as a state of consciousness, that we need to be aware of. I introduce them to the traditional literature in the field, as well as more cutting edge issues about it. And validate the fact that it will remain a discomfort zone for the rest of their lives. They're never going to solve this. You know, there will always be only partial realities that get represented.

Josephine discussed the possibility of resistance and how change is a slow process. Not everyone is excited about change or will immediately embrace new ideas. Although she considers her branch manager thoughtful and forward thinking, she acknowledged issues facing diversity:

> I'm aware of [diversity], certainly, I'm certainly aware of the fact that we're in a white middle class community that has a growing, um, Hispanic population…The reference librarian I report to is very tolerant, but I guess libraries don't change that quickly and I guess there's lots of reasons not to change.

Other students discussed the role of diversity in libraries. Several mentioned the need for more diversity within the library staff, primarily focused on professional positions. Mary commented on how diversity could improve the library overall.

> I think diversity is definitely a respect for other people being different…is very important. I think it is usually understated when you talk about the work environment. Um, but it definitely would be nice if more diversity was brought into the whole profession because I think that it also expands the collection, it expands the culture, and you know, the language, and all the other aspects that come with diversity.

Nathan also discussed the importance of diversity to the library "because there's a lot more ideas…[t]here are a lot of different backgrounds…what people are looking for, what type of service, different view points and stuff like that."

Sondra perceived a role for diversity in empowering people through access to information in the library. It did not matter who was looking for information, a diverse library could fill the information needs of anyone.

> Those are the things that we have to fight for. So this, I don't know, like I said, this whole thing, we need to create programming, we have to meet them…to really find people where they are, we have to empower, I know that my empowerment came from that knowledge I gained, so we need to try to empower that same way…that's a really big part of being diverse. Being able to make, have…to make all types of information accessible to all types of people.

The participants' comments reflect a challenge to many current views of diversity. Integration of culture and community is central to the students' vision of diversity. Additionally, the participants recognized the concepts of change, conflict, and discomfort as part of the diversity process. The library's purpose for diversity needs to be something beyond just looking at ethnic groups and focusing on information needs and the tools to fill them.

DISCUSSION

The intent of this research was to gain some insight into the motivations of ethnic minority LIS students in choosing LIS as a career. Its purpose is two-fold: to highlight successful diversity initiatives and to draw attention to what may have been missed. Understanding why certain people select a career may also uncover reasons why others do not. Although this research is not comprehensive, the findings do have some strong implications regarding ethnic minority student recruitment as well as other diversity initiatives in LIS.

The motivations for choosing a particular career vary depending on the individual. Decisions can be based on cultural influences, economic status, family background, and knowledge of a profession (Bandura, 2001; Brown, 2002; Durodoye & Bodley, 1997). These factors can result in challenges for ethnic minorities that Caucasian individuals do not face. The importance of family considerations and expectations over individual goals can be restrictive. Other limitations such as access to education, visibility of careers, and availability of opportunities may create obstacles. In some professions, these challenges are minimal, but in others, the barriers can seem insurmountable. A profession that requires graduate work such as LIS can be seen as too difficult or almost impossible because of the additional educational commitment, especially when familial concerns and economic hardship are factored in. Yet, despite these concerns, some ethnic minorities do pursue graduate degrees for professional careers.

Much of the information presented in the findings supports concepts presented in LIS literature. The majority of the participants were library users from an early age, which is a common characteristic of LIS professionals regardless of ethnic heritage (Van House, 1988; Gordon & Nesbeitt, 1999). The importance of reading is also a cited characteristic of LIS professionals in general (Weihs, 1999). Although family expectations and encouragement were important, individual participants, library experiences were also very influential on their educational and career decisions. Being a library user and working in a library were two of the primary motivations for choosing LIS as a career.

It is important to note that not all the participants were library users from an early age. Sadie commented on discovering the library in college. Steve did not spend time in libraries until high school, and Rick remarked on not realizing the importance of libraries until he was working in a library. Mary discovered the library as a way to find romance novels and then connected her interest in reading with scholastic achievement. These students show that it is possible to attract individuals to the library at various ages. Although it may make a larger impact at a younger age, introduction to the library and acceptance within the institution is effective regardless of age. Individuals do not need to be library users since childhood for the library to influence their lives. The implication is that library service is essential to diversity initiatives and that outreach should extend to all parts of the community.

The library as a place was an oft-mentioned influence on library use. Libraries were described as safe havens, as a source of tools for learning, and as comfortable, accepting locations. It is a place where the participants could envision working because they enjoyed spending time there. In this context, the library acted as both a tool of cultural hegemony and an escape from the pressures of society. Although it was not an immediate realization, the majority of the students eventually recognized that their love of the library could translate into a career.

The significance of these findings is not that they are unusual, but rather that library use and reading are common motivations for LIS professionals, regardless of ethnic background. The individuals coming into LIS are already aware of the library as a welcoming place, as a social institution, and a community resource. For the most part, the participants did not find the library after looking for a career, but rather discovered a way to combine their love of the library with their career focus. All these characteristics reflect the larger LIS student population (Van House, 1988; McClenney, 1989; Gordon & Nesbeitt, 1999; Weihs, 1999; O'Brien, 2002; Ard et al., 2006). Although it does not provide any new insights into why students choose LIS, it does highlight the importance of library services to underserved populations. To recruit ethnic minorities into the profession, LIS needs to ensure that they first establish the value of the institution within ethnic minority communities. The more LIS can create a place where all can feel acceptance and ownership of the organization, individuals from ethnic minority groups may choose to access the library and its resources, which may improve the chances of diversifying the profession.

Almost half of the participants also had some work experience in libraries, which is also a common motivator for LIS students. It illustrates the potential of programs and recruitment efforts aimed at current library staff. Several of the participants commented on supervisors or librarians who suggested LIS as a career. However, several other students remarked on that they only received encouragement after they decided to apply to a LIS program. Molly and Mary also commented on encouragement from LIS professionals, but only after having made the decision to pursue the MLIS. This raises the question of who may be missed because librarians and other staff are reluctant to suggest LIS as a career option.

The findings may also suggest limitations in recruitment efforts, especially in regard to where to recruit students and who to recruit. The participants were interested in libraries before their decision to pursue the MLIS. These are individuals who are already deeply tied to libraries and who understand the nature of LIS. Although the profession may not have been visible, the institution of the library is an important part of the participants' lives. LIS needs to continue recruitment of students such as the participants, but LIS also needs to expand its focus. Because of their ties to libraries, the participants understand the institution and have tacit knowledge of how to work within the profession. This suggests that by recruiting those who already know the library, the profession is looking for individuals who are most like them, those who understand the inherent restrictions and barriers to diversity and who are willing to work within the system. The implication is that many recruitment efforts limit themselves to those already comfortable and accepting of LIS in its current state or those who believe that change must evolve slowly and within the established framework. This limits the introduction of new ideas, new perspectives, and new approaches, creating barriers to real change in the profession.

There are several steps needed to help LIS recruitment efforts expand their focus. The first is to improve the perception and location of libraries in society. The visibility of the library and the profession is central to recruitment. Most of the participants did not see LIS as a visible profession. However, they did view the library as an important social or public institution.

The participants' comments connect the importance of service and outreach to improve diversity in the library and in the professions. The findings also supported other concepts often presented in LIS literature, such as the role of librarians in diversity, the importance of mentors, and the need for strong support systems (Patterson, 2000; Guerena & Erazo, 2000; Totten, 2000; McCook & Lippincott, 1997a; McCook & Lippincott, 1997b; Neely, 1999a; Buttlar & Caynon, 1992). These concepts are often mentioned in connection with diversity initiatives. Interactions with librarians can either encourage or discourage individuals from library use (Adkins &

Hussey, 2004). Mentors are perceived as having a positive influence on ethnic minorities during the educational process (Buttlar & Caynon, 1992; Knowles & Jolivet, 1991; McCook & Lippincott, 1997b) and in the retention of ethnic minority librarians in the profession (Bonnette, 2004). Support systems, both within and outside of LIS, help build stability and create a more accepting atmosphere for many ethnic minority students, which helps foster success academically and professionally (McCook & Geist, 1993).

With the participants' strong ties to libraries, it is interesting to consider the role of librarians in the participants' decisions. Although many students discussed a librarian who influenced them, several others could not even remember a single librarian with whom they had interacted. For these students, librarians were simply part of the organization, a means to an end for locating materials and conducting research. Rather than diminish the role of librarians, these comments actually support the need for good, high-profile, caring service, and well-trained professionals. It also underscores the need for librarians to reach out and build bridges to library users.

Although there were negative comments such as absences of service or strict authoritarians working in the profession, most of the participants had mainly positive connections to librarians. What this illustrates is that it is not as important for a librarian or staff member to be remembered as it is for the experience to be positive. In other words, service should be a central consideration in diversity initiatives and programs, as well as part of the everyday responsibilities of LIS professionals. Interactions with LIS professionals can help build the welcoming and comfortable atmosphere of the library or they can alienate patrons from the institution. Service to the community is the first step in recruitment to the profession.

Mentors, like librarians, played a prominent role in participants' decisions to pursue a career within LIS, but was not a universal motivator. The role of mentors reflects much of the literature in LIS (Buttlar & Caynon, 1992; Knowles & Jolivet, 1991; McCook & Lippincott, 1997b). Much of the literature highlights the importance of mentors to ethnic minority students and several of the participants remarked on the assistance and encouragement of their mentors, especially those who were also ethnic minorities. This is not surprising, but does identify a potential problem in LIS; there are simply not enough ethnic minority professionals to act as mentors for current LIS students (U.S. Department of Labor, 2004; ALISE, 2004).

Despite the prominence of mentors and other influential individuals in the discussion of support, the majority of participants commented on how important familial support for education was essential to their success. Those without strong families created familial structures with friends and within a cultural framework. Either way, education was a central focus for the participants.

The importance of education to the participants and their families demonstrates the influence of both cultural hegemony and discursive formations. The significance of strong family ties shaped many participants' educational goals, but these goals were still impacted by social expectations. Family expectations inform the individual discursive formations, which had a strong effect on their educational choices and pursuits.

The experience of the Asian-American participants was unique among the ethnic groups. Although the pursuit of the MLIS was often perceived as unusual for all the participants, the reason for this perception differed. Many African-American, Native American, and Hispanic/Latino students remarked on being one of the few in their family or the first member of their family to work toward a graduate degree. Their level of education often set them apart from others in their community and culture. However, in the case of the Asian-American participants, it was not graduate education that was unusual, but rather the degree selected. For the Asian-American participants, education is central to their culture. All of the Asian-American students made comments that reflected this idea. Most children are expected to at least pursue a bachelor's degree as well as advanced degrees. The decision to pursue a graduate degree is a reflection of cultural expectations. Their individual discursive formations included the need to achieve academically as part of the cultural background. However, the choice of major often conflicted with the expectations of their families and their communities. When Dean, Maggie, and Seta discussed their concerns regarding family expectations and their career choices, they also mentioned coming to realization that they had to make the decision to not to follow family wishes. Their actions reflected a more individualistic outlook, which illustrates the influence of cultural hegemony. All three participants made choices placing individual priorities before family considerations.

For some of the participants from other ethnic minority backgrounds, the stress on education was perceived as unusual within their culture. Several of the Hispanic/Latino students commented on how their families were different from others because of their focus on education. For these participants, education was seen as a way to make a better life, to improve their social and economic standing, and to become more like those in power in their communities. All the Native American participants commented on how they were unusual in their educational achievements.

The educational background of the participants' families varied from doctorate degrees to dropping out of the educational system before high school. The familial educational level determined the influence of discursive formations and cultural hegemony on the students' academic goals. Those from highly educated families came from backgrounds where achievement was important. The discursive formations were tightly tied to goals of cultural hegemony with regards to education. However, the participants who were the first, or among the first, to receive a college education reveal the influence of cultural hegemony. Education represents a tool for the improvement of social and economic status, a way to move away from their culture at least in terms of status. Although there were still strong ties to the individual discursive formation such as strong work ethics and wanting to give back to the community, education can be seen as an unconscious acceptance of the majority culture's focus on academic achievement.

LIS programs themselves were also part of the discussion. The majority of students spoke positively about the LIS programs they attended. Although not central to the initial motivation to pursue this career, LIS programs did influence some of the students' decisions to enter the LIS profession. Most students selected programs based on location and financial resources, although the participants also stressed the importance of reputation and the quality of the academics. Scholarships and financial aid are important to the participants because they were financial independent and any assistance made the educational process easier. However, for the majority of the participants, financial aid was not the deciding factor. The implication is that money is not the only tool needed for recruitment of ethnic minority students. Flexible schedules and location of classes play a significant role in selecting a particular LIS program.

Diversity and support were also addressed in the context of the LIS program. The LIS programs offered coursework on diversity and serving ethnic communities. However, most of the diversity classes are broad, all-encompassing multicultural courses. This type of course may provide a good introduction to diversity, especially to Caucasian students, but it can also be perceived as a half-hearted attempt at introducing the idea of diversity to the profession. In these classes, students are given the opportunity to learn about multiculturalism using broad and general concepts that simplify a very complex subject. However, the concepts taught in multicultural classes are often not tied into the rest of the curriculum and, therefore, can be perceived to emphasize separateness rather than inclusion.

The participants also discussed their career plans as part of their motivations for entering LIS, and these plans mirror the literature. The majority want to work in public libraries where they can focus on their community. Many perceived LIS as an admirable profession in service-focused organizations and see working in a library provided the opportunity to give back to their communities and to society. This generally translated into an aspiration to work in a public or school library. They were also the types of library of which almost all of the students tied their own positive experiences. This was especially obvious with the participants who described the library as social or public institutions, which can be tied back to the desire to give back to the community. There is an implicit understanding in the LIS literature that ethnic minority professionals want to focus on their own communities and other underserved populations (Gomez, 2000; Watkins, 1999a, 1999b; McCook & Lippincott, 1997a, 1997b; Adkins & Espinal, 2004), and this is supported by answers offered by these participants.

However, not everyone wanted to work with ethnic minority communities, to be the minority representative on staff, or even to be considered an ethnic minority within the profession. This point of view was more common among the Asian-American student. However, it was also mentioned by the African-American participants of Caribbean heritage. Some of these students wanted to work in academic libraries because of the higher prestige attached to the institution and the possibility of working with a more educated community. A few others did not want to work with the public at all either because they were not comfortable interacting with strangers or they were tired of dealing with belligerent or rude patrons. This challenges the often unspoken assumption that ethnic minority librarians want to work on diversity issues and focus on outreach to underserved communities. Some just want to be LIS professionals with all the same opportunities as the majority, an attitude that highlights the problems with visual diversity. Some ethnic minority librarians do not want to be perceived as different and diversity initiatives are built on the basis of difference. The implicit assumptions created through diversity initiative may not fit with the ambition and goals of the individuals selected to fill the positions.

As with the general student population, the majority of the participants were entering LIS as a second career. However, it is important to consider the exceptions. Three students went straight from their undergraduate program to the LIS program and one student took a year off to work and find a way to pay for graduate school. For all four participants, the library was deemed to be a visible career options either because of the influence of an individual or work experience in the library.

The findings related to libraries, librarians, support, and mentors are not overly surprising. Although there are some unusual characteristics or comments, these concepts fit well with previous research and support many of the goals and objectives of diversity initiatives. However, the discussion of ethnic identity, acculturation, and the definition of diversity highlights some gaps in LIS research and some of the problems with diversity initiatives.

Ethnic identity was important to the majority of the participants, but did not necessarily influence their career goals and educational decisions. Yet, this theme provides some insight into the decision process of the participants to select LIS as a career. It also reflects influences of both cultural hegemony and discursive formations.

Ethnic identity is an essential component of how the participants perceived themselves within society, their community, and the LIS profession. Although many feel that they are tightly tied to their ethnic heritage, they also recognized their unusual status within their culture. Dean and Maggie both commented on how their choices did not fit with "traditional" Asian families. Sadie remarked on the difference in her mind-set when she realized that she did not want to limit herself to just her culture. Alanna, Jill, and Luisa all discussed situations where they were rejected by other Hispanic/Latinos, because of either poor language skills or light skin tones. Identity is not an individual, private process, but one that must be acknowledged by others. Additionally, identity is not a static concept, but rather evolves as individuals move and function within society (Trimble et al., 2003).

For the participants, there was some recognition that as they progressed through their education, their place in society changed and their identity was altered. They did not belong to majority culture, but did not quite fit within their own ethnic community. However, this was generally perceived as a positive characteristic in that they could act as role models for other ethnic minorities, which reflects the influence of cultural hegemony and a bridge between majority and minority communities. The majority of participants discussed their plans to work with ethnic minority communities and the positive influence they hope to have in these communities. In this discussion, there was a tacit recognition of separation from their culture. With the Native American, African-American, and Hispanic/Latino participants, this difference was because of the amount of education. For Asian-American students, it was due to their pursuing educational preparation for career that was outside those that conveyed prestige in their culture. Either way, the participants realized that their career choice may distance themselves from the culture of their families.

The acculturation of the participants indicates, at least tacitly, the acknowledgement of the library as a white or majority culture institution. Even those students who were tied into their ethnic culture made comments about the need to work within the culture of the library that it was different from their own culture, even if the library was clearly a part of that community. The participants recognize the power structures inherent in social and ethnic cultures and understand how to work within the boundaries of culture and power.

The acculturation of the participants also reflects the fact that LIS is recruiting those who can easily adapt to existing library culture. This does not mean that the participants are rejecting their own cultural backgrounds. Rather, the implication is that, by focusing on ethnic minority concerns, the students are fulfilling majority culture expectations. As with fellowship programs and diversity initiatives, hiring librarians of color may be a reaction to the need for visual diversity rather than an attempt to influence organizational culture. Some librarians of color recognize the irony of being "hired to serve their ethnic respective communities yet are told that they act 'too ethnic on the job'" (Balderrama, 2000, p. 199). By failing to recognize the influence of majority culture in libraries, diversity initiatives may result in the "relegation of members of historically excluded groups to positions that interface with their own communities" (Linnehan & Konrad, 1999, p. 404).

The definitions of diversity illustrate an implicit understanding of acculturation and assimilation within LIS. The participants are pretty clear in their desire to be included in, but not subsumed by, another culture, and reflect the participants' discursive formations as members of under-represented or oppressed groups. Most of the participants' definitions of diversity are constructed from the position of an outsider. Their focus is on how the individual or ethnic group can be integrated into organizations and institutions rather than how the individual or ethnic group can be fitted into the existing structure. From the participants' point of view, diversity ought to provide the opportunity for various groups within the community to share and explain their culture as they view it rather than providing an example of an ethnic culture formed through the perception of the majority culture.

The importance of inclusion without assimilation is interesting, especially when one considers how the participants have already been influenced by majority culture. The stress was not on equal representation, but actual recognition. In other words, there was an aspiration for "legitimate" recognition of the right to be included "as is," rather than made to fit within the existing structure. "Individuals may privately know who they are, but certain social forces and groups can and do deny or limit self-declaration" (Trimble et al., 2003, p. 242). Recognition provides legitimacy, which may grant some level of influence. This influence can create opportunities for cross-cultural influence on majority culture.

The discussion of diversity highlights another issue – the role of conflict in diversity. Many participants recognized that diversity is change and change creates discomfort. "One of the first challenges in any paradigm of diversity is overcoming a long history of antagonistic attitudes towards difference..." (Potts & Watts, 2003, p. 66). This is not an issue that is commonly addressed in LIS literature, but many participants anticipated some level of discomfort inherent in any change, including the diversification of the profession. This is perhaps because they have actually experienced discomfort or conflict when trying to integrate into some aspect of majority culture without being assimilated. It also raises another issue with diversity initiatives: the lack of recognition of majority culture identity and the privileges automatically given to members of majority culture.

> To redesign social systems we need first to acknowledge their colossal unseen dimensions. The silences and denials surrounding privilege are the key political tool here...[m]ost talk by whites about equal opportunity seems to me now to be about equal opportunity to try to get into a position of dominance while denying that systems of dominance exist. (McIntosh, 1998, p. 152)

Many participants recognized the privileges of majority culture and what is required of them if they are to successfully function within a white institution. However, their perceptions contradict the general belief that privilege and racism do not exist in LIS (St. Lifer & Nelson, 1997; Neely, 1999b, 1998; Josey, 1999; Hankins et al., 2003). The concept of white privilege is not unique to LIS, but reflects a larger trend in American society. Very few members of the majority culture in the United States acknowledge even having a culture beyond being American, and those in the majority often perceive libraries as an integral part of American society, institutions open to all who want to access the resources within. Yet, very few recognize the role libraries can and often do play in privileging one culture over another. There is an assumption that, if individuals do not use the library, it is because they do not want to, not that they cannot find value in it. Until LIS can acknowledge these issues, the profession will not change. For diversity recruitment to be successful, the first step is to review assumptions and consider different views of libraries, such as those presented by the participants in this research.

CONCLUSIONS

Although this research is not generalizable beyond the participants, its findings do support many assumptions regarding ethnic minority recruitment in LIS. The findings related to libraries, librarians, mentors, and support illustrate that many recruitment initiatives are starting in the right place. There is also an implication that LIS may confine itself by limiting recruitment efforts to individuals who will easily fit within the profession. However, the most noteworthy findings were those that centered on identity, acculturation and diversity because they dealt issues that are not often considered or discussed by many in the profession outside of ethnic minority organizations. Related studies will continue to be required to fill the holes in our understanding of the dynamics of diversity and how those dynamics are evolving.

At the heart of the problems with diversity in LIS is power. In the United States, class structures and power inequality are rarely acknowledged, especially by those in power. Member of the majority culture are given privilege simply because of their position in society and with this privilege comes power and influence. Most Caucasians do not recognize an ethnic identity or culture beyond a symbolic "attachment to their grand-parents' origins" (Trimble, et al., 2003, p. 246). "Whites are taught to think of their lives as morally neutral, normative, and average, and also ideal" (McIntosh, 1998, p. 148), which implies that majority culture provides the example of what "others" should try to achieve, the basis of cultural hegemony.

The power structure and influence of cultural hegemony are reflected in LIS. Libraries are information centers and cultural repositories. Rather than being bastions of diversity, they act as a tool of cultural hegemony through service, policies, and collection (Wiegand, 1999). These actions and intentions are generally not overt or even openly acknowledged, which creates challenges and barriers to diversity initiatives. Introducing diversity to a profession as ethnically homogenous as LIS necessitates large-scale change. "When we privilege the knowledge of the oppressed or outsiders, we reveal aspects of the social order that previously have not been exposed" (Allen, 1998, p. 577). The first step is to recognize the role of majority culture in libraries and the unequal power relations between various cultures within our society. "To ignore white ethnicity is to redouble its hegemony by naturalizing it" (Roediger, 1991, p. 6).

However, much of the LIS literature implies that diversity can be achieved through individual programs that will gradually introduce new ideas and programs without addressing the problems inherent in change. Real change involves conflict because change requires sacrifice and effort. For diversity to succeed, those in power must first acknowledge their power and privilege and then surrender at least some of the power and privilege. This cannot happen without conflict, but very few in LIS have addressed this issue.

Evaluation of diversity initiatives often focuses on what was done well and what fits well into the existing system rather than trying to change the system. Mistakes or mis-steps are rarely discussed, which further complicates diversity as it is possible to learn as much from mistakes as from successes. However, mistakes and failures may draw attention to the subtle racism and inherent white privilege that acts as barriers to diversity. Grass roots projects can have an influence on larger organizations, but until LIS is willing to address unearned privilege, power relationships and inequality of opportunity, the profession will continue to struggle when trying to attract ethnic minorities into LIS and diversify both its workforce and its attitudes and programs.

NOTES

1. Male students are identified by (M) after their names.
2. All names have been changed by the author to ensure privacy.
3. For a complete breakdown of the participants, refer to the Appendix.

REFERENCES

Adkins, D. (2004). Latino librarians on becoming LIS educators: An exploratory investigation of barriers in recruiting Latino faculty. *Journal of Education for Library and Information Science*, *45*(2), 149–161.

Adkins, D., & Espinal, I. (2004). The diversity mandate. *Library Journal, 7*, 52–54.

Alire, C. (2001). Diversity and leadership: The color of leadership. *Journal of Library Administration, 32*(3/4), 99–114.

ALISE. (2004). *Library and information science education statistical report.* State college, PA: ALISE.

ALISE. (2005). *Library and information science education statistical report.* State college, PA: ALISE.

Allen, B. J. (1998). Black womanhood and feminist standpoints. *Management Communication Quarterly, 11*(4), 575–586.

American Library Association. (2005a). ALA homepage. Available at http://www.ala.org. Retrieved on March 4, 2005.

American Library Association. (2005b). Recruitment for diversity. Available at http://www.ala.org/ala/diversity/divrecruitment/recruitmentdiversity.htm. Retrieved on March 6, 2005.

Anderson, K., & Jack, D. C. (1991). Learning to listen: Interview techniques and analyses. In: S. B. Gluck & D. Patai (Eds), *Women's words: The feminist practice of oral history.* New York: Routledge.

Ard, A., Clemmons, S., Morgan, N., Sessions, P., Spencer, B., Tidwell, T., & West, P. J. (2006). Why library and information science? The results of a career survey of MLIS students along with implications for reference librarians and recruitment. *Reference and User Services Quarterly, 45*(3), 236–247.

ASHE. (2005). The challenge of diversity. *ASHE Higher Education Report, 31*(1), 1–90.

Association of Research Libraries. (2006). ARL homepage. Available at http://www.arl.org. Retrieved on May 30, 2006.

Association of Research Libraries. (2006). Diversity initiatives: Initiative to recruit a diverse workforce. Available at http://www.arl.org/diversity/init/index.html. Retrieved on May 30, 2006.

Balderrama, S. R. (2000). This trend called diversity. *Library Trends, 49*(1), 194–214.

Bandura, A. (2001). Self-efficacy beliefs as shapers of children's aspirations and career trajectories. *Child Development, 72*, 187–206.

Berry, J. (2004). Knowledge river. *Library Journal, 7*(April 15), 55.

Bogdan, R. C., & Biklen, S. K. (2003). *Qualitative research for education: An introduction to theories and methods.* Boston, MA: Allyn and Bacon.

Bonnette, A. E. (2004). Mentoring minority librarians up the career ladder. *Library Administration and Management, 18*(3), 134–139.

Brewer, J., & Winston, M. D. (2001). Program evaluation for internship/residency programs in academic and research libraries. *College and Research Libraries, 62*(4), 307–315.

Brown, D. (2002). The role of work and cultural values in occupational choice, satisfaction, and success: a theoretical statement. *Journal of Counseling and Development, 80*, 48–57.

Budd, J. (2001). *Knowledge and knowing in library and information science: A philosophical framework.* Lanham, MD: Scarecrow Press.

Buttlar, L., & Caynon, W. (1992). Recruitment of librarians into the profession: The minority perspective. *Library and Information Science Research, 14*, 259–280.

Cogell, R. V., & Grunwell, C. A. (2001). *Diversity in libraries: Academic residency programs.* Westport, CT: Greenwood Press.

Cresswell, J. W. (2003). *Research design: Qualitative, quantitative, and mixed methods approaches* (2nd ed.). Thousand Oaks, CA: Sage Publications.

Diversity dictionary. (2000).Available at http://www.inform.umd.edu/EdRes/Topic/Diversity/ Reference/divdic.html. Retrieved on March 4, 2005.

Durodoye, B., & Bodley, G. (1997). Career development issues for ethnic minority college students. *College Student Journal, 31,* 27–33.

Foucault, M. (1972). *The archeology of knowledge.* New York: Pantheon Books.

Garrison, L. (1993). Professionals of the future: Will they be female? Will they be ethnically diverse? *Roeper Review, 15,* 161–165.

Glaser, B. G., & Strauss, A. L. (1967). *The discovery of grounded theory: Strategies for qualitative research.* Chicago: Aldine Publishing.

Gollop, C. J. (1999). Library and information science education: Preparing librarians for a multicultural society. *College and Research Libraries* (July), 385–395.

Gomez, M. (2000). Who is most qualified to serve our ethnic-minority communities? *American Libraries,* 39–41.

Gordon, R. S., & Nesbeitt, S. (1999). Who we are, where we're going: A report from the front. *Library Journal, 124*(9), 36–39.

Grover, M. L. (1983). Library school recruitment of Spanish-speaking Americans: problems and prospects. *Catholic Library World, 55,* 163–168.

Guerena, S., & Erazo, E. (2000). Latinos and librarianship. *Library Trends, 49,* 182–193.

Hankins, R., Sanders, M., & Situ, P. (2003). Diversity initiative vs. residency programs: Agents of change? *College and Research Library News, 64*(5), 308–315.

Hawley, L. (2001). Impact of socioeconomic status on family and career. *Career Planning and Adult Development Journal, 17,* 106–114.

Hepburn, P. (2001). Residency programs as a means of nurturing new librarians. *Feliciter, 47*(3), 142–144.

Horrocks, C. (2001). *Introducing Foucault* (2nd ed.). Lanham, MD: Totem Books.

Howland, J. S. (1998). Diversity deferred. *Law Library Journal, 90,* 561–575.

Josey, E. J. (1999). Diversity: Political and societal barriers. *Journal of Library Administration, 27*(1/2), 191–202.

Josey, E. J., & Abdullahi, I. (2002). Why diversity in American libraries. *Library Management, 23,* 10–16.

Knowles, E. C., & Jolivet, L. (1991). Recruiting the underrepresented: Collaborative efforts between library educators and library practitioners. *Library Administration and Management, 5,* 189–193.

Lears, T. J. J. (1985). The concept of cultural hegemony: Problems and possibilities. *The American Historical Review, 90*(3), 567–593.

Linnehan, F., & Konrad, A. M. (1999). Diluting diversity: Implications from intergroup inequality in organizations. *Journal of Management Inquiry, 8*(4), 399–414.

Lowe, A. (1996). An explanation of grounded theory. *Swedish School of Economics and Business Administration Working Papers, 336,* 1–18.

Lynch, M. J. (2004). ALA recruitment and retirement survey. Available at http://www.ala.org/ ala/ors/reports/recruitretire/recruitmentretirement.htm. Retrieved on November 12, 2004.

McClenney, E. G. (1989). *Why students choose careers in information and library science: Factors that affect the decision-making process.* Unpublished master's thesis, University of North Carolina, Chapel Hill.

McConnell, C. (2004). Staff and leadership shortages? Grow your own. *American Libraries,* *35*(9), 34–36.

McCook, K. P., & Geist, P. (1993). Diversity deferred: Where are the minority librarians? *Library Journal* (November 1), 35–38.

McCook, K. P., & Lippincott, K. (1997a). Library schools and diversity: Who makes the grade? *Library Journal,* 30–32.

McCook, K. P., & Lippincott, K. (1997b). *Planning for a diverse workforce in library and information science professions.* Tampa, FL: University of South Florida.

McCook, K. P., & Moen, W. E. (1992). Patterns of program selection: Ranked factors in the choice of a master's degree program in library and information science. *Journal of Education for Library and Information Science, 33*(3), 212–225.

McIntosh, P. (1998). White privilege: Unpacking the invisible knapsack. In: M. McGoldrick (Ed.), *Re-visioning family therapy* (pp. 147–152). New York: Guilford Press.

Moen, W. E. (1988). Library and information science student attitudes, demographics and aspirations survey: Who we are and why we are here. In: W. E. Moen & K. M. Heim (Eds), *Librarians for the new millennium* (pp. 93–109). Chicago, IL: American Library Association Office of Library Personnel Resources.

Mosley, M., Jr. (1999). Perceptions of African-American law school students toward law librarianship as a career choice. *The Journal of Academic Librarianship, 25*(3), 232–234.

Neely, T. Y. (1998). Diversity in conflict. *Law Library Journal, 90,* 587–601.

Neely, T. Y. (1999a). Diversity initiatives and programs: The national approach. *Journal of Library Administration, 27*(1/2), 123–144.

Neely, T. Y. (1999b). African American librarians in the profession: Education, recruitment, and success – Discrimination, racism, and sexism. In: *Conference proceedings of the 3rd National Conference of African American Librarians* (pp. 285–291). Newark, NJ: Black Caucus of the American Library Association.

Neely, T. Y., & Abif, K. K. (Eds). (1996). *In our own words: The changing face of librarianship.* Lanham, MD: Scarecrow Press.

Niemann, Y. F. (2003). The psychology of tokenism. In: G. Bernal, J. E. Trimble, A. K. Burlew & F. T. L. Leong (Eds), *Handbook of racial and ethnic minority psychology* (pp. 100–118). Thousand Oaks, CA: Sage Publications.

O'Brien, E. (2002, March 1). What are we doing right? Why LIS students have chosen our profession. *Ex Libris, 133.* Available at http://maylaine.com/exlibris/elib133.html. Retrieved on July 10, 2006.

Patterson, L. (2000). History and status of Native Americans in librarianship. *Library Trends, 49,* 194–214.

Peterson, L. (1999). The definition of diversity: Two views. A more specific definition. *Journal of Library Administration, 27*(1/2), 17–26.

Potts, R. G., & Watts, R. J. (2003). Conceptualization and models: The meaning of difference in racial and ethnic minority psychology. In: G. Bernal, J. E. Trimble, A. K. Burlew & F. T. L. Leong (Eds), *Handbook of racial and ethnic minority psychology* (pp. 65–75). Thousand Oaks, CA: Sage Publications.

Raber, D. (2003). Librarians as organic intellectuals: A Gramsican approach to blind spots and tunnel vision. *Library Quarterly, 73*(1), 33–53.

Ricoeur, P. (1992). *Oneself as another.* Chicago: University of Chicago Press.

Roediger, D. (1991). *Wages of whiteness: Race and the making of the American working class.* New York: Verso.

Rossman, G. B., & Rallis, S. F. (1998). *Learning in the field: An introduction to qualitative research.* Thousand Oaks, CA: Sage Publications.

Sassoon, A. S. (1987). *Gramsci's politics* (2nd ed.). Minneapolis, MN: University of Minnesota Press.

Siann, G., & Knox, A. (1992). Influences on career choice: The responses of ethnic-minority and ethnic majority girls. *British Journal of Guidance & Counseling, 20,* 193–205.

Silverman, D. (2001). *Interpreting qualitative data: Methods for analyzing talk, text and interaction* (2nd ed.). Thousand Oaks, CA: Sage Publications.

St. Lifer, E., & Nelson, C. (1997). Unequal opportunities: Race does matter. *Library Journal, 122,* 42–47(from EBSCOhost database Academic Search Elite, available at http://www. library.arizona.edu/indexes/links/academicsearchelite.shtml. Retrieved on September 23, 2002).

Totten, H. L. (2000). Ethnic diversity in library schools: Completing the education cycle. *Texas Library Journal, 76,* 16–19.

Trimble, J., Helms, J., & Root, M. (2003). Social and psychological perspectives on ethnic and racial identity. In: G. Bernal, J. E. Trimble, A. K. Burlew & F. T. L. Leong (Eds), *Handbook of racial and ethnic minority psychology* (pp. 239–275). Thousand Oaks, CA: Sage Publications.

U.S. Census Bureau. (1980). 1980 Statistical abstracts of the United States. Available at http://www2.census.gov/prod2/statcomp/documents/1980-01.pdf. Retrieved on September 2009.

U.S. Census Bureau. (2000). 2000 Statistical abstracts of the United States. Available at http://www.census.gov/prod/www/abs/statab1995_2000.html. Retrieved on September 2009.

U.S. Department of Labor. (2004). *Occupational outlook handbook, 2004–2005 edition.* Available at http://www.bls.gov/oco/. Retrieved on November 17, 2004.

Van House, N. A. (1988). MLS students' choice of a library career. *Library and Information Science Research, 10,* 157–176.

Vang, V. (2002). Expectations, realities, and diversity: A personal account. *American Libraries, 33,* 48–51.

Watkins, C. (1999a). Chapter report: Libraries, communities, and diversity. *American Libraries, 30*(7), p. 13.

Watkins, C. (1999b). A community mirror: Reflections on the color of librarianship. *American Libraries, 30*(10), 64–66.

Weihs, J. (1999). The birth of a librarian. *Technicalities, 19*(9)1, 8–10.

Weissinger, T. (2003). Competing models of librarianship: Do core values make a different? *The Journal of Academic Librarianship, 29*(1), 32–39.

Wetherell, M., Taylor, S., & Yates, S. J. (2001). *Discourse as data: A guide for analysis.* Thousand Oaks, CA: Sage Publications.

Wiegand, W. (1999). Tunnel vision and blind spots: What the past century tells us about he present: Reflections of the twentieth-century history of American librarianship. *Library Quarterly, 69,* 1–19.

Williams, H. E. (1987). Experiences of blacks in predominantly white library schools, 1962–1974: An era of transition. In: M. L. Bundy & F. J. Stielow (Eds), *Activism in American librarianship, 1962–1973* (pp. 153–161). New York: Greenwood Press.

Winston, M. (1998). The role of recruitment in achieving goals related to diversity. *College and Research Libraries* (May), 240–247.

AN UNRELENTING NEED
FOR TRAINING

Barbara J. Stites

ABSTRACT

Changes in the format of library materials, increased amounts of information, and the speed at which information is being produced have created an unrelenting need for training for library staff members. Additionally, library employees are retiring in greater numbers and their accompanying expertise is being lost. The purpose of this study was to document evaluation practices currently used in library training and continuing education programs for library employees, including metrics used in calculating return-on-investment (ROI). This research project asked 272 library training professionals to identify how they evaluate training, what kind of training evaluation practices are in place, how they select programs to evaluate for ROI, and what criteria are important in determining an effective method for calculating ROI.

INTRODUCTION

Library services have been transformed by the rapid development of information technology and the new knowledge economy (Bryson, 2001). As changes to library tools, products, and formats continue to occur, library staff members experience a persistent need for training (Massis, 2004;

Advances in Library Administration and Organization, Volume 28, 219–282
Copyright © 2009 by Emerald Group Publishing Limited
All rights of reproduction in any form reserved
ISSN: 0732-0671/doi:10.1108/S0732-0671(2009)0000028008

Hallam, 2007). Staff training is no longer an intermittent luxury but a critical strategy to provide quality services.

Not only have the formats of information changed but also the amount of information being produced. According to Lyman and Varian (2003) newly stored information grew approximately 30% per year between 1999 and 2002. The amount of this new information is estimated to be 5 exabytes, comparable to the size of the holdings of 37,000 Libraries of Congress. Most of this information (92%) is stored in magnetic format on diskettes, DVDs, and hard disk drives (Lyman &Varian, 2003; Heber, 2007).

The amount of new information is substantial, but the rapidity of the creation of information is even more dramatic. Estimates of the amount of information created before the year 2000 is 12 exabytes (129 billion gigabytes; approximately the size of 1.3 billion personal computers). In less than 3 years, by the middle of 2002, the total doubled to over 24 exabytes. It took thousands of years to create the first 12 exabytes of information and only 3 additional years to double it (Lyman & Varian, 2003).

In addition to the increase in the amount of information and the increase in its speed of production, there also has been a significant change in the formats and containers through which information is delivered. Traditional formats of paper books, periodicals, microfiche, and microfilm are rapidly being duplicated by digitized versions and remodeled by interactive online media. The world's largest bibliographic database producer, Online Computer Library Center (OCLC), claims that "information has left the container" (OCLC, 2004). New information containers, such as streaming video, webcasts, and blogs have become ubiquitous. In 2003, Lyman and Varian estimated that there were over 3 million recognized blog sites and approximately 10,000 new blogs were added to the Web every day and the growth continues. In 2007, there were an estimated 70 million blogs and 120,000 added daily (Sifry, 2007).

These changes in the format of library materials, amount of information, and the speed at which information is being produced have created an unrelenting need for training. This quantitative study used survey research methods and employed a cross-sectional field survey to explore training evaluation practices in library staff training. The dependent variables are: reaction to training, learning, use of the learning on the job, organizational impact, plus return-on-investment (ROI) (Kirkpatrick, 1959a, 1959b; Phillips, 1994). The independent variables are divided into four categories: training provider characteristics, training evaluation process, perceived need for training, and barriers to evaluation.

BACKGROUND OF THE PROBLEM

Not only have changes in the format of library materials, amount of information, and the speed at which information is being produced created an unrelenting need for training; there are additional factors involved. Skill depreciation, retirements, and short career ladders also add to the training dilemma.

Problems of Skill Depreciation, Retirements, and Short Ladders

Like other service organization leaders, library administrators find themselves dealing with the resulting problem of skill depreciation among employees (van Loo, de Grip, & de Steur, 2001; van Loo & Rocco, 2006). As technology evolves, human capital depreciates and suffers from obsolescence if not engaged in ongoing training (MacDonald & Weisbach, 2001). In fact, employees with higher levels of education, such as librarians, are more affected by skill depreciation than other workers (Neumann & Weiss, 1995).

Also complicating the task of providing high-quality library and information service is the rapid graying of the profession (Lenzini, 2002; Steffen, 2004; Wilder, 2007). Librarianship is losing large numbers of long-term professionals and their accompanying expertise. The latest national survey, according to *American Libraries* editor John Berry, reports that by 2009, 25% of librarians will be turning 65, and 58% will reach retirement age by 2019 (Berry, 2002).

Stanley Wilder, University of Rochester Libraries Associate Dean, (1995, 2007) suggests that one reason for rising retirement rates is due to the 1960s hiring increases in academic libraries, in particular, of baby boomers (Lenzini, 2002). In addition, he notes that the increase in the age of library school students over the last 12 years has increased, making the typical library professional 40% more likely to be over the age of 45, than a professional in another field.

One indicator of the considerable concern for this issue of impending retirements is the recent grant announcement from the Institute of Museum and Library Services (IMLS). The University of North Carolina – Chapel Hill has been awarded a $994,369 IMLS grant to study the future of librarians in the workforce. The two-year study will identify labor shortages, determine the skills that are necessary to fill such positions, and will recommend effective approaches to recruiting and retaining staff to fill those positions (Institute of Museum and Library Services, 2004).

Workforce demographics are changing and career ladders are shortening. As librarians are hired to fill these vacant positions and move more quickly through the ranks to management and administrative positions, these new professionals will need opportunities for continuing education to support them in their new roles (Webb, 1995; McCarthy, 2005). Large amounts of information are being created at an unprecedented rate driving the need to address skill depreciation and its effect on the bottom line.

American businesses know that investing in training improves financial success (Bassi, Ludwig, McMurrer, & Buren, 2002) but what does the library field know about training's impact? Financial implications for libraries regarding returns from library staff training have not been described. Studies have not been conducted even though libraries spend almost as much on training as the for-profit sector. We do know however, something about what both the business sector and libraries are spending on training.

According to the American Society of Training and Development (ASTD), in 2001 businesses spent an average of 1.9% of their payroll on training and staff development whereas public and academic libraries spent an average of 1.26% of total payroll on training (Lynch, 2001). By 2003, ASTD reported that businesses training expenditures increased to 2.31% and in 2006 they spent 2.33% of their payroll on training. No statistics are available for library training expenditures after 2001.

According to the 2006 ASTD State of the Industry Report, spending for training per person has grown. Spending per day per employee rose from $734 in 2001 to $812 in 2004 to $1,040 in 2006. Hours of training also increased. Time spent per employee in training sessions increased from 24 h in 2001 to 30 h in 2004 (Sugrue, 2004).

With rising expenditures and increasing training needs, the library community is beginning to give increased attention to evaluation. In the library instructional community this focus is reflected in the American Library Association's (ALA) newest Research Agenda for Library Instruction and Information Literacy (Association of College and Research Libraries [ACRL] Instruction Section [IS] Research and Scholarship Committee, 2005). One of its suggested research question, "What are the most cost-effective methods for assessment of learning outcomes?" directly relates to evaluation. The American Association of Law Libraries also has a number of research agenda items that focus on staff development, including, "How well are law librarians served by their local, regional, and national professional organizations in matters of continuing education, public relations, and promotion of common interests?" (American

Association of Law Libraries' Research Agenda, 2000). Another national professional library organization, the Medical Library Association, also lists training program evaluation as a research priority (Homan, McGowan, & Lilly, 2002).

The problems of skill depreciation and the hiring of a large number of new managers and leaders are driving the library communities' research agenda toward more accountability in training. Being able to show funding agencies that training is effective and whether or not it changes employees' behavior, impacts service and information products, and that it provides a ROI is more important now than ever (Craven & McNulty, 1994). Unfortunately proving that training is working has been given little attention among librarians.

We Just Don't Know

As a profession, we are unclear about the state of current evaluation practices in library training programs. According to the Library Literature & Information Science Index, there has been no research reported that provides information about how library training organizations are evaluating the success of their work. We do not know how library training organizations are assessing participants' satisfaction with the training experience or how organizations are assessing actual learning. There has been no research to show how library staff members have taken what they have learned and applied it back on the job or that the new skills and behaviors are making a difference in the library workplace. In addition, no work has been done to support the claim that library staff training is creating a ROI for not only the individual, but also the organization and the customers. A final gap in what we know about training evaluation is how evaluation data is being used to improve training programs.

Another problem is that there is no generally accepted library training evaluation model to follow. A review of the curriculum of graduate library programs shows that many training programs in library settings are developed and staffed by librarians with no background in human resource development or training. Not unlike the early days of library computing when librarians interested in computing were made systems administrators, librarians who enjoy teaching have often found themselves head of training departments. I spoke to at least a dozen training leader during both the 2004 and the 2005 ALA Continuing Library Education Network and Exchange

(CLENE) Training Showcase who found themselves in just that position-thrilled to have the position, but realizing there is more to develope library staff members than having an outgoing personality and enjoying teaching. The data collected as part of this study does in fact show that few are members of professional training organizations such as the ASTD, the Academy of Human Resource Development (AHRD), or the International Society for Performance Improvement (ISPI).

The increase in the number of courses about ROI for training and articles about ROI seems to indicate an interest in understanding felt need to comprehend and use evaluation models, especially those having to do with ROI. Searches using both Google and ProQuest reveal increased attention to ROI.

Google search results for the keywords, *ROI workshops* and *training about ROI*, significantly increased from 2000 to 2004. Only 39 hits on the Google search (*roi workshop* and *training*) appear for 2000, at least 129 appear for the year 2004 (Stites, 2005) and 258 for the year 2007 (Stites, 2007). Although the meaning of these numbers cannot be determined without further research, they appear to indicate an increased interest in the subject.

The number of articles about training's ROI has also increased. A database search ((*ROI*) AND *training*) in the citation and abstract fields, between January 1997 and December 2000 in the ProQuest Global database, cited 30 scholarly articles. The same search executed for the years 2001 through the end of 2004, resulted in 53 scholarly articles, an increase of almost 18% (Stites, 2007). Another 48 articles were added in 2005 and 2006, almost doubling the increase again.

So What Do We Need To Do?

Assuming that training can impact performance and is necessary to provide quality library service, and that library organizations want a return on their investment in training, we must establish workable evaluation models. We need to begin by documenting evaluation practices currently used in training programs for library staff members, including metrics used in calculating ROI.

This study focused on two research questions: (1) What are the current training evaluation practices used in library staff training programs? (2) Which training evaluation models would best fit library staff development needs?

ASSUMPTIONS

The following assumptions were made in the design of the study:

1. Training is necessary to provide quality library service.
2. Library organizations want a return on their investment in training.
3. Training can impact performance.
4. Libraries need to make decisions regarding the distribution of financial and human resources.
5. Members of the ALA's subgroups the Continuing Library Education Network and Exchange Roundtable (CLENERT) and the Interlibrary Cooperation and Networking Section (ICAN), U.S. State Libraries, and library cooperatives constitute "library staff training providers."
6. Members of the ALA's subgroups CLENERT and ICAN, State Libraries, and other library cooperatives are knowledgeable about industry practices.

RATIONALE

This research rests on the Human Resource Development (HRD) field and its foundational theory of psychology. According to Swanson and Holton (1997), psychological theory encompasses the main human components of developing human resources and serves as one of the three legs on which HRD is based. Although this study is based on the foundational theories of psychology and learning theory, the theoretical framework guiding this study is comprised of instructional design theory, the instructional system design model, *ADDIE*, and finally various aspects of evaluation (Fig. 1).

Instructional Design Theory

Instructional System Design Model (ADDIE)

Evaluation Models and Metrics

Fig. 1. Theoretical Framework.

The major underpinning of this research is instructional design theory which provides a number of instructional system design models (e.g., Dick & Carey Model, ADDIE Model, Kemp Model, ICARE Model, and ASSURE Model) on which instructional designers base their work (McGriff, 2005). This study focuses specifically on the evaluation component from the *ADDIE* model (Fig. 2).

There are at least three factors fueling the need to describe current training evaluation practices used in libraries, and to refine an ROI model that library administrators and staff training professionals could use to establish the value of training. First, there have been no research studies that focus on libraries' current training evaluation practices for library staff development. In addition, there are no research studies about the ROI for training library staff. And finally, the profession does not have a generally accepted evaluation and ROI model.

In 2003, Patricia Pulliam Phillips studied evaluation practices in the public sector and the variables that influenced the use of different levels of evaluation (Phillips, 2003a, 2003b). Based on her work and two previous studies from the business sector (Twitchell, 1997) and healthcare (Hill, 1999), she suggested further study of training evaluation using the variables: organization characteristics, stakeholder perspective, manager experience, need for training, barriers to evaluation, criteria for selecting programs, and the training process (Phillips, 2003a, 2003b).

By exploring similar variables and trends in evaluation of library staff training, library training providers will have additional ways to improve

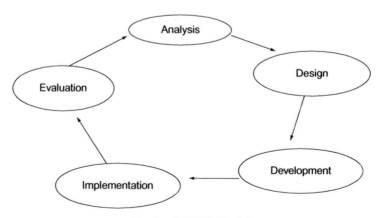

Fig. 2.   ADDIE Model.

learning and performance. Library administrators will be able to use this information about evaluation to make better decisions regarding use and distribution of financial and human assets.

STATEMENT OF HYPOTHESES

The hypotheses were adapted from *Training Evaluation in the Public Sector* (Phillips, 2003a, 2003b) with permission.

H1. Training for library staff is evaluated primarily at Levels 1(reaction) and 2 (learning).

H2. There is no generally accepted method of evaluating return-on-investment in library staff training.

H3. Differences in percentage of evaluation conducted at the five levels are associated with library organization characteristics.

H4. Differences in percentage of evaluation conducted at the five levels (reaction, learning, behavior, organizational impact, and ROI) are associated with library organization training practices, including the need for training and the training process.

SCOPE AND DELIMITATIONS OF THE STUDY

The scope and parameters of this quantitative study were limited in several ways. First, data was collected using survey research methods during 2006 from library trainers operating only in face-to-face training sessions in the United States. Data from interventions other than face-to-face sessions will not be collected. For example, data regarding evaluating web-based training interventions will not be collected. Web-based and computer-based training continue to increase, making evaluation of this type of delivery mechanism critical; however, it is not directly addressed in this study.

Delimitations of this study also include items within the researcher's influence that may affect external validity (Locke, Spirduso, & Silverman, 1987). In this study, external validity is the extent to which the findings can be applied to other library trainers and library training organizations beyond those that were studied (Gall, Borg, & Gall, 1996).

The results of this study were expected to be generalized to the library training population. The validity of that population was expected to be high because the sample was randomly selected from a nationwide group of library trainers and training organizations. The target sample included all of the members of the continuing education and training division of the ALA, training leaders in U.S. public and academic libraries, and all of the U.S.-based library cooperatives. Library cooperatives typically provide large programs of continuing education and training (Curry & Baughman, 1997; Bolt, 1998) and are established in every geographic region in the U.S. The results of this study were not intended to be generalized beyond the library training community.

Furthermore, this study did not attempt to calculate the ROI of any particular training program or provide information about causation. It was not the intent of this study to actually assign an actual ROI estimate to any of the participants' training programs or sessions. In addition, the data collected in this study did not provide any descriptions of causality. For example, just because a variable such as larger staff size may seem to be linked to higher use of Level 5 evaluation, it does not suggest that larger staff size actually causes more use of Level 5 evaluation.

Limitations (Charles, 1998) of this study that were beyond the control of the researcher included loss of participants during the study, as well as biased results from participants. Because the research data was collected via self-reporting on survey instruments rather than by testing or experimental means, another limitation was the subjective nature of the instrument used.

DEFINITIONS OF TRAINING EVALUATION

One challenge in analyzing the literature about training evaluation is that it is often unclear what researchers mean when they use the term *evaluation*. In 1989, Marguerite Foxon undertook a meta-analysis of the training evaluation literature published between 1970 and 1986 and the resulting report detailed numerous definitions (Foxon, 1989). These definitions of evaluation fall into two distinct categories, beginning with Williams (1976) and Harper and Bell (1982) who viewed evaluation as assessing or enabling judgments about value or worth of training to the organization. Both researchers wrote specifically about the importance of evaluation so that decisions regarding support for training programs could be made. Foxon identified other uses of the term *evaluation* to mean determining a training program's effectiveness (Snyder, Raben, & Farr, 1980; Goldstein, 1986,

1993) and also as a process used to make program improvements (Rackham, 1973; Smith, 1980; Morris, 1984; Tyson & Birnbrauer, 1985; Foxon, 1986). Of all the various descriptions, Hamblin's (1974) definition of evaluation is cited most often, perhaps because it encompasses all of these ideas: *Any attempt to obtain information (feedback) on the effects of a training programme, and to assess the value in the light of that information* (Hamblin, 1974).

LITERATURE REVIEW

History and Models of Measurement and Evaluation

Wang and Sptizer (2005) described HRD measurement and evaluation (M & E) as evolving through three stages. They identified the first stage as practice-oriented and atheoretical, spanning the years 1950–1987. This initial stage of measurement and evaluation was dominated by Kirkpatrick's (1959a, 1959b, 1960a, 1960b) practice-oriented levels and scant theoretical research is found during this first stage (Wang & Sptizer, 2005).

The second stage, referred to as *process-driven operational* (1987–present) expands on the first stage with the introduction of Dr. Jack J. Phillips' method for calculating ROI and other researchers more in-depth analysis of previous M & E efforts (Phillips, 1987; Alliger & Janak, 1989). The final stage, according to Wang and Sptizer (2005), is a research-oriented, practice-based comprehensive period (2000–present) and is being driven by accountability and a need for HRD theory building.

Stage One: Practice-Oriented (1950–1987)
Stage One begins with the earliest mention of training evaluation in the literature which was made by Kirkpatrick (1959a, 1959b, 1960a, 1960b) in a series of articles that outlined his four "levels." According to Kirkpatrick (1959a, 1959b), evaluation of training could be conceptualized into four distinct outcomes: reaction, learning, behavior, and results (Table 1).

Numerous evaluation models evolved from Kirkpatrick's four level design and most practitioners have continued to view evaluation through this programmatic and practice-oriented lens for decades (Wang & Wang, 2005). Some of these models incorporate additional steps or levels, for example, adding training design and needs analysis on the front end (Warr, Bird, & Rackham, 1970). Additional models have appended enhancements to the back end, such as societal impact and ROI (Phillips, 1994, 1995; Kearns & Miller,

Table 1. Kirkpatrick's Four Levels of Evaluation.

Level	Questions
1. Reaction	Were the participants pleased with the program?
2. Learning	What did the participants learn in the program?
3. Behavior	Did the participants change their behavior based on what was learned?
4. Results	Did the change in behavior positively affect the organization?

Table 2. Phillips' Five Level ROI Framework.

Levels	Description
Reaction and planned action	Measures participant's reaction to the program and outlines specific plans for implementation
Learning	Measures skills, knowledge, or attitude changes
Job applications	Measures change in behavior on the job and specific application of the training material
Business results	Measures business impact of the program
Return on investment (Phillips, 1994)	Measures the monetary value of the results and costs for the program, usually expressed as a percentage

1997). Others have added to both sides (Kaufman et al., 1995; Molenda, Pershing, & Reigeluth, 1996). At least six researchers have expanded the Kirkpatrick model to serve as an evaluation model for an entire training program, not just of a single intervention (Warr et al., 1970; Brinkerhoff, 1987; Bushnell, 1990; Sleezer, 1992; Bernthal, 1995; Swanson & Holton, 1999).

Second Stage: Process-Driven Operational (1987–Present.)
Phillips (1994) introduced a fifth level to Kirkpatrick's model that would provide information about the financial impact of training interventions. An early response to the increasing pressure from CEOs and other administrators to demonstrate accountability and illustrate the value of training, Phillips' work was responsible for providing practitioners with tools to establish the financial impacts of training (Table 2).

The KPMT model (Kearns & Miller, 1997) is also very similar to Kirkpatrick and Phillips. KPMT simply combines job application and business results into the KPMT Level 3 labeled *Transfer to the Workplace/ Behavior* and revises Phillips' Level 5 (ROI) to include only hard measures. Like Fitz-enz (2000), Kearns and Miller emphasize that training must directly influence a business objective. Evaluators must be persistent and

Table 3. KPMT Model (Kearns & Miller, 1997).

KPMT Model (Kearns & Miller, 1997)	Similar to
Reaction	Kirkpatrick Level 1
Learning	Kirkpatrick Level 2
Transfer to workplace/behavior	Kirkpatrick Levels 3 and 4
Bottom line added value, measured in relation to the base level measures taken	Phillips' Level 5

continue to ask questions until tangible outcomes from training are revealed (Kearns & Miller, 1997; Table 3).

Kaufman et al. (1995) added a number of additional considerations to Kirkpatrick's four steps, including a final process to evaluate societal outcomes of the intervention. This model was the first to suggest the notion that costs can be examined at each stage, using efficiency measures at the input level to utility costs at the highest level (Kaufman et al., 1995; Table 4).

The Indiana University approach (Molenda et al., 1996) added activity accounting (e.g., number of training sessions and number of trainees) to the front of the Kirkpatrick (1959a, 1959b) model and added social impact to the end. Also, similar to Kirkpatrick, especially Levels 3 and 4, Fitz-enz (1994) describes his Training Validation System (TVS) approach as including situation analysis, intervention, impact, and value. Central to the TVS approach is ascertaining needs and training gaps. Brinkerhoff's (1987) six stage model also evaluates the whole process of HRD, not just the training itself. It includes goal setting, program design and implementation, learning outcomes, usage outcomes, impacts, and worth.

Similar to the CIRO Model (Warr et al., 1970), Bushnell's IPO Model (input, process, and output) focuses more on inputs to training with the outputs and outcomes aligning with Kirkpatrick's Levels 1–4 (Bushnell, 1990). Intervention planning under the IPO Model requires indicators of performance to be set for each of the IPO stages: input, process, output, and outcomes. Notably similar to Kirkpatrick's Levels 3 and 4, Bushnell's third stage, *Output*, includes reactions, knowledge and skills gained, plus improved job performance. The final stage in Bushnell's IPO Model, *Outcomes*, includes not only a financial impact measure, much like that of J. J. Phillips (1994), but also a measure of customer satisfaction.

Another training evaluation model similar to Kirkpatrick's is the Training Effectiveness Evaluation (TEE) Model (Swanson & Sleezer, 1987). TEE is similar to the Kirkpatrick model because it scores satisfaction, learning, and performance indicators. Similar to J. J. Phillips' (1994) model, it includes a

Table 4. Kaufman et al. (1995) Evaluation Model.

Level 1: input	Similar to Kirkpatrick's but added role, usefulness, appropriateness and contributions of the methods and resources used
Level 2: process	Similar to reaction level but includes an analysis of whether the intervention was implemented properly in terms of achieving its objectives
Level 3: micro (acquisition)	Similar to learning level and examines both individual and small group mastery and competence
Level 4: micro (performance)	Like behavior level
Level 5: macro	Relates to the results level and examines organizational contributions and payoffs
Level 6: mega	An additional level which looks at societal outcomes

cost–benefit analysis (CBA) tool. TEE expands on these earlier models to include components for not only planning evaluation tasks, but also for measuring and reporting effectiveness.

Although not as well known, Bernthal's (1995) four-step model expands the context level by including identification of the organization's values and linking them with skills, knowledge, and attitudes. Bernthal's model ties the outcome of training to the organization's strategies (Step 1) by linking employee skills, knowledge, and attitudes (Step 2) to the scope and purpose of the evaluation (Step 3). Finally, Step 4 identifies a process to determine valid and reliable evaluation data sources.

In 1999, Swanson and Holton suggested that using language that more nearly reflects for-profit vocabulary would improve communication between HRD practitioners and corporate stakeholders. Since for-profit businesses use the words *assessment, performance,* and *measurement* instead of *evaluation,* Swanson and Holton (1999) warned that using the term *evaluation,* an educational and governmental term, may lead to a negative image towards the work of HRD professionals. Swanson and Holton expanded the five-level evaluation model (Phillips, 1994), to more nearly reflect the language of the for-profit culture and created the Results Assessment System which includes the core components of Process, Domains, Results Assessment Planning, and Assessment Tools.

The first component, *Process,* mimics that of outcome-based evaluation beginning with specifying the expected results, planning the assessment, developing measures, collecting and analyzing the data, and reporting the results assessment. The second component, *Domains,* measures performance, learning, and perception results, and is essentially identical, although

Table 5. Swanson and Holton's (1999) Results Assessment System.

Domains	Core	Compared to Kirkpatrick/ Phillips Model
Performance results	System measures in units (how many cars were made?)	Level 4 Business impact
	Financial results	Level 5 ROI
Learning results	Knowledge	Level 2 Learning
	Expertise	Level 3 Behavior
Perception results	Participant perceptions of the training	Level 1 Reaction
	Stakeholder perceptions (does the boss think the training did what it was designed to do?)	None

the levels are inverted, to evaluation at Kirkpatrick's Levels 1–5. The third component is *Planning* and describes which domains get measured, how data is collected and analyzed, and what tools and information is needed to compare the results. The final component, *Tools*, provides techniques for developing measures of results, as well as, how to conduct an assessment when interventions have not been connected to up-front analysis (Swanson & Holton, 1999; Swanson, 2005; Table 5).

Most recently, Holton (2005) described a revised HRD Evaluation and Research Model. Holton's model has evolved to include motivation theory and has identified specific variables that should be measured within each of the domains (Holton, 1996). The model has not yet been tested and Holton continues to work on the organizational performance domain.

Third Stage: Research-Oriented, Practice-based Comprehensive Period (2000–Present)

Wang and Wang (2005), concerned with the lack of methodologies and techniques to support evaluation services to for-profit businesses, described a systems approach to overcome these barriers. They discuss three barriers to successful training evaluation: business, technical, and analytical and have developed a conceptual model for conducting evaluations to determine the business impact of training.

The first business barrier is one of the perspectives. Like the field of accounting, current HRD evaluation practice involves reviewing intervention outputs and reporting the results. The field of finance, however, focuses more on looking forward and attempting to predict the effects of current forces on the future. Wang and Wang (2005) suggest that the differences

Table 6. Conceptual Model for Conducting HRD Evaluations
at the Fourth Level (Wang & Wang, 2005).

Input		Output/Business Impact
HRD – reaction, learning, and performance	Process	Monetary (continuous [sales] or discreet [productivity])
Operations Marketing		Non-monetary (continuous [turnover, time] or discreet [job satisfaction; customer satisfaction])

between accounting and finance are similar to the differences between
current training evaluation models and what new models might provide.
They posit that evaluation is like accounting and provides a picture of past
performance, in contrast to finance which predicts future outcomes.

Like Spitzer (2005), Wang and Wang (2005) agree that current evaluation
practices describe what training accomplished in the past, but is not predicting
what training impacts we could expect from employees or organizations in the
future. If evaluation were more like the field of finance, where results are
projected rather than like accounting where the past is reported, we would be
able to increasingly develop a market for HRD services.

The second barrier to evaluation is a technical one and refers to the
validity of ROI analysis. Current measurement and evaluation methods are
too simplified and do not isolate the effect of HRD. Wang and Wang (2005)
suggest that by using econometric or statistical processes it is, in fact,
possible to measure the net effect of HRD programs. However, until we get
theories and methodologies in place to measure and predict, we may
eventually hinder further development toward the market for HRD services.

The last hurdle, the analytical barrier, is that HRD professionals need to
reframe their conception of measurement and evaluation. This rearrange-
ment and reclassification of the Kirkpatrick Levels 1–3 (reaction, learning,
and performance) as inputs to an analytical framework will assist with
providing a clear connection between the Levels 1–3 taxonomies and the
Level 4 evaluation model (Table 6).

Alternative Models

Although numerous training evaluation models have been based on
Kirkpatrick (1959a, 1959b), there have been other models, especially in

the past decade whose perspective is decidedly different. A number of evaluation researchers have described evaluation activities by looking at the purpose of the evaluations. For example, Pulley (1994) focuses on communicating the evaluation results to decision makers. In his responsive evaluation model it is critical to identify the decision makers and find out what they need to know. Once the data about the intervention is collected, it must be translated into meaningful information to keep decision makers involved and informed.

Taking a more qualitative approach to evaluation, Preskill and Torres (1999) focus on organizational change, as well as, individual, team, and organizational learning. Their model of evaluation rests on four primary learning processes: dialogue, reflection, asking questions, and identifying and clarifying values, beliefs, assumptions, and knowledge. As the HRD field increases its embrace of qualitative methods such as collaborative inquiry and action inquiry technologies (Brooks & Watkins, 1994) collaboration between researchers and participants may increase.

Another qualitative approach, the Success Case Method (SCM) (Brinkerhoff, 2003), was developed to evaluate the business effect of training. Its success lies in its simplicity and the fact that it produces actual evidence of the impact of training. The method is two-part and begins by first identifying individuals or teams that are successfully using a skill or process that was learned through a structured training initiative. The second step is to interview participants using naturalistic inquiry and case study techniques. Including individuals and teams that are not experiencing success with the skill or process taught can also be a valuable way of learning more about the individual, team, or organizational performance the training was intended to impact.

Models Using Different Measures

In the Balanced Scorecard, Kaplan and Norton (1996), assert that we need to measure not only learning, but also finance, customers, and internal business processes. Measures of learning and innovation are as important as financial measures in evaluating a company's competitive position. The concepts of "pay back" and "pay forward" introduced by Lee (1996), describe the distinction between short- and long-term benefits of training. Lee outlines how evaluation practices and relationships change as an organization's level of maturity regarding training changes. He suggests that organizations move through six different levels of operationalizing training: no systematic training, isolated tactical training, training integrated with operational management, training as the means for implementing corporate strategy and achieving change, training and leaning possibilities help to shape strategy, and training and learning are the processes through which strategy is formulated.

Evaluation Studies

A review of the literature revealed four recent training evaluation studies (Twitchell, 1997; Hill, 1999; Strunk, 1999; Phillips, 2003a, 2003b), none however, in libraries. These studies describe the amount of evaluation taking place in organizations and at which of Kirkpatrick's and Phillips' levels they are being evaluated. The studies also indicated what kind of instruments or processes were in place to collect the evaluation data, and why some organizations did not evaluate various levels.

The first study (Twitchell, 1997) surveyed 146 ASTD technical and skills trainers from all types of organizations. The results found that although many organizations evaluated training programs at Kirkpatrick's Level 1 (reaction), less than half evaluated learning (47.05%), behavior (30.54%), and organizational results or ROI (20.82%). Similar results were found by Hill (1999) when she surveyed 244 ASTD Healthcare Forum members. Hill (1999) found that healthcare organizations had no generally accepted method of evaluating training, and that evaluation planning more often than not does not occur. Hill also found that ROI evaluations were effective when they were perceived as credible and appropriate for a variety of programs. Use of evaluation Levels 2–5 increased when results of training programs were normally reported to management. When training departments were not required to report training outcomes to management, use of evaluation Levels 2–5 was reduced.

Strunk (1999) studied a group of 186 ASTD HRD and ROI Network members from all types of organizations. Her results indicated that more organizations were evaluating at a higher level, perhaps due to the population surveyed. Since the participants in the survey were all from the HRD and ROI sections of ASTD, it would not be unusual to expect that this group would have a higher use rate, because of their assumed interest in HRD and ROI.

Phillips (2003a, 2003b) also found that more evaluation occurs at the reaction level (Level 1) than at any other level. Phillips' study also revealed

Table 7. Comparison of Training Evaluation Studies.

Evaluation Level		Twitchell (1997)	Hill (1999)	Strunk (1999)	Phillips (2003a, 2003b)	Stites (2007)
		Technical and Skills Trainers	Healthcare	HRD/ ROI Members	Public Sector	Libraries
Level 1	Reaction	72.74	80.85	78.0	72.18	82.30
Level 2	Learning	47.05	52.59	88.7	31.65	33.60
Level 3	Behavior	30.54	30.77	75.7	20.42	19.43
Level 4	Organizational impact	20.82	16.97	50.5	12.21	23.63
Level 5	ROI	Included in level 4	3.73	(Part of Level 4)	5.25	05.50

that expectations of management increased the level of evaluation used (Table 7).

Summary

The historical description of training evaluation highlighted the strong and continued role of practice-oriented evaluation as developed by Kirkpatrick (1959a, 1959b, 1960a, 1960b). Its evolution to a more process-driven method including Phillips' (1994) ROI calculations led to the newest stage, which is a research-oriented, practice-based period driven by accountability (Wang & Sptizer, 2005). Four previous studies were noted which described training evaluation practices used by technical and skills trainers, in the healthcare industry, among ASTD HRD/ROI members, and in public sector organizations. Although there were library staff that provided technical and skill training and were ASTD HRD/ROI members employed in the healthcare field and in the public sector, there was no indication in any of these studies that library staff were among the respondents except in the Phillips (2003a, 2003b) study. In this study at least one of the participants had a master's degree in library science. The lack of literature describing training evaluation in library settings formed the basis for this study.

METHODOLOGY

The purpose of this quantitative study was to explore evaluation practices used in library staff training and development programs. The study addressed important questions including:

(1) What are the current training evaluation practices used in library staff training programs?
(2) What training evaluation models would best fit library staff development needs?

Research Design

This study used survey research methods and employed a cross-sectional field survey to explore the dependent and independent variables. The research design for collecting and analyzing the data involved surveying

Table 8. Kirkpatrick's Four Levels, Adapted to Include Phillips' Measure for Return on Investment.

Level	Dependent Variable	Description
1	Reaction and planned action	Were the participants satisfied with each workshop and what were their perceptions about what they learned? Were the methods of presentation, content, use of audio-visual materials, class materials effective? Were the participants pleased with the program?
2	Learning	What skills, knowledge, and abilities were affected by the training?
3	On-the-job application	What new or improved changed skills, knowledge, or abilities were applied on-the-job? What new tasks, processes, or procedures were implemented as a result of this new learning?
4	Business results	How did the participants' changed skills, knowledge, or abilities impact the library? How was service to internal and external customers impacted? Did the on-the-job applications produce measurable results?
5	Return-on-investment	Did the financial value of the results of the training exceed the cost?

training professionals about current evaluation practices used in library training programs. The web-based survey instrument measured the dependent variable, training evaluation practices, for five levels of evaluation. The five levels of evaluation referred to Kirkpatrick's four-level evaluation model of reaction, learning, use of the learning on the job, business impact plus Phillips' fifth measure, and ROI (Kirkpatrick, 1959a; Phillips, 1994). The decision to use Phillips' five levels as the dependent variables was based on the popularity and familiarity of the levels with training professionals. The five dependent variables are described in Table 8 that follows. The independent variables shown in Table 9 were divided into five categories: training provider characteristics, training evaluation process, perceived need for training, barriers to evaluation, and criteria for selecting programs to evaluate.

Survey research is a basic quantitative method for library-related research (Powell, 1991) and surveys are most often used in quantitative research to describe attitudes, behaviors, or characteristics of a population (Creswell, 2002). This study will employ a self-administered web-based survey to gather data about training evaluation practices in library settings.

Surveys requiring self-reporting, rather than in-person interviews or telephone questionnaires are increasing (Dillman, 1999). As a culture, we are transitioning to a self-service model of information acquisition and information transfer. Self administration of many day-to-day activities is not only common, but also required. Usage of ATM machines, prescription refill systems, and online banking are a few of the common tasks that have moved to self-service in the past decade (Dillman, 1999).

The literature reflects three primary concerns regarding Web-based surveys: visual design factors, response rates, and participants' levels of web access (Dillman, 1999). There have been questions about whether web-based surveys are equivalent to the traditional pencil and paper survey. King and Miles (1995) found no evidence to support the inferiority of web-based instruments. Penny (2003) found that survey delivery methods indicated little evidence that the method of delivery affected the answers to surveys' questions.

One reason researchers support the use of web-based surveys is that response time is faster than that of paper questionnaires and surveys, and the cost is nominal. A study by Bachmann, Elfrink, and Vazzana (2000) revealed that the mean return time for e-mail surveys was 4.3 days and mail surveys took 18.3 days to be returned.

Although response times are very positive with electronic surveys, response rates continue to be a concern. Until recently, most surveys were

Table 9.   Independent Variables.

Category	Variable
Training provider characteristics	Type of provider Staff size Evaluation policy
Training evaluation process	Timing of evaluation planning Evaluation reporting Number of employees responsible for evaluation
Need for training	Acquire new attitude Perform at a set level Training as a reward Activity for all employees Compliance with regulation or certification Change in organizational outcomes
Barriers to evaluation	Cost in hours, expenses, and capital Lack of training or experience Not required by organization Little perceived value to the organization Policy prohibits the evaluation of employees Union opposition
Criteria for selecting programs	Operational goals Cost of program Visibility of program Expected life cycle of program Management interest Perceived need for program

printed and mailed via U.S. Postal Service or a ground delivery provider (Penny, 2003). According to Michigan State University researchers Kaplowitz, Hadlock, and Levine (2004), web-based surveys can garner comparable response rates, however, if the web-based surveys lead with a traditional mail-based notification to participants. Study participants that are notified that they will be asked to complete a web-based survey are more likely to submit a response (Kaplowitz et al., 2004).

A letter alerting participants in this study of the upcoming web-based survey was mailed before the web-based survey was released. Two weeks after the alert letter was mailed, participants received an e-mail with an embedded link to the survey. When participants opened the weblink, they were automatically placed at the introduction to the web-survey.

Discussions in the literature about web-based surveys have suggested that lack of access to the Internet would implement barriers to participants (Tse, 1998). The dramatic increase in Internet access, however, has virtually removed that barrier. Internet access has become ubiquitous and virtually all library staff members have access to the Internet. In a 1999 U.S. Department of Education study, 92% of public libraries across the United States reported that they provided access to the Internet for adults (National Center for Education Statistics, 2000; Bureau of the Census, 2003). In Florida, the most recent public library statistics report that 100% of Florida's public libraries provide Internet access (State Library and Archives of Florida, 2004). Statistics regarding access to the Internet in U.S. public schools were reported at 99% and in Florida, 100% of the public schools provide Internet access (National Center for Education Statistics, 2004). Internet access as a barrier to web-based surveys is not expected to influence the response rate or cause a significant coverage error.

Pilot Studies

A pilot survey was tested with three training coordinators from the Southwest Florida ASTD Chapter. The suggestions generated from this pilot were used to improve the survey design.

Population and Sample

The population that could provide information to answer the research questions included trainers and staff responsible for evaluating U.S. library staff training programs. The target sample population was drawn from three groups: trainers and staff from State Library Agencies, ALA members involved in training, and training directors from U.S. libraries.

State Library Agencies have been established in each of the 50 states and according to the 2003 State Library Agency Survey, all 50 agencies engage in providing training directly to library staff. Each State Library training department was included in the population and 10 participated in the survey.

The second group that was asked to participate in the online survey included members of certain subgroups of the ALA. The Association has over 64,000 members worldwide and includes all types of library staff, trustees, and a variety of vendors, and includes dozens of Divisions, Sections, and Round Tables. The members of two of its subgroups, the

CLENERT and the ICAN were included in the sample for this study. The ALA's subgroup, CLENERT, is made up of 56 training organizations and 333 personal members; ICAN includes 123 individuals employed by library cooperatives that provide training. The final group included in the target sample was made up of any additional library training professionals identified from library literature and not already included.

The mailing lists of the target sample were combined and duplicate names removed so that only one survey was mailed to each person. Decisions about who within an organization should receive the survey were made based on position titles. The surveys were sent to employees holding titles that indicate the highest level of training administration (e.g., Training Director, Manager, or Coordinator).

Once the target sample was identified, representative simple random sampling techniques were used to select the sample population. Using a confidence level of 95% and a confidence interval of $+/-4$, and considering the target population is estimated to be 560, the sample size needed was 275. To begin the final sample selection, each member of the target sample was assigned a number (e.g. 1–560). The final sample of 272 participants was selected using a Random Numbers Table. Alert letters and online surveys were distributed to this final sample.

Instrumentation

The data was collected via a survey instrument slightly modified from the survey *Training Evaluation in the Public Sector* (Phillips, 2003a, 2003b) to reflect the nomenclature of librarianship. Both the survey instrument and the letter of permission to use the survey and to modify the language to reflect the library field's nomenclature is shown in Appendix B. Phillips' survey, from which the instrument in this research is based, was developed from two previous instruments, *Evaluation: Present Practices in U.S. Business and Industry Technical Training* (Twitchell, 1997) and *Survey of Present Practices in Training Evaluation: U.S. Healthcare Industry* (Hill, 1999).

Validity and Reliability
Three common categories of validity: content validity, criterion validity, and construct validity are important to consider if instruments are to measure what they are designed to measure (Swanson & Holton, 1997). They must contain questions that are representative of what could be asked (Creswell, 2002). An instrument may be very reliable, with the results being able to be

replicated, but if the measurements do not relate to the research questions and do not measure what was intended, the result will not be valid (Powell, 1991). Criterion validity questions whether the measure actually predicts the dependent variable it is supposed to predict and construct validity is associated with the meaning of the instrument scores and whether they can be safely generalized.

Content validity is particularly important since it indicates that the survey items actually measure what was desired. According to Lynn (1986), establishing content validity is a two stage process beginning with the developmental stage, which involves domain identification, item generation, and instrument formation. Next, the second stage of judgment-quantification for cognitive measures requires assertion by at least five experts that the items and entire instrument are content valid (Lynn, 1986). The content validity of this study is based on that of its predecessors, *Evaluation: Present Practices in U.S. Business and Industry Technical Training* (Twitchell, 1997), *Survey of Present Practices in Training Evaluation: U.S. Healthcare Industry* (Hill, 1999), and *Training Evaluation in the Public Sector* (Phillips, 2003a, 2003b).

The earliest of the three surveys on which this instrument is based is Twitchell's (1997) survey which was designed by training evaluation leaders, Dr. Ed Holton, III and Dr. Jack Phillips and reviewed by a group of students from a graduate research class, training managers and supervisors, academic researchers, and two business and training experts. Based on expert judgment, it provided the necessary content validity from which Hill (1999) developed the *Survey of Present Practices in Training Evaluation: U.S. Healthcare Industry*. Before administering the actual survey, Hill randomly selected 12 individuals involved and experienced in training to field test the survey to further establish content validity. Responses from seven individuals were collected and used to improve the instrument. Hill implemented additional validity checks by engaging a panel of experts using a structured procedure as described by Lynn (1986) where eight training evaluation professionals ranked each question's relevance to each research question on a scale of 1–4. The team evaluating the content validity of the questions agreed that the survey items did map to the research questions.

Field Procedures

Five mailing lists were rented from the ALA. The first list consisted of approximately 220 members of the Continuing Education Network

Exchange (CLENE); the second list was from the 123 members in the ALA Interlibrary Cooperation Network Section (ICANS). The third rented list included the State Library Agency Section members (110). The last two lists included public and academic libraries which hold ALA membership. Additions to the overall mailing list were compiled from library directories, library literature, and suggestions from the field. The mailing list was developed in an Excel spreadsheet and duplicates were removed.

Once the mailing label spreadsheet was developed, any missing contact information, including e-mail addresses was added. Missing contact information was located in a number of ways, including the consulting of print library directories and other library literature, in addition to phone calls and Internet searches.

Once completed, this spreadsheet was used to produce mailing labels for the alert letters that were mailed two weeks before the online link to the actual survey was activated. Once the survey was activated and ready for participants' input, they were notified via e-mail. Invitations to participate were mailed to 272 randomly selected individuals and 94 answered some or all of the items.

Data Collection and Recording
Data was collected from library trainers, training departments, and organizations throughout the United States via a web-based questionnaire in April and May 2006. The survey was hosted on the web by a MarketTools, a commercial firm, at http://zoomerang.com. Both quantitative and narrative data was collected at the web site and archived on the MarketTools' server. The researcher has used MarketTools' Zoomerang survey site in over 50 previous surveys and has found it dependable. The server has experienced no unplanned downtime and the data backup procedures follow standard accepted practices. Zoomerang customers include DuPont, Tyco Electronics, PeopleSoft, the American Association of School Administrators, and Levi Strauss & Co. Dr. Scott McLeod, Co-Director of the University of Minnesota School Technology Leadership Initiative (STLI), reports that "With Zoomerang we get better feedback. It seems people are more comfortable with a keyboard than with a pen and paper. So (with online surveys) we get longer and richer responses."

The data was password protected and could be viewed only by the researcher. The data was accessible throughout the collection period and a final data export occurred once the survey was closed and data collection completed. Once the survey was closed, the web site would not accept any further input from participants.

The data was exported from the web site into a Microsoft Excel spreadsheet and then transferred into the statistical analysis software, SPSS, Version 11.0. SPSS was used to develop descriptive statistics and inferential statistics, including correlations and one-way analysis of variance (ANOVA).

Data Processing and Analysis
Once the archived data from the completed surveys were retrieved in Excel format, each data point was assigned a name (e.g., QA1, QA2), and then imported into the statistical analysis software, SPSS Version 11.0. SPSS was used to describe or test each of the four hypotheses using the statistical tools shown in Appendix C.

Methodological Assumptions

Scores from any two individuals are independent of one another.
Population scores are normally distributed.

Limitations

There were a number of limitations of this study that were beyond the control of the researcher. First was that the online survey software did not provide a way for participants to move back to pages already completed if they wanted to. Once the answers on one page of the questionnaire were completed and submitted, no changes could be made. Future research would gain by being conducted with a product that would allow forward and backward movement throughout the instrument. Next, an additional limitation is that some biased results from participants may have been included. Because the research data was collected via self-reporting on survey instruments rather than by testing or experimental means, a limitation was the subjective nature of the instrument used.

Summary

Survey research methodology formed the basis of this study and 272 library staff trainers were asked to complete a web-based survey regarding their training evaluation practices. The resulting data was analyzed to answer questions about how library training is evaluated and correlated with organizational characteristics, the training process, need for training, barriers to evaluation, and criteria for selecting programs.

RESULTS

An analysis of the data provided evidence for each of the four hypotheses and three sub-questions. Each was tested using descriptive statistics, ANOVA, or correlations and results are presented in this chapter. The chapter is arranged of the hypotheses and begins with a review of the methodology and a presentation of the results, continues with discussion that ties the findings together in relation to the review of literature, and concludes with a summary.

Methodology

The target sample population was made up of trainers and staff responsible for evaluating U.S. library staff training programs and was drawn from three groups: trainers and staff from state library agencies, ALA members involved in training, and training professionals from U.S. libraries and library training organizations.

Once the target sample was identified, representative simple random sampling techniques were used to select the sample population. Using a confidence level of 95% and a confidence interval of $+/-4$, and considering the target population was estimated to be 560, the sample size needed was estimated to be 272. The final sample of 272 participants was selected using a Random Numbers Table. Alert letters and links to the online questionnaire were distributed to this final sample.

The online questionnaire was filled out by 94 respondents for a return rate of 34%, which is well within appropriate sampling guidelines for useful inferences to be drawn (Bartlett, Kotrlik, & Higgins, 2001). In their 2001 article, Bartlett and colleagues, provide procedures for determining sample size for population sizes from 100 to 10,000 in increments of 100. For populations of 100, the sample size needed for an alpha of 0.05 is 55; for a population of 200 for a 0.05 alpha, the authors identify the minimum returned sample must be at least 75 participants.

A reminder e-mail with a link to the survey was sent to all nonrespondents twice during the collection period to increase the number of responses.

Three potential participants contacted the researcher to request that the questionnaire be sent to another employee in the organization who would be better able to provide the information, and this was done.

Demographics

Responses came from various types of libraries and library training organizations. However, not all respondents identified their type of organization. For questions which required *type of organization* data, these cases ($n = 26$) were removed. Among the participants who identified the type of organization in which they worked, the two largest groups were 25 academic libraries (approximately 37%) and 21 library networks or consortium (31%). Other types of organizations represented among the responses were: 10 public libraries and 10 state libraries (both approximately 15%), as well as two consulting/training organizations (2%) (Table 10).

Most of the organizations identifying their size ($n = 53$) had less than 200 employees and 16 organizations reported employing more than 200. Only two responses were submitted from organizations with over 2,000 employees (Table 11).

Question 55 asked participants to identify the number of years that they had been involved in training by selecting one of the three possible answers: 1–5 years, 6–10 years, and 11 or more years. The largest group of participants (32%) reported being involved in training more than 11 years ($n = 30$), the next largest group (20%) reported between 6 and 10 years of experience ($n = 19$) and the final group (19%) reported five or less years of

Table 10.   Return Rates for Questionnaire by Type of Organization.

Type of Organization	Returned		Mailed	
	$n = 94$	%	$n = 272$	%
Network/Consortium	21	30.9	43	15.8
Public	10	14.7	44	16.2
Academic	25	36.8	138	50.7
School	0	0	0	0
Special	0	0	5	1.8
State Library	10	14.7	32	11.8
Consulting/Training	2	2.9	10	3.7
Type not identified	26	2.9		

Table 11.   Return Rate by Size of Library Organization ($n = 94$).

Number of Employees	n	%
1–10	14	15
11–20	10	11
21–40	6	6
41–75	8	9
76–100	5	5
101–200	10	11
201–500	8	9
501–750	2	2
751–1,000	1	1
1,000–2,000	2	2
Over 2,000	2	2
Unidentified size	26	28

experience (18%). Most respondents were female (88%) and 12% were male. Respondents indicated a high level of education; 91% had a master's degree or higher. Membership in professional organizations focused on training were held primarily in the ALA's Continuing Library Education Network and Exchange ($n = 28$), American Society of Training and Development ($n = 12$), American Management Association ($n = 3$), Academy of Human Resource Development ($n = 1$), and International Society of Performance Improvement ($n = 0$).

Library Training Evaluation Usage

The purpose of this study is to document evaluation practices currently used in training programs for library staff members, including metrics used in calculating ROI. The results that follow describe how library organizations evaluate their training, how ROI is determined, and how it depicts the nature of the relationship among organizational characteristics and training practices of library organizations.

Levels Most Used

The frequencies and means for Questions 1, 7, 13, 19, and 25 support the first hypothesis that *Training for library staff is evaluated primarily at Levels 1 and 2.* The mean percentage scores for both Levels 1 and 2 usage show that library training organizations evaluate almost 90% of their training sessions for Level 1 *reaction* and over 30% for Level 2 *learning*. Much less used are Level 3 *on-the-job application* (16%), Level 4 *organizational outcome* (19%), and Level 5 *ROI* (4%) (Table 12).

Of the five levels of training evaluation (Kirkpatrick, 1959a, 1959b, 1960a, 1960b; Phillips & Phillips, 1994), library organizations most often use Level 1 *reaction*; in fact, 52% of the respondents reported using Level 1 evaluation for all of their training sessions. Another 36% reported evaluating Level 1 between 75% and 99% of the time. Five percent of the respondents reported using Level 1 50–74% of the time, another 5% use it for 1–4% of their training and 2% never evaluate for Level 1.

Generally Accepted Methods of Evaluating Return on Investment

Hypothesis One focuses on all levels of evaluation usage, whereas Hypothesis Two focuses more specifically on one type of evaluation, return on investment. Hypothesis Two was tested by Question 26 and asked participants to indicate the method and the frequency of use of that method to calculate their training programs' ROI (Level 5). The questionnaire provided the participants with eight methods for calculating ROI and asked that they select all that applied and to indicate the percentage of time they employed the selected methods. The question also provided participants with the option *other* to indicate they used a method not listed and provided space to describe the method. The eight methods, defined in Chapter one from which to select were: traditional ROI calculation (ROI), CBA, payback period (PP), net present value (NPV), internal rate of return (IRR),

Table 12. Library Training and Use of Training Evaluation ($n = 58$).

Percentage of Evaluation Used	M	SD	Standard Error (SE)
Level 1 *reaction*	86.74	22.97	.03
Level 2 *learning*	30.66	36.81	.05
Level 3 *on-the-job application*	16.24	27.69	.04
Level 4 *organizational outcomes*	18.71	32.51	.04
Level 5 *ROI*	4.14	16.01	.02

Note: Cases ($n = 36$) that did not provide usage data for all five levels were removed for the purposes of testing this hypothesis.

Table 13. Methods of Determining Return on Investment ($n = 73$).

Percentage of Use (%)	ROI	CBA	PP	NPV	IRR	UA	BalSc	CoNTr	Other
0	90.4	90.4	93.2	90.4	91.8	93.2	93.2	89.0	95.9
0–19	2.7	1.4	1.4	2.7	2.7	2.7	1.4	1.4	–
20–39	–	–	–	–	–	–	–	–	–
40–59	4.1	4.1	5.5	4.1	4.1	4.1	4.1	5.5	2.7
60–79	1.4	2.7	–	1.4	–	–	1.4	1.4	1.4
80–100	1.4	1.4	–	1.4	1.4	–	–	2.7	–

Note: Dashes indicate that no data was reported.

utility analysis (UA), balanced scorecard (BalSc), and consequences of not training (CoNTr). The usage percentile ranges provided were 0%, 1–19%, 20–39%, 40–59%, 60–79%, and 80–100%.

Very few respondents reported using any of these methods to determine ROI. Of the 73 responses to this question, the most usage reported was for CoNTr ($n = 8$). Seven participants reported using traditional ROI, CBA, and NPV; six reported using IRR, and five reported PP, UA, and BalSc. Following the procedures used in Phillips (2003a, 2003b), nonresponses to this question were treated as though the participant selected 0%. Although response rates to the questionnaire were adequate overall, there was a great deal of missing data for this question. The results support the second hypothesis that *no generally accepted method of evaluating ROI in library staff training exists* (Table 13).

Generally Accepted Methods for Evaluating Levels 1–4

A sub-question for Hypothesis Two used Questions 2, 8, 14, and 20 to estimate the percentage of training sessions for which participants' organization uses each of the methods listed for Levels 1–4. Percentage ranges from which to select were: (1) 0%; (2) 1–10%; (3) 20–39%; (4) 40–59%; (5) 60–79%; and (6) 80–100%. Using frequencies and means, the most reported methods are presented in Table 14 that follows.

Use of Evaluation and Characteristics of Libraries

A one-way analysis of variance was conducted to test Hypothesis Three: The differences in percentage of evaluation conducted at the five levels are

Table 14. Preferred Evaluation Methods for Levels 1–5.

Evaluation Levels	Method	n	M	SD	Standard Error (SE)
Level 1 *reaction*	Reaction questionnaires	80	5.53	0.97	.11
Level 2 *learning*	On-the-job demonstration	38	3.42	1.54	.25
Level 3 *on-the-job application*	Anecdotal information	34	4.00	1.69	.29
Level 4 *organizational outcomes*	Anecdotal information	29	4.03	1.68	.31
Level 5 *ROI*	Cost-benefit analysis	73	1.32	1.31	.12

associated with library organization characteristics. An ANOVA was used to test for differences among the means of organizational characteristics (type, size, and evaluation policy) and the use of each evaluation level. In the first test, the independent variable was the type of library, and included seven categories: Library Network/Cooperative; Public Library; School Library; Special Library; State Library; Training/Consulting Organization, and Other. In the second ANOVA, the independent variable was the size of the organization and included 10 categories indicating number of employees (1–10; 11–20; 21–40; 41–75; 76–100; 101–200; 201–500; 501–750; 1,000–2,000; and Over 2,000). The third test's independent variable was whether or not an evaluation policy existed in the organization and was indicated by Yes or No.

The dependent variable for each of the three ANOVAs (type, size, and evaluation policy) was the percentage of use of each of the five training evaluation levels. In addition, correlation coefficients were computed among the five levels of evaluation and each of the organizational characteristics (type, size, and evaluation policies) to further test Hypothesis Three. The results of these tests support the third hypothesis that the *differences in evaluation usage are associated with organizational characteristics* and are discussed later.

Type of Library and Mean Use of Evaluation
The first of the three organizational characteristics in Hypothesis Three, type of library organization, are discussed in the following three sections. First, Question 48 asked participants to identify the type of library organization in which they work. Choices provided were: Library Network/ Cooperative, Public Library, School Library, Special Library, State Library, Training/Consulting Organization, and Other. An additional category Did Not Indicate Type was added during the data analysis process to reflect the nine respondents who did not indicate type of library. No responses were

received from Special Libraries or School Libraries. Three responses coded Other (University Department of Library Instruction, School of Library and Information Science, and State Regional Library System) were received but were moved to the Training/Consulting category where they better reflected their training evaluation role.

The results suggest that Library Network/Cooperatives, State Libraries, and Consulting/Training Organizations evaluate training more often than other types of library organizations. Table 15 provides usage data for organizations that use each Level of evaluation the most.

One type of library organization (consulting/training organizations, $n = 2$) was removed before testing the differences in use of evaluation levels by different types of libraries. Only two consulting/training organizations answered this question and because both cases reported identical usage for three of the five levels (L1, 100%; L4, 0%; and L5, 0%) determination of equality of variance was impossible. Once these two cases were removed, it became possible to determine equality of variance and select the appropriate test to employ. Two tests, ANOVA and Welch, were selected based on the results of the Levene homogeneity test.

Both the ANOVA and the Welch tests were used to identify significant mean differences in the evaluation levels used by various types of library

Table 15. Percentage of Evaluation Most Used and
Type of Organization.

Evaluation Level	Type of Training Organization	n	M	SD	Standard Error (SE)
Level 1: % evaluating reaction	State Library	9	.98	.04	.01
	Library Network/Cooperative	19	.94	.13	.00
Level 2: % evaluating learning	Consulting/Training Organization	2	.60	.57	.40
	Library Network/Cooperative	19	.36	.45	.10
	Public Library	10	.36	.24	.08
Level 3: % evaluating on-the-job application					
	Consulting/Training Organization	2	.55	.64	.45
	Library Network/Cooperative	19	.22	.33	.08
Level 4: % using organizational outcomes					
	Library Network/Cooperative	19	.28	.43	.10
	State Library	9	.27	.37	.12
Level 5: % using ROI	Library Network/Cooperative	19	.05	.16	.04
	State Library	9	.03	.07	.02

Table 16. Significant Differences of Evaluation Use
and Organization Type.

	Type (a)	*M* (a)	Type (b)	*M* (b)	Mean Difference	Standard Error (SE)
Level 1: Reaction	State Library (*n* = 9)	.9833	Academic Library (*n* = 22)	.7627	.2206*	.0633

Note: Correlations with a (*) were significant at $p < .05$.

organizations depending on the degree of variance present. ANOVA was used to test Levels 3 and 5 since both showed homogeneous variances; Welch was used to test Levels 1, 2, and 4 since their variances differed significantly, not meeting the criteria for using ANOVA.

No significant results were identified via the ANOVA; however, the Welch test showed significance for Level 1 usage, $F(3,25.25) = 5.965$, $p = .003$. A Games-Howell post hoc analysis was conducted to investigate the nature of the difference and found that the means of the Level 1 evaluation usage reported by State Libraries and Academic Libraries differed significantly at the .05 level (see Table 16). This difference suggests that State Libraries evaluate Level 1 training more than Academic Libraries; however, this result cannot be generalized due to the small number of responses in each subset.

Size of Library and Mean Use of Evaluation

The second factor in Hypothesis Three, size of library, is addressed in Question 49 which asked respondents to identify the size of their organizations by selecting 1 of the 11 ranges (1–10; 11–20; 21–40; 41–75; 76–100; 101–200; 201–500; 501–750; 751–1,000; 1,000–2,000; and Over 2,000). Most library organizations reported evaluating training for participants' reactions (Level 1) with a range of use between 60% (76–100 employees) and 100% (over 1,000 employees). Level 2 evaluation usage ranged from 16% (41–75 employees) to 100% (over 2,000 employees). The range of Level 3 usage spanned from 0% (76–200 employees) to 50% (over 2,000 employees). The ranges for Level 4 were 0% (1,000–2,000 employees) to 75% (over 2,000 employees) and for Level 5 0–50%. In each instance, the largest library organizations, those with over 2,000 employees (*n* = 2), reported the highest usage of evaluation. The next highest usage of all evaluation levels was reported by the smallest library organizations (Table 17).

Using ANOVA, a significant difference was found between the means of the largest library organizations using Level 5 (ROI) evaluation and the

Table 17. Percentage of Evaluation Use and Size
of Organizations ($n = 59$).

Levels	1–10	11–20	21–40	41–75	76–100	101–200	201–500	501–750	1,000–2,000	Over 2,000
n	11	10	5	8	5	9	6	2	2	1
L1	0.95	0.89	0.94	0.90	0.60	0.76	0.85	0.85	1.00	1.00
L2	0.46	0.24	0.29	0.16	0.30	0.29	0.32	0.38	0.38	1.00
L3	0.31	0.08	0.19	0.11	–	–	0.31	0.25	0.03	0.50
L4	0.32	0.24	0.06	0.14	0.12	0.16	0.20	0.30	–	0.75
L5	0.05	–	0.02	–	–	–	0.05	–	–	0.50

Table 18. Comparison of ROI Use and Organization Size ($n = 66$).

Size of Organization	n	M	Mean Difference	Standard Error (SE)
1–10	14	.036	.489	.053
11–20	10	.000	.525	.055
21–40	6	.017	.508	.058
41–75	8	.000	.525	.056
76–100	5	.000	.525	.059
101–200	10	.000	.525	.055
201–500	7	.043	482	.057
501–750	2	.000	.525	.071
1,000–2,000	2	.000	.525	.071
Over 2,000	2	.525	.035*	.025

means of smaller organizations using Level 5 (ROI) evaluation,
$F(9,49) = 5.167$, $p < .001$. Because the ANOVA showed significance, a post
hoc test, Tukey's HSD test (Tukey, 1953), was conducted to evaluate
differences among the means. This test was selected because it is recommended for unplanned comparisons (Sheskin, 2004). Using Tukey's HSD
test, the mean score for organizations with over 2,000 employees differed
significantly with all other groups as indicated by an asterisk in Table 18. This
meets the test of significance but the difference in the higher percentage of
large organizations using ROI evaluation as compared to other size organizations cannot be generalized due to the small sample sizes of the sub-groups.

Existence of an Evaluation Policy and Mean Use of Evaluation
The third factor addressed in Hypothesis Three, the existence of an
evaluation policy and the use of evaluation is explored by Question 40. This

Table 19. Existence of Written Training Policies ($n = 61$).

Type of Organization	Yes	%	No	%	Total
Library Network/Cooperative	3	5	17	26	20
Public Library	1	2	9	14	10
Academic Library	3	5	22	33	25
State Library	1	2	8	12	9
Consulting/Training Organization	2	3	0	0	2

Table 20. Evaluation Use and Written Evaluation Policy.

	Written Policy	n	M	SD	Standard Error (SE)	F	Significance
Level 1	Yes	8	0.975	0.071	.025	9.360	0.004
	No	51	0.845	0.245	.034		
Level 2	Yes	8	0.575	0.471	.167	3.300	0.106
	No	51	0.260	0.338	.047		
Level 3	Yes	8	0.463	0.472	.167	3.780	0.090
	No	51	0.132	0.234	.033		
Level 4	Yes	8	0.344	0.481	.170	0.890	0.374
	No	51	0.178	0.312	.044		
Level 5	Yes	8	0.063	0.177	.063	0.172	0.680
	No	51	0.037	0.157	.022		

question asked participants whether or not a written training evaluation policy is in place in their organization. There were two possible answer choices, Yes or No. Of the 66 answers, 15% reported Yes (they have a training evaluation policy) and 85% replied No. Library Network/ Cooperatives and Academic Libraries reported only slightly higher rates (5%) of having an evaluation policy than Public and State Libraries (3%) (Table 19).

Table 20 shows that on average, 98% of programs evaluated at Level 1 are done so when an evaluation policy is in place. The Welch test was used to identify significant differences among the means of evaluation levels for organizations that have written evaluation policies in place. The Welch test was used because the Levene statistic indicated that not all the variances were equal, and although that is not fatal to ANOVA (Box, 1954), using the Welch statistic instead of the F statistic is considered a more powerful and conservative approach (Brown & Forsythe, 1974). The Welch statistic showed that mean use of Level 1 evaluation $F(1, 38.9) = 9.36$, $p = .004$ differs significantly for organizations with written evaluation policies in place.

Organizational Characteristics
In addition to identify the levels of evaluation usage for each of the three organizational characteristics, additional tests indicated if a relationship was present between the evaluation levels and the characteristics. Correlation coefficients were computed among each of the five levels of evaluation and the three organizational characteristics (type of organization; size of organization; and evaluation policy) and two relationships were found. A negative correlation was identified between having a written evaluation policy in place and usage of Level 2 evaluation. This correlation indicates that having a policy predicts less use of Level 2 evaluation use, $r(61) = -.278$, $p = .03$. A similar negative correlation between having a written evaluation policy in place and the usage of Level 3 evaluation indicates that having a policy predicts less use of Level 3, $r(61) = -.382$, $p = .002$. Although the results of the tests meet the test of significance, these results cannot be generalized due to the small sub-group sample sizes (Table 21).

Use of Evaluation and Organizational Training Practices

The fourth hypothesis, differences in percentage of evaluation conducted at the five levels are associated with library organization training practices including the need for training and the training process was investigated using four factors. For the purpose of this study, the factors relating to organizational training practices include: use of evaluation planning (Question 31), evaluation reporting (Question 47), percentage of employees responsible for evaluation (Question 33), and the need for training (Question 32). ANOVA was used with the first three factors to test their mean differences and Pearson's correlation was used to identify any relationship between the need for training with the use of each evaluation level.

Planning
Data regarding the first factor in Hypothesis Four, planning was collected via Question 31 and asked participants to identify when they begin planning the evaluation process. The six possible answers were: before program development, as the first step in program development, during program development, after program completion, when training program results must be documented, or evaluations are not implemented. Most

Table 21. Bivariate Correlations among Evaluation Levels and Organizational Characteristics (*n* = 61).

		Percentage of Evaluating Reaction	Percentage of Evaluating Learning	Percentage of Evaluating On-the-Job Application	Percentage of Evaluating Organizational Outcomes	Percentage of Using ROI
Evaluation policy	Pearson Correlation	−0.218	−0.278	−0.382	−0.166	−0.015
	Significance (2-tailed)	0.092	*0.030	**0.002	0.202	0.907
Organizational type	Pearson Correlation	0.131	−0.012	−0.006	−0.069	−0.203
	Significance (2-tailed)	0.313	0.924	0.963	0.599	0.117
Organizational size	Pearson Correlation	0.047	0.120	0.012	−0.035	−0.070
	Significance (2-tailed)	0.717	0.359	0.928	0.789	0.593

* Correlation is significant at the 0.05 level (2-tailed).
** Correlation is significant at the 0.01 level (2-tailed).

Table 22.   When Does the Planning for Evaluation Begin? ($n = 58$).

Point When Planning Begins	n	%
Before program development	11	19
As the first step in program development	13	22
During program development	8	14
After program completion	3	5
When training program results must be documented	11	19
Evaluations are not implemented	12	21

organizations (22%) indicated that they begin planning for evaluation as the first step in program development (Table 22).

A one-way analysis of variance was conducted to evaluate the relationship between when evaluation planning begins and which levels of evaluation library organizations use. The independent variable included the five levels of evaluation. The dependent variable included six points related to when evaluation planning might begin. Both ANOVA and the Welch test were used. ANOVA was used with Level 2 evaluation to identify differences in the means of use of when evaluation planning begins and the Welch test was used to identify differences in the remaining four evaluation levels because their variances were not homogeneous and did not meet the criteria for using ANOVA.

The Welch identified significant differences in means of when organizations begin planning if they evaluate using Level 1 (reaction) $F(5,13.5) = 3.08$, $p = .05$ and also for organizations evaluating using Level 3 (on-the-job application) $F(5,13.7) = 3.4$, $p = .03$. Further investigation using Games-Howell did not reveal any additional significance.

Reporting

The second factor for Hypothesis Four, reporting evaluation results, was investigated by Question 47 and asked if training program evaluation information is routinely reported to executive management. The question provided two possible choices: Yes and No. Respondents ($n = 54$) using Level 1 evaluation reported that they routinely report training evaluation information 60% of the time. For respondents reporting no use of Level 1 evaluation, evaluation information is routinely reported 40% of the time.

The Welch statistic was used to evaluate the relationship between whether evaluation is routinely reported to executive management and the use of each evaluation level. The Welch statistic was computed in addition to a

Table 23. Differences When Evaluation Information
is Routinely Reported.

	Reported?	*n*	*M*(%)	Significance
Level 1: % evaluating reaction	Yes	32	59	.019
	No	22	41	
Level 4: % using organizational outcomes	Yes	32	59	.013
	No	22	41	

one-way analysis of variance because Levene's test indicated that the variances were not homogeneous. Both tests were significant for both Level 1 and Level 4 evaluation. Although the Welch showed that the means were significantly different for Level 1, $F(1,31.7) = 6.14$, $p = .019$, the effect size was small to modest. The partial η^2 was just .012, which means that Level 1 by itself accounted for only 1.2% of the overall (effect + error) variance. In addition, although Level 4 showed significance $F(1,41) = 6.68$, $p = .013$, the strength of the relationship between reporting and evaluation levels was also small to modest and only accounted for 3% of the overall variance. This data suggests that reporting training evaluation information to executive management may be aligned with the use of Levels 1 and 4 (Table 23).

Staffing
Question 33.1 focused on the third factor of Hypothesis Four and asked participants to indicate the approximate percentage of staff who are involved in training evaluation. There were six answers from which to choose: 0%, 1–19%, 20–39%, 40–59%, 60–79%, and 80–100%. Table 24 presents the means and standard deviations of the percentage of staff members involved in evaluation when certain evaluation levels are used. The means decrease markedly for Levels 2–5.

A one-way analysis of variance between subjects was conducted to evaluate the relationship between the percentage of staff involved in training evaluation and the use of the five levels of evaluation. The ANOVA was significant for Level 1, $F(5,52) = 2.36$, $p = .05$, however the effect size was modest. The partial η^2 was .185, indicating that Level 1 by itself accounted for approximately 19% of the overall variance.

A Pearson's correlation between the percentage of staff involved in training evaluation and levels of evaluation resulted in one significant relationship. The positive correlation between percentage of training staff involved in evaluation and usage of Level 1 evaluation, indicated that

Table 24. What Percentage of Training Staff Members are
Involved in Evaluation? ($n = 58$).

Evaluation Levels	M	SD	F	Significance
Level 1: % evaluating reaction	.86	.23	2.36	.05
Level 2: % evaluating learning	.31	.37	.82	.54
Level 3: % evaluating on-the-job application	.18	.30	.88	.50
Level 4: % using organizational outcomes	.20	.34	.99	.44
Level 5: % using ROI	.04	.16	.53	.75

Table 25. Bivariate Correlations among Evaluation Levels and
Percentage of Training Staff Members Involved in Evaluation ($n = 61$).

Factor		% Level 1	% Level 2	% Level 3	% Level 4	% Level 5
Level 1	Pearson Correlation	.360**	.141	.053	.113	.162
	Significance (2-tailed)	.006	.293	.691	.400	.225

Note: Correlations marked with an asterisk (*) were significant at $p < .05$.
Correlations marked with two asterisks (**) were significant at $p < .01$.

increasing the number of training staff involved in evaluation predicted an
increase of Level 1 evaluation use, $r(61) = .360$, $p = .006$ (Table 25).

Need for Training
The final factor investigated related to Hypothesis Four was the need for
training. Question 32 asked participants to indicate the reasons staff were
sent to training by the following question "Employee development
programs are delivered for a variety of reasons and have different levels
of participation. Please indicate the percentage of your currently active
programs that match the descriptions listed." The possible answers were:
(1) training is a reward; (2) all employees or a special group are sent; (3) to
acquire a new attitude; (4) to be able to perform at a set level; (5) to change
organizational outcomes. The percentages from which to choose were: 0%,
1–19%, 20–39%, 40–59%, 60–79%, and 80–100%. Table 26 presents
frequencies for each factor in the reason organizations send employees to
training.

Results indicate that the least likely reason for training is *as a reward* and
the most likely reason is that *all employees or a special group attends. To be
able to perform at a set level* and *to acquire new attitude* had nearly identical
positions and *to change organizational outcomes* trailed only slightly behind.

Table 26. Reasons for Sending Employees to Training.

Factors	How Often This Factor Influences the Reason for Training					
	0%	1–19%	20–39%	40–59%	60–79%	80–100%
Training as a reward	55.74	24.59	9.84	4.92	3.26	1.64
All employees or special group attend	11.1	12.70	14.29	22.22	22.22	17.46
To acquire new attitude	8.20	16.39	26.23	24.59	16.39	8.20
To be able to perform at a set level	9.84	11.48	27.87	24.59	19.67	6.56
To change organizational outcomes	16.13	20.97	20.97	20.97	16.13	4.84

Table 27. Correlations among Evaluation Levels and Reasons for Training ($n = 61$).

Factors		Level 1	Level 2	Level 3	Level 4	Level 5
Training is as a reward	Pearson Correlation	.117	.328*	.405**	.141	.181
	Significance (2-tailed)	.422	.021	.004	.334	.214
All or special group sent	Pearson Correlation	−.016	.058	.427**	.381**	.156
	Significance (2-tailed)	.911	.693	.002	.007	.283
To acquire new attitude	Pearson Correlation	.051	.187	.048	.243	.297*
	Significance (2-tailed)	.725	.198	.743	.093	.038
To be able to perform at a set level	Pearson Correlation	−.111	.383**	.274	.085	.336*
	Significance (2-tailed)	.448	.007	.056	.561	.018
To change organizational outcomes	Pearson correlation	.053	.146	.200	.416**	.297*
	Significance (2-tailed)	.718	.317	.168	.003	.038

Note: Correlations marked with an asterisk (*) were significant at $p < .05$.
Correlations marked with two asterisks (**) were significant at $p < .01$.

Correlation coefficients were computed among each of the five levels of evaluation and five reasons for training (training as a reward, all employees or special group sent, to acquire a new attitude, to be able to perform at a set level, to change organizational outcomes). The results of this correlational analyses, presented in Table 27, show that eight out of 25 correlations were statistically significant and were less than or equal to .05. Significant correlations were found between *Training as a reward* and Levels 2 and 3 evaluations, *All employees or a special group is sent*; Levels 3 and 4 evaluations, *To acquire a new attitude*; Level 5 evaluation, *To be able to perform at a set level*; and Levels 2 and 5 evaluations, and finally, *To Change organizational outcomes* is correlated with Levels 4 and 5 evaluations.

ROI Criteria

The investigation of Hypothesis Four *concludes with an exploration of two sub-questions:* What criteria are used in selecting programs to evaluate for ROI *and* What criteria are important in determining an effective method for calculating ROI? The first question (Question 43) asked participants to rank the ten items in Table 28 below from 1–10 (with 1 being low) according to the items' importance in selecting training programs for evaluation at the ROI level. As the table shows, the most highly rated reason to evaluate at the ROI level is that a program *has the interest of top executives* and the least important reason reported was *important to strategic objectives.* Although a number of respondents indicated that *Other* reasons would compel them to select a training session for evaluation at the ROI level, only one identified that criterion (interest level of staff involved).

Table 29 below presents the results from Question 45 that asked for additional factors to consider when choosing a method of calculating ROI. Library organizations reported that the most important factors when they calculate ROI for training are being able to account for other factors, having it be applicable with all types of data, and being able to account for all program costs.

Summary

This research project asked 272 library training professionals to respond to a web-based questionnaire regarding four training evaluation hypotheses. Responses were received from 94 individuals representing network/

Table 28. Criteria Used to Select Programs to Evaluate at Level 5 ROI.

Factors	*n*	*M*	SD
Have the interest of top executives	48	6.13	2.69
Have high visibility	46	5.85	2.38
Have a comprehensive needs assessment	51	5.75	2.53
Take a significant investment of time	47	5.57	2.18
Are expensive	46	5.20	2.87
Expected to have long life cycle	47	5.09	2.07
Involves large target audience	49	4.90	2.66
Links to operational goals and issues	45	3.89	2.72
Important to strategic objective	45	3.84	3.26
Other	13	9.08	2.57

Table 29. Important Factors When Deciding How to Calculate ROI.

Factors	*n*	*M*	SD	Standard Error (SE)
Account for other factors	36	5.64	1.97	.33
Be applicable with all types of data	38	5.05	2.13	.35
Account for all program costs	43	4.93	2.32	.35
Have successful track record	47	4.72	2.2	.32
Simple economical	44	4.41	2.67	.40
Be appropriate for a variety of programs	41	4.05	2.33	.36
Theoretically sound	39	4.00	2.14	.34
Credible	42	3.98	2.61	.40
Other	8	8.38	1.41	.50

consortiums, public and academic libraries, state libraries, and library consulting/training organizations. Twenty-six participants did not identify their organization type.

On average, most participants in this research were women with a master's degree in Library Science working in an organization with less than 100 employees. Typically participants' title included the word Director or Coordinator and they have been working in the training field for at least five years but do not belong to a professional organization for training (e.g., ASTD). Training budgets were reported to be is less than 20% of the total budget and averaged approximately $64,533.

Training for library staff is evaluated primarily at Levels 1 and 2, although some organizations use Levels 3 and 4 evaluations in certain situations. Generally accepted methods for evaluating training are: Level 1 (reaction), reaction questionnaires; Level 2 (learning), on-the-job demonstration; Level 3, anecdotal information; Level 4, anecdotal information. Respondents reported that Level 5 (ROI) is seldom used and there is no generally accepted method of evaluating ROI.

In the aggregate, differences in the percentage of evaluation conducted at the five levels are associated with library organization characteristics (type, size, and written training evaluation policy). The results suggest that Library Network/Cooperatives, State Libraries, and Consulting/Training Organizations evaluate training more often than other types of library organizations and that small library organizations (under 40 employees) evaluate a great deal more than larger ones. The existence of a written training evaluation policy in an organization was related to higher use of Level 1 evaluation; however, only 15% of respondents indicated having such a document. No one type of library was more likely to have a written policy in place than another.

The differences in the percentage of evaluation conducted at the five levels are also associated with library organization training practices (planning, reporting, and staff involved in evaluation). Library training professionals indicated that they begin planning the evaluation process at various times, including: before program development, as the first step in program development, during program development, after program completion, when training program results must be documented, or not at all. The results suggest that reporting training evaluation information to executive management is aligned with the use of Levels 1 and 4.

There is a significant relationship between the use of Level 1 evaluation and employees who are responsible for evaluation. Less than one-half of library training staff members have had formal preparation in training evaluation and yet approximately two-thirds of library training staff are involved in evaluation in some way.

There tended to be agreement that the least likely reason for training is *as a reward* and the most likely reason is that *all employees or a special group attends. To be able to perform at a set level* and *to acquire new attitude* had nearly identical positions and *to change organizational outcomes* trailed only slightly behind. Each of the factors involved in the need for training are positively correlated with one or more levels of evaluation.

Library trainers tend to select programs to evaluate at Level 5 (ROI) based on the interest of top executives and programs that have high visibility. Less than 3% of library training organizations use Level 5 evaluation. When they do calculate ROI, library organizations report that the most important criteria for ROI to include are being able to account for other factors, having it be applicable with all types of data, and being able to account for all program costs.

DISCUSSION

Changes in the format of library materials, increased amounts of information, and the speed at which information is being produced have created an unrelenting need for training for library staff members. Additionally, library employees are retiring in greater numbers and their accompanying expertise is being lost (Berry, 2002). With rising expenditures and increasing training needs, the library community is beginning to give increased attention to evaluation.

Summary of the Findings

The purpose of this study is to document evaluation practices currently used in training programs for library staff members, including metrics used in calculating ROI. This study focuses on two research questions: (1) What are the current training evaluation practices used in library staff training programs? (2) Which training evaluation models would best fit library staff development needs?

Analysis of the data provided possible answers to the primary research questions. The first research question was: *What are the current training evaluation practices used in library staff training programs?* The data suggests that current training evaluation practices are similar to those in healthcare, business, and the public sector (Twitchell, 1997; Hill, 1999; Phillips, 2003a, 2003b). Library training is primarily evaluated for participants' reaction by using reaction questionnaires. When learning is evaluated, the preferred way to assess it is by on-the-job demonstration. Although Level 3 (on-the-job application) evaluation is not often used, when it is, anecdotal information is used to assess. When Level 4 evaluation is used, anecdotal information is also the preferred assessment method. There is not a generally accepted method of evaluating ROI.

The second research question: *Which training evaluation models would best fit library staff development needs?* is answered by the analysis of a number of factors including noting why trainers evaluate. The most frequently cited reasons for evaluating training were Improving Programs and Demonstrating Value. Improving facilitator performance, improving processes to track, and making training investment decisions were the next highest reasons given for evaluation. An evaluation model would have to be able to provide a way to respond to all of these needs. In particular when employing these types of evaluations, it would be important to note the top reasons respondents gave for employing those levels. Although no one training evaluation model will fit each organization's needs, evaluation designs should be developed with the end outcome in mind. Research results suggest that for each type of evaluation below, certain factors should be included:

Level 1:	improving programs, improving facilitator performance
Level 2:	improving programs, demonstrating value
Level 3:	demonstrating value; improving processes to track skills
Level 4:	improving programs, demonstrating value
Level 5:	demonstrating value, making training investment decisions

Discussion

Hypothesis One. *Training is evaluated primarily at Levels 1 and 2.*

Consistent with previous studies (Twitchell, 1997; Phillips, 2003a, 2003b), the usage reported by this study beyond Level 1 begins to decline. According to the results reported in three seminal HRD training evaluation studies (Twitchell, 1997; Hill, 1999; Phillips, 2003a, 2003b) the level of evaluation usage varies as does the usage in this study. Comparisons among the frequency and means made in this research, show that library usage of Levels 1 and 4 is higher than in both Hill's (1999) healthcare study and Phillips' (2003a, 2003b) public sector study. Reasons for the higher levels for evaluating reaction and organizational outcomes may be related to the funding sources for much of libraries' technology training. Reaction and outcomes evaluation is often required by library funding agencies. For example, training grants awarded by State Libraries, the Institute for Museums and Libraries, and the Gates Foundation all require evaluation of outcomes for grant objectives (Table 30).

Findings of this study are consistent with other studies that also report Level 1 evaluation as most highly used, followed by Level 2 (Twitchell, 1997; Hill, 1999; Phillips, 2003a, 2003b). Twitchell (1997) studied technical training programs in U.S. businesses and reported 73% Level 1 usage and over 47% Level 2 usage. In 2003, ASTD reported that the percentage of its organizations using Level 1 evaluation has remained consistently in the 70% range since 1999. In 2005, ASTD asked its' Benchmarking Forum, 18 large

Table 30. Library Training and Use of Training Evaluation ($n = 58$).

Levels of Use	Library Profession		Public Sector (Phillips, 2003a, 2003b)		Healthcare (Hill, 1999)	
	M	SD	*M*	SD	*M*	SD
Level 1 *reaction*	86.74	22.97	72.18	36.53	80.85	26.82
Level 2 *learning*	30.66	36.81	31.65	34.32	52.59	32.57
Level 3 *on-the-job application*	16.24	27.69	20.42	29.03	30.77[a]	30.77[a]
Level 4 *organizational outcomes*	18.71	32.51	12.21	24.74	16.97	25.53
Level 5 *ROI*	4.14	16.01	5.26	17.09	3.73	12.18

Note: $n = 58$ for Library Profession.
[a]These numbers appear identical because of rounding, but differ at the fifth decimal point.

Fortune 500 companies and public sector organizations, about their program evaluation methods and these results along with those from the Corporate Leadership Council study (*Reframing the Measurement*, 2002) are compared to the library results in Table 31.

In this study and the others in Table 31, evaluation at Levels 1 and 2 is reported to be the most widely used and Levels 3, 4, and 5 less often.

Hypothesis Two. *Generally Accepted Methods of Evaluating Return-on-Investment.*

Very few participants (*n* = 10) responded to Question 26 regarding what methods they use to determine ROI. Although response rates to the questionnaire overall were adequate, there was a large amount of missing data for this question. This is similar to other comparable studies regarding training evaluation (Twitchell, 1997; Hill, 1999; Phillips, 2003a, 2003b) which may suggest a lack of knowledge about the various ways to determine ROI. In Florida, a full-day workshop was presented at the 2005 Public Library Directors' Meeting regarding ROI for general library operations.

Table 31. Mean Percentage of Evaluation Usage Comparisons.

Variable	Library Organizations	Twitchell (1997)	Training (2005)	Training (2003)	Corporate (2002)
Percentage of evaluating Level 1 *reaction*	86.74	72.74	91.3	74	–[c]
Percentage of evaluating Level 2 *learning*	30.66	47.05	53.9	41	–[c]
Percentage of evaluating Level 3 *on-the-job application*	16.24	30.54	22.9	14	–[c]
Percentage of evaluating Level 4 *organizational outcomes*	18.71	20.82	7.6	8	27
Percentage of evaluating Level 5 *ROI*	4.14	–[a]	5.3[b]	–[c]	11

Note: n = 58 for Library Organizations.
[a]Twitchell included ROI in Level 4.
[b]Combination of Level 5 (projected) and Level 5 (actual).
[c]Dashes indicate that no data was reported.

Since this was the first time ROI training was made available in the library community and the information has not been widely shared with library training managers and directors, it is not surprising that there is still lack of ROI expertise not only in Florida, but elsewhere.

Hypothesis Three. *Use of Evaluation and Characteristics of Libraries.*

The results of the statistical tests support the third hypothesis that the differences in evaluation usage are associated with organizational characteristics. There were differences in the percentage of evaluation conducted at the five levels that are associated with library organization characteristics (type, size, and evaluation policies); however, the differences were not found at each level for each characteristic. Differences regarding size were noted for Level 5 evaluation and two sizes of library organizations (Table 16) but the number of responses in each subgroup were too small to generalize; Differences for type of organization and evaluation usage were noted for State Libraries' and Academic Libraries' Level 1 usage, but the number of subgroup responses were also too small to generalize (Table 15).

Type of Library and Mean Use of Evaluation
Special libraries were included on the mailing list, but no responses were received from the five special libraries who received the questionnaire. Special libraries by their nature have small numbers of employees and although their employing agency or firm may have a manager of staff development, the position is not normally found within the library. However, because a number of special libraries were ALA/CLENE members, they were not excluded. In addition, no school libraries were members of any of the library training professional groups, so questionnaires were not mailed to school libraries. Since K-12 school libraries are departments of larger school, county, or district organizations, it would be unusual for them to have a library employee fully or even partially dedicated to library staff training.

The research results suggest that Library Network/Cooperatives, State Libraries, and Consulting/Training Organizations may evaluate training more often than other types of library organizations. Since State Libraries often fund their training programs with federal grant funds, this difference may be explained by grant regulations. Typical grant funders (e.g., Institute of Museums and Library Services) regularly require grantees to evaluate using outcomes measurement.

Size of Library and Mean Use of Evaluation

For Level 1 evaluation, small organizations evaluate almost three times more than organizations with 41–200 employees. An explanation could be related to the responses from 20 library networks/cooperatives which are often smaller regional organizations. These organizations typically play a primary role in library training around the U.S. and frequencies reported in this study indicate that they have the highest likelihood of having memberships in professional training organizations (e.g., ASTD and CLENE) and the most years of experience in training.

Hypothesis Four. *Use of Evaluation and Organizational Training Practices.*

For the purpose of this study, organizational training practices include four factors: use of evaluation planning (Question 31), evaluation reporting (Question 47), percentage of employees responsible for evaluation (Question 33), and the need for training (Question 32).

Reporting

Question 47 asked if training program evaluation information is routinely reported to executive management and provided two possible choices: Yes and No. Respondents using Level 1 evaluation reported that they routinely report training evaluation information 63% of the time. For respondents reporting no use of Level 1 evaluation, evaluation information is routinely reported 37% of the time.

In a 2003 study of training evaluation in the public sector, all five levels of evaluation were shown to have a significant relationship with those training professionals who routinely report evaluation information to their administrators (Phillips, 2003a, 2003b).

Staffing

Less than one-half of library training staff members have had no formal preparation in training evaluation and yet approximately two-thirds of library training staff are involved in evaluation in some way. Using ANOVA, results suggest that there is not a significant difference in the means of the percentage of employees responsible for evaluation and the use of each evaluation level.

Results indicate that the least likely reason for training is *as a reward* and the most likely reason is that *all employees or a special group attends. To be able to perform at a set level* and *to acquire new attitude* had nearly identical positions and *to change organizational outcomes* trailed only slightly behind.

Implications for Human Resource Development

This study contributes not only to the human resource development literature, but also provides HRD practitioners who work in the library environment with additional information to improve learning and performance. This research offers important, new knowledge to the HRD field about how training evaluation is used and what training evaluation factors are deemed important. It informs the field more broadly and provides a more integrated understanding of factors that may be useful in developing new models for establishing return on investment.

In addition, this study provides descriptive information that is available to assist library training organizations to plan and assess human resource development interventions. For the first time, library administrators will have access to information about library training evaluation to make better decisions regarding use and distribution of financial and human assets.

Limitations of the Study

Limitations of this study that were beyond the control of the researcher included loss of participants during the study, as well as biased results from participants. Because the research data was collected via self-reporting on survey instruments rather than by testing or experimental means, another limitation was the subjective nature and the length of the instrument. There were a number of participants who either did not complete the questionnaire or skipped questions throughout the instrument. Missing data was primarily handled by deleting cases with unanswered questions from the analysis on a hypothesis by hypothesis basis.

Demographic data was collected at the end of the survey and 26 participants did not indicate type or size of their library organization. This missing data impacted the study's ability to generalize the results found between type and size of the organization with the use of some evaluation levels. The analysis showed significance between characteristics of library organizations and evaluation levels used but because the sub-group sizes were too small, no generalizations about written evaluation policies or type of libraries that evaluate are possible.

Recommendations for Future Studies

This study provided a glimpse at how library organizations use evaluation; however, further work is needed. To decrease the amount of missing data, it is suggested that future research studies adjust the questionnaire to limit the number of possible selections on certain questions. I recommend using a scale from 1 to 4 instead of 1–10 to provide larger sub-groups of responses so that significant findings will be more likely to be able to be generalized.

A second consideration for future research is to use a different web-based survey tool. The online survey software "Zoomerang" performed reliably and as expected with one exception. Participants could not "go back" to any previous pages to amend or change answers. Being able to return to a previous page, as well as, putting the survey "on hold" then returning to complete it at a later date, are both important survey functions.

Another instrument design improvement for future studies is to collect the demographic data earlier in the questionnaire. Because the questions about size and type of library were placed toward the end problems with data loss were magnified. The data submitted from participants that did not complete the questionnaire was incomplete.

Suggestions for future research include an expanded focus on ROI and training budgets. Although the questionnaire asked participants to identify their annual training budgets, more work could be done to identify the origin of the funds and where they are dispersed. To calculate ROI for training, more research is necessary regarding library training budgets, revenue, and expenditures.

CONCLUSIONS

Training for library staff is evaluated primarily at Level 1 (reaction) and Level 2 (learning). The reaction of participants (Level 1) is typically assessed after the training via reaction questionnaires which informs us about what attendees thought about the training session, for example, whether staff enjoyed the session, found the handouts helpful, and liked the presenter. Training is also evaluated for learning (Level 2), usually by demonstrating the learning to a supervisor. Unless we evaluate further, however, we still cannot assess if employees are using what they learned back on-the-job (Level 3) and whether it makes any difference in the organization as a whole (Level 4). This research suggests that evaluation at Levels 3 and 4 rarely take place because of a number of barriers. These obstructions to evaluating Level 3 are: lack of experience, not required, cost in hours or capital, and unavailability of data. Similar reasons were identified as barriers to assessing organizational impact of training: not required, cost in hours or capital, and lack of training and experience in using this type of evaluation.

Unless instances of higher level training evaluation and assessment increase, the opportunities for additional library professionals to gain experience in conducting these assessments will be limited. An initial step towards gaining that experience could be addressed by requiring measurement and assessment at those levels. The key to developing a richer pool of experienced evaluators lie with whether administrators of library organizations and accrediting bodies will require higher levels of training assessment. For example, library grant funding agencies could require evaluation of not only training participants' reactions to classes, but also evidence of learning, on-the-job application of what was learned and how this is making a difference in libraries' outcomes. As training evaluators practice higher levels of evaluation, they may no longer perceive lack of experience as a barrier.

Training organizations have a long history of engaging in best practices once they are aware of them. Increasing knowledge of more sophisticated training evaluation models through library literature, graduate education programs and continuing education may serve to encourage training professionals to develop opportunities for practice. However, providing training about evaluation, requiring higher levels of evaluation and expanding experience must be balanced by recognizing that measurement is costly.

No organization can justify evaluating every learning session at all levels all of the time. Barriers to evaluation because of limited funding are not trivial but are possible to address. Keeping evaluation plans realistic, limiting the number of courses evaluated at higher levels and taking advantage of work that has already been done by colleagues and other library organizations provide sensible first steps.

Although Levels 1–4 have generally accepted methods of evaluation, Level 5 evaluation does not. There is no one way that library training organizations tend to account for ROI for training. With the focus on financial accountability across all sectors, being able to relate how training brings back financial and other types of results to an organization continues to be difficult.

REFERENCES

Alliger, G. M., & Janak, E. A. (1989). Kirkpatrick's levels of training criteria: Thirty years later. *Personnel Psychology, 42*(2), 331–342.
American Association of Law Libraries. (2000). *American association of law libraries' research agenda* (2005). Chicago, IL: American Association of Law Libraries.

American Society of Training and Development. (2001). *State of the industry: ASTD's annual review of U.S. and international trends in workplace learning and performance.* Alexandria, VA: ASTD.

Association of College and Research Libraries [ACRL] Instruction Section [IS] Research and Scholarship Committee. (2005). *Research agenda for library instruction and information literacy.* Washington, DC: Association of College and Research Libraries.

Bachmann, D. P., Elfrink, J., & Vazzana, G. (2000). E-mail and snail mail face off in rematch. *Marketing Research, 11*(4), 10–15.

Bartlett, J. E., Kotrlik, J. W., & Higgins, C. C. (2001). Organizational research: Determining appropriate sample size in survey research. *Information Technology, Learning, and Performance Journal, 19*(1), 43–50.

Bassi, L. J., Ludwig, J., McMurrer, D. P., & Buren, M. V. (2002). Profiting from learning: Firm-level effects of training investments and market implications. *Singapore Management Review, 24*(3), p. 61.

Bernthal, P. R. (1995). Evaluation that goes the distance. *Training & Development, 49*(9), 41–44.

Berry, J. (2002). President's message: Addressing the recruitment and diversity crisis. *American Libraries, 33*(2), p. 7.

Bolt, N. (1998). *Strategic planning for multitype library cooperatives: A planning process.* Washington, DC: American Library Association.

Box, G. E. P. (1954). Some theorems on quadratic forms applied in the study of analysis of variance problems. *Annuals of Statistics, 25,* 290–302.

Brinkerhoff, R. O. (1987). *Achieving results from training.* San Fransico: Jossey-Bass.

Brinkerhoff, R. O. (2003). *The success case method: Find out quickly what's working and what's not.* San Francisco: Berrett-Koehler Publishers.

Brooks, A., & Watkins, K. E. (1994). *The emerging power of action inquiry technologies.* San Francisco: Jossey-Bass.

Brown, M. B., & Forsythe, A. B. (1974). The small sample behavior of some statistics which test the equality of several means. *Technometrics, 16*(1), 129–132.

Bryson, J. (2001). Measuring the performance of libraries in the knowledge economy and society. *Australian Academic & Research Libraries, 32*(4), 332–342.

Bureau of the Census. (2003). Current population survey: Table 425: Use of the internet, U.S. Department of Commerce. 2005: unpublished data; table prepared 2003.

Bushnell, D. S. (1990). Input, process, output: A model for evaluating training. *Training and Development Journal, 44*(3), 41–43.

Charles, C. M. (1998). *Introduction to educational research.* New York: Longman.

Craven, B. M., & McNulty, M. B. (1994). Management training and development expenditures: Perspectives from auditing, economics and human resource management. *Managerial Auditing Journal, 9*(6), p. 3.

Creswell, J. W. (2002). *Educational research: Planning, conducting, and evaluating quantitative and qualitative research.* Upper Saddle River, NJ: Pearson Education, Inc.

Curry, E. A., & Baughman, S. A. (1997). *Strategic planning for library multitype cooperatives: Samples and examples.* Washington, DC: American Library Association.

Dillman, D. A. (1999). Mail and other self-administered surveys in the 21st century: The beginning of a new era. *Gallup Research Journal,* Available at http://survey.sesrc.wsu.edu/dillman/papers/svys21st.pdf. Retrieved on 12/23/04 11:29 am.

Fitz-enz, J. (1994). Yes…you can weigh training's value. *Training, 31*(7), 54–60.

Fitz-enz, J. (2000). *The ROI of human capital: Measuring the economic value of employee performance*. New York: Amacom.

Foxon, M. J. (1986). Evaluation of training: The art of the impossible. *Training Officer, 22*(5), 133–137.

Foxon, M. J. (1989). Evaluation of training and development programs: A review of the literature. *Australian Journal of Educational Technology, 5*(2), 89–104.

Gall, M. D., Borg, W. R., & Gall, J. P. (1996). *Educational research: An introduction*. White Plains, NY: Longman.

Goldstein, I. L. (1986). *Training in organizations: Needs assessment, development, & evaluation*. Pacific Grove, CA: Brooks/Cole.

Goldstein, I. L. (1993). *Training in organizations: Needs assessment, development, & evaluation*. Monterey, CA: Brooks-Cole.

Hallam, G. (2007). Don't ever stop! The imperative for career-long learning in the library and information profession. *ALIA Information Online 2007: 13th Annual Conference*. Sydney.

Hamblin, A. C. (1974). *Evaluation and control of training*. New York: McGraw-Hill.

Harper, E., & Bell, C. (1982). Developing training materials: An evaluation-production model. *Journal of European & Industrial Training, 6*(4), 24–26.

Heber, J. (2007). Information storage. *Nature Materials, 6*(11).

Hill, D. R. (1999). Evaluation of formal, employer-sponsored training in the U.S. healthcare industry. *Doctoral dissertation*. Austin, TX: University of Texas, 1–170.

Holton, E. F., III. (1996). The flawed four-level evaluation model. *Human Resource Development Quarterly, 7*(1), 5–21.

Holton, E. F., III. (2005). Holton's evaluation model: New evidence and construct elaborations. *Advances in Developing Human Resources, 7*(1), 37–54.

Homan, J. M., McGowan, J. J., & Lilly, R. (2002). The Medical Library Association: Promoting new roles for health information professionals. *Journal of the Medical Library Association, 90*(1), 80–85.

Institute of Museum and Library Services. (2004). *IMLS announces national research study on the future of librarians in the workforce*. Washington, DC: Press release.

Kaplan, R. S., & Norton, D. P. (1996). *The balanced scorecard*. Boston, MA: Harvard Business School Press.

Kaplowitz, M. D., Hadlock, T. D., & Levine, R. (2004). A comparison of web and mail survey response rates. *Public Opinion Quarterly, 68*(1), 98–104.

Kaufman, R., Keller, J., & Watkins, R. (1995). What works and what doesn't: Evaluation beyond Kirkpatrick. *Performance and Instruction, 35*(2), 8–12.

Kearns, P., & Miller, T. (1997). *Measuring the impact of training and development on the bottom line*. London: Pitman Publishing.

King, W. C., Jr., & Miles, E. W. (1995). A quasi-experimental assessment of the effect of computerizing noncognitive paper-and pencil measurements: a test of measurement equivalence. *Journal of Applied Psychology, 80*, 643–651.

Kirkpatrick, D. L. (1959). Techniques for evaluating training programs. *Journal of the American Society for Training Directors, 13*(11), 3–9.

Kirkpatrick, D. L. (1959). Techniques for evaluating training programs: Part 2-learning. *Journal of the American Society of Training Directors, 13*(12), 21–26.

Kirkpatrick, D. L. (1960). Techniques for evaluating training programs: Part 3-Behavior. *Journal of the American Society of Training Directors, 13*(3), 13–18.

Kirkpatrick, D. L. (1960). Techniques for evaluating training programs: Part 4-results. *Journal of the American Society of Training Directors, 14*(2), 28–32.

Lee, R. (1996). The pay-forward view of training. *People Management* (2), 30–32.

Lenzini, R. T. (2002). The graying of the library profession: A survey of our professional association and their responses. *Searcher, 10*(7), 88–97.

Locke, F. L., Spirduso, W. W., & Silverman, S. J. (1987). *Proposals that work. A guide for planning dissertations and grant proposals*. Newbury Park, CA: Sage Publications.

Lyman, P. & Varian, H. R. (2003). How much information. Available at http://www.sims.berkeley.edu/research/projects/how-much-info-2003/. Retrieved from University of California, Berkley.

Lynch, M. J. (2001). *Spending on staff development*. Chicago, IL: American Library Association. 2004.

Lynn, M. R. (1986). Determination and quantification of content validity. *Nursing Research, 35*, 382–385.

MacDonald, G., & Weisbach, M. S. (2001). The economics of has-beens. *Journal of Political Economy, 112*(1), 289–310.

Massis, B. (2004). *Practical library trainer*. Birmingham, NY: Haworth Press.

McCarthy, J. (2005). Planning a future workforce. *New Review of Academic Librarianship, 11*(1), 41–56.

McGriff, S. J. (2005). ISD knowledge base/instructional design & development/instructional systems design models. Available at http://www.sjsu.edu/depts/it/mcgriff/kbase/isd/ISDModel.html. Retrieved on August 30, 2005.

Molenda, M., Pershing, J. A., & Reigeluth, C. M. (1996). Designing instructional systems. In: R. L. Craig (Ed.), *The ASTD training and development handbook*. New York: McGraw-Hill.

Morris, M. (1984). The evaluation of training. *Industrial & Commercial Training, 16*(2), 9–16.

National Center for Education Statistics. (2000). *Fast response survey system; Survey for programs of adults in public library outlets*. Washington, DC: U.S. Department of Education.

National Center for Education Statistics. (2004). *Digest of education statistics* (2005). Washington, DC: Department of Education.

Neumann, S., & Weiss, A. (1995). On the effects of schooling vintage on experience-earnings profiles: Theory and evidence. *European Economic Review, 39*(5), 943–955.

OCLC. (2004). *2004 information format trends: Content, not containers* (2005). Dublin, OH: OCLC.

Penny, J. A. (2003). Exploring differential item functioning in a 360-degree assessment: Rater source and method of delivery. *Organizational Research Methods, 6*(1), 61–80.

Phillips, J. J. (1987). *Recruiting, training, and retaining new employees*. San Francisco: Jossey-Bass.

Phillips, J. J. (1994). *Measuring return on investment: Volume I*. Alexandria, VA: American Society for Training and Development.

Phillips, J. J., & Phillips, P. P. (1994). *Measuring return on investment*. Alexandria, VA: American Society for Training and Development.

Phillips, P. P. (2003). *Measuring ROI in the public sector*. Canada: The Canadian Centre for Learning and Development.

Phillips, P. P. (2003). Training evaluation in the public sector. *DAI, 64*(09A), p. 3162.

Powell, R. R. (1991). Guides to conducting research in library and information science. In: C. R. McClure & P. Hernon (Eds), *Basic research methods for librarians*. Norwood, NJ: Ablex.

Preskill, H., & Torres, R. T. (1999). *Evaluative inquiry for learning in organizations*. Thousand Oaks, CA: Sage.

Pulley, M. L. (1994). Navigating the evaluation rapids. *Training & Development, 48*(9), 19–25.
Rackham, N. (1973). Recent thoughts on evaluation. *Industrial & Commercial Training, 5*(10), 454–461.
Sheskin, D. J. (2004). *Handbook of parametric and nonparametric statistical procedures*. Boca Raton, FL: Chapman & Hall.
Sifry, D. (2007). *State of the Blogosphere/State of the Live Web*. Available at http://www.sifry.com/stateoftheliveweb/. Retrieved on 03/08/2008 10:00 am.
Sleezer, C. M. (1992). Needs assessment: Perspectives from the literature. *Performance Improvement Quarterly, 5*(2), 34–46.
Smith, M. E. (1980). Evaluating training operations and programs. *Training & Development Journal, 34*(10), 70–78.
Snyder, R., Raben, C., & Farr, J. (1980). A model for the systematic evaluation of human resource development programs. *Academy of Management Review, 5*(3), 431–444.
Spitzer, D. R. (2005). Learning effectiveness measurement: A new approach for measuring and managing learning to achieve business results. *Advances in Developing Human Resources, 7*(1), 55–70.
State Library and Archives of Florida. (2004). *Florida library directory with statistics*. Tallahassee, FL: State Library and Archives of Florida.
Steffen, N. (2004). *Retirement, retention and recruitment: The future of librarianship in Colorado*. Available at http://www.lrs.org-documents-closer_look-RRR_web.pdf. Retrieved on February 20, 2007.
Stites, B. J. (2005). *Google search*. 2007. Retrieved on January 4.
Stites, B. J. (2007). *Google search*. 2007. Retrieved on February 20.
Strunk, K. S. (1999). Status of and barriers to financial impact evaluations in employer-sponsored training programs. *DAI, 60*(06A), p. 2128.
Sugrue, B. (2004). *State of the industry: ASTD's annual review of trends in workplace learning and performance* (1–24 pp.). Alexandria, VA: American Society of Training and Development.
Swanson, R. A. (2005). Evaluation, a state of mind. *Advances in Developing Human Resources, 7*(1), 16–21.
Swanson, R. A., & Holton, E. F. I. (Eds). (1997). *Human resource development research handbook*. San Francisco: Berrett-Koehler Publishers.
Swanson, R. A., & Holton, E. F. I. (1999). *Results: How to assess performance, learning, and perceptions in organizations*. San Francisco: Berrett-Koehler Publishers, Inc.
Swanson, R. A., & Sleezer, C. M. (1987). Training effectiveness evaluation. *Journal of European Industrial Training, 11*(4), 7–16.
Tse, A. C. B. (1998). Comparing the response rate, response speed and response quality of two methods of sending questionnaires: E-mail vs. mail. *Journal of the Market Research Society, 40*(4), 353–361.
Tukey, J. W. (1953). *The problem of multiple comparisons*. Princeton, NJ: Princeton University.
Twitchell, S. (1997). Technical training program evaluation: Present practices in United States' business and industry. *The School of Vocational Education*, Louisiana State University and Agricultural and Mechanical College, Baton Rouge, LA, pp. 1–152.
Tyson, L. A., & Birnbrauer, S. (1985). High-quality evaluation. *Training & Development Journal, 39*(9), 33–37.
van Loo, J., de Grip, A., & de Steur, M. (2001). Skills obsolescence: Causes and cures. *International Journal of Manpower, 22*(1/2), 121–137.
van Loo, J., & Rocco, T. S. (2006). Differentiating CPE from training: Reconsidering terms, boundaries, and economic factors. *Human Resource Development Review, 5*(2), 202–228.

Wang, G. G., & Sptizer, D. R. (2005). Human resource development measurement and evaluation: Looking back and moving forward. *Advances in Developing Human Resources, 7*(1), 5–15.

Wang, G. G., & Wang, J. (2005). HRD evaluation: Emerging market, barriers, and theory building. *Advances in developing human resources, 7*(1), 22–36.

Warr, P., Bird, M., & Rackham, N. (1970). *Evaluation of management training.* London: Gower Press.

Webb, R. (1995). Continuing education: Mandate or option?. *Journal of Education for Library and Information Science, 36*(3), 261–264.

Wilder, S. J. (1995). *The age of demographics of academic librarians: A profession apart.* Washington, DC: Association of Research Libraries.

Wilder, S. J. (2007). *The ARL youth movement: Reshaping the ARL workforce.* Washington, DC: Association of Research Libraries.

Williams, G. (1976). The validity of methods of evaluating learning. *Journal of European Industrial Training, 5*(1), 12–20.

APPENDIX A. ALERT LETTER

Letter to be mailed to potential participants two weeks before survey is released.

Barbara J. Stites
510 Wildwood Parkway
Cape Coral, Florida 33904
(239) 225-4225
[date]

[Participant mailing address]

Dear Staff Development Colleague,

In approximately two weeks you will receive a weblink so that you can participate in the first nationwide survey to determine library training evaluation practices.

Great libraries depend on well-trained library staff and successful training depends upon effective evaluation methods to ensure the best use of staff development resources.

By surveying library training organizations and training contractors, I hope to identify effective evaluation methods, including metrics used to establish return-on-investment.

Your participation is very important and your name and organization will remain confidential; only aggregated results was published. All participants will receive a summary of the research results and a bibliography of training evaluation literature upon the completion of the study.

Please do not hesitate to contact me with questions or concerns at bstites@fgcu.edu.

Barbara J. Stites
Doctoral Candidate, Barry University

Research supervised by:
Dr. Betty Hubschman
Dr. Madeline Doran
The Adrian Dominican School of Education, Human Resource Development Department
Barry University
Miami, Florida

APPENDIX B. PERMISSION TO USE QUESTIONNAIRE

[Email from Dr. Patti Phillips]

From: TheChelseaGroup@aol.com [mailto:TheChelseaGroup@aol.com]
Sent: Sunday, December 05, 2004 10:55 PM
To: Stites, Barbara
Subject: Re: ROI and Evaluation Dissertation Question for Dr. Patti Phillips

Hi Barbara:

Sorry for the delay in responding to your email. I've been traveling the past week and have gotten way behind on all email.

I'd be delighted for you to use my questionnaire; I read your first chapter and the study sounds interesting. When you have completed your study, I'd love to get a copy or at least a summary; we'd like to quote you and your research in some of our publications if you are okay with it.

Thanks so much for the email. Please feel free to use the questionnaire. If I can help you with your dissertation in any other way, please don't hesitate to contact me again.

Thanks,

Patti Phillips

APPENDIX C. HYPOTHESES AND TESTS

Hypotheses	Statistic	Procedure	Survey Questions	Data Type
H1: Training for library staff is evaluated primarily at Level 1 and Level 2	Descriptive	The frequency and means of the use of each evaluation level	Independent variables: evaluation levels used (Q1, Q7, Q13, Q19, Q25)	Interval
H2: There is no generally accepted method of evaluating return-on-investment in library staff training	Descriptive	The frequency of participants who selected various ways to establish ROI	ROI method used (Q26); evaluation levels used (Q1, Q7, Q13, Q19, Q25)	Nominal
Sub-question: What are the generally accepted methods for evaluating training at Levels 1, 2, 3, and 4	Descriptive	The frequency of participants who selected various ways to evaluate at Levels 1, 2, 3, and 4	Method used (Q2, Q8, Q14, Q20, Q26)	Nominal
H3: Differences in percentage of evaluation conducted at the five levels are associated with library organization characteristics	One-way ANOVA	Will test the difference in the means of three library organizations' characteristics (type, size, and evaluation policies)/use of each evaluation level	Independent variables: Organizational characteristics (Q40, Q48, Q49, Q50, Q53); dependent variables: evaluation levels used (Q1, Q7, Q13, Q19, Q25)	Nominal/interval
	Correlation	Will determine the relationship between library organizations' characteristics (type,	Independent variables: Organizational characteristics (Q40, Q48, Q49, Q50, Q53);	Interval

APPENDIX C. (Continued)

Hypotheses	Statistic	Procedure	Survey Questions	Data Type
		size, and evaluation policies) and the use of the various levels of evaluation	dependent variables: evaluation levels used (Q1, Q7,Q13, Q19, Q25)	
H4: Differences in percentage of evaluation conducted at the five levels are associated with library organization training practices including the need for training and the training process	One-way ANOVA	Will test the differences in the use of evaluation planning, reporting, percentage of employees responsible for evaluation/use of each evaluation level	Independent variables: training process (Q31, Q33, Q47); dependent variables: evaluation levels used (Q1, Q7,Q13, Q19, Q25)	Nominal/interval; interval
	Correlation	Will test the differences in percentages of the need for training with the use of each evaluation level	Independent variables: need for training (Q32); dependent variables: evaluation levels used (Q1, Q7,Q13, Q19, Q25)	Ordinal; interval
Sub-question: What criteria are used in selecting programs to evaluate at Level 5, ROI?	Descriptive	The frequency of the criteria used	Independent variables: criteria for selecting ROI method (Q43)	Nominal
Sub-question: What criteria are important in determining an effective method for calculating ROI?	Descriptive	The frequency of the criteria selected as important	Independent variables: criteria ranking for best ROI method (Q45)	Nominal

APPENDIX D. OVERVIEW OF FINDINGS

1. Hypothesis One (accepted): Training is evaluated primarily at Level 1 and Level 2.
2. Hypothesis Two (accepted): There is no generally accepted method of evaluating return-on-investment.
   2.1. Sub-question for Hypothesis Two: Generally accepted methods of evaluating are: Level 1, reaction questionnaires; Level 2, on-the-job demonstration; Level 3, anecdotal information; and Level 4, anecdotal information.
3. Hypothesis Three (partially accepted): Differences in percentage of evaluation conducted at the five levels are associated with library organization characteristics (type, size, and evaluation policies).
   3.1. Having written training policies in place is associated with using Level 1 evaluation.
4. Hypothesis Four (accepted): Differences in percentage of evaluation conducted at the five levels are associated with library organization training practices including the need for training and the training process (planning, reporting, and number of staff involved with evaluation).
   4.1. Evaluation *reporting* is related to the use of Levels 1 and 4 evaluations.
   4.2. The percentage of the *staff involved* in evaluation is associated with Level 1 evaluation.
   4.3. There is a difference in the percentage of evaluation conducted at the five levels and the *need for training*.
      4.3.1. There is a correlation between using training as a reward and using Levels 2 and 3 evaluations.
      4.3.2. There is a correlation between sending all staff or a group to training and the use of Levels 3 and 4 evaluations.
      4.3.3. There is a correlation between sending employees to training for organizational outcomes and using Levels 4 and 5 evaluations.
      4.3.4. There is a correlation between sending employees to training to change an attitude and the use of Level 5 evaluation.
   4.4. First sub-question for Hypothesis Four: Criteria used in selecting programs to evaluate at Level 5 are that (1) the program has the interest of top executives and (2) has high visibility.
   4.5. Second sub-question for Hypothesis Four: Criteria important in determining an effective method for calculating ROI are that (1) it must account for other factors and (2) be applicable with all types of data.

APPENDIX E. SURVEY INSTRUMENT

Training Evaluation Practices and Return on Investment in Libraries

Thank you for participating in this survey research project. This survey gathers data on training evaluation used by libraries and library training organizations. The survey is adapted from a survey originally developed by Dr. Dianne Hill in Survey of Present Practices in Training Evaluation: U.S. Healthcare Industry and later modified by Patricia Pullium Phillips for Training Evaluation in Public Sector Organizations.

Training includes any employer-sponsored training or continuing education that addresses knowledge and skills needed for library staff development. This includes both employer-delivered and contract-provided training.

Sections A – E that follow address reaction, learning, on-the-job application, organizational outcomes, and return on investment. Section F addresses general evaluation practices within the organization. Section G gathers general and demographic data. If your duties include education/training outside the United States please respond based on education/training that occurs only in the United States.

Participation in this research is completely voluntary and participation may be discontinued at any time without penalty or prejudice. The Survey Form # listed at the top of the survey form is used to secure sampling adequacy, and to facilitate follow-up on unreturned surveys. All respondents will receive a summary copy of the results.

To maintain confidentiality, the list that matches your name to the Survey Form # will be destroyed after responses are coded and a mailing list is compiled for survey results. No individual response information will be released to anyone before or after this list is destroyed. After completion of the research project, the individual responses will be destroyed and only summary information will be retained.

This project has been reviewed by Barry University's Internal Review Board (IRB), which ensures that research projects involving human participants follow federal regulations. Any questions or concerns about rights as a research participant should be directed to the Institutional Review Board point of contact, Ms. Avril Brenner, at (305)899-3020.

If you have questions regarding this research project, please contact:
Barbara J. Stites
12751 Westlinks Drive
Building III, Unit 7
Fort Myers, FL 33913
Telephone: (239) 225-4225
Fax: (239) 225-4229
e-mail: bstites@fgcu.edu

LIBRARY FACULTY AND COLLECTIVE BARGAINING: AN EXPLORATION

Stephen H. Aby

ABSTRACT

Faculty unionization is growing, and library faculty members are included in many collective bargaining units. Yet there is a dearth of information on how well collective bargaining contracts address the sometimes unique nature of library faculty work. This article explores contracts in a number of Ohio universities and from selective institutions around the country to see how well they accommodate the professional and work-related needs of librarians. Major contractual issues addressed include governance, academic freedom, workload, salary, and the retention, tenure, and promotion (RTP) of faculty, among others.

INTRODUCTION

The purpose of this article is to explore the degree to which collective bargaining agreements in higher education address some of the specific interests and concerns of library faculty members. This analysis is premised on the fact that, while faculty unionization is growing and librarians are included in many faculty bargaining units, there is a dearth of information

Advances in Library Administration and Organization, Volume 28, 283–321
ISSN: 0732-0671/doi:10.1108/S0732-0671(2009)0000028009

on librarian-related contractual issues (Spang, 1993; Garcha & Phillips, 2001; Bentley, 1978; Kennelly, 1976).[1] A number of questions can be raised. To what extent are academic librarian concerns reflected in contract articles such as governance, academic freedom, and salary? What are the difficulties or challenges that might be posed by trying to negotiate contract provisions that apply to differently situated constituencies? What are some of the common contract problems addressed by library and teaching faculty? What are examples of librarian-specific or librarian-friendly provisions that one can find in contracts in Ohio and around the country, and what are their advantages?

On many unionized campuses, librarians are part of the bargaining unit, whether they are formally classified as faculty or librarian-equivalent faculty. Not surprisingly, these contracts vary widely in their attentiveness to the sometimes unique nature of library faculty work. In this article, many examples will be drawn from colleges and universities in the state of Ohio, eleven of which are unionized with the American Association of University Professors (AAUP), with librarians included in a number of these bargaining units.[2] Additional examples will be drawn from collective bargaining agreements around the country that illustrate unique or interesting contractual features and language related to library faculty.[3] The focus of this analysis will be on contractual language in four-year institutions.

We need to begin this exploration by discussing the broader historical trends in unionization and providing the context for the growth and attractiveness of faculty unionization in particular. The core motivations for unionization, representing one's interests and establishing more control over one's work, are a constant, whether we are talking about blue collar work, white collar work, or the professional work engaged in by library and teaching faculty. However, the dynamics and trajectory of faculty unionization is somewhat different from that of unionization elsewhere in the economy. Understanding these differences is essential to understanding the dynamics generating faculty unionization and the issues confronted by library and teaching faculty. For library and other faculty, the trend in higher education is toward an erosion of shared governance and the involvement of faculty in decisions affecting their work and professional lives as academics. As will be shown, faculty unionization is one means by which library and teaching faculty can reassert their proper role. Contracts are the means by which these roles are guaranteed. Thus, the language in the contracts on key issues is critical in defining the shared governance and other rights of library and teaching faculty.

UNIONIZATION TRENDS

National data indicate that, overall, unionization is declining. From a high of 32.5% of the workforce in 1953, the unionized workforce is now about 12% (Labor Research Association, 2007; Bureau of Labor Statistics, 2007). While some may argue that the decline indicates the growing lack of appeal of unionization among workers (Blum, 1990; Will, 2005), this explanation is arguable. Surveys of workers report that 32% of nonunion workers, and a majority of all workers, want union representation (Freeman, 2007). As an example, in the past four years, the AFL-CIO's Working America initiative has added two million individual, nonunionized members to the AFL-CIO, suggesting the desire on the part of many workers for some collective representation, albeit indirect in this instance (Broder, 2007; Von Bergen, 2006).

However, numerous obstacles to collective bargaining exist. Some of these are a result of state law and regulation, others derive from federal law and regulation, and still others are a consequence of court decisions. At the state level, there are 23 "right-to-work" states that prohibit both mandatory membership in unions and the collection of involuntary union dues or agency fees from workers. Agency or "fair share" fees are those fees that unions may assess nonmembers for the services rendered in negotiating and enforcing the contract. Furthermore, many states have no enabling legislation to structure the process of forming public sector unions and resolving collective bargaining disputes. These states make it more difficult for unorganized employees to organize in the face of management opposition, an opposition that has grown since the Taft-Hartley amendments to the National Labor Relations Act in 1947 and the Landrum-Griffith amendments in 1959 (Ross, 2004, p. 194).[4] Even for those states that do have enabling legislation, their statutes are idiosyncratic. In Ohio, for example, the Ohio Revised Code statute that regulates public sector unionization (ORC 4117) prohibits part-time (contingent) faculty and graduate student employees from unionizing under the protection of that statute. In Wisconsin, faculty members at public two-year institutions are allowed to engage in collective bargaining under their statute, but faculty at public four-year institutions are not (American Federation of Teachers, n.d.a). In Alaska, the opposite is the case (National Education Association, 2007). Most recently, the governors of Maryland, Indiana, and Missouri rescinded the collective bargaining rights or agency fee ("fair share") rights of state employees and their unions (Preciphs, 2005; Union busting, midwest-style, 2005), causing another setback to collective bargaining.

At the federal level, President Reagan's firing of air traffic controllers in the 1981 PATCO strike also dealt a serious blow to the labor movement that has had lasting effects (Busch, 2006; Twarog, 2006; Rothstein, 1997). Also, in recent years, the National Labor Relations Board (NLRB) has consistently ruled against worker and collective bargaining rights, gradually eroding the rights that are supposed to be protected by the National Labor Relations Act (Hall, 2007). For example, in 2004, the NLRB ruled that graduate assistants on private college campuses are ineligible for unionization, reversing a previous ruling and thus prohibiting organizing among that group of campus employees (Smallwood, 2004a, 2004b). In 2007, this trend in NLRB decisions elicited severe criticism from 58 labor law professors in a letter submitted to a joint committee of Congress addressing the effect of the NLRB's decisions on workers' collective bargaining rights (Brudney & Estlund, 2007).

There have also been court decisions that have impeded collective bargaining in both the public and the private sectors, including among academics. The Supreme Court's Yeshiva University decision in 1980 declared that private college and university faculty are administrators or management and are therefore ineligible for collective bargaining under the National Labor Relations Act (Finkin, 1980; Metchick & Singh, 2004). This ruling effectively eliminated any further growth in unionization among faculty in private colleges and universities, and, in fact, some private institutions that had faculty collective bargaining lost it (Metchick & Singh, 2004).

There are also structural issues that make unionization, especially among faculty, challenging. Most notable is the fact that higher education faculties are becoming increasingly composed of contingent or part-time faculty. Between 1975 and 2003, the percentage of those faculty members who are tenured or tenure track shrank from approximately 57% to 35% with part-time (contingent) and non-tenure track (term) faculty appointments rising from 43% to 65% (Curtis & Jacobe, 2006, p. 5). In Ohio, if one adds graduate teaching and research assistants into the totals for contingent teaching labor, the percentage for all contingent instruction rises to over 70% at some institutions (Curtis & Jacobe, 2006, p. 31). Contingent faculty are the quintessential disposable labor force: hired just-in-time; often denied health and other benefits; and paid a fraction of what full-time faculty are paid for the same work while generating the same instructional income to the university. These figures represent a stunning decline in the traditional target population for faculty unionization. Furthermore, it is widely acknowledged that contingent faculty have, at best, a tenuous hold on academic freedom, a fundamental concern of library and teaching faculty.

Although the increase in part-time employment among academic librarians has not been well studied, research from the late 1980s suggested that the growth in part-time academic librarians comprised a "sizable proportion of the workforce" (Brustman & Via, 1988), not unlike the trend for teaching faculty. Furthermore, the motivations for this increase (i.e., flexibility, reduced costs) seemed to be similar to those causing the precipitous growth in part-time or contingent teaching faculty. While the professional faculty associations, like the AAUP, and unions, like the National Education Association (NEA) and American Federation of Teachers (AFT), are increasingly trying to organize this new segment of contingent faculty, the altered composition of the faculty has created a stark contrast from the previous faculty landscape, and thus an organizing challenge.

Yet, despite the obstacles, surprisingly, unionization among college and university faculty has shown substantial growth in the past 30 years. Both the growth and the reasons for it are important. An "American Faculty Poll," conducted by the NEA in 2000, indicated that one-third of surveyed faculty were on campuses with faculty unions, and fully two-thirds of those unionized campus respondents were union members (NEA Higher Education Research Center, 2000). Even 37% of non-unionized faculty support unionization, and 52% "favor creating an organization to help represent their interests," though not necessarily a union (Jaschik, 2005). As of 2006, approximately 318,000 faculty were unionized (Directory of faculty contracts and bargaining agents in institutions of higher education, 2006, p. vii). This figure had grown by some 62,000 faculty since 1998, with that growth being reflected equally in the expansion of existing bargaining units and the addition of 78 new ones (Directory of faculty contracts and bargaining agents in institutions of higher education, 2006, pp. iii, viii). Furthermore, faculty members at some private colleges have won the right to hold collective bargaining elections despite Yeshiva (Gravois, 2005; Leatherman, 2000a, 2000b, 2000c). On many campuses that are unionized, library faculty members are included in the bargaining unit. Of the approximately 575 academic union contracts that the *Directory of Faculty Contracts and Bargaining Agents in Institutions of Higher Education* has reviewed, librarians are included in the bargaining unit in 301 of them (Directory of faculty contracts and bargaining agents in institutions of higher education, 2006).[5] These are conservative numbers, given that some agreements are multi-campus agreements covering larger systems with distinct campuses.

Growth in Faculty Unionization

Why has there been this growth, and what do library and teaching faculty have to gain in collective bargaining? The standard rationale given for why professionals such as university faculty do not need unions is that they are highly educated and have much discretionary control over their professional work. Unions, so the argument goes, are for blue collar workers whose on-the-job functioning is under more direct managerial control. Faculty members, by contrast, supposedly have involvement in shared governance through collegial mechanisms such as faculty senates. Shared governance is the decision-making model premised on the belief that many campus decisions are best made by the constituency closest to the core mission of the institution, the faculty.

However, a trend in higher education over the past couple of decades has undermined the practice of shared governance. As many authors have argued and documented, universities are becoming increasingly corporatized and entrepreneurial, both in their values and in their management (Johnson, Kavanagh, & Mattson, 2003; Bousquet, 2008; Herman & Schmid, 2003; Readings, 1996; Giroux, 2007; Nelson & Watt, 2004; Moser, 2001; Witt, 2007; Slaughter & Rhoades, 2004). In the latter area, the introduction of management structures that mimic those in business and government diminishes the traditional role of faculty in shared governance and, specifically, the professional discretion that faculty have traditionally exercised. Where once decisions were made by faculty and administrators together in a climate of collegial decision-making, now they are increasingly made by administrators exercising their management rights in a corporate model of governance. These can include not just areas such as budgetary and facilities planning, but even the selection of faculty and curricular planning, which are supposed to be staples of faculty decision-making in higher education (Jaschik, 2007; Bourdaghs, 2008). As will be explored later, some trends within academic librarianship may also weaken library faculty discretion in the face of budgetary crises and the more concentrated corporate provision of information and materials. In general, these developments have narrowed faculty prerogatives and constrained shared governance.

Growing administrative discretion and corporatization manifests itself in other areas as well. Once, the knowledge created on campus became part of the information commons, freely shared with other researchers and scholars. Now, such knowledge has increasingly become owned, privatized, and commercialized, with attendant limits on its availability (Washburn, 2005; Bollier, 2002). Part of this was fostered by the passage of the Bayh-Dole Act of 1980, which facilitated the commercialization of knowledge produced in the course of campus based research (Association of University Technology Managers, n.d.). Often, this knowledge was generated with public funds, and in the new environment, it increasingly becomes proprietary, with accompanying risks of bias or reduced access by the "scientific commons" (Fenwick & Zipp, 2007; Jelinek, 2005). Certainly, open access to knowledge is one of the fundamental principles of the library profession, as noted in the ALA's Library Bill of Rights (American Library Association, 1980).

These trends toward corporatization may also partially be in response to diminished state financial support and the necessity for colleges and universities to be more economically self-sustaining (Ehrenberg & Rizzo, 2004). The concomitant rise in commercialized research-based knowledge and, unfortunately, student tuition and fees is part of this trend. These developments contribute to making higher education less of a public good, deserving of public support, than a consumer item to be purchased based on a personal cost-benefit analysis.

These dynamics explain, in part, the growth of faculty unionization. Collective bargaining can be seen, increasingly, as a non-traditional mechanism for trying to gain, or recapture, a quite traditional value: shared governance. While many articles on the desirability or advisability of collective bargaining focus on its possible economic benefits, or lack thereof, for library and teaching faculty (Lee, Rogers, & Grimes, 2006; Ehrenberg, Kezsbom, Klaff, & Nagowski, 2004), actual collective bargaining campaigns on campuses repeatedly focus on the loss of shared governance as the root cause for unionization (North central state faculty association AAUP chapter, n.d.; American Association of University Professors, 1998, 2001, 2003; American Association of University Professors, University of Akron, 2002; Govea, 1998). Researchers may disagree about the potential economic benefit of faculty unionization, but library and teaching faculty on campuses often view the inattention to salary issues as just one of a number of symptoms of the core problem: lack of a faculty voice in governance. As faculty supporting collective bargaining campaigns view it, a contract is a way of ensuring that they have a voice in governance, at least on the dozens of topics negotiated there. Shared governance is the crystallization of many of the day-to-day activities that library and teaching faculty engage in. These include academic freedom in the classroom and one's interactions with students, the development and dissemination of knowledge, the evaluation of one's professional colleagues, the review of one's administrative leaders, the development and approval of curricula, and the shaping of the direction of one's department and institution. Nothing could be more central to the professional lives of library and teaching faculty. Therefore, how these and other issues are treated in faculty collective bargaining agreements is crucial in shaping library faculty work. Furthermore, given the dominance of teaching faculty on any campus, it remains an open question as to how well contracts, in attempting to reassert the faculty role, attend to the sometimes distinct needs of library faculty.

LIBRARY FACULTY

While library faculty are part of many faculty bargaining units, a preliminary issue that has been raised is whether they should be included in these units and whether librarians share a "community of interest" with other faculty. Community of interest is the labor law term used to indicate that employees share similar enough features in their work that they should be included in the same bargaining unit. Do library faculty members share a community of interest with teaching faculty? On this point, a 1977 decision in the Supreme Court of New Hampshire is instructive. It upheld a decision by the Public Employee Labor Relations Board that library faculty in the University of New Hampshire System did indeed share this community of interest with teaching faculty, and, therefore, should be considered part of the faculty bargaining unit:

> The PELRB found that librarians "are given faculty rank and tenure based on qualifications and share in the same benefits as faculty members;" that they "participate in a measurable degree in the related teaching process;" and that "[a] community of interest with academic faculty is apparent ..." These findings were supported by testimony given at both the initial hearing and the rehearing, as well as by written evidence submitted by interested parties. There was evidence that the librarians hold faculty rank. Tenure and promotions are determined in the same manner as for other faculty members. Librarians also serve on university committees in the same capacity as other ... faculty members. Although the job of a librarian is not the same as that of other faculty members, librarians are nevertheless engaged in the instruction of students, both on an individual and on a classroom basis ... In their relationship to both students and faculty, librarians are an integral part of the university's teaching, learning, and research processes. (Supreme Court of New Hampshire, 1977)

In support of this rationale, the ruling noted similar state labor relations board and NLRB decisions that included librarians in the bargaining units at the University of Massachusetts, the University of Vermont, Rensselaer Polytechnic Institute, and New York University. The Association of College and Research Libraries (ACRL), a division of the American Library Association (ALA), takes a similar position supporting library faculty in faculty bargaining units (Association of College and Research Libraries, 2007).

As academic librarians know, their appointments may be exactly equivalent to faculty with academic rank, or they may, in other cases, have their own, parallel designations. While teaching faculty can have appointments such as Instructor, Assistant Professor, Associate Professor, or Full Professor, library faculty may have designations such as Beginning Librarian, Assistant Librarian, Associate Librarian, Associate Senior Librarian, and Senior Librarian, which is the case at the University of Cincinnati. On other campuses, such as at the University of Akron or the University of Toledo, the library faculty designations are exactly the same as those for teaching faculty. In either case, librarians may form a distinct subset of academic faculty. The distinctiveness in terms of their work, and the possible implications for the fit and appeal of the collective bargaining agreement, is the subject of this article. To be clear, the purpose of this chapter is not to debate whether collective bargaining is good for faculty or academic librarians. Rather, it assumes the reality of collective bargaining for many faculty and librarians and attempts to assess both the process and the outcomes of negotiating agreements that apply to academic librarians.

GOVERNANCE

A premise of this article, as indicated by various collective bargaining campaigns, is that faculty unionization is often inspired by a desire for shared governance. How does a bargaining agreement address this desire in these cases? If one breaks down a contract, shared governance can be manifested both in the process of implementing the agreement and in the content of the various contract articles. Library faculty members have a stake in both areas, and existing contracts reveal the ways in which their concerns are and are not addressed. In some cases, such as collegial decisions embedded within contracts, library faculty share similar concerns with teaching faculty. In other areas, such as academic freedom, or even the definition of what constitutes a department, their concerns may be more unique and somewhat under-addressed. This would also be true in areas such as salary and workload, as we will see.

Collegial Decisions in Contractual Environments

Some features of collective bargaining agreements may require a more traditional looking process of collegial shared governance. Take for example, the development, approval, and revision of guidelines for the retention, tenure, and promotion (RTP) of faculty. At the University of Akron, the 2005–2009 contract's Article 13 provides the broad parameters of such guidelines, and each department's individual guidelines must fit within those parameters (Collective bargaining agreement between the University of Akron and the American Association of University Professors, University of Akron chapter, 2005). These include features such as application dates, various subsequent decision dates, criteria categories (i.e., teaching, research, service), and appeal procedures. However, every department's faculty are also empowered to write their own specialized or discipline-specific guidelines within these parameters, as they should be. These guidelines would tease out the discipline-specific criteria for demonstrating one's accomplishments in the areas of teaching/work, research, and service. Once written, the contract specifies that the guidelines must be approved by the Dean and then the central administration. The guidelines, then, are faculty-driven, yet reviewable by administration. This is an inherently collegial process, not unlike what is followed on non-collective bargaining campuses. In such a process, library faculty are empowered to write RTP guidelines that are especially suited to their disciplinary expectations and educational mission.

Contracts vary in the degree to which they explicitly empower faculty directly, in various contract articles, as opposed to giving (library) faculty the right to develop and implement a departmental faculty handbook that addresses multiple internal governance issues. These handbooks can enshrine numerous procedures that may be found elsewhere in other contracts; yet, they still have the force of law and the contract. So, for example, in Kent State University's contract with AAUP-KSU, every department's or unit's faculty, including library faculty, is empowered to write a handbook that outlines features such as RTP guidelines; faculty workload expectations and procedures for arriving at these; and much more. The Kent State contract states (Article VI, Section 7):

Section 7. Implementing Handbooks

A. Each department, college, independent school, and regional campus, as well as the University Libraries and Media Services and the Regional Campuses System shall establish a handbook to implement University policies within their respective units. Departmental handbooks shall be developed by the departmental FAC and Chairperson and shall be subject to final approval by the Dean.

In reviewing handbooks or proposed revisions to handbooks, the Dean may request revisions before lending final approval. If these revisions are not adopted at the department level, the Dean shall consult the College Advisory Committee with regard to the provisions in dispute before making a final determination and certifying final approval of the handbook. Collegial handbooks shall be developed by the CAC and the Dean and shall be subject to final approval by the Office of the Provost. The Provost shall consult with the Provost's Advisory Committee before making final determination on any provision in dispute. Regional campus handbooks shall be developed by each regional campus Faculty and the Dean of each regional campus and shall be subject to final approval by the Provost. The Provost shall consult with the Regional Campuses Faculty Advisory Council before making final determination on any provision in dispute. The Regional Campuses System handbook shall be developed by the RCFAC and the Chief Academic Officer for the Regional Campuses and shall be subject to final approval by the Office of the Provost. (Collective bargaining agreement, effective August 23, 2005, Kent State University and the tenure-track unit of the American Association of University Professors, Kent State chapter, 2005)

The list of subjects covered in such handbooks includes (Article VI, Section 7.b):

B. It is recognized that all handbooks will cover such items as may be mandated from time to time by University policy and may contain such other subjects as are reasonably related to the mission of the unit. These include but are not limited to:

• tenure and promotion criteria and procedures;
• search procedures for appointment of new Faculty;
• reappointment, nonreappointment and dismissal;
• role and responsibilities of non-tenure track and other instructional faculty within the unit, if and as applicable;
• responsibilities, structure, election procedures, and terms of members of committees, including appropriate representation of Regional Campus Faculty;
• Faculty workload specification and workload equivalent duties;
• workload equivalent for off-campus teaching assignments, if and as appropriate;
• evaluation criteria and process relating to salaries and merit increases;
• access to opportunities for summer, intersession and overload assignments;
• teaching assignments and class schedules;
• research and other leaves;
• procedures for teaching evaluations;
• procedures for resolving complaints and disputes;
• procedures for student complaints; and
• a statement of professional ethics and responsibilities.

(Collective bargaining agreement, effective August 23, 2005, Kent State University and the tenure-track unit of the American Association of University Professors, Kent State chapter, 2005)

The document for Libraries & Media Services at Kent State University is known as the *Libraries and Media Services Handbook* (Libraries & Media Services, Kent State University, 2008). This document operationalizes many of the rights granted to library faculty under the contract and its authorization of the handbook. This handbook discusses the creation of the School Advisory Committee (SAC), the creation of other standing committees and the elections of faculty to them, the collegial process for providing input to the Dean on Handbook-related matters, and so on. The SAC is, in effect, a mini-advisory body involved in the internal governance of the unit. Other processes provided for in the Handbook include search committees and the initial appointment of faculty, workload, professional leaves, retention/promotion/tenure guidelines, and much more. In short, what the contract at Kent State University does is authorize such handbooks and create mini-governance bodies in each college or unit, specifying the functional entities, their scope of decision-making, and the overall parameters of governance in the unit. For library faculty, having the authority to address many internal governance matters in a broad document of their own creation is an excellent opportunity to craft contractual rights in their discipline.

An issue in such contract provisions is whether faculty rights are granted without qualification or are empowered as part of a collegial process of approval that moves up the administrative chain. At Kent State, the latter is the case, and the language in Article VI, Section 7 of contract specifies the time frames for the review of submitted guidelines:

Administrators responsible for approving handbooks or proposed handbook revisions shall acknowledge receipt of handbooks forwarded for approval no later than ten (10) days after the receipt of the handbook. The relevant administrator must provide the academic unit his/her substantive response to handbooks or revisions within ninety (90) days of initial receipt of the handbook. If any new handbook or proposed revision is rejected, the relevant administrator shall provide the unit with a substantive response, i.e., a written rationale for his/her decision and suggestions for acceptable alternative wording. If no response has been received within ninety (90) days of the most recent submission to the relevant administrator of the handbook or handbook revisions, the proposed new handbooks or revisions to existing handbooks shall become effective and shall remain in full force and effect on an interim basis until and unless the relevant administrator either indicates formal approval or submits suggestions for modifications and revisions, as described above. Upon receipt of the relevant administrator's substantive response, the academic unit will re-submit the revised handbook to the administrator within sixty (60) days of receipt. The relevant administrator will provide subsequent substantive responses to the academic unit within thirty (30) days. If no substantive response has been received within one hundred thirty-five (135) days of initial receipt by the relevant administrator, or within ninety (90) days of the most recent re-submission from the academic unit, the proposed new handbook shall be considered as having received final approval of the relevant administrator, and become effective. Once approved, a copy of the handbook will be made available to the Association by the Office of Faculty Affairs and Curriculum. (Collective bargaining agreement, effective August 23, 2005, Kent State University and the tenure-track unit of the American Association of University Professors, Kent State chapter, 2005)

As noted here, there are explicit time frames involved, with the contract specifying that a lack of administrative action or approval after a specified period of time will result in the automatic approval of the submitted guidelines. This language was introduced when negotiating the Kent State collective bargaining agreement by the faculty in response to persistent problems of inaction by the administration in such approvals (D. Smith, personal communication, November 8, 2007). This is an inherent problem in relying on collegial mechanisms in a contractual environment, and it is one shared by library and teaching faculty alike. Administration has the right to approve in a collegial process, but the time frame and expectations are left to its discretion, unless otherwise constrained by contract language.

A similar issue arose in the University of Akron contract between faculty and the university. The first contract specified that faculty had the right to develop discipline-specific merit pay guidelines that would have to be approved by the administration. The same collegial process was specified for the development and approval of RTP guidelines, as well as chair review guidelines. However, the collegial implementation of the merit guidelines proved problematic. Faculty wrote the guidelines, but the administration, from the department chairs to the Deans to the Provost, had its own ideas about what those guidelines should be. Thus, a long and drawn-out negotiation ensued, with some departments' faculty writing and re-writing guidelines to attempt to meet administrative expectations, while still holding firm to their conception of merit within their field. The delay in approval led to a delay in contractually guaranteed salary increments, which, in turn, led to a union grievance and, ultimately, to arbitration. The possible lesson concerning collegial mechanisms within the contract, such as those from Kent State and the University of Akron, may be that more constraints on implementation must be specified. If, in fact, issues relating to the effectiveness of shared or collegial governance, as has been argued, are a root cause of faculty unionization, then it is not surprising that its continued operation may be problematic.

Faculty-of-the-Whole vs. Departments

Another potential issue for library faculty in terms of governance is whether they should function as a faculty-of-the-whole or in their distinct departments. Shared governance in contracts often devolves down to faculty within their departments. Libraries are generally composed of departments, such as reference, collection development, serials, and cataloging. These departments may have their own chairs or department heads as well. However, librarians, while sharing different functional specialties, may see themselves as colleagues in the same way that faculty in a history department do in that academic specializations within the field do not separate them from their library faculty community of interest. This would suggest that they should function as a faculty-of-the-whole. If the language in the contract allows this, other issues may arise. For example, if their department heads function as other department heads on campus do, and come up for review within the shared governance provisions of the contract, who will review them? Will it be only the faculty within that department, or will it be all library faculty, regardless of their specialization? If the latter, then one would have faculty out of that department reviewing chairs working in areas beyond their expertise and with whom they may have limited professional contact.

Of course, library work is inherently collaborative and, if you will, interdisciplinary. As a result, it might be appropriate for a cataloger to evaluate a chair of collection management, or a collection management librarian to evaluate a chair of the reference department. Would the reverse be as suitable? That is, if library faculty implemented the contract on a departmental basis, and chairs were only reviewed by the faculty within that department, would that provide a sufficiently broad review given the nature of library work?

There is a related question as to how easily a contract might be implemented in a library operating as a faculty-of-the-whole as opposed to a collection of departments. Take the review of chairs as an example. If such review is done within a department that happens to be small, with only three or four library faculty, how could one preserve anonymity among the faculty respondents? Currently, at the University of Akron, there are library departments that have one, two, three, and four faculty members. There is no guarantee that faculty within those departments could fill out an evaluation of a chair that would remain anonymous. Furthermore, how would there be enough faculty in such a department to staff a chair review committee and provide a balanced review, particularly if both the faculty and the administration are allowed to make appointments or elect faculty to such a committee?

SALARY PROVISIONS

Salary contract articles may often include components such as across-the board raises, merit raises, market adjustments, or gender equity adjustments, among other things. At one level, these components may seem to be equitable in their application to faculty across departments. There are some standard challenges that could face any campus when negotiating salary provisions: how much of the salary is devoted to each of these components; to whom does one compare oneself for the purposes of market adjustments; how is merit determined, and by whom; are raises in percentages, or based on dollar amounts for accomplishments, or both? As complicated as some of these questions may be for the teaching faculty, buried within them are additional challenges for library faculty.

Merit Pay

Collective bargaining contract articles on salary or compensation may include not only across-the-board components but also merit pay components. The potential problems with merit pay are many. First, the criteria used for administering merit pay are often considered subjective, with decisions on awarding merit residing in the hands of department heads or Deans. Second, merit is not truly merit, since one's merit award is often contingent upon the size of the merit pool of money. Third, merit is most often a zero-sum game, with one person's higher merit necessitating another's lower merit. It is not necessarily criterion-based.

One response to these issues is to have all across-the-board salary increases, such as is the case in the 2007–2010 University of Cincinnati – AAUP collective bargaining agreement (Collective bargaining agreement between the University of Cincinnati and the American Association of University Professors University of Cincinnati chapter, 2007). Alternatively, at Kent State University, their bargaining philosophy in the past has been to backload merit pay at the end of the contract in, typically, the last year, with prior years designated for across-the-board increases. This allows those faculty interested in merit pay to accumulate accomplishments for that event. Another option, not mutually exclusive, is to have faculty-driven merit pay guidelines, as is the case at the University of Akron, in addition to across-the-board components. These guidelines would specify the discipline-specific criteria for the achievement of merit, as determined primarily by the faculty.

Within libraries, the merit pay issue can be somewhat more complicated than for distinct academic departments within a college. If a library faculty functions as a faculty-of-the-whole, then a percentage of all of their salaries would comprise the merit pool, which would then be distributed to faculty based on their accomplishments. The Kent State library faculty, for example, does function as a faculty-of-the-whole. Therefore, they are required to develop merit criteria that apply equally well across the various sub-disciplines or specialties within librarianship. How easily can one compare the work-related accomplishments of, say, a cataloger to that of a reference librarian? Who gets to make this comparison and based on what criteria?

The alternative model would be to have library faculty be evaluated for merit pay on a library department-by-department basis. That is, librarians within reference, cataloging, collection management, or other units would each fully comprise the unit of administration for purposes of salary and merit. In this case, the salary pool would be divided only among those members in that particular department, comparing apples to apples. An issue inherent in this is the possible effect of the size of the department. Taken all together, the entire library faculty may not be any larger than a good sized teaching department. However, subdivided into library departments, these faculties can shrink to rather small numbers. At the University of Akron, for example, the current departments with library faculty have one, two, three, or four faculty members. With so few faculty members, the zero-sum feature of merit pay is more telling. In a department of two, one faculty member's extraordinarily productive year may completely overshadow and diminish the more modest yet reasonable accomplishments of their only other colleague. In a more extreme case, in a department of one, that lone faculty member could receive all of a merit pay pool by default, depending of course on the basis for distribution. While this may be viewed as an unavoidable consequence of a certain administrative structure (i.e., small departments), it nonetheless contradicts an underlying and debatable assumption of merit pay: the value of competition for salary increases.

If library and other faculty have merit as one component of a salary increase, and if they are empowered to develop their own merit guidelines, to what extent are library faculty disadvantaged by one or the other of the models? That is, if they function as a faculty-of-the-whole, will they be able to write broadly applicable merit guidelines that are sufficiently nuanced to do justice to library faculty in more specific specialty areas? At the University of Akron, merit pay is applied on a library department-by-department basis, with faculty in each department writing their own merit guidelines. While these guidelines have certain commonalities, they are understandably quite different as they relate to the detailed work of departmental faculty. Ultimately, if the goal of shared governance is to empower faculty in the activities closest to their practice, merit pay models and procedures need to be evaluated by their ability to be faithful to this principle.

Minimum Salary per Rank

Beyond merit, and how to assess it, one of the more interesting provisions in an academic salary contract is the minimum salary per rank. This has special value for library faculty. For each rank in the bargaining unit from, for example, Instructor through Professor, there can be a specified minimum salary for the lowest paid faculty member in that rank. In some contracts (e.g., Kent State University), this figure changes with each year of the contract. In other cases (e.g., University of Cincinnati), there is one figure for the start of the contract, with the stipulation that there are regular percentage increases to the minima over the life of the contract. Thus, a minimum salary provision can be viewed as a one-time contract cost to bring those below the minimum up to standard, albeit with compound interest on those raises or specified increases in each subsequent year. Cincinnati's 2007–2010 contract also distinguishes between regular faculty minima and library faculty minima at each librarian rank, though in fact the numbers are virtually the same as for teaching faculty:

12.1 The minimum base salary for all Bargaining Unit members shall be as follows:

Effective 9/1/2007
Professor $62,718
Assoc. Professor $51,050
Asst. Professor $42,298
Instructor $36,464
Senior Librarian $62,718
Assoc. Sr. Librarian $54,113
Assoc. Librarian $49,590
Asst. Librarian $42,298
Beg. Librarian $36,464

Faculty Members earning a base salary below the effective minima shall move to the new minima and receive any across-the-board increase under Article 10.1 on his or her minima. (Collective bargaining agreement between the University of Cincinnati and the American Association of University Professors University of Cincinnati chapter, 2007)

What is present in some contracts, however, is particularly attractive to many library faculty members. Often, librarians work 12-month contracts. Therefore, the minimum per rank for nine-month faculty may not do justice to the added weeks and months of employment for these faculty librarians. The salary contract article at Kent State University addresses this issue. It includes minima by rank, as well as by nine-month and 12-month appointment. Thus, 12-month faculty members receive a higher minimum for their added time at work over the course of the year. More importantly, the Kent State contract (Article XII.5.A–C) does not distinguish between teaching and library faculty as faculty, but does tease out 12-month equivalent minima for each year of the contract. In the final year of its current contract, 2007–2008, these minima are:

C. The minimum annual contract salaries for Faculty members at each of the professional academic ranks for the academic years 2007–2008 shall be as follows:

	9 mo. Contract	12 mo. contract
Professor	$66,000	$80, 667
Associate Professor	$55,000	$67,222
Assistant Professor	$44,000	$53,777
Instructor	$40,000	$48,888

(Collective bargaining agreement, effective August 23, 2005, Kent State University and the tenure-track unit of the American Association of University Professors, Kent State chapter, 2005)

Since library faculty might comprise a significant proportion of 12-month faculty, this means that their minimum salaries might compare more favorably to their teaching colleagues. They are being paid for their lengthened academic year despite the fact that it might be difficult to find other employment that paid as well (absent a comparable salary contract article). That said, 12-month library faculty are ineligible for the summer teaching compensation that many teaching faculty can use to supplement their nine-month salaries. Thus, the 12-month supplement to the salary minima seems perfectly reasonable.

Comparing these Kent State salary figures to Association of Research Libraries (ARL) annual salary data, which have average salaries by ranges of years of experience, one finds that these minima correspond to 12-month librarians with 28–31 years of experience for Professors, between 16–19 and 20–23 years of experience for Associate Professors, between 4–7 and 8–11 years of experience for Assistant Professors, and between 0–3 and 4–7 years of experience for Instructors, on average (and regardless of specialty)(Association of Research Libraries, 2007). Since the AAUP does not include library faculty salaries in its data, ARL data, imperfect as they are for comparisons by rank, may be the closest thing to a national dataset for library faculty.

One finds salary minima for academic and calendar year librarians in other contracts as well, such as the agreement between United University Professions (UUP) of New York and the Executive Branch of the State of

New York. UUP is one of the largest multi-campus units in the country, along with the California State System, and is a joint affiliate with both the AFT and the AAUP.[6] Its contract article on salary minima for the July 1, 2008, year states the following (Article 20.4d.1):

e. Salary minimums shall be established for the following ranks or grades or positions equated to them and shall be effective on the dates of the salary increases provided pursuant to subdivision (a) of this section:

Academic Employees	Academic Employees Academic Year	Academic Employees Calendar Year
Professor	$51,609	$61,734
Librarian		
Associate Professor	$41,643	$49,770
Associate Librarian		
Assistant Professor	$35,200	$42,103
Lecturer		
Sr. Assistant Librarian		
Instructor	$30,755	$36,735
Assistant Librarian		

(Agreement between the State of New York and United University Professions July 2, 2007–July 1, 2011, 2007).

This is followed by additional years of contractually guaranteed increases in these minima at each rank, as specified in prior and following subsections of the direct compensation contract article (Article 20), culminating in a 12-month minimum salary for Professor/Librarian of $66,129 in 2010. One may note here that these minima are decidedly less than the minima for 12-month librarians at Kent State University, cited previously.

Market Adjustments

The lack of library faculty salary data in the annual AAUP salary survey, and the breakdown of ARL salary data by specialty and years of service, but not academic rank, raises another challenging issue: market adjustments. It is not uncommon for faculty contracts to include provisions for market adjustments for faculty who may fall below similar faculty in comparator institutions. The question then becomes: where does one find suitable comparative salary data? If one relies on national datasets, such as the College and University Professional Association-Human Resources

(CUPA-HR) salary data, or the AAUP or ARL data, one finds that they are not comparable. CUPA-HR includes data for library faculty who teach in schools of library and information science, but not for library faculty members working within libraries. Similarly, as mentioned above, the AAUP data do not include library faculty since librarians are not considered faculty at all institutions. Finally, the ARL data, possibly reflecting the same inconsistency regarding librarians and faculty status, report data by years of experience and library specialty (e.g., collection development, cataloging, reference). In all of these cases, then, the datasets would be inadequate for calculating a market adjustment for library faculty at various academic ranks.

Evaluating library faculty for market adjustments requires, therefore, either the hand assembling of data from a cohort of comparable institutions (i.e., those with library faculty) or some alternative approach. At the University of Akron, the 2005–2009 collective bargaining agreement required use of CUPA-HR data, and their inadequacy for library faculty (as well as eight other departments) led to an agreed upon alternative evaluation of librarians by specialty and years of experience using ARL data. In this instance, the years of experience in the ARL data served as a rough surrogate for academic rank, though clearly they are not the same.

The University of Toledo and its AAUP chapter also included a market adjustment salary provision in their most recent contract. They, too, utilized the CUPA-HR salary dataset for doing salary comparisons. Not surprisingly, they found that the dataset did not provide data comparing library faculty with their counterparts at similar institutions. As noted above, the only data available were for faculty teaching in schools of library science. That deficiency aside, the University of Toledo administration and faculty went ahead and used those CUPA-HR data as the closest available data for library faculty market adjustment purposes (M. Dowd, personal communication, April 11, 2008).

Depending on the collective bargaining agreement, and the nature of library faculty appointments, the issue of market adjustments may be somewhat difficult to administer. As indicated by the examples above, the lengths to which one might have to go to create a dataset for library faculty will depend on the two parties' willingness to accept comparative data that may not be fully faithful to the populations being compared. Of course, there is nothing inherently correct or incorrect in how one handles this issue. Such contractual features are negotiated and it is within the right of the parties to make accommodations as they see fit.

ACADEMIC FREEDOM

Intellectual freedom and the free exchange of ideas is an acknowledged core concern of the library profession, including academic librarians (Association of College and Research Libraries, 2000). Academic librarians should have as much vested interest in a sound academic freedom policy and contract article as any teaching faculty. The ACRL and ALA statement on behalf of intellectual freedom in academic libraries delineates the key principles of such support. Among these key principles are support for the ALA's *Library Bill of Rights*, library user privacy, a diversity of perspectives within collection development, open access to the Internet and facilities and resources, equitable and open access to the diversity of users, and the preeminence of research and instructional needs of selector preferences, among others (Association of College and Research Libraries, 2000). These are certainly fundamental or core principles to which any academic librarian could subscribe. Some of them relate to providing library users with access to information rather than the rights of the library faculty themselves. To what degree do academic freedom contract articles reflect these concerns? Beyond that, what other possible issues are neglected, if any? Are there any more unique concerns of academic librarians that can and should be reflected in, or at least protected by, an academic freedom contract article?

At the University of Cincinnati, there is both an academic freedom article, applicable to all faculty, and a faculty rights and responsibilities article, which singles out the distinctive interests of both teaching and library faculty. The latter article (Article 3, Academic Safeguards and Responsibilities, in the 2007–2010 contract) closely parallels the AAUP's *Statement on Professional Ethics* (American Association of University Professors, 2006b) and reads, in part, as follows:

3.1 The AAUP and the University recognize the following:

3.1.1 That in the practice of their profession, Faculty Members' principal academic functions are teaching, discovering, creating, and reporting knowledge.

3.1.2 That in the practice of their profession, Librarians select, acquire, and provide access to scholarly information according to the duties and responsibilities contained in their individual job descriptions. As part of their professional responsibilities they may also participate in teaching, discovering, creating, and reporting knowledge.

3.1.3 That in order to carry out these functions, special protections are acknowledged to be essential by the parties to this agreement. These protections are known as academic freedom and tenure.

3.2 The general statements which follow take as their source and guide the "1940 Statement on Academic Freedom and Tenure" and the "1987 Statement on Professional Ethics" found in the *Policy Documents and Reports of the AAUP* (the Redbook). ...

3.6 As teachers, Faculty Members and Librarians encourage the free pursuit of learning in their students.... Faculty and Librarians make every reasonable effort to foster honest academic conduct and to assure that their evaluations of students reflect their true merit. They respect the confidential nature of the relationship between teacher and student. They avoid any exploitation of students for their private advantage and acknowledge significant assistance from them. They protect students' academic freedom...

3.8 As principals of an academic community, Faculty Members and Librarians accept that active participation in the governance in their academic units, colleges, and the University cannot always be coterminous with their teaching responsibilities. ....

3.9 As members of their institution, Faculty Members and Librarians seek above all to be effective teachers and scholars. Although they observe the stated regulations of the institution, provided they do not contravene academic freedom, they maintain their rights to criticize and seek revision. ...

3.10 As members of their community, Faculty Members and Librarians have the rights and obligations of all citizens....As citizens engaged in a profession that depends upon freedom for its health and integrity, members of the academic community have a particular obligation to promote conditions of free inquiry and to further public understanding of academic freedom.

3.11 The responsibilities of members of the academic community encompass many professional functions appropriate to their varied roles. The responsibilities of individual Faculty Members and Librarians will vary depending upon the specific areas of activity in which they are engaged. It is recognized that the protections afforded by academic freedom are not to be taken lightly. Academic freedom protects Faculty Members and Librarians in refusing to accept specific responsibilities they find morally, politically, or intellectually reprehensible; but, this does not imply that the safeguards of academic freedom may be used on unprincipled grounds. (Collective bargaining agreement between the University of Cincinnati and the American Association of University Professors University of Cincinnati chapter, 2007)

One thing that is apparent in these excerpts is not only that the academic freedom of librarians is given parity with teaching faculty but also that their roles as providers and creators of knowledge are acknowledged, albeit in a cursory fashion. This, in fact, is openly expressed in the AAUP, ACRL, and Association of American Colleges (AAC) *Joint Statement on Faculty Status of College and University Librarians* (quoted in the ACRL document), which declares that:

College and university librarians share the professional concerns of faculty members. Academic freedom, for example, is indispensable to librarians, because they are trustees of knowledge with the responsibility of ensuring the availability of information and ideas, no matter how controversial, so that teachers may freely teach and students may freely learn. Moreover, as members of the academic community, librarians should have latitude in the exercise of their professional judgment within the library, a share in shaping policy within the institution, and adequate opportunities for professional development and appropriate reward. (Association of College and Research Libraries, 2000)

The academic freedom contract article at the University of Cincinnati takes language directly from AAUP policy statements (e.g., the *Statement on Professional Ethics*) and simply adds "and librarians" after mentions of the faculty. It should also be noted that there are no detailed elaborations of the actual work of faculty librarians such as might be found in intellectual freedom statements by the American Library Association (2007). This document appeals to the common status of all faculty, as reflected in the AAUP's 1940 *Statement of Principles on Academic Freedom and Tenure* (American Association of University Professors, 2006a), a document that is also cited in the Cincinnati contract.

In the University of Toledo contract article on academic freedom (Article 5.1), there is also a modest effort to distinguish the intellectual and academic freedom interests of librarians. It states that:

5.1.4 Librarians shall be free to choose books and other materials and to provide services for the interest, information and enlightenment of all members of the academic community. In no case shall materials be excluded from University libraries because of their author(s) or their scientific, economic, social, political, or religious views. No library materials shall be proscribed or removed from the libraries because of partisan or doctrinal disapproval. (Tenured Tenure-Track CBA 2004–2007 (Toledo), 2004)

Like the University of Cincinnati article, this singles out the information acquisition, management, and dissemination functions of academic librarians. The article's ban on the censorship of library materials, while heartening, is not exceptional by academic library standards.

By contrast, neither the University of Akron nor Kent State University contracts include any specific language in their academic freedom contract articles that speak to the practice of academic librarians, though both contracts liberally cite and draw language from the broader AAUP statements on academic freedom and professional ethics. At Kent State, however, the Libraries & Media Services Faculty Handbook also includes statements on intellectual freedom and professional ethics in its Appendix 3 (Libraries & Media Services, Kent State University, 2008). Here, one finds the handbook quoting directly from the University Policy Register, which acknowledges the AAUP's *1940 Statement of Principles on Academic Freedom and Tenure* as the standard for academic freedom. This basically reiterates the academic freedom contract article in the collective bargaining agreement. However, the accompanying section of this Appendix details the ethical responsibilities of the faculty to students, colleagues, the university, and the profession. This is comparable to, though more elaborate than, the AAUP's *Statement on Professional Ethics*. The language here assumes a teaching faculty model; none of this language acknowledges any of the special concerns of library faculty. Appendix 4, however, includes the ALA *Code of Ethics* and the ALA's *Library Bill of Rights*, both of which are library-specific. Their focus, however, is on the obligations of librarians to provide equitable, open, and unbiased service and access to information. While these are praiseworthy ethical standards, there is not much focus on the academic freedom rights of library faculty as faculty members as distinct from their role as service providers.

Since the academic freedom language from the AAUP's *1940 Statement* is the industry norm in higher education faculty contracts, there may be no need to worry about or tease out the particular features of academic library work. Nor do there appear to be a rash of attacks on academic librarians' rights to select materials as required by their educational mission or their rights to conduct research as their interests dictate. In fact, the *Kent State Library & Media Services Faculty Handbook* has a detailed review of the kinds of research that the service-oriented library profession might find valuable. That said, other growing practices within the field of librarianship that are not yet acknowledged in contract language on academic freedom may be subtle incursions into the professional discretion and academic freedom of faculty librarians. Some of these developments relate to the previously discussed corporatization of higher education, particularly as it manifests itself in the library field.

In Ohio and nationally, some academic librarians are engaged in a collection development practice that raises more nuanced questions about their independence of judgment and academic freedom in the selection of materials. As part of OhioLINK, its statewide consortium, almost every academic library in the state participates in a book approval plan. In this plan, librarians specify the parameters of books they want for the various subjects and disciplines in which they collect, at least for their core collections. The book vendor matches those parameters to newly published books and sends what it believes to be matching titles to the library. In most libraries, the librarians then have the opportunity to review received titles and to send back those that, in their judgment, do not meet their needs. Ultimately, approval plan profiles can be adjusted so that the received titles are better suited to the collection needs of the institution.[7]

This is a cost-conscious strategy on the part of a library. But it also raises the question as to how much collection development is fully in the hands of the subject librarians. The approval plan already concedes some collection development decision-making to the professionals employed by the vendor who make the initial decisions as to what subject and non-subject parameters would apply to each book. This, in turn, would dictate whether a title is actually one that the target library would want based on its approval plan profile. This ceding of discretion is rooted in the approval plan for the particular disciplines, a plan formulated by the subject librarian in conjunction with the vendor. If further discretion to reject titles is given up by librarians toward the goal of saving money, is this an acceptable trade-off? Is this an academic freedom issue? The question here is not based on any intent of vendors to infringe on the academic freedom of librarians in their collection development activities. If anything, these well-meaning developments may suggest instead one of the subtle ways in which corporatization manifests itself in libraries. That is, approval plans create discounts, expedite the delivery of desired materials, and even facilitate the cataloging and labeling of materials. In an age of spiraling materials costs (especially for serials), declining state support for higher education (as a percentage of student instructional costs), one could see these developments as a sort of a benign version of corporatization within academic libraries. The logic of these decisions seems almost inescapable within the budgetary context that is given. With the risks of shrinking state support and declining budgets, library faculty may be grateful for such options. Nonetheless, we need to ask whether this logic simultaneously does harm to library faculty discretion in the selection of materials. That said, it could be that discretion over approval plan profiles is more than sufficient to assuage any apprehension over possible limitations to a library faculty member's discretion.

Similar issues can be raised with regard to full-text journal article databases. Increasingly, these databases include more and more full-text titles. Under the principle of more-is-better, librarians may not flinch at this growth in full-text, despite the fact that it may include journals that would not have been selected otherwise. Some databases, such as InfoTRAC Custom, do allow some crafting of the list of full-text journals to be included, as long as the titles are drawn from its master list of available titles (http://www.gale.cengage.com/title_lists/). However, the dynamics of the industry seem to be moving toward decreasing the purchaser's discretion and possibly the academic freedom of academic librarians as it applies to determining what is to be available within the library's collection. With the escalating costs of materials (especially serials), and the accompanying demand for full-text journals via packaged databases, this trend may be inevitable and unavoidable. That said, is it acceptable? Is it something that should be addressed on behalf of academic librarians in an academic freedom contract article? At what point do the bureaucratization and economies of scale of the acquisition of information impinge on the academic freedom and discretionary rights of library faculty members who are charged with the acquisition and dissemination of knowledge?

RETENTION, TENURE, AND PROMOTION: DEPARTMENTAL CRITERIA

A necessary feature of collective bargaining agreements on RTP guidelines is the fact that they must specify broad parameters that apply across campus. However, they also empower each individual department or unit to write its own specific guidelines within those parameters. Such a process is stated concisely in the University of Toledo contract in its *Article 9: Evaluation*:

> 9.1.1.4. The faculty of each college, in agreement with its Dean, shall establish specific elaborations of the criteria set forth by April 15, 2006. Such elaborations must be approved by the Provost, be applied fairly and equitably to all members in that college. College elaborations cannot be in conflict with the terms of this Agreement. All such elaborations must be published and provided to new members upon entering the college. Copies of elaborations will be provided to the UT-AAUP for review and comment twenty (20) days prior to the review and approval of the Provost.
>
> 9.1.1.5 The faculty of each department, in agreement with its Chairperson, shall establish specific elaborations of the criteria and college elaborations thereon set forth by April 14, 2007. Such elaborations must be approved by both the dean of that department's college and the Provost, be applied fairly and equitably to all members in that department and not conflict with any approved college elaborations of the criteria set forth above or with the terms of this Agreement. All such elaborations must be published and provided to new members upon entering the department. Copies of elaborations will be provided to the UT-AAUP for review and comment twenty (20) days prior to the review and approval of the Provost. (Tenured Tenure-Track CBA 2004–2007 (Toledo), 2004)

Consequently, library faculty are allowed to write RTP guidelines that reflect the specific expectations of their field in the areas of research, work/ teaching, and service. Since library faculty may not all have teaching as part of their overall constellation of work duties, that particular function may not take on the substantive role that it plays in the evaluation of teaching faculty.

Returning to our issue of the library faculty-of-the-whole vs. a departmental organization, the University of Cincinnati contract with faculty provides an interesting acknowledgment of and variation on this issue in its treatment of the composition of the library faculty retention, promotion, and tenure (RPT) committee. While operating as a faculty-of-the-whole, the contract mandates that the RPT committee include members from at least two "jurisdictions" within the library:

> 7.6.6.1 Composition. The Library Faculty shall have a RPT Committee composed of full-time Library Faculty in the Bargaining Unit from at least two (2) library jurisdictions. Except for these restrictions, the Library Faculty shall determine by democratic means the structure, size, and method of selection of the Committee. (Collective bargaining agreement between the University of Cincinnati and the American Association of University Professors University of Cincinnati chapter, 2007)

At Cincinnati, these jurisdictions refer to the various branch libraries such as Clermont, Raymond Walters, University Libraries (the main library), and Law. Though retaining a faculty-of-the-whole structure, this provision does seem to acknowledge some potential inherent challenges in evaluating faculty across different jurisdictions within the library, though, in this case, the jurisdictions are distinct libraries. It acknowledges the fairness to candidates of a diverse committee for the reviewing the candidate's accomplishments.

Of course, it is critical that library faculty write their own RTP guidelines, consistent with their disciplinary standards, their institutional mission, and their workload. Most librarians work a 40-hour week, or close to it, and so, the demands on that workload need to be figured in to the work, service, and scholarship expectations of library faculty. To what extent are workload expectations for library faculty equitable and mindful of distinctions between library faculty and teaching faculty? We explore some of these issues in the next section.

WORKLOAD

Workloads for teaching faculty are typically calibrated to credit hours of teaching and also, for graduate faculty, to graduate teaching and research, for which workload credit is given. For example, a full teaching faculty load at a teaching-intensive institution might be 12 credit hours per semester, which is the equivalent of four three-hour classes. For faculty teaching at the graduate level, with more stringent research requirements, thesis and dissertation supervision, and grant-getting requirements, they may receive three or six credit hours of release time from that starting load requirement. They might also be given release time for quasi-administrative functions such as being the graduate program advisor or the like. Of course, this is just a crude approximation of the structure of an academic workload in a teaching department. Surveys of faculty work time show that instructional faculty and staff work 53.3 hours per week, which is well above a 40-hour workweek and includes all of the time they devote to teaching, service, and scholarship (Pattillo, 2004). Certainly, some of this work is done in a discretionary manner, outside of class and away from the institution.

How then do library faculty workloads compare to this? What are the models? While Ohio contracts are the primary laboratory for this exploration, they are not ideal as they address this particular topic. As a consequence of a 1993 state law mandating increased faculty workloads, which would no longer be negotiable under the state collective bargaining statute, the Central State University AAUP chapter sued, arguing that the law denied their right to negotiate workload. The Ohio Supreme Court initially (1998) ruled in favor of the Central State University AAUP in this lawsuit. However, on appeal to the U.S. Supreme Court, this decision was overturned, and, in 1999, the Ohio Supreme Court decreed that workload could not be a mandatory subject of bargaining under the state's collective bargaining statute (Euben, 2003). While not being able to negotiate workload seems counter-intuitive, it nonetheless is true that workload in Ohio is a permissive, not mandatory, subject of bargaining. The exception to this might be those institutions, such as the University of Cincinnati and Kent State University, whose union-ization predated the states collective bargaining law of the mid-1980s. That said, most Ohio contracts are relatively silent on workload for any faculty, library, or otherwise, though some selective negotiation over workload can be found in various contracts. In these instances, workload was bargained as a permissive subject. The faculty contract at Cleveland State University (Agreement between Cleveland State University and American Association of University Professors, CSU Chapter, Effective August 16, 2006 through August 15, & 2009, 2006), for example, does include language on workload (Article XIII), though their contract does not cover librarians and is less relevant to our focus here. It should also be pointed out, however, that while workload may not be a mandatory subject of negotiation, its consequences could be. That is, salary and other benefits could be tied in negotiation to workload, which in and of itself may not be negotiable.

At Kent State University, whose collective bargaining agreement predates Ohio's collective bargaining statute, there is both contractual language on workload and library handbook language on the subject. According to Kent's most recent contract (Collective bargaining agreement, effective August 23, 2005, Kent State University and the tenure-track unit of the American Association of University Professors, Kent State chapter, 2005), *Article IX (Workload)* cites the University Policy register statement on workload as the operative standard. It states in Addendum D of the contract that

> (D) Since the nature of work differs among departments, load regulations cannot be applied uniformly. Therefore, each department chairperson, along with the departmental faculty advisory committee, shall specify which kinds of loads shall be the equivalents of twenty-four credits of formal course teaching per academic year, with appropriate adjustments being made for graduate teaching, research involvement, direction of laboratory and studio sections, and excessive number of preparations by a new faculty member, and unusually large class sections. Upon approval by the collegial dean, these specifications shall be filed with the dean and the human resources. All regular full-time faculty in the department shall be informed of these departmental understandings. (Collective bargaining agreement, effective August 23, 2005, Kent State University and the tenure-track unit of the American Association of University Professors, Kent State chapter, 2005)

This is clearly written for teaching faculty, and so one must turn to the library faculty handbook to find the workload that would be equivalent to the 24 credit hour standard for teaching faculty. In fact, the *Libraries & Media Services Faculty Handbook* does this. Section 6.06 of the *Handbook* specifies the annual process by which library faculty and their supervisors review projected workload equivalencies in the areas of job responsibilities, special projects, and committee assignments. Once refined and agreed to, these responsibilities comprise the Workload Equivalency Statement (Library & Media Services, Kent State University, 2008). In Section 6.10, *Statement on Additions to Faculty Load*, the *Handbook* not only acknowledges that a 40-hour week is standard, but also specifies the duties in a footnote:

> 1. Typical faculty workload will include regularly scheduled duties (e.g.cataloging, liaison responsibilities, office hours, individual and group instruction, public service desk duty) and irregularly scheduled duties (e.g. committee/task force assignments, planning, preparation of instructional sessions, supervision of staff and/or students). (Library & Media Services, Kent State University, 2008)

This handbook section goes on to specify how additions to, and adjustments of, workload would be made within the parameters of a 40-hour workweek. "Limited or selected administrative responsibilities," up to a certain point, would lead to workload adjustments. Past a certain point, administrative duties would be substantial enough to disqualify the faculty member from membership in the bargaining unit. Interestingly, library faculty are given 200 hours of research time per year, roughly four hours a week

(Library & Media Services, Kent State University, 2008.). Given their 40-hour workweek, this is an essential acknowledgment that research time needs to be structured in to their load.

The University of Cincinnati also has a librarian workload statement that, while not part of the contract, is both vague and somewhat intriguing (University of Cincinnati workload guidelines for library faculty, 1994). This statement specifies that librarians work more than a 40-hour workweek because they are "independent professionals" and their work is not constrained by time or place. It clearly equates the professional commitment of library faculty to that of teaching faculty, who structure their own time to accomplish their professional duties. This document notes that time and place do not constrain professional work, and the practice at Cincinnati is to allow librarians much the same type of flexibility in their work schedule enjoyed by teaching faculty. It should also be noted, as an aside, that this workload statement follows upon the Ohio Supreme Court ruling on the Central State workload lawsuit. Central State lost that lawsuit, and, thus, public university faculty around the state were obliged to demonstrate that they were teaching the additional 10% mandated by state law and upheld by the court decision (Euben, 2003). The University of Cincinnati library workload statement affirms that the library faculty is engaged in teaching, and "is committed to increasing this effort by 10 percent" (University of Cincinnati workload guidelines for library faculty, 1994).

Interestingly, the above-mentioned document has never been a functional document regarding workload. Rather, it captures or reflects what has been the evolving past practice of library faculty at the University of Cincinnati. While library faculty are indeed expected to put in a 40-hour week, they have latitude to structure their workdays and workweeks as they see fit, not unlike teaching faculty. This includes taking research days to complete articles, for example. As long as library faculty take care of the functional requirements of their positions, they are given the freedom to structure their work. However, this flexibility is not guaranteed by the contract.

While 21 other states had some legislative expectations on faculty workload in the mid-1990s (Euben, 2003), there are current examples of how workload for librarians has been worked out in other collective bargaining contracts. Hofstra University, though a private institution in New York, is represented by the AAUP and has a faculty contract that is quite detailed on issues of workload for librarians. Much of the detail on library faculty is found in the substantial Appendix B of its 2001–2006 contract (Hofstra Chapter of the American Association of University Professors, & Hofstra University, 2001).

Library faculty at Hofstra are required to work 190 days during the academic year. The length of the workweek and workday changes during the summer, going from an academic year norm of 35 hours a week and 7 hours a day, to 32.5 hours a week and 6.5 hours a day (Hofstra Chapter of the American Association of University Professors, & Hofstra University, 2001, Appendix B.1). The contract is quite specific in matters such as overload and the mechanisms by which library faculty can receive overload compensation. Specifically, overload can be compensated in the form of either overload payments or compensation time. There is also a provision for banking overload compensation time up to 31.5 days per year and 94.5 days over three years. Library faculty may convert banked days into overload compensation.

Since overload in an academic contract is typically defined as a teaching overload, with compensation for extra classes, the Hofstra contract makes a good faith effort both to define and to compensate for library overload. In light of the possible overload demands of evening bibliographic instruction, for example, such provisions could bring some structural parity to library faculty compensation. No contract in Ohio covering librarians, even those at institutions that predate the Central State workload court decision, includes such provisions. Given the law in effect when they unionized, Kent State and Cincinnati may be able to negotiate such language if they choose; other institutions can only demand to negotiate for the inclusion of language about compensation for overload and not about workload itself. This could include negotiating overload salary compensation or for compensatory time.

Library faculty in the California State University system are represented by the multi-campus California Faculty Association (CFA) in its contract with the California State University Board of Trustees. The workload article in their current contract (California Faculty Association, 2007) does specify the workload requirements for librarians. It states that

20.9 The assignment of a librarian employee may include, but shall not be limited to, library services, reference services, circulation services, technical services, online reference services, teaching in library subject matter, service on systemwide and campus committees and task forces, and activities that foster professional growth, including creative activity and research. The nature of such assignments shall correlate closely with activities expected of librarian employees to qualify for retention, tenure, and promotion and, following tenure, activities expected of librarian employees in order to maintain their role as contributing members of the bargaining unit. Such assignments shall be made by the appropriate administrator after consultation with the librarian employee. (California Faculty Association, 2007)

More to the point on workload, the contract specifies (subsection 20.10) not only a 40-hour workweek within a seven-day time span but also allows librarians to opt for 12-month or 10-month appointments, given sufficient coordination with administrators, prior notice, and prior time on the job (Sections 20.12–20.24).

What this contract does not specify is workload credit for research or scholarly endeavors, which is and should be as important a part of library faculty appointments as it is for teaching faculty. Of the various contracts that we have reviewed so far, including Ohio, the CFA, Hofstra, and UUP, only the Kent State University contract specifies workload credit for research. They grant 200 hours for research. At Akron, past practice has been to grant library faculty four hours of research time a week, to be taken as individual faculty members see fit. However, this practice is not specified in the contract. In the UUP contract in New York, there is some concern about the status inequities of library faculty vis-à-vis teaching faculty. The lack of appreciation by administrators that library faculty research is as important to them as research is to teaching faculty is one such concern (A. Perry, personal communication, June 24, 2008).

Beyond the acknowledgment, or lack thereof, of the research needs of library faculty, one can raise the question as to the adequacy of the 200-hour standard. Teaching faculty with a 24-hour load per year would teach 12 hours per term. The standard metric is that two hours are required outside of class for every hour taught. Thus, a 12-hour teaching load would take up 36 hours of a teaching faculty member's time. Remaining time would be spent between service and scholarship. No wonder faculty workloads, in practice, are well over 50 hours per week, though faculty may have lower teaching loads if their research expectations are higher, thus building research release time into their workload. For library faculty, would 200 hours of release time for research, or four hours per week, be equivalent to that available to teaching faculty? As we saw earlier in the definitions of academic freedom for librarians, those contractual statements seemed to emphasize access to information by others or freedom from censorship. But there was little in the way of detail about the actual research expectations of library faculty. That is left to requirements agreed upon by the librarians and their administrators.

The status inequities articulated by library faculty in UUP also relate to the lack of the discretionary use of one's professional time, as compared to teaching faculty. When teaching faculty are not in the classroom, their constraints are the office hours they set at their discretion, committee meetings, and discretionary research time. Teaching faculty do have a considerable amount of discretion in the structuring of their non-class hours. As librarians in UUP note, library faculty in New York have no such discretion. They are tied to their 40-hour workweek, and the UUP librarians also note that they have no readily available options for telecommuting to do one's work. Not one of the contracts alluded to in this analysis has provisions for the flexibility of work schedule that teaching faculty enjoy, other than Hofstra's option for a 10-month or 12-month contract. It seems to be assumed that librarians should work approximately 40 hours a week despite the fact that much library work, such as collection development, cataloging, or systems, lend themselves to remote work or telecommuting. Yet, no contracts allow library faculty the latitude to structure their hours in a manner that is comparable to teaching faculty.

CONCLUSION

Collective bargaining agreements are necessarily reflections of the interests of faculty and administrations on the particular campus. Local features of that relationship will inevitably impact the language of the contract, making many of them seem somewhat idiosyncratic. That said, it also seems true from the above exploration that many features of the work of library faculty are underrepresented in teaching faculty-oriented contract language. Where contracts are silent on the particular needs of library faculty, workarounds are required. This is no doubt true of other features of contracts, particularly new ones. Still, this very brief review suggests that library faculty need to be involved in drafting contractual provisions to address some of their more unique faculty needs. There also seems to be a need for the sharing of more contractual language and features by librarians in bargaining units around the country. This is important for a few reasons. First, there is no need to reinvent the wheel on important provisions and the language that can accomplish these, as long as one remembers that contractual language is the result of negotiation and therefore may not have been the language one started with. Second, given the paucity of discussion of contractual features for library faculty, it is important that the library faculty community begin to share such ideas on many of the topics briefly touched on here, as well as others. All contracts are works in progress, and, over time, they can be refined and improved. Hopefully, this article, exploratory as it is, will encourage the dialog and further exploration needed to refine the contractual language and conditions of employment for library faculty around the country.

NOTES

1. The case of library faculty and collective bargaining at Wayne State University in Detroit, as described by Spang, reflects some of the idiosyncrasies of the campus

316 STEPHEN H. ABY

and the joint representation effort by the American Association of University Professors (AAUP) and the United Auto Workers. Nonetheless, this is an interesting case study, spanning twenty years (1960s–1980s), of early efforts to address faculty status, salary, governance, and other important issues from an academic librarian perspective.

2. Ohio bargaining units that include librarians are the University of Akron, the University of Toledo, Kent State University, the University of Cincinnati, and Cuyahoga Community College.

3. These contracts are accessible either in the AAUP contract database, or on relevant AAUP, National Education Association (NEA), and American Federation of Teachers (AFT) bargaining agent web sites.

4. As quoted in William Osborne's *Labor Union Law and Regulation*:

Professor Archibald Cox identified three "sources of pressure for the enactment of [the LMRDA] in 1959": (1) organizations, such as the American Civil Liberties Union, concerned with the individual rights of union members; (2) legislative bodies, like the McClellan Committee of the U.S. Senate, seeking to remedy union corruption; and (3) employer organizations "whose primary object appears to have been to use the outcry against corruption within labor unions as an occasion for reversing [the law] in a manner which would weaken unions." (Osborne, 2003, p. 5)

5. Three major organizations have been at the forefront of this faculty unionization movement: the AAUP, the NEA, and the AFT. The AAUP was exclusively a faculty professional association (technically, a charitable organization) until the early 1970s, when it voted to support those campus chapters that wanted to pursue collective bargaining as a means of promoting and ensuring faculty rights and values (Davis, 1971). Now, over half of the faculty who are members of the AAUP are on the 70+ collective bargaining campuses (American Association of University Professors, 2007). At the two-year college level, both the NEA and the American Federation of Teachers have significantly unionized this sector (NEA almanac of higher education, 2007; American Federation of Teachers, n.d.b). Both organizations represent four-year college and university faculty as well.

6. The list of UUP campus chapters includes Albany, Alfred State, Binghamton, Brockport, Buffalo Center, Buffalo State, Canton, Cortland, Environmental Science and Forestry, Farmingdale, Fredonia, New Paltz, Oneonta, Optometry, Plattsburgh, Potsdam, Purchase, Stony Brook, Stony Brook HSC, System Administration, Upstate Medical University (http://www.uuphost.org/).

7. At the University of Akron, there is an interesting twist on this practice, motivated by a desire to stretch collection dollars. Given that approval plan practice had indicated that only a very small percentage of titles had been returned, the university libraries negotiated a larger discount with the vendor if the library kept all of the sent approval titles. Furthermore, the automatically kept titles would be sent with accompanying cataloging records and shelf labels. Thus, the library would keep some titles it might not have otherwise, but it would save costs on shipping back those titles, as well as saving via a larger discount on titles it did receive. It would also save on professional time involved in cataloging and labeling these pre-accepted books.

REFERENCES

Agreement between Cleveland State University and American Association of University Professors, CSU Chapter, Effective August 16, 2006 through August 15, 2009. (2006). Retrieved August 21, 2009, from http://www.csuohio.edu/organizations/aaup/contract/0609contract/complete.html

Agreement between the State of New York and United University Professions July 2, 2007–July 1, 2011. (2007). Retrieved September 8, 2008, from http://www.uupinfo.org/agreement.pdf.

American Association of University Professors. (1998). AAUP wins election at Wright State University. Retrieved July 11, 2007, from http://www.aaup.org/AAUP/newsroom/prarchives/1998/Wright.htm

American Association of University Professors. (2001). Faculty at UVM vote to unionize in high-turnout election. Retrieved July 11, 2007, from http://www.aaup.org/AAUP/newsroom/prarchives/2001/UVM.htm

American Association of University Professors. (2003). University of Akron faculty elect Akron-AAUP as collective bargaining representative. Retrieved July 11, 2007, from http://www.aaup.org/AAUP/newsroom/prarchives/2003/Akron.htm

American Association of University Professors. (2006a). 1940 statement of principles on academic freedom and tenure, with 1970 interpretive comments. In: *Policy documents & reports* (10th ed.). Washington, DC: American Association of University Professors.

American Association of University Professors. (2006b). Statement on professional ethics. In: *Policy documents and reports* (10th ed.). Washington, D.C: American Association of University Professors.

American Association of University Professors. (2007). Collective bargaining chapters. Retrieved October 10, 2007, from http://www.aaup.org/AAUP/About/cbc/colbargainchap.htm

American Association of University Professors, University of Akron Chapter. (2002). Why UA needs collective bargaining. Retrieved November 8, 2007, from http://www.akronaaup.org/clearinghouse/howto/flyerbank/whyua.html

American Federation of Teachers. (n.d.a). *Collective bargaining laws in higher education (public sector)*. Unpublished manuscript.

American Federation of Teachers (n.d.b). *AFT higher ed institutions*. Unpublished spreadsheet.

American Library Association. (1980). Library bill of rights. Retrieved March 27, 2009, from http://www.ala.org/ala/aboutala/offices/oif/statementspols/statementsif/librarybillrights.cfm

American Library Association. (2007). Intellectual freedom principles for academic libraries: An interpretation of the library bill of rights. Retrieved March 27, 2009 http://www.ala.org/ala/aboutala/offices/oif/statementspols/statementsif/interpretations/intellectual.cfm

Association of College and Research Libraries. (2000). Intellectual freedom principles for academic libraries: An interpretation of the library bill of rights. Retrieved March 27, 2009 from, http://www.ala.org/ala/aboutala/offices/oif/statementspols/statementsif/interpretations/intellectual.cfm

Association of College and Research Libraries. (2007). Guideline on collective bargaining. Retrieved August 24, 2009, from http://www.ala.org/ala/mgrps/divs/acrl/standards/guidelinecollective.cfm

Association of Research Libraries. (2007). *ARL annual salary survey 2006–07* (Retrieved on September 8, 2008. Available at http://www.arl.org/bm~doc/ss06.pdf). Washington, D.C: Association of Research Libraries.

Association of University Technology Managers. (n.d.). Bayh-Dole Act. Retrieved August 24, 2009, from http://www.autm.net/Bayh_Dole_Act.htm

Bentley, S. (1978). Collective bargaining and faculty status. *Journal of Academic Librarianship*, 4(2), 75–81.

Blum, D. E. (1990). 10 years after high court limited faculty bargaining, merits of academic unionism still hotly debated. *Chronicle of Higher Education*, 36(20), A15–A16.

Bollier, D. (2002). *Silent theft: The private plunder of our common wealth*. New York: Routledge.

Bourdaghs, M. K. (2008). The right and wrong ways to celebrate, June 16. Message posted to http://bourdaghs.com/blog.html?p = 484

Bousquet, M. (2008). *How the university works: Higher education and the low-wage nation*. New York: New York University Press.

Broder, D. (2007). Labor flexed muscle last week, but wait for '08. *Akron Beacon Journal* (November 11), p. 15.

Brudney, J. J., & Estlund, C. (2007). Letter. Senate Subcommittee on Employment and Workforce Safety and House Subcommittee on Health, Employment, Labor, and Pensions. *Recent decisions and their impact on workers' rights, The national labor relations board*. Available at http://www.aflcio.org/joinaunion/upload/scholarsletter_nlrb.pdf. Retrieved on September 4, 2008.

Brustman, M. J., & Via, B. J. (1988). Employment and status of part-time librarians in U.S. academic libraries. *Journal of Academic Librarianship*, 14(2), p. 87.

Bureau of Labor Statistics. (2007). Union members summary. Retrieved July 2, 2007, from http://www.bls.gov/news.release/union2.nr0.htm

Busch, A. (2006). Ronald Reagan and the firing of PATCO workers. Paper presented at the annual meeting of the American Political Science Association, Marriott, Loews Philadelphia, and the Pennsylvania Convention Center, Philadelphia, PA, August 31, 2006. Available at http://www.allacademic.com/meta/p153618_index.html. Retrieved on September 28, 2008.

California Faculty Association and the California State University Board of Trustees. (2007). Contract. Retrieved September 29, 2008, from http://www.aaupuc.org/0710contract.pdf

Collective bargaining agreement between the University of Akron and the American Association of University Professors, University of Akron chapter. (2005). Retrieved September 8, 2008, from http://www.akronaaup.org/documents/CBA031706.pdf

Collective bargaining agreement between the University of Cincinnati and the American Association of University Professors University of Cincinnati chapter. (2007). Retrieved September 8, 2008, from http://www.aaupuc.org/0710contract.pdf

Collective bargaining agreement, effective August 23, 2005, Kent State University and the tenure-track unit of the American Association of University Professors, Kent State chapter (2005). Retrieved August 18, 2008, from http://www.aaupksu.org/AAUP-KSU_TT_Folder/indexContent/2005_TT_CBA.pdf

Curtis, J. W., & Jacobe, M. F. (2006). *AAUP Contingent Faculty Index 2006*. Washington, DC: American Association of University Professors.

Davis, B. H. (1971). Council position on collective bargaining. *AAUP Bulletin*, 57(4), 511–512.

Directory of faculty contracts and bargaining agents in institutions of higher education. (2006). New York, NY: National Center for the Study of Collective Bargaining in Higher Education and the Professions, Hunter College of The City University of New York.

Ehrenberg, R. G., Kezsbom, A., Klaff, D., & Nagowski, M. (2004). Collective bargaining in American higher education. In: *Governing academia* (pp. 209–232). Ithaca, NY: Cornell University Press.

Ehrenberg, R. G., & Rizzo, M. J. (2004). Financial forces and the future of American higher education. *Academe, 90*(4), 28–31.

Euben, D. R. (2003). Lives in the balance: Compensation, workloads, and program implications. Retrieved April 30, 2008, from http://www.aaup.org/AAUP/protect/legal/topics/livesbalance.htm

Fenwick, R., & Zipp, J. (2007). Faculty liberalism and university corporatism. In: S. H. Aby (Ed.), *The academic bill of rights debate: A handbook* (pp. 91–107). Westport, CT: Praeger.

Finkin, M. W. (1980). The Yeshiva decision: A somewhat different view. *Journal of College and University Law, 7*(3), 321–327.

Freeman, R. B. (2007). *Do workers still want unions? More than ever* (Retrieved on September 4, 2008. Available at http://www.sharedprosperity.org/bp182.html). The Economic Policy Institute.

Garcha, R., & Phillips, J. C. (2001). US academic librarians: Their involvement in union activities. *Library Review, 50*(3), 122–127.

Giroux, H. A. (2007). *The university in chains: Confronting the military-industrial-academic complex.* Boulder: Paradigm Publishers.

Govea, R. M. (1998). The unionization of Cleveland State. *Academe, 84*(6), p. 34.

Gravois, J. (2005). Labor board sides with faculty union in religious-freedom case. *Chronicle of Higher Education, 52*(4), A25.

Hall, M. (2007). Leading labor law scholars say Bush NLRB undermining U.S. labor laws, December 21. Message posted to http://blog.aflcio.org/2007/12/21/leading-labor-law-scholars-say-bush-nlrb-undermining-us-labor-laws/

Herman, D. M., & Schmid, J. M. (Eds). (2003). *Cogs in the classroom factory: The changing identity of academic labor.* Westport, CT: Praeger.

Hofstra Chapter of the American Association of University Professors, & Hofstra University. (2001). Collective bargaining agreement by and between Hofstra University and the Hoftstra chapter of the American Association of University Professors, September 1, 2001 - August 31, 2006. Hempstead, New York. Retrieved July 30, 2008, from http://www.aaup-hofstra.org/CBA.pdf

Jaschik, S. (2005). Will professors sign up? *Inside Higher Ed,* April 22 Retrieved September 4, 2008, from http://www.insidehighered.com/layout/set/print/news/2005/04/22/poll

Jaschik, S. (2007). Hoover in the heartland. *Inside Higher Ed,* Retrieved June 18, 2008, from http://www.insidehighered.com/news/2007/09/20/illinois

Jelinek, M. (2005). Academic entrepreneurship: University spinoffs and wealth creation/ivory tower and industrial innovation: University-industry technology transfer before and after the Bayh-Dole act. *Administrative Science Quarterly, 50*(1), 131–136.

Johnson, B., Kavanagh, P., & Mattson, K. (Eds). (2003). *Steal this university: The rise of the corporate university and the academic labor movement.* New York: Routledge.

Kennelly, J. R. (1976). The current status of academic librarians' involvement in collective bargaining: A survey. In: M. Abell (Ed.), *Collective bargaining in higher education.* Chicago: American Library Association.

Labor Research Association. (2007). Union membership: Overall (1948–2004). Retrieved November 26, 2007, from http://workinglife.org/wiki/index.php?page = Union +Membership%3A+Overall+%281948-2004%29

Leatherman, C. (2000a). NLRB lets stand a decision allowing professors at a private college to unionize. *Chronicle of Higher Education, 46*(44), A14.

Leatherman, C. (2000b). A private college's professors try for a unionizing breakthrough. *Chronicle of Higher Education, 47*(16), A12.

Leatherman, C. (2000c). Union movement at private colleges awakens after a 20-year slumber. *Chronicle of Higher Education, 46*(20), A16.

Lee, D. O., Rogers, K. E., & Grimes, P. W. (2006). The union relative wage effect for academic librarians. *Industrial Relations, 45*(3), 478–484.

Libraries & Media Services, Kent State University. (2008). Libraries & media services faculty handbook. Retrieved May 13, 2008, from http://extra.lms.kent.edu/page/14043

Metchick, R. H., & Singh, P. (2004). Yeshiva and faculty unionization in higher education. *Labor Studies Journal, 28*(4), 45–66.

Moser, R. (2001). The new academic labor system. Retrieved November 26, 2007, from http://www.aaup.org/AAUP/issues/contingent/moserlabor.htm

National Education Association. (2007). *Collective bargaining rights for educational employees in the United States*. Unpublished manuscript.

NEA almanac of higher education (2007). Washington, DC: NEA Communications Services. Retrieved from http://www2.nea.org/he/healma2k7/index.html

NEA Higher Education Research Center. (2000). The American faculty poll. *Update, 6*(3).

Nelson, C., & Watt, S. (Eds). (2004). *Office hours: Activism and change in the academy*. New York: Routledge.

North central state faculty association AAUP chapter. (n.d.). Retrieved November 8, 2007, from http://www.ncscaaup.org/

Osborne, W. O. (Ed.) (2003). *Labor union law and regulation*. Washington, DC: Bureau of National Affairs, Inc.

Pattillo, G. (2004). Faculty work load. *College & Research Libraries News, 65*(9), 570.

Preciphs, J. (2005). Three republican governors hit unions. *Wall Street Journal – Eastern Edition, 246*(29), A4.

Readings, B. (1996). *The university in ruins*. Cambridge, MA: Harvard University Press.

Ross, R. J. S. (2004). *Slaves to fashion: Poverty and abuse in the new sweatshops*. Ann Arbor, MI: The University of Michigan Press.

Rothstein, R. (1997). Union strength in the United States: Lessons from the UPS strike. *International Labour Review, 136*(4), 469.

Slaughter, S., & Rhoades, G. (2004). *Academic capitalism and the new economy: Markets, state, and higher education*. Baltimore, MD: Johns Hopkins University Press.

Smallwood, S. (2004a). Labor board rules against TA unions. *Chronicle of Higher Education, 50*(46), A1–A21.

Smallwood, S. (2004b). The NLRB's ruling on collective bargaining. *Chronicle of Higher Education, 50*(47), A10.

Spang, L. (1993). Collective bargaining and faculty status: A twenty-year case study of Wayne State University librarians. *College & Research Libraries, 54*, 241–253.

Supreme Court of New Hampshire. (1977). University System of New Hampshire v. State of New Hampshire, Nos. 7579, 7580.

Tenured, Tenure-Track CBA 2004–2007 (Toledo). (2004). Retrieved September 8, 2008, from http://www.utaaup.com/tenurecontract.htm

Twarog, J. (2006). Remembering PATCO: U.S. labor movement still feeling effects after 25 years. *Massachusetts Nurse, 77*(7), 8–10.

Union busting, midwest-style. (2005). *National Journal, 37*(3), 89.

University of Cincinnati workload guidelines for library faculty. (1994). Unpublished manuscript.

Von Bergen, J. M. (2006). Labor movement thinks outside bargaining unit: Advocates take up where traditional unions leave off with worker agenda. *Akron Beacon Journal* (April 16), D4.

Washburn, J. (2005). *University, Inc.: The corporate corruption of American higher education.* New York: Basic Books.

Will, G. F. (2005). Labor since the overpass. *Newsweek, 146*(7), 54.

Witt, D. D. (2007). Higher education in the time of the corporate university: Repeating the call for faculty activism. In: S. H. Aby (Ed.), *The academic bill of rights debate: A handbook* (pp. 108–120). Westport, CT: Praeger.

WORK IN MOTION/ASSESSMENT AT REST: AN ATTITUDINAL STUDY OF ACADEMIC REFERENCE LIBRARIANS – A CASE STUDY AT MID-SIZE UNIVERSITY (MSU A)

Bella Karr Gerlich

ABSTRACT

It is reasonable to assume the existence of a new "dynamic" that influences how to measure reference services in libraries and how we evaluate the reference librarians who provide those services. Traditional, face-to-face delivery of reference services is reported to be declining, and there is myriad evidence, albeit largely uncollated and little evaluated, which suggests reference librarians are delivering significant and increasing amounts of the services they render in network environments. These trends raise questions, in turn, about how well we understand the current state of affairs in reference services, particularly where the management and evaluation of reference services in network environments are concerned.

The purpose of this study is to investigate relevant circumstances and conditions bearing – directly and indirectly – on changes in the nature, form, substance, and effects of reference services – through the reference librarian experience. Specifically, this attitudinal study will account for and assess changes in reference services (in the context of a medium-sized

Advances in Library Administration and Organization, Volume 28, 323–371
ISSN: 0732-0671/doi:10.1108/S0732-0671(2009)0000028010

*private university with a national reputation for successfully integrating
information technologies into the educational process), with the further
aim of developing an understanding of how to capture statistics and
evaluate reference services and personnel in this dynamic environment.
Reference librarians at a second mid-sized public university library were
also interviewed for comparative data analysis in this study. Select
portions of this paper have appeared in other publications in shorter,
focused, introductory articles.*

INTRODUCTION

There is an abundance of evidence suggesting that the nature of reference work
is changing dramatically. This available evidence of change is confusing and
scattered, meaning that there is no wholly reliable source of data; nor is it clear
that the overall demand for reference services is growing or declining. This lack
of cohesive observation is felt especially in the academic community, where
both library and technology infrastructures are commonly well developed and
organizationally mature. There is also reason to believe that the statistics
gathered and standards by which the performance of reference librarians is
evaluated have evolved, at least in recent times, at a pace substantially slower
than that of reference work itself. A recent study published in 2002 by the
Association of Research Libraries (ARL) to determine the state of statistical
reporting in academic libraries "hoped that the survey results would reveal
current best practices, but instead, they revealed a situation in flux":

> The study reveals a general lack of confidence in current data collection techniques.
> Some of the dissatisfaction may be due to the fact that 77% of the responding libraries
> report that the number of reference transactions has decreased in the past three years.
> With many librarians feeling as busy as ever, some have concluded that the reference
> service data being collected does not accurately reflect their own level of activity
> (Novotny, 2002).

While the dissonance is regarded by at least some influential reference
librarians to be a significant problem, it is not yet clear whether it will achieve
the proportions genuinely warranting the status of a "serious problem". But it
would also be fair to say that the failure to study the causes of this
dissatisfaction might well guarantee that the conflict between service
assessment standards and service practice in professional work grows into a
serious problem within the library profession. The organization that produced
the SPEC Kit, the ARL, currently has projects underway to address this issue.

Data from this study could be useful for an in-depth illustration of a single point of view and for information comparison purposes. The information collected in this study will determine if these issues are also experienced in a non-ARL setting, while adding to subsequent research efforts by the ARL and other professional associations or organizations a mine of qualitative data that focuses on the reference librarian's unique point of view.

The primary purpose of this investigation was to:

1. collect information on the perceptions of librarians at an academic library on the contemporary nature and state of reference work;
2. compare those findings to the structure and content of current standards for reference librarians; and, on the basis of that analysis
3. collect information on the perceptions of reference librarians regarding satisfaction with their work, perceptions of current position responsibilities, perceptions on value of work (theirs, users, and administrators), their perceptions on the value of statistical and evaluative measures of academic library reference.

The investigation focused entirely on the reference practice of one mid-sized University Library (identified as MSU A) with strong programs in computer science, engineering, the arts and a significant long-term investment in both information infrastructure and digital library services. Additionally, reference librarians were interviewed at a similar, though public, mid-size university (identified as MSU B) for the purpose of comparison. As institutions, both MSU A and MSU B are known leaders in technology research and curriculum –so, studying the library and their practices regarding reference work, assessment and data gathering provided additional information on how these librarians feel services and personnel assignments might change in the current environment, and their perceptions as to whether assessment of the model as it emerges continues to rely on traditional methods.

The survey done in 2002 of ARL, of which MSU B is a member to gather information on current reference statistics and assessments gives supporting evidence that many academic institutions are not completely satisfied with the usefulness of the statistics gathered, but collecting data that defines reference services in today's networking environment has thus far been elusive, noting that 'the migration of reference activity to areas beyond the traditional reference desk (e-mail, chat, office consultations), has further motivated many libraries to re-examine and modify current practices' (Novotny, 2002, p. 12). A scan of library literature databases also supports the idea that there are a number of academic libraries and consortia of all sizes that are experimenting with new ways to collect statistics related to reference work.

Because MSU A is not an ARL member, a case predicated on the perceptions of professional librarians at this library should provide additional information regarding how librarians feel regarding reference issues in the academic library community that is not represented by the ARL survey.

This case study employed a qualitative research methodology using the grounded theory approach. Semi-structured interviews of library reference personnel, library administrators, and users were conducted, and interviews transcribed, coded, and analyzed by question using the qualitative analysis tool HyperRESEARCH, version 2.6.1.

Case study methodology using interview techniques enabled the researcher to focus on naturally emerging language and meanings assigned by individuals to particular work-life experiences. Elements representing behavior, routine, personal experiences are left to surface in the participant's time with their value systems in place, allowing patterns to emerge naturally among the group. Qualitative research is inductive and naturalistic, taking place in an open system in a dynamic reality, where a close relationship is developed between the researcher and the subject.

LITERATURE REVIEW

Book Reviews

SPEC Kit 268, *Reference Service Statistics & Assessment*, Eric Novotny, published in September 2002 paints a clear picture of changing reference services and stagnant assessment measures of the same in research libraries.

This SPEC Kit surveys and documents how ARL libraries are collecting and using reference service transactions data. Reference transactions were defined as "an information contact that involves the knowledge, use, recommendations, interpretation, or instruction in the use of one or more information sources by a member of the library staff" and did not include directional queries, library instruction or database or Web site usage.

This survey described in its executive summary confusion and angst surrounding modern reference work as libraries scramble to collect data. Many institutions noted that they changed dramatically how they gathered statistics – that is, went from daily data gathering to sampling or visa versa but continue to value above all else the total number of transactions as the primary measure of service. The next most popular method was through a survey of users such as LibQUAL or user interviews. However, there is no mention of tapping the reference librarians for what they feel should be measured or judged to be a "successful" reference transaction. The reasons for collecting data also seem to be mired in the traditional – staffing needs, budget, reporting figures to appropriate bodies, and, to some extent, user satisfaction. There is no mention of improving reference quality, developing employees or recognition of work effort. The study did not distinguish between a successful or an unsatisfactory transaction.

Many of the changes made to gathering data come in the form of new electronic methodologies. But the survey was limited in its scope of how a reference transaction is defined, and as a result, it does not recognize the search for information by a user using Web research guides authored by reference librarians. Although it recognizes the use of electronic tools to gather data, there is a failure to recognize the librarian's use of electronic tools to distribute information in any sense outside of the narrow confines of a count of "transactions."

This study was most useful in that it painted a picture that the system of reference assessment in use by ARL libraries appears to be in flux. In its micro, traditional definition of transactions, the survey also supported the idea that there is a great disconnect between (a) what is defined in our modern era non-traditional reference work effort/transactions in a networked society and (b) how we should assess and evaluate this work.

Rebecca Watson-Boone's book, *Constancy and Change in the Worklife of Research University Librarians* (1998) is a study that interviewed and observed 29 (non-administrative) librarians at a large anonymous Midwest Public Research-I University (MIRI-U). The study comprises observations and attitudes expressed by and about librarians and their experiences and feelings about the work and work-life that is librarianship. Watson-Boone chose to use a constant comparative approach of grounded theory, which she describes in detail in the appendix of the book, including stages, site selection, participating librarians, data collection and analysis, coding data, assumptions, and limitations. Watson-Boone used several types of data-gathering techniques such as the interview, note gathering, personal journals, and observation.

In the introduction to *Constancy and Change*, Watson-Boone states her intention for the study to act as a benchmark for what it is like to work in a large U.S research University in the mid-1990s. Watson-Boone suggests that this benchmarking is important because although much has been written about recent changes in libraries (such as technological advances), there is a clear lack of studies that correlate the relationship between change and its effect on the librarian's jobs, and, ergo, work-life attitudes. Because library literature has little to offer in attitudinal studies of librarians, Watson-Boone turned to numerous studies regarding worker attitudes from other professions. Most oft referenced is the 1987 survey by the Meaning of Working International Research Team (MOW IRT), an eight-country study of 15,000 workers. These references to other studies outside the library-specific realm spoke to the heart of Watson-Boone's rationale for a study of this magnitude. Likewise, it provided a model in applying qualitative research methodologies in this area of inquiry.

Watson-Boone also stresses that the movement from a manufacturing to a service economy that has been occurring in the United States for decades is the basic work-related change facing and effecting librarianship. This new service economy has resulted in what Mike Hales (1980) called "thinkwork" – a term Watson-Boone uses throughout the text to describe librarians' tasks or efforts. In addition to setting a historical path of work attitudes, Watson-Boone's study acquaints readers with the social–psychological approach to the study of work which Watson-Boone says holds that "to understand a librarian's work, one must both understand the librarians and the work they do" (p. vii). She defines the meaning of working through the study of the psychology of work, giving examples of how librarianship can be studied from either a psychological or a sociological perspective, providing a clear understanding of why a combined social–psychological approach best represents and encompasses the social behaviors and individual inflections of the librarians. In the first chapter, Watson-Boone uncovers shared realities of coworkers and what is "real" and how professional cultures are formed. She introduces the concept of *work centrality*, defined as "the extent to which a person defines himself through work or commitment to work" (p. 9). The author also introduces two other work meanings to discern reality for a group, *extrinsic features* centering on job tasks, and *intrinsic features* focusing on physiological motivators. Watson-Boone's study ponders where librarians would fall in the reality of their work meanings.

In the second chapter, "Tell Me What You Do," Watson-Boone's work focuses on librarians' own descriptions of their positions. The author's categories of jobs: collection work, catalog work, reference work, and learning-teaching-training work are broad representations of traditional librarian roles. These categories constitute the librarians' primary work, as defined by such factors as time increments, personal likes, and how they defined their position. There were differences between the reference services librarians (those in the public eye) and the technical services librarians who work behind the scenes in the values placed on the primary tasks that they were expected to perform. Reference services librarians place high value on interacting with patrons, whereas technical services people value the ability to work alone and on their own. The majority of the participants shared a higher value on the work than salary or prestige.

Within each category, Watson-Boone goes into detail, breaking down the tasks and the degrees to which they affected job satisfaction. In the chapter "The University and the Library," Watson-Boone examines the relationship between the librarians, their administration, and the institution at large. Watson-Boone first sets the stage of the relationship between the university and its employees as being "adhocratic" – that is, one that places emphasis on continuous skill development, involves more lateral than upward career mobility, and has a flatter organizational structure.

Waston-Boone observes, "The librarians' sense of life-at-work is centered on their primary tasks, their unit and their colleagues. Within their units they are 'we' – outside it is 'they', though the strength of this statement depends on the topic being discussed at the time" (p. 80). The librarian interviews did not aspire to administration, and they were critical and suspicious of the highest tier of administration, equating the large numbers of managers to bureaucracy and assigning to them the blame for poor communication and the resulting dissatisfaction that came out of this failure to communicate well.

In the next chapter, "Expressions of Self," Watson-Boone asserts that job conditions are affected by personality and that individuals' work meanings influence motivation and performance. Specific concepts with regard to primary work and their work setting create a physiological and organizational sense of self and an overall sense of work identity. In this chapter, the librarians' statements sometimes contradict earlier statements and feelings. For example, it seems ironic that autonomy was the primary job characteristic that the librarians valued, but they could not recognize its value in their leadership.

The primary goal of the final chapter, "The Post Industrial Future," was to document the librarians' view of their work life and shared realities of the organization. But the failure to share with librarians the kinds of changes predicted for libraries and recording their reactions to these predictions and their thoughts about where librarianship is going left key questions unanswered.

The Academic Library (1998a, 1998b, 1998c) by John M. Budd supplements any research in academic librarianship. It is designed to give the reader an understanding of the history of academic libraries, its professional culture, and the relationship between the library and higher education. Most relevant to this study is his chapter on the history of Higher Education and Academic Libraries in the United States. Budd suggests that outside influences shaped library culture and subsequent group dynamics and reference interactions with users in ways that still resonate. These, in turn, shaped the perceptions of librarians and their users and their relationship. In the earliest days of academia in the New World, books were few. Libraries were open an average of 10 hours a week, access was usually restricted to faculty, and collection management practices were poor. Tired of restrictions and inaccessibility, students formed societies where membership dues paid for securing large book collections. Budd then paints a grim portrait of the profession: the role of librarian was not regaled. Librarianship was not a profession, but a task assigned generally to the least senior faculty member at each college. Their job was to keep a strict inventory of the books in the library, and there were no expectations for service. Not until the end of the nineteenth century did the idea that a functioning library was a key element in the curriculum emerge, and then only after the traditional English model of instruction was replaced by German styled institutions. Budd referenced Arthur Hamlin (1981), with an excerpt of a conversation to Daniel Coat Gilman (librarian of Yale) from then president of Yale Woolsey on hearing of his resignation had this to say: "In regard to your leaving your place my thoughts have shaped themselves thus: the place does not posses that importance which a man of active mind would naturally seek...with the facilities you possess...you can in all probability secure for yourself a more lucrative, a more prominent and a more varied as well as stirring employment..." (p. 34, Budd). This changed just before the advent of the twentieth century when the focus of campuses shifted to research and librarianship became a distinct profession.

Budd's historical overview helps paint a picture of the librarian as worker over time. Budd's work suggests organizational memory and organizational culture play key roles in the study of librarianship and outlines the perceptions that librarians have with regard to their work, professional status, and value for their services within the organization. In this study, interviews with librarians expanded upon Budd's research to define the librarian's role in the university by including current perceptions of work value and assessment of services.

Articles

A New Classification for Reference Statistics by Debra G. Warner (2001) provides a small insight into the attitudes of librarians and library staff members who tested an alternative reference data-gathering model. The impetus for creating this classification model came out of need for training and triage at a new single point of service desk at East Carolina University rather than an interest in studying attitudes regarding capturing statistics that reflect the evolution of reference work in a networked environment. Warner takes the reader through the development, deployment, and methodology of the study, which used a three-point scale based on question difficulty to those staff working at the combined service point. Subsequently, employees were polled for their reactions to use the scale to evaluate service as compared to only recording number of questions. Interviewing participants provided an opportunity to enrich the data gathering, information in depth, and direct quotes relating to user and staff satisfaction. In the course of the study, Warner changed from the daily collection of data that was used for the first three months to one that polled the staff on a randomly selected day once a month. Warner suggested that the mean numbers derived using this sampling paralleled those of previous collected data without offering corroborating data. However, Warner's research and subsequent decision to change the data collection in this case introduces the prospect that alternative methods exist for gathering statistics and that the opportunity exists for the validation of the data collected.

An article by Brian Quinn, *Beyond efficacy; the exemplar librarian as a new approach to reference evaluation* (1994), suggests using qualitative methods of evaluating reference librarians by first asking "what makes a reference librarian great?" From survey responses, the author suggests a profile that includes three dimensions: attitude, professional skills, and interpersonal skills. Quinn asserts that good reference behavior is learned and that cultural preparation is a must. The study also found that a combination of skills rather than any one single factor makes a librarian great. Quinn's study also found that the most important characteristic described by librarians was exemplar mastery of skills, and this is a proficiency that he believes can be measured through testing and training. Quinn ends his article calling for "moving beyond the tunnel vision that presently characterizes reference evaluation" (p. 172). Quinn's article focuses on behavioral aspects of reference librarianship, to include position responsibilities, attitudes, and perceptions about users/administrators and seeks to capture those behavioral qualities and efforts in a meaningful statistic.

Personalized library portals as an organizational culture change agent by Amos Lakos and Christopher Gray (2000) suggests that, by initiating a new service and introducing new technologies, an organization can experience cultural chance. Lakos and Gray begin their article talking about important future trends identified by the Library and Information Technology Association (LITA) experts for technologies in the libraries at the 1999

American Library Association (ALA) Midwinter meeting. The LITA group emphasized the user-focused approach with the emphasis in this chapter on personalized library portals as the trend of the future. The authors contend that by creating these dynamic library portals, libraries will become more customer centered. They also believed that library organizational cultures will begin to include continual assessment strategies to better serve clients and, in so doing, will change the way library staff work.

This study suggests that the work of the librarian may change as these portals develop. However, it is difficult to assume library culture will change if the strategies for gathering evaluative data are not also reassessed. Lakos and Gray give an overview of what organizational culture is and suggest how external factors influence that culture. But they do not explain how a personalized portal will change the culture of a library internally. The authors also list a number of new tasks librarians would have to do to assist portal customers. This list approximates the job description for an online computer assistant, and it supports the assertion that the work of librarians has changed significantly since the introduction of the networked environment. It does not address the value of intellectual work, suggesting instead that there is a need to improve technology skills in reference librarians. Likewise, there is no discussion regarding how one might assess or measure the effects of this training or recognize that the culture of an organization is changing. But, this research takes some of the ideas proposed to the next level by including attitudinal studies.

In the article *Server Logs: Making Sense of the Cyber Tracks* (2003), Darlene Fichter walks the reader through the hows and whys of Web log analysis. With major headings that include identifying user patterns and what access logs can tell observers, Fichter makes a compelling argument for using Web log analysis. Fichter does make a point of saying that Web log files only tell a part of the story, and are best used as part of an iterative process with other evaluative measures. Like Fichter, this study seeks to use a combination of evaluative measures, including Web log analysis, to more accurately reflect the work of the today's librarians and lead to better and an understanding of their responsibilities.

REFERENCE LIBRARIANSHIP IN THE CONTEXT OF MODERN LIBRARIANSHIP

Samuel Rothenstein (1955) referenced David Bendel Hertz' observation that the publishing boom of scientific literature after World War II was a primary reason for an increase of the responsibilities of reference librarians as researchers and recognized that the sheer volume of new materials alone was impossible for any one scientist to keep abreast of. The introduction of the networked environment was just as profound a change as the publication explosion for reference librarians, as this change to delivery of information using electronic formats brought with it new challenges and roles for reference librarians: "The computer is the single biggest agent of change in reference work in the twenty-five years that I have been a reference librarian. In the early 1970's none of us had a clue that by 1980 our working lives would revolve around the idiosyncrasies of this box on the desk" (Fairchild, 1991, p. 62).

Technology, or more specifically, computers and the connections between them, has changed reference services "forever" (Kelly & Robbins, 1996). Cindy Faries (1994) wrote that the most significant change for reference librarians and users was the introduction of the online catalog in the 1980s:

> Patrons could access holdings of their libraries more quickly, and this often led to a greater demand for increased services and collections. The patron might now surmise, "If I can find out what my library owns, when can I find out what library *x, y* or *z* holds down the road? Also, when will I be able to access journal articles from the online catalog?" Furthermore, reference librarians were now forced to learn much of that mysterious stuff only their cataloging colleagues previously knew such as authority control; expert manipulation of Library of Congress subject headings; and the interpretation of a MARC record. The online catalog also introduced the reference librarian to the technical side of the computer and forced a growing collaboration with programs and technicians. (Cindy Faries, 1994, p. 18)

The information needs of the electronic user bring new labor demands on the reference librarian as well. New information resources are often very expensive to own and require librarians to constantly train and retrain if they are to stay abreast of database changes (Shaw, 1991). Reference librarians who once created extensive bibliographies, indexes, and abstracts on paper now turn their efforts to Web authoring and content control, creation, and continuity to insure that users are finding the information they need when researching online, because users can become easily lost in cyber space and will seek directions through Web transactions. Librarians must be flexible and adapt to changing technologies and new services, features, and products at the same pace at which they are developed. With more choices available to access the same data, reference librarians must carefully weigh the pros and cons of each format and service to make well-informed decisions, a process that can take valuable time (Faries, 1994).

This study included data from librarian interviews to determine the extent to which they feel that the current practices of recording statistics and evaluative measures are adequate and if they reflect the augmentation that has occurred in reference librarians' responsibilities with the introduction of the networked environment and the expectation that they offer reference services electronically. Interviews of librarians also determined the extent to which in-person interactions at the point of service are a necessary and satisfying learning experience for users and librarians alike, and, during periods of low patron activity, how the productivity of the librarian might be re-directed to other tasks that are needed to meet user demands for information. Interviews of library administrators and users are used for comparative purposes.

EVOLUTION OF REFERENCE SERVICES

Analog

Reference transactions before the networking age were primarily communicated through in-person consultations. Information that may have seemed foreign, unreachable, or just too difficult to find for many users meant traffic lines at information desks. Also, users were typically localized citizens or researchers associated with an institution. Reference librarians assisted faculty and students with their research and collection needs, and provided library instruction. They helped find accurate and the most up-to-date information, made notations in card catalogs, created pathfinders and bibliographies, located remote resources, and paved the way for researchers with letters of introduction and collaborative relationships. Putting data in a prescribed order and helping with the proper annotation of citations were also expected. Work was focused primarily on satisfying in-person queries for information and working with common tools – typewriters, phone, and books – and the work was often redundant. With the introduction of the digital realm came diversity in the user population with online and offline clientele, and new tools added to the complexity of the work. This study sought to determine the value of traditional point-of-contact action and the degree to which librarians are committed to that kind of action.

Digital

Almost all academic libraries now use the Web as the primary gateway to their resources. With the presence of the library now assured in this virtual world, there is a shift, not only in how users interact with reference services or what they might expect from them, but in who is being served. With physical boundaries effectively erased by technology, reference librarians now have the world's population as potential clients. The Web interfaces of academic libraries are available to anyone who wants to utilize them (excepting those databases that require campus user authentication) and are accessible and used by many on and off campus on a daily basis. The intellectual work done by a reference librarian identifies resources or outlines course needs. This action may lead to inquiries.

As most academic reference desk services find themselves expanding beyond the physical campus through the Internet, communication skills and cultural awareness on a global scale are required in effectively fulfilling reference requests.

With the potential to reach an audience through networked systems, reference librarians offer "virtual" services such as providing real time live "chat," reference services through the Web to assist online users just as they would help a person at a desk. One volume of *The Reference Librarian*, Numbers 79/80 (2002), is dedicated entirely to digital reference service issues. With this shift from manual searching to online access comes an expectation on the part of proficient Web surfing students, referred to on occasion as Generation Netters, of speed and instant gratification (Alch, 2000). This generation is the first to grow up exclusively in the Digital Age. Even with their well-developed computer skills, information gratification can be difficult to achieve without the assistance of a well-versed, knowledgeable reference librarian who is familiar with the current licensing packages, intricacies of Boolean searching, and subject headings. Additionally, along with accelerated growth of electronic information and related services comes a host of changing (or "upgraded") instruction issues that can cause confusion for that same user who can easily find and download an audio MP3 (Moving Pictures Expert Group – level 3 compressed file) but has trouble (a) knowing what Library of Congress terms to use for a successful search strategy and (b) discerning which is the best database to use for their particular research need amongst the hundreds to which the library subscribes.

More critical still is the need to introduce a new user – the virtual client who may never set foot in the library building, but who requires the same level for assistance in navigating databases mounted on numerous platforms. The interactions of a virtual interview, while similar to a live consultation, may be more difficult and time consuming due to the nature of the asking and answering process. Challenges include typing and waiting for a typed response when conducting the "reference interview"; assisting the multitasking clients who take their attention away from the interview at hand; explaining steps in information retrieval techniques by screen, taking more time than in-person interviews, especially if the native languages of librarian and the user are different, making case word selection more crucial. There also can exist a host of other problems unique to services dependent on technology. The reference interview in a traditional setting provides the librarian many more cues than just words (Taylor & Porter, 2002). And, with virtual users, there can be all kinds of communications challenges, issues with compatibility and connectivity, and technical problems.

Hybrid

State of the art reference services must include a hybrid of traditional and electronic services in addition to added responsibilities for librarians. At the MSU A Libraries, where Live Chat and Email reference are offered as two methods of communicating with reference staff, users still value the human point of contact when seeking information in the library (Fig. 1):

- Virtual clients likewise seek the expertise of reference librarians and access to the Web research guides is actively pursued.
- Libraries today provide services and resources in a hybrid-operating environment. There is the physical library and there is the electronic one (Bertot, McClure, Davis, & Ryan, 2004). The explosion of Web publishing and digital products has added new challenges in reference

Reference Transactions by Type, MSU A Libraries 2003 -2004

Email 1,227   Chat 485

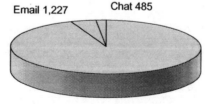

Personal Contact 26,793*

*Personal Contact Transactions include directional and reference queries, phone and walk up

Fig. 1.   Reference Transactions by Type, MSU A.

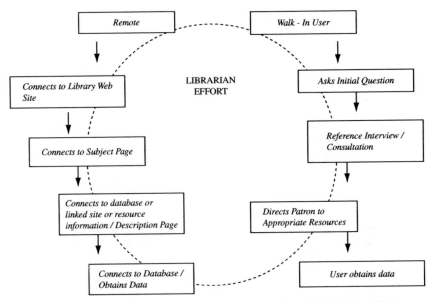

Fig. 2. Relationship between Digital Services and Traditional Modalities of Reference Work.

services while increasing the opportunities for reference librarians to serve a new user group – virtual customers. Interviews with reference librarians uncovered their reactions to serve this clientele and what statistics they feel should reflect the new reference services developed for the online user as well as the traditional physical reference "desk" interaction.

The relationship between digital services and traditional modalities of reference work was explored and is illustrated here (Fig. 2):

- The reference interaction as suggested here demonstrates that the digital transaction requires the same cognitive traits of the reference librarian, but it only tells part of the story. How do reference librarians feel about providing services in the networked environment? Are adequate considerations given to this aspect of their positions?

In addition to querying librarians about their contribution to the electronic medium, this study assessed through the interview process whether the ongoing importance of the physical presence/comfort/interactions that occur at the reference desk continues to play an important role for both the user and the reference librarian in reference activities:

> One of the great strengths of reference librarianship is this commitment of a set of humanistic values that puts a high premium on person-to-person relationships. Because of these values, reference service has a remained labor-intensive, helping profession. Thus it is possible for the reference department to incorporate high technology into its services while maintaining a caring attitude toward students and faculty alike. (Shaw, 1991, p. 56)

REFERENCE LIBRARIANSHIP AS A PROFESSIONAL SPECIALIZATION

The manifestation of specialization in reference services has seen the emergence and evolution of competencies and performance standards. The *Guidelines for Behavioral Performance* first published in 1996 by ALA's Reference and User Services Association (RUSA) with the intent that it would be used in the training and development, or the evaluation of library professionals and staff provide standards for the measurement of effective reference transactions. These *Guidelines* do not emphasize quantitative data gathering for determining effective reference services but focus instead on qualitative measures that might be applied to assessment and evaluation. Updated in 2001 and 2004, the *Guidelines* reflect the changes in the reference profession to include the networked environment. The five main areas (approachability, interest, listening/inquiring, searching, and follow up) remain the same (since developed in 1996), but three distinct categories have been added (where appropriate) under each. They are:

- *General.* Guidelines that can be applied in any type of reference interaction, including both in person and remote transactions.
- *In Person.* Additional guidelines that are specific to face-to-face encountersand make the most sense in this context.
- *Remote.* Additional guidelines that are specific to reference encounters by telephone, email, chat, etc., where traditional visual and non-verbal cues do not exist (RUSA Reference Guidelines – Guidelines for Behavioral Performance, 2004).

Listing the reference responsibilities/tasks/services in the pre- and post-network environment at MSU A University Libraries, the shift in services, expectations, and professional work likewise becomes profoundly noticeable. Yet assessment measures for these services and personnel remain unchanged, and the statistics gathered are rooted in the traditional at the organizational level. This appears to be the norm rather than the exception.

For example, data gathering as recommended by the Association for College and Research Libraries (ACRL) in June 2004 recommends the following ratios when evaluating reference services: a ratio of reference questions (sample week) to combined student and faculty FTE; a ratio of material/information resource expenditures to combined total student and faculty FTE; a ratio of number of students attending library instructional sessions to total number of students in specified target groups. Likewise, an overwhelming majority (96%) of members of the ARL surveyed in 2002 indicated that the primary methodology used to evaluate reference transactions was quantitative in nature – number of transactions either in total or based on sampling strategies.

In the pre-network environment at MSU A University, librarians were classified as staff, and faculties from various departments were responsible for collection development as they were the experts in their respective fields. The curriculum was more structured; users were primarily the campus community and the tasks of the librarians were localized (Table 1).

The changes observed in the duties of reference librarians over time at MSU A Libraries are typical, as illustrated by the recently updated RUSA *Guidelines for Behavior* listed earlier. The post-network environment at MSU A demonstrates the addition of reference services/skills/tools with the introduction of a networked community. Faculty began to rely on librarians, first as a point of contact, then as experts in various disciplines; curriculum is more interdisciplinary and less structured with the ability to transcend subject matter, interconnect themes, and communicate through the Web; users have expanded far beyond the local community to an

Table 1. MSU A Pre-Network Environment Reference Services.

Tools/Skills	Tasks	User	Curriculum	Faculty/Researcher
Pre-network environment librarian as staff member				
Print resources	Questions	Local	Structured	Collection development
Telephone	Office consultations			Expert in research
Fax	Bibliographies			resources
Typewriter	Subject guides			
Mail	Abstracts			
Knowledge	File documents			
Communication	Committee work			
Writing				
Terminology				
Print resources				
Telephone				

international audience; librarians at MSU A Libraries are recognized as faculty and are expected to conduct their own independent research as outlined in the promotion process (Table 2).

PERFORMANCE EVALUATION OF REFERENCE SERVICES AND LIBRARIANS

The SPEC Kit published in 2002 by the ARL "hoped that the survey results would reveal current best practices, but instead, they revealed a situation in flux" (p. 9). The executive summary also reports that "reference transactions no longer occur solely at the reference desk and libraries are attempting to capture data from a number of service points"(p. 9). How can libraries capture all the different types of questions? And how then should reference visits in the networked environment, virtual and in person, be analyzed to satisfy the standards of the profession, the work value for the reference librarian, and the manager's need to assess and improve services for the academic community?

Even though there is general dissatisfaction among librarians with the current data gathering methodology for academic reference services as reported by the ARL researchers, the statistics gathered for reference still continue to primarily value volume (i.e., number of interactions at a particular service point): 96% of the survey respondents indicated they tracked the number of reference transactions as a way to evaluate effective reference services, followed by user surveys and focus groups, with less than 16% including analysis of email and chat activities. Of these respondents, 99% reported manually recorded transactions using tick marks on paper, with less than 8% indicating that they track hits on subject Web pages. When asked to indicate impressions about the quality of their library's assessment activities with respect to recording, analyzing, and using reference transaction data, as a group the respondents rated their performance *below* minimum performance level in analysis and use of transaction data, just above bare *minimum* for perceived performance in recording transactions, and in collection, analysis and use of data performance was deemed to fall far short of desired performance levels. "Although the reasons for poor self-ratings were not disclosed, the scores clearly indicate widespread dissatisfaction with current practices relating to reference transaction data" (ARL SPEC Kit 268, Reference Services & Assessment).

MSU A University librarians were asked whether they felt that current data gathering in their libraries adequately reflects their effort or the value

Table 2. MSU A Post-Network Environment Reference Services.

Tools/Skills	Tasks	User	Curriculum	Faculty/Researcher
Post-network environment librarian as faculty				
Computer	Questions	Local	Inter-disciplinary	Requests purchases
Online catalog	Bibliographies	National	Less Structure	Use librarians as Resources
Print resources	Indexes	Inter-national		
Electronic resources	Subject guides	Virtual		
Internet search tools	Abstracts			
Intranet	Review databases			
Fax	Tests catalog/products			
Mail	Bibliographic instruction			
E-mail	Create online tutorials			
Live chat	Review web sites			
Online resources	Create/update web pages			
Knowledge	Troubleshoot equipment			
Technology	HTML creation			
Terminology	Collection development			
Communication	Continuing education			
Database searching	Department liaison			
HTML	Work with vendors to create/test tools/content			
Writing	Committee work			
	Subject specialist			
	Chat reference			
	Office consultations			
	Research/professional work (as faculty)			
	Selects content for digitization			
	Create databases			

they assign to various elements of reference work, whether in the traditional sense or within the networked community. Traditionally, libraries have used statistics to secure more funding, personnel, professional standing, etc. as indicated by responses from the ARL SPEC Kit survey participants, and so the decline of the total number of at-the-desk reference transactions over a period of time is viewed unfavorably. This issue has real world consequences because of the way libraries compete for resources. But are these declines real, or is it more accurate to say that the data gathered does not include the added reference dimensions and the shift in resources and responsibilities required to deal with the introduction of the networked environment? Are the changes in library practice moving at such a rapid pace that the current methodologies for statistical gathering are in need of recalibration to reflect current services and user trends? If reference librarians truly feel a lack of confidence in the statistics gathered for evaluative purposes, how does this reflect on their attitudes toward their work, their profession, their users, their administration?

One example that demonstrates a current work dimension that is not measured for its value as a reference service is the amount of time librarians spend creating Web pages for users to visit 24/7, time that might have been previously spent answering questions in person. There is no prescribed formula for assessment of these virtual visits vis-à-vis the *reference* transaction, but could there be? Are declines in reference transactions at the reference desk due in some part to these virtual visits to online research guides created by the librarians? Web pages are counted, and the parent institution analyzes hits, but without the important link to credit the author for the "reference service" the virtual user received. Another ARL project, the E-Metrics project, is an ongoing effort to explore the feasibility of defining and collecting data on the use and value of electronic resources. Interviews with reference librarians in this study can help determine the amount of time librarians estimate that they spend on creating Web pages, the value they place on this activity, and whether a dichotomy exists between position expectation and service.

Reference librarians were asked what the role of these research/subject guides play in reference services. Is the work/function/transaction recorded? The virtual client is, on a simplistic level, no different than a personal contact reference transaction at the service point. The user needs guidance about using resources for his or her topic (wants assistance and goes to the library Web site), selects the appropriate Web guide (an electronic "reference desk" for the subject that is either discovered by the user or introduced in a library instruction session), and follows the guide the librarian has prepared (if looking for databases, encyclopedias, etc. these are the best ones for this subject "X"). The differences between in-person and virtual users are likewise simplistic: proximity and time (home base of clientele and open hours of facility), personal preference or learning styles (in-person interaction more effective), ability to use resources locally (resources not available through the Web), and curricula (assignments of professors for specific tasks). The opportunity to interact with a virtual visitor in real-time is difficult or impossible in the best of circumstances, especially when there is a potential for platform/program/hardware/linguistic/cultural compatibility issues. Yet there is little support for the idea that these transactions are being given even minor consideration in terms of accountability or accolades for individual performance, and little effort has been expended determining whether the guide is effective or reaching its intended audience. Interviews in this study determined where the librarians place this job function within their priorities.

RECORDING POINT OF SERVICE
REFERENCE TRANSACTIONS

At MSU A University Libraries, the following figures for total reference transactions (includes email, phone, Chat, directional and reference queries) were reported for 1998–2002 (Table 3).

When viewed in isolation, the 12% decline in reference transactions from 2001/2002 to 2002/2003 may appear significant, although over time the number of transactions is steady, with approximately 30,000 transactions per year. However, without additional information about librarian responsibilities, work productivity, costs associated with a networked office etc., these figures cannot reflect the librarians effort/effectiveness with regard to traditional

Table 3. Total Reference Transactions, MSU A.

Reference Transactions	1998/1999	1999/2000	2000/2001	2001/2002	2002/2003
Reference transactions include chat, email, phone as well as in person transactions. Margin of error information not available	29,421	27,236	30,209	30,409	26,793

inquiries. Is this a meaningful decline? Are the declines symptomatic of a serious problem? Why are there fewer questions? Anne G. Lipow, in her keynote address at the *Information Online & On Disc, '99: Strategies for the Next Millennium* conference in Sydney, Australia (1999) suggested that:

> One reason must certainly be that their Internet-using clients are answering more questions on their own. And if that is indeed the reason and the only reason, then it is right that we should disappear. But is that the only reason, or is it even the reason at all? There's a good chance, even when the reference desk is within eyesight, that for at least some people the reason they don't ask is simply that to leave a workstation and go to the reference desk with a question risks losing their seat to someone waiting for it. Others might think that having to explain their problem by leaving their workstation and trying to repeat the symptoms on the librarian's computer is too complicated, so they don't ask. (Lipow, 1999, p. 110)

Lipow admitted these were just guesses, but she further emphasized that, without further investigation into causality (or meaningfulness of said decline), these figures can have an effect on operations of a library and the attitude of reference workers:

> However, administrators and funders of libraries don't guess. With no one to contradict them, they believe the reason we're getting fewer questions is that the search engines can now do the job – and better than we can. So, as they reorganise library work, reference gets downsized, downgraded, or eliminated. Anthropologist Bonnie Nardi explains that librarians are prime targets for elimination because our work is invisible – to our clients, to our administrators, even sometimes to ourselves. In her introduction to a recent issue of *Computer Supported Cooperative Work* devoted entirely to perspectives on this important concept of invisible work, Nardi says of librarians that no-one recognises that real work is being done or that it is of value, or they don't understand the importance of what librarians do, and so administrators are willing to cut library funds. She says that the methodologies used in studies that purport to analyse and measure the work of intermediaries such as librarians do not uncover their non-repetitive, non-routine, conceptual work. You can imagine, for example, that if you measure your reference service simply by dividing your hourly wage by the number of questions you answer on average in an hour, that comes to an expense that keeps going up as the number of questions answered per hour goes down till it reaches a point where it seems very expensive. (Lipow, 1999, p. 111)

Interviews with librarians provided information on how helpful they perceive gathering these statistics to be. Using Lipow's suggestion that one reason for the declining number of reference inquiries might be users answering their own questions vis-à-vis the Internet, the following data were gathered in the same time period, recording significant virtual visits to reference librarians' Web research guides (significant visits recorded at MSU A University Libraries are defined as continuous, uninterrupted 20-minute plus Web session from a single IP address) (Table 4).

Table 4. Reference Research Guide Web Visits, MSU A.

1998/1999	1999/2000	2000/2001	2001/2002	2002/2003
Reference research guides-user web visits				
143,818	160,861	400,000	587,367	634,485

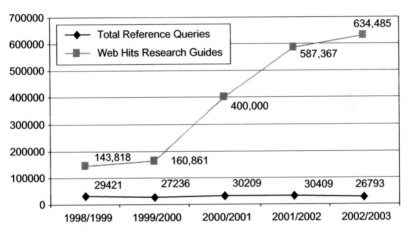

Fig. 3. Total Reference Queries and Web Visits, Research Guides at MSU A Libraries, 1998–2003.

These figures show an increase of 8% from 2001/2002 to 2002/2003 of online activity at 57 research guides – activity where users are seeking a specific knowledge base created by reference librarians that address research needs in a particular subject area – just as they actively select which reference desk to approach based when addressing their information needs. The rise in virtual visit activity since 1998 shows a more dramatic increase of 340%. When virtual visits and traditional reference desk counts are correlated together, the results are as follows (Fig. 3):

The decline in traditional reference transactions appears less dramatic when paired with the increased use of Web research guides and a more accurate view of reference work with reference librarians creating research guides so that users can more easily access information independently in an organized way, in this case, by subject area. Patron reference traffic, although lower than in previous years, continues to be a stable, albeit steadily declining, sought after service that users have not yet abandoned.

Currently, reference statistics collected at most academic institutions rely primarily on quantitative measures as accepted standards. This method that uses accumulated hash marks over a prescribed period of time only counts transactions between the user and the librarian. In most instances, no other data describing the interaction or information delivery is mined. Although the ARL survey recorded a small number of libraries among their respondents that recorded types, time to answer, and difficulty of question, these measures were in the minority, and in no way evaluated librarian effort. The ARL executive report noted that "With as many librarians feeling as busy as ever, some have concluded that the reference service data being collected does not accurately record their level of activity" (Novotny, 2002, p. 12). Reference transaction figures are gathered by sampling or accumulation over 12 months and categorized into "reference" and "directional" categories and reported to professional organizations such as the ACRL. These figures are published in various formats and used for benchmarking, reporting to accreditation bodies, and in most instances, staffing service points.

This supports in part the notion posited anthropologist Bonnie Nardi (Lipow, 1999) that librarians' work is invisible because "the methodologies used in studies that purport to analyze and measure the work of intermediaries such as librarians do not uncover their non-repetitive, non-routine, conceptual work." Interviews with librarians determine what these activities and tasks might be, and how they perceive assessment on such responsibilities is carried out.

CRITERIA FOR THE DEVELOPMENT/SELECTION OF METHODS TO BE USED IN THE STUDY

Statistical gathering measures have remained arithmetical and non-descriptive. The most obvious response for libraries has been to change data gathering from the user's perspective. External survey tools such as LibQUAL, while useful for determine client satisfaction, are not telling as much what the library is doing, but only the effects that are valued by the clients. There is no insight as to the reference librarian activities/position responsibilities other than those perceived by the public encounter. The primary focus of gathering statistics when it comes to reference transactions continues to be one of numbers – with the total number of transactions used for a measure of "success" and still essentially non-descriptive.

As the ARL study suggests, many librarians feel the methodology for keeping reference statistics, which counts transactions only, does not adequately portray the level of activity of the reference librarian, whose services have "migrated beyond the traditional reference desk" (p. 12).

METHODOLOGY AND TOOLS

Descriptive case study methodology was used here, with MSU A University Libraries as the case study institution and MSU B as the comparative institution. Descriptive case exploration, as defined by Bruce L. Berg (2004) in *Qualitative Research Methods*, requires that the investigator present a descriptive theory which establishes the overall framework that will be followed throughout the study. The five-component elements recommended by R. K. Yin (1994) for descriptive case study design were also used. These included study questions; study propositions or a theoretical framework; identification of the units of analysis; logical linking of data to propositions; and criteria for interpreting findings.

MSU A is a representative case institution on a number of levels. As one of the private institutions classed in the Doctoral/Research Universities-Extensive category by the Carnegie Classification of Institutions of Higher Education, MSU A represents a growing class of educational institutions that recognize the need for consortial relationships, digital content, and it is a member of national and local organizations. As a result, a case predicated on the attitudes and opinions of its professional librarians may be expected to have larger meaning on a number of levels in the academic library community. The data gathered at a second public institution (MSU B) enabled the researcher to compare results to determine whether attitudes about reference work are similar at different universities (see Profiles, Appendix A).

As discussed earlier, one of the rationales for undertaking such a study at this time is that the survey of members of the ARL in 2002 to gather information on current reference statistics and assessments found that there is a "general lack of confidence in current data collection techniques" (p. 12) and "the dramatic decline in recorded reference desk activities appears to have generated renewed interest in addressing the problem of developing meaningful measures of reference activity" (p. 12). The study also cited some librarians as concluding "that reference service data being collected does not accurately reflect their own level of activity" (p. 12) and fails to recognize the impact the network environment has had on traditional reference services and how data should be gathered, noting that "the migration of reference activity to areas beyond the traditional reference desk (e-mail, chat, office consultations), has further motivated many libraries to re-examine and modify current practices" (p. 12). This research may inform the future direction of reference statistics and assessments in academic library communities by providing additional information and comparative analysis on the attitudes of librarians at two academic institutions, one outside of ARL and one an ARL member.

A scan of library literature databases also supports the idea that there are a number of academic libraries of all sizes and consortia that are experimenting with new ways to collect statistics related to reference work. This study sought to contribute additional information on the attitudes of reference librarians. For example, like most academic libraries, reference librarians at MSU A continue to staff reference desks in both the physical (phone, in-person) and the virtual (chat, email) sense. Reference librarians in academia are often responsible for appropriate subject specialization as well as for general reference assistance. Staffing/management of service points is decided, in large part, by the quantitative statistics gathered at the physical reference desk. Like other academic libraries, the introduction of the digital environment has seen a necessary shift in reference services and work with position descriptions and responsibilities dictated by networking capabilities and new user groups.

As institutions, MSU A and MSU B are known leaders and innovators in the use of technology. They study their practices in reference service assessment at the library level and provided additional information on personnel and change in library environments and whether the perception of these librarians is that assessments continue to rely on traditional methods. Likewise, evidence from the SPEC survey kit demonstrates that the overwhelming majority of ARL, also continue to gather statistics in traditional ways but are struggling to determine what data to gather and why.

As a case study, librarian interviews gathered data that provide additional information on academic librarians' perceptions of:

1. the current nature and state of reference work;
2. comparisons of such findings to the structure and content of current standards for reference librarians;
3. current position responsibilities, the value of work (theirs, users, and administrators), and the value of statistical and evaluative measures as they exist today.

Interviews of library administrators and users were conducted to compare their perceptions of reference services to those of librarian perceptions. Qualitative research methodology was used and semi-standardized interviews conducted of library reference personnel (Appendix B). These interviews were transcribed, coded, and analyzed by question. A blending of manifest and latent content analysis strategy was used. The following elements were considered when coding the interviews: words, themes, concepts, and semantics. Open coding methodology was conducted, and 80 codes were devised using the master themes of evaluative measures, job satisfaction, job satisfaction challenges, perception, perception responsibility ranks, perception role use of study research guides, work habits time, reference experience, reference experience changes, responsibilities, and statistical measures (Appendix C).

RELEVANT VARIABLES (THEMES IN ANALYSIS)

Watson-Boone (1998) noted that "centering a study on job content or design can lead to ignoring the people who perform the work" (p. vii). This study proposes that, by interviewing academic reference librarians, we can begin to understand the responsibilities of today's networked librarian and the great effects the virtual environment has had on determining tasks, evaluations and statistics relating to the psyche of the academic reference librarian. The information gathered in these interviews will support further retooling of staffing strategies to utilize the skills of the academic librarian more fully and to explain what they do. That is it will help librarians' increase their self-awareness, develop a more positive image of the professional, more accurately describe the work they do, and gain recognition for the intellectual work that they do.

Primary themes in this study are:

A. Perceptions of reference librarianship
  1. Librarian view
  2. User view
  3. Administrator view
B. Responsibilities
  4. Tasks
  5. Primary function
  6. Responsibility rankings in order of importance
  7. Time spent on specific tasks
  8. Typical reference desk shift
  9. Role of research/subject guides
C. Reference experience
  1. Changes
  2. Constancy

    3. Best experience
    4. Worst experience
  D. Job satisfaction
    1. Most and least satisfying component
    2. Challenges of the workplace
  E. Statistical measures
    1. What is counted
    2. What value do they hold for the librarian?
    3. Perceptions of decisions made with data sets
    4. What would they count?
  F. Evaluation measures
    1. What tasks are they evaluated on?
    2. Desired measures

RESULTS AND SIGNIFICANT FINDINGS

The primary purpose of this investigation was to:

1. collect information on the perceptions of librarians at an academic library on the contemporary nature and state of reference work;
2. compare such findings to the structure and content of current standards for reference librarians and on the basis of analysis;
3. collect information on the perceptions of reference librarians regarding satisfaction with their work, perceptions of current position responsibilities, perceptions on value of work (theirs, users, and administrators), and their perceptions on the value of statistical and evaluative measures of academic library reference.

CONTEMPORARY NATURE AND STATE OF REFERENCE WORK

1. Collect information on the perceptions of librarians at an academic library on the contemporary nature and state of reference work:

Librarians reported technology as the number one reason for change in reference services, while people and the need to mediate information were listed as the as the number one constant in their work. With technology, librarians have been able to expand the reference desk globally and provide services 24/7, but this work is invisible and undervalued. Emails are not counted. Web page creation is neither counted nor promoted. Librarians themselves value highly the work of their colleagues on subject guides, consulting them when they need to assist users in an area they are not familiar with. This use goes uncounted, as do the hits from outside the library environment. In addition, librarians are responsible for the acquisition of electronic resources. The users in this study mention many of these resources, yet are they aware that they have been selected, tested, and approved by a reference librarian?

The State of Reference Work

1. *Typical reference work.* 100% of respondents at both institutions listed answering questions as an activity at the desk. The next most recorded activities were collection development, email, professional development/ committee work, project work, liaison and computer skills, and Web page creation/modification. Again, these activities mirror primary function/responsibilities/rankings described earlier, suggesting that even when librarians are not answering questions or assisting people they are working on a variety of complex tasks.
2. *Role of research/subject guides.* The expansion of reference services/creating ready reference options to save time was the number one perceived role, with the support of 100% of MSU A librarians and administrators and 90% of MSU B librarians and 100% of its administrators. The second most common role was to assist reference librarians themselves, with the support of 30% from MSU A and 50% from MSU B.

Contemporary Nature of the Reference Work

- *Changes.* There was a 100% consensus from MSU A and MSU B study participants that technology was the most significant change in reference services over time. The "amount of resources" was second – and this factor relates directly to the technology issue.
  1. *Constancy.* Both MSU A (76%) and MSU B (90%) librarians reported constancy in terms of answering/assisting with reference questions, people interaction, mediation of services – human elements associated with reference services.
  2. *Best experience/worst experience.* Reference librarians at both institutions listed the human element and subject knowledge (or lack thereof) as the best/worst experiences as reference librarians.

The reference desk is recognizable as both place and function. In its current state, reference work is a series of complicated but invisible tasks aimed at providing premium service/information options for clients. Although the traditional role of the reference librarian, assisting users with their information needs on a personal level, continues to be most valued, new responsibilities that support this work have evolved but appear not to be appreciated/evaluated on a task level. Subject guides are used as a reference source for librarians, suggesting they value the intellect/information knowledge of their colleagues, but recognition for this work is on an insider level. To acknowledge/evaluate the current state of reference work, librarians and administrators should:

1. Recognize that the exchange of information is key, and develop ways to evaluate/recognize value in the transaction/information exchange at the traditional service point;
2. Acknowledge that additional tasks are performed at the reference desk that support the primary responsibility and devise evaluative/rewarding measures for this work;
3. Recognize/reward the intellectual/reference value of subject guides – some possible ways include:
   a. Peer to peer blind Web site evaluations
   b. Survey of clientele/promotion of Web guides
   c. Involvement of clientele in the design process
   d. Develop a standardized way to count use of Web pages as a reference transaction such as following a user's activities through the site and time spent at the site
4. Reference librarians/libraries have two constants – technology and service to users. Skills developed in these areas should be rewarded/measured in standardized ways, for example:
   a. Established competencies/training for technology skills
   b. Established point of contact "humanistic" skills

STRUCTURE AND CONTENT
OF CURRENT STANDARDS

- Compare such findings to the structure and content of current standards for reference librarians.

Typical reference shifts were described as busy work environments – most often described first in terms of helping people in great detail and when not helping patrons as a portable office. No one suggested that reference desks close. Again, their primary function and reason for wanting to be a reference librarian was expressed in terms of helping people. When not assisting users, librarians spend their time fulfilling the other responsibilities assigned to them. It appears that a large amount of their liaison correspondence, collection development, computer skills, and answering reference emails in particular (often not recorded) is done at the desk.

Working at the reference desk/consulting/helping patrons was also listed as the part of the job that was most time consuming by both librarians and administrators. This included because whether it was an assigned number of hours at the desk or it was helping people with their research needs.

Challenges described at the institutions mirrored the responses received when describing a least satisfactory reference experience. They ran the gamut and appeared to be secondary in nature, though lack of funding found the most common ground amongst the librarians.

The RUSA Professional Competencies for Reference and User Services Librarians (2006) focus on the abilities, skills, and knowledge that make reference and user services librarians unique from other professionals:

- Access
  1. Responsiveness
  2. Organization and design of services
  3. Critical thinking and analysis

- Knowledge base
  1. Environmental scanning
  2. Application of knowledge
  3. Dissemination of knowledge
  4. Active learning

- Marketing/awareness/informing
  1. Assessment
  2. Communication and outreach
  3. Evaluation

- Collaboration
  1. Relationships with users
  2. Relationships with colleagues

3. Relationships within the profession
4. Relationships beyond the library and the profession

- Evaluation and assessment of resources and services
  1. User needs
  2. Information services
  3. Information resources
  4. Information interfaces
  5. Information service providers

Responses from study participants listed tasks/responsibilities that fall into categories as outlined earlier:

1. *Tasks.* Eleven tasks were reported by librarians at both institutions, with the top seven in order being reference, instruction, liaison, collection development, professional development, computing skills, and consulting. Only two categories – cataloging and development – were listed by librarians at MSU A but not at MSU B. The following responsibilities were listed by librarians, but not listed by Administrators at MSU A: consulting, supervising, chat, cataloging, and development. At MSU B, administrators did not list the following: computer skills, consulting, supervising, chat, cataloging, development, and email. Overlap occurred for supervising, chat, cataloging, and development.

2. *Primary function.* Four primary functions were identified: reference, instruction, liaison, and supervisory. The majority (61%, MSU A, 40% MSU B) listed reference as their primary function. Administrators agree (100% from both institutions).

3. *Responsibility rankings in order of importance.* When giving a response, these data follow the same pattern – reference first, liaison second, collection development third. The majority of librarians at both institutions preferred not to give ranks to tasks beyond the third tier, indicating that all of their tasks were important.

4. *Time spent on specific tasks.* Combined responses at both institutions place reference service work/desk schedule first (40% or 11 of 27), balancing of projects (25% or seven of 27) second, and collection development (14% or four of 27) as the third most time consuming element overall. These responses mirror the primary function and responsibility rankings listed earlier.

WORK SATISFACTION, RESPONSIBILITIES, VALUE OF WORK

1. Collect information on the perceptions of reference librarians regarding satisfaction with their work, perceptions of current position responsibilities, perceptions on value of work (theirs, users, and administrators), their perceptions on the value of statistical and evaluative measures of academic library reference.

Reference work in today's networked environment is a dynamic, service-driven function of the modern academic library. Reference librarians and administrators agree that responsibilities have expanded exponentially, yet there is little recognition/promotion of these functions/tasks in terms of either evaluative measures or statistical data gathering. When asked whether they felt current reference statistic gathering practice reflected their effectiveness as a reference librarian, the overwhelming majority, including administrators, said no. There was a resounding dissatisfaction with data gathering in general, and an expressed interest in seeking new methods of recording effort/knowledge/work value.

Perceptions of Reference Librarianship

1. *Librarian view.* When asked whether they had to describe to someone "what it means to be a reference librarian," 100% of the study participants used words and phrases describing the activity associated with a reference transaction and assisting patrons in their quest for finding information such as help or helping, investigate/detective work/how to find, research, teaching, interpreting, needs, mediate (information needs), and making yourself available (for the consultation). All responses were social in nature, describing an interaction with receptive communication, user needs and teaching roles emphasized, suggesting that the librarian places high value on the "meaning" of being a reference librarian.
2. *User view.* The majority of users in this study had a similar perception of what it means to be a reference librarian, using the same descriptive terms expressed by the librarians themselves. This validates the importance of the interaction and functionality of the reference librarian and point of service transactions that occur.

3. *Administrators.* Administrators from both institutions (4, 100%) talk about the reference transaction component when describing what it means to be a reference librarian. When other duties are also included in the description (10%), reference desk responsibilities are mentioned first, suggesting it is the primary function. Except for the lone administrator at MSU A who described three additional distinct components and the administrator from MSU B who used personal experience as a former reference librarian, these responses mirror the reference librarians' "meaning" attached to their being: the interaction with the user, the answering of questions, mediating information sources, is the fulcrum of the reference librarian position, suggesting it is the single most defining criteria of the position.

Job Satisfaction

- *Most and least satisfying component.* Most librarians at both institutions said that working with/helping people was the most gratifying component of their job with a response rate of 69% (16 of 23). This was a response that is personal in nature, one that focused on of "what it means to be a reference librarian" where helping people was the most common response (100%). This supports Mabel Shaw's (1991) observation that there is a level of commitment on the part of reference librarians that puts "a high premium on person-to-person relationships." Similarities across both MSU A and MSU B reinforce the earlier findings that interaction with users is paramount to the work/experience of the reference librarian and attitudes of reference librarians at any academic institution will reflect this sentiment.

There was no consensus when it came to describing the least satisfying aspects of their work as reference librarians. The components were widely varied, suggesting that dissatisfaction on a more personal level was individualized; where there is commonality between both institutions, the majority is personnel/support related. Because there are no significant similarities or differences between MSU A and MSU B, it can be determined that dissatisfaction of reference librarians at any academic institution will be localized and personal in nature, depending on training, resources, governance, etc.

The manifestation of specialization in reference services has seen the emergence and evolution of competencies and performance standards.

The ALA's RUSA created Guidelines for Behavioral Performance to serve as the standards for measurement of effective reference transactions. The Guidelines reflect the changes in the reference profession to include the networked environment:

1. Approachability
2. Interest
3. Listening/inquiring
4. Searching
5. Follow up

Each standard includes three distinct categories (where appropriate). They are:

1. *General.* Guidelines that can be applied in any type of reference interaction, including both in person and remote transactions.
2. *In person.* Additional guidelines that are specific to face-to-face encounters and make the most sense in this context.
3. *Remote.* Additional guidelines that are specific to reference encounters by telephone, email, chat, etc., where traditional visual and non-verbal cues do not exist.

The statistics/evaluative measures outlined earlier are not reflected at MSU A or MSU B.

Statistical Measures

- Librarians at both institutions all reported (23 of 23 responses) the recording of reference transactions that occur at the reference desk. Seventy-five percent (three of four) of the administrators listed that statistic as something they counted. The rest of the statistics reported as being counted are not statistically significant (instruction, three responses; consultations, seven responses; computer skills, one response) – which is significant because these four of the measures are specific position responsibilities that both librarians and administrators listed in previous responses.
  1. Do they hold value for the reference librarian? Sixty-nine percent of the librarians indicated no, 75% of the administrators agreed – the rest were non-committal, suggesting they had no stake in the process.
  2. Perceptions of decisions made with data sets: Librarians' perceptions are mostly in sync with administrators'. Service hours (30% of MSU A

and 50% of MSU B) were noted as one possible outcome of statistics gathering. One administrator (25%) acknowledges this management activity. Staffing decisions for the reference desk (30% of MSU A and 50% of MSU B) were also listed as a possible outcome of the statistics gathered. The majority 75% (three of four) of the administrators listed this as a management directive based on reference statistics. It is interesting to note that, with the number of hours and staffing decisions made with the statistical data, it is obvious that the reference activity is somewhat valued, but there is no determination to look beyond the pure number of transactions to staffing ratio.

3. What would they count? At MSU A, where reference transactions are recorded as either "directional" or "reference" the majority suggested collecting additional qualitative data related to the questions they assisted patrons with (61%). At MSU B, there was no clear statistical winner though the most responses matched those of MSU A's dominant choice (30%) of more qualitative data when it came to question type, even though MSU B's statistical data for reference transactions already includes a number of categories such as technology, database query, etc. for each question. The other areas where additional statistics gathering was suggested with three or more responses were subject knowledge, Web pages, collection development, library instruction, and question by user type. It is important to note that all but one of these – question type – directly reflect the position responsibilities listed earlier in this study by both librarians and administrators.

Evaluation Measures

1. What tasks are they evaluated on? Work responsibilities/tasks are not reflected in the evaluative process or the statistical measuring processes. The highest-ranking list of evaluative measures by librarians and administrators were self-evaluation, professional development, and goals – none of which are task specific. Reference is absent all together. Eight major responsibilities were identified by librarians and administrators, but administrators only listed evaluating performance based on professional development/goals.

2. *Desired measures*. Librarians were then asked to describe any measures they might like to be assessed on or "given credit" for work being done. These desired measures mirror the responsibilities listed by librarians/

administrators as well as reflect primary functions listed and responsibility rankings: reference desk, collection development, instruction, and liaison.

Reference librarians and administrators alike identify that the reference transaction is the defining characteristic, the most important function and the most time consuming responsibility of the reference librarian's work. Reference librarians also equate this activity as the most satisfying component of their profession; however, statistical data and evaluative measures do not capture this activity in any meaningful way. Reference librarians also list a number of other work responsibilities that are likewise not recorded, measured, or rewarded except anecdotally at best. Suggested ways to bring their activities to light include:

1. Find new statistical measures.
   a. Introduce qualitative data gathering techniques to supplement the quantitative data gathered, such as a tool that measures the effort/knowledge/skills of the librarian expended during the reference transaction;
   b. Recognize the use of technology in the field, and count use of subject guides as a type of reference transaction;
   c. Recognize subject specialization and define measures for expertise in consulting during the reference transaction;
   d. Recognize that transactions away from the traditional service point are often not counted, and measures must include ways to account for this activity, either in person or through electronic means (chat, email).
2. Find new evaluative measures.
   a. Acknowledge the importance of personal contact and customer service at the reference desk and evaluate/reward librarians in their humanistic approaches and user satisfaction through peer-to-peer evaluations, observation techniques, client surveys;
   b. Recognize the importance of collection use with regard to collection development/reference activity, and use circulation activity, database use and curriculum comparisons locally and with peer institutions as measures of success or realignment need in this area;
   c. Develop local measures for evaluating liaison activities, such as consulting with assigned department head, faculty and students, recording activity in collection development areas, recording subject specific consultations or activities in the department such as instruction, class specific Web guides or committee work;

   d. Recognize that librarians must continually test library systems such as the online catalog, new databases, and so forth, and develop criteria for measuring/rewarding this activity such as finding anomalies and reporting problems, self-proclaiming expertise by attaching their moniker to a specific tool, disseminating search strategies, features, and so forth to appropriate clientele;

   e. Develop library instruction evaluations with regard to users knowledge (pre & post testing of material introduced, student surveys) and effectiveness (developing lesson plans, instructor evaluations by peers or managers);

   f. Develop standards for Web pages created and evaluate librarians for this work as well as applying strategies for increasing use;

   g. Develop standards for technology expertise vis-à-vis hardware, software and evaluate librarians in this activity where appropriate.

Possible additional uses and long-term implications of the information collected in this research include:

1. A study which compiles and contrasts librarian's attitudes with regard to using other measures to support the idea that there is a need for academic libraries to consider librarians' unique perspectives;
2. Investigate alternatives to transaction data gathering techniques that assess/evaluate/appreciate the "humanistic value" of reference librarianship and reflect current responsibilities and the networked environment;
3. Generate ideas for creating new ways to gather statistics for traditional/ non traditional reference services/transactions;
4. Establishes a place in time to benchmark similar data collection in the future;
5. Develop local and standard practical applications for evaluative measures, training opportunities, recognition mechanisms, and assessment in general.

Reference librarianship is a multi-faceted profession. Technology has changed the work of the reference librarian, but its strong service component and initial calling – helping people find information – remains constant. Reference librarians, administrators, and users rate the "humanistic value" of the transaction above all other position responsibilities – yet there appears to be little or no recognition or evaluative measures that reflect these knowledge/skills/experience, resulting in a lack of confidence in data collection techniques felt by librarians and administrators alike. Reference librarians appear ready to move beyond the traditional quantitative statistics gathered primarily for transactions and seek varied and inclusive measures for recording reference interaction data that incorporates the value-added skills, knowledge, and effort in all aspects of their work.

REFERENCES

Alch, M. L. (2000). Get ready for the net generation. *Training & Development, 54*(2), 32–34.

Berg, B. L. (2004). *Qualitative research methods for the social science.* New York: Pearson.

Bertot, J. C., McClure, C., Davis, D. M., & Ryan, J. (2004). Capture usage with e-metrics. *Library Journal, 8,* 30–32.

Budd, J. (1998a). A brief history of higher education and academic libraries in the United States. In: *The academic library: Its context, its purpose, and its operation* (pp. 24–48). Englewood, CO: Libraries Unlimited. Chap. 2.

Budd, J. (1998b). Organizational culture and higher education. In: *The academic library: Its context, its purpose, and its operation* (pp. 49–79). Englewood, CO: Libraries Unlimited. Chap. 3.

Budd, J. (1998c). Libraries and money. In: *The academic library: Its context, its purpose, and its operation* (pp. 194–217). Englewood, CO: Libraries Unlimited. Chap. 8.

Fairchild, C. A. (1991). A look back at twenty-five years behind the desk. *The Reference Librarian, 33,* 59–65.

Faries, C. (1994). Reference librarians in the information age: Learning from the past to control the future. *The Reference Librarian, 43,* 9–28.

Fichter, D. (2003). Server logs: Making sense of the cyber tracks. *Online,* 47–50.

Hales, M. (1980). *Living think work: Where do labour processes come from?* London: CSE Books.

Kelly, J., & Robbins, K. (1996). Changing roles for reference librarians. *Journal of Library Administration, 22*(2/3), 111–121.

Lakos, A., & Gray, C. (2000). Personalized library portals as an organizational culture change agent. *Information Technology and Libraries, 19*(4), 169–174.

Lipow, A.G. (1999). Serving the remote user: Reference service in the digital environment. *Proceedings of the Ninth Autralasian Information Online and On Disc 99: Strategies for the Next Millennium,* January 19–21, 1999, pp. 106–126.

Novotny, E. (2002). *Reference service statistics & assessment (ARL Spec Kit #268).* Washington, DC: ARL.

Quinn, B. A. (1994). Beyond efficacy: The exemplar librarian as a new approach to reference evaluation. *Illinois Libraries, 76,* 163–173.

Rothstein, S. (1955). *The development of reference services.* Chicago, IL: ACRL.

RUSA Professional Competencies for Reference and User Services Librarians. (2006). *American Library Association.* Available at http://www.ala.org/ala/rusa/rusaprotools/referenceguide/professional.htm. Retrieved on November 12, 2006.

Shaw, M. W. (1991). Technology and service: Reference librarians have a place in the '90s. *The Reference Librarian, 33,* 51–58.

Taylor, D., & Porter, G. S. (2002). The problem patron and the academic library web site as virtual reference desk. *Reference Librarian, 36*(75/76), 163–172.

Warner, D. G. (2001). A new classification for reference statistics. *Reference & User Services Quarterly, 41*(Fall), 51–55.

Watson-Boone, R. (1998). *Constancy and change in the worklife of research university librarians.* Chicago, IL: ACRL.

Yin, R. K. (1994). *Case study research: Design and methods.* Thousand Oaks: Sage Publications.

APPENDIX A. PROFILES, MSU A AND MSU B INSTITUTIONS, SERVICE POINTS, AND STUDY PARTICIPANTS

Profiles – Case Study Subject, MSU A University Libraries

MSU A University was founded in 1900. Today, MSU A is a top-ranked university composed of seven colleges and numerous research institutes. MSU A is a multidisciplinary research institution of 7,200 students, 1,070 faculty, and 3,350 staff. The university offers more than 140 named degrees, graduate and undergraduate, professional and academic. The academic units are complemented by some 57 research centers, institutes, and groups dedicated to specific subject areas. MSU A is a private, coeducational university incorporated under the laws of its state.

Reference Service Points and Staff
There are four service points located in three buildings for users seeking reference assistance at MSU A University Libraries: Business, Humanities & Social Sciences Reference; Arts & Special Collections; Engineering Reference; Biological Sciences Library.

Staffing for these service points includes 14 liaison/reference librarians who are subject specialists, plus graduate students, and staff associates. Librarians are faculty appointments. Only librarians were interviewed. Thirteen librarians participated in the study (one participant had left the institution).

Two of the librarians interviewed are department heads for their reference unit. For the purposes of this study, they were included in the librarian group (supervisory responsibilities being only a portion of their responsibilities).

There is one dean and one associate dean who supervise reference staff that were interviewed for a total of two administrators participating.

Users
A call for volunteers to answer a set number of questions for a $5.00 stipend was advertised on a popular listserv at MSU A (Appendix A). Twelve

volunteers self-nominated and participated in the study, with the target number being 6–12. This number was selected as it is equal to the recommended number of participants needed for a focus group study.

Identification
Participants of this study were given a letter and number identifier. MSU A librarians were identified with the letter "P" followed by a number, administrators "PA" and number, and users "UP" and number.

Reference Service Hours of Operation
Each service point schedules and maintains its own service hours. These hours are posted on the Libraries' Homepage and advertised in a number of printed venues when applicable (such as packets for incoming freshman and graduate students).

Locations, schedules, and concentrations of reference service points, MSU A University Libraries:

Business, Humanities, and Social Sciences Reference
This desk is the central point for general reference help and information. Subject specialties include business, humanities, and the social sciences. Hours of operation during the semester are:

Monday – Thursday	9 am–8 pm
Friday	9 am–5 pm
Saturday	1 pm–5 pm
Sunday	1 pm–8 pm
Responsible for 7 hours of live chat per week.	

Arts and Special Collections Reference
Subject specialties include art, architecture, design, music, drama, and special collections (rare books, artists' books, related archives). Hours of operation during the semester are:

Monday – Thursday	9 am–8 pm
Friday	9 am–5 pm
Sunday	5 pm–8 pm
Responsible for 6 hours of live chat per week.	

Engineering Reference
Subject specialties include computer science, engineering, mathematics, physics, and robotics. Hours of operation during the semester are:

Monday – Thursday	9 am–8 pm
Friday	9 am–5 pm
Saturday	1 pm–5 pm
Sunday	5 pm–8 pm

Responsible for 6 hours of live chat per week.

Biological Sciences Reference
Subject specialties include biological sciences, chemistry, and chemical engineering. Hours of reference operation are:

Monday – Friday	9 am–5 pm

Responsible for 1 hour of live chat per week.

Comparative Subject, MSU B University Libraries (ARL Member)

MSU B was founded in 1885 and is a top ranked research university, distinguished by its commitment to improving the human condition through advanced science and technology.

MSU B's has over 16,000 undergraduate and graduate students that receive a focused, technologically based education. MSU B one of 34 public institutions of higher education, which comprise the Public University System of its Home State.

Reference Service Points and Staff
There is one service point at the main MSU B Library with 21 liaison/reference librarians who are subject specialists, plus students, and staff associates. Librarians are faculty appointments. Only librarians were interviewed. There is one additional department library; however, the librarian declined to participate in the study. Eleven librarians agreed to participate in the study. One recorded interview was not usable – the recording device failed. This study reflects 10 total librarian interviews.

Two of the librarians interviewed have some management oversight for the reference unit. For the purposes of this study, they were included in the librarian group (supervisory responsibilities being only a portion of their responsibilities).

The dean and the head of public services that manages reference personnel were interviewed for a total of two administrators participating in the study.

Users

A call for volunteers to answer a set number of questions for a $5.00 stipend was advertised on a popular listserv at MSU B (Appendix A). Six volunteers self-nominated and participated in the study, with a target of 6–12. This number was selected as it is equal to the recommended number of participants needed for a focus group study.

Identification

Participants of this study were given a letter and number identifier. MSU B librarians are identified with the letter "L" followed by a number identifier; administrators "LA" and number; users "UL" and a number.

Reference Service Hours of Operation

Sunday – Thursday	24 hours a day
Friday	12:01 am–6 pm
Saturday	9 am–6 pm

Chat and email services are available during the same service hours schedule above.

APPENDIX B. INTERVIEW GUIDES FOR LIBRARIANS, ADMINISTRATORS, AND USERS

Interview Guide for Reference Librarians

The Position (Responsibilities)

The rationale for this group of questions is to establish the responsibilities each librarian has, how they differ, how they are the same – then it is to get their personal feelings about what they view is the most important aspect of their position.

- If you had to describe to someone what it means to be a reference librarian, what would you say?

- How do you think your constituents might describe a "reference librarian"? (Rationale: says how a librarian thinks they are seen and how they might interact with customers)
- *What do you think an administrator thinks a reference librarian does?* (Rationale: does the librarian's perception match with the administrator? Do these perceived values match reward systems/statistical data gathered?)
- *What would you say is the primary* function *of your job?* (Rationale: is the primary function the same as perception listed earlier?)
- *Can you list for me your job responsibilities/tasks?* (Rationale: are additional responsibilities listed here not mentioned in the first question?)
- *Can you rank your job responsibilities in order of importance?* (Rationale: does the rank differ from the responsibilities order giving more importance to one function that the other? Is the order of importance also reflected in the perceptions of what it means to be a reference librarian for the participants?)
- *What aspect of your job gives you the most personal satisfaction?* Why? (Rationale: will give personal insight)
- *What aspect of your job gives you the least personal satisfaction?* Why?
- *Can you describe a typical reference shift for you?* (Rationale: trying to establish what the librarian feels is typical for being at the desk, what other tasks might be getting done when not helping patrons and given ratio of task expectations.)
- *What part of your job do you spend the most amount of time on?* (Rationale: is what they see as most important and the percentages jibe? How does this equate into work given ratio of desk service hours vs. other scheduled time?)
- *Using the your own personal experience, during the time you have been a reference librarian, what has changed for you the most over the course of time?* (Rationale: will identify outside factors, trends, etc. that influence either the position responsibilities or the librarian. Will this reflect on how they value public services? How will respondents' opinions differ?)
- *What has remained constant?* (Rationale: will librarians differ on constancy in the profession?)
- *What role do subject/research guides play in reference?* (Rationale: does this coincide with responsibilities/users expectations/perceived declines experienced at the reference desk?)
- *Can you tell me about a "best experience" as a reference librarian you have had?* (Rationale: gives personal insight)
- *Can you tell me about a "worst experience"?* (Rationale: gives personal insight)

About Reference Service Evaluation and Statistics

- *What's the most challenging thing about being a reference librarian at (LIBRARY)?* (Rationale: gives personal insight. Are challenges external or internal?)
- *How are you evaluated as a reference librarian?* (Rationale: are evaluated measures tied to specific tasks/responsibilities listed?)
- What statistics are gathered and reported for reference services? *(Rationale: what statistics are gathered that reflect work or expectations)*
- How do these statistics reflect the work you do or your effectiveness as a reference librarian? *(Rationale: personal insight on the collecting and reporting of statistics as a reflection of work effort/responsibilities)*
- What management decisions do you think are made with this data? *(Rationale: personal insight as to perception of data collection purposes. Does answer reflect any of the responsibilities or perceived importance of position?)*
- What kind of statistics might you gather that would be meaningful to you as a reference librarian? *(Rationale: personal insight on importance of statistics/librarian interest)*
- What of your tasks would you like to be assessed on? *What might be meaningful?* *(Rationale: personal insight on desire for recognition or performance)*

Interview Guide for Library Administrators

These questions match those of the reference librarian interview, to enable a comparative analysis of perceptions.

The Position (Responsibilities)

- If you had to describe to someone who a reference librarian is, what would you say?
- Can you list their responsibilities?
- What would you say is the primary function of a reference librarian's job?
- What job task do they spend the most amount of time on?
- In the course of your career as a librarian/administrator, what would you say has changed the most about reference librarianship? (Rationale: are they cognizant of changes in reference services? Do they perceive the same changes as the librarians?)
- What has remained constant?

About Reference Service Evaluation

- What's the most challenging thing about being a reference librarian at (LIBRARY)?
- How are reference librarians evaluated?
- What statistics are gathered and reported for reference services?
- What management decisions are made with this data?
- How do these statistics reflect the work effectiveness of a reference librarian?

Interview Guide for Library Users

These questions match those of the reference librarian interview, to enable a comparative analysis of perceptions. Additional demographic data were gathered to describe randomness or sameness in participation.

Faculty, Staff or Student?
Major: (if student)
Year:

- If you had to describe to someone what a reference librarian does, what would you say?
- Have you ever asked a reference librarian a question?
- If they say yes, ask how did the librarian assist you? Did you learn anything?
- Ask how do you find information/resource materials you need for assignments/papers?
- Do you use the subject research guides on the library Web site? If they say yes, ask what they found useful – if they say no, ask why not?

APPENDIX C. THEMES/MASTER CODE LIST

Evaluative measures
   Cataloging
   Collection development
   Computer skills
   Desired

Knowledge
Liaison work
Library instruction
Management
Personal skills
Reference
Research professional dev
Self-evaluation
Web page

Job satisfaction
Least satisfying
Most satisfying

Job satisfaction challenges of workplace
External
Internal

Perception
Administrator
Administrator management decisions
Librarian administration viewpoint
Librarian management decisions
Librarian viewpoint
Primary function
User
Librarian user viewpoint faculty
Librarian user viewpoint student

Perception responsibility ranks
Rank most important first
Rank most important second
Rank most important third

Perception role use of study research guides

Work habits time
Most time consuming
Time rank order first
Time rank order second
Time rank order third

Reference experience
  Best experience
  Worst experience
  Job sameness
  Most important
  Typical shift

Reference experience changes
  Changes in job
  Job sameness
  Technology
  Amount of resources

Responsibilities
  Collection development
  Liaison work
  Research professional dev
  Web page
  Cataloging
  Computer skills
  Consulting
  Development
  Library instruction
  Other
  Chat
  Reference desk
  Email
  Supervising

Statistical measures
  Effectiveness
  Chat transactions
  Desired
  Email transactions
  Instruction
  Off-desk
  Other
  Phone transactions
  Point of contact transactions
  Web logs

APPENDIX D. TEXT FOR
ADVERTISEMENTS FOR USERS

Email message was posted to appropriate market listservs advertising position opportunities for the campus communities. Flyers were not posted.

It was determined that 6–10 users would be sufficient to interview. This was based on the recommended number of participants for a focus group session.

Ten subjects needed for a paid research study opportunity – earn $5.00 to answer five questions!

The purpose of this study is to gather data about select library services. Participation is open to any interested library user.

One day only (DATE). Interested participants should contact (RESEARCHER EMAIL) indicating available time. Participants should allow 15–20 minutes for the interviews.

Participants will receive $5.00 in compensation for their time and effort.

Study will be held in (LOCATION).

ABOUT THE AUTHORS

Stephen H. Aby is professor and education bibliographer at The University of Akron. He has an MLS from Kent State University, a Ph.D. in Foundations of Education from SUNY-Buffalo, and a B.A. and M.A. in Sociology from the University of Texas and the University of Houston, respectively. He is past president of the University of Akron chapter of the American Association of University Professors (AAUP), chair of the Ohio Conference AAUP Committee A on Academic Freedom, and a current member of the AAUP national Council. His books include *The Academic Bill of Rights Debate: A Handbook* (Praeger, 2007).

Bella Karr Gerlich has over two decades of academic library experience and is university librarian at Dominican University in River Forest, IL. Her prior administrative appointments include Associate University Librarian at Georgia College & State University and Head, Arts & Special Collections at Carnegie Mellon University. Gerlich has a BFA from VCU, a MPM from Carnegie Mellon, and a Ph.D. in Library and Information Science from the University of Pittsburgh. Her research interests focus on library organization, management, assessment, and attitudinal studies.

Donald L. Gilstrap, B.A., M.A., M.L.S., Ph.D., is associate dean of Libraries for Technical Services at the University of Oklahoma. He has worked as a library administrator for 10 years and has served on the Executive Committees of the Connecticut Council of Academic Library Directors and the Oklahoma Council of Academic Library Directors. He has been active in higher education assessment and accreditation, serving on the ACRL Standards and Accreditation Committee and as an evaluator for the New England Association of Schools and Colleges and the North Central Association's Higher Learning Commission. Serving on two editorial boards, he also teaches graduate courses on organizational development and publishes actively on leadership, organizational dynamics, complex systems, and assessment of learning.

Lisa K. Hussey is an assistant professor at Simmons College in Boston. She received her Masters of Arts in Information Resources and Library Science from the University of Arizona and her Doctorate in LIS from the University of Missouri. She has taught for the University of Arizona, University of Missouri, University of British Columbia, San Jose State University, and Simmons College, focusing in management. Additionally, Lisa has worked as a school librarian, a prison librarian, and an academic librarian.

Catherine Maskell holds two Bachelor of Science degrees from McMaster University in Hamilton, Ontario, Canada, and an MLIS and Ph.D. from the University of Western Ontario in London, Ontario, Canada. She currently works at the University of Windsor's Leddy Library as Associate University Librarian. The research reported in this article is drawn from her doctoral research: *Consortia Activity in Academic Libraries: Anti-competitive or in the Public Good?*, completed in 2006 and winner of the 2006 Emerald/EMFD Outstanding Doctoral Research Award.

Jean K. Mulhern has been the director of the S. Arthur Watson Library at Wilmington College (Ohio) since 2005. Previously she was director of the Rembert E. Stokes Library at Wilberforce University (Ohio) from 1982 to 2005. She has a B.A. degree in Secondary Education from Heidelberg College, an MLS and additional courses from Kent State University, and a Ph.D. in educational leadership from the University of Dayton that includes coursework at Syracuse University. She has held recent elective offices on the OPAL consortium Executive Council, the OHIONET Board of Trustees, and the Southwest Ohio Council on Higher Education Library Council. She also serves on the OHIOLINK Independent Colleges Directors Council.

Barbara J. Stites is the associate director for Florida Gulf Coast University Library in Fort Myers, FL. Formerly, she was the executive director of the Southwest Florida Library Network (1999–2006) and Tampa Bay Library Consortium (1991–1995); she has also been employed as a school librarian, an elementary school teacher, a law librarian, and as a business information specialist. Barbara continues to serve in leadership roles with the Florida Library Association and the American Library Association and is the editor of the journal *Resource Sharing & Information Networks*.

AUTHOR INDEX